Networking:
A Beginner's Guide

BRUCE **HALLBERG**

Osborne/**McGraw-Hill**

Berkeley   New York   St. Louis   San Francisco
Auckland   Bogotá   Hamburg   London   Madrid
Mexico City   Milan   Montreal   New Delhi   Panama City
Paris   São Paulo   Singapore   Sydney
Tokyo   Toronto

Osborne/**McGraw-Hill**
2600 Tenth Street
Berkeley, California 94710
U.S.A.

For information on translations or book distributors outside the U.S.A., or to arrange bulk purchase discounts for sales promotions, premiums, or fund-raisers, please contact Osborne/**McGraw-Hill** at the above address.

Networking: A Beginner's Guide

1234567890 AGM AGM 019876543210

ISBN 0-07-212226-9

Publisher
Brandon A. Nordin

Associate Publisher and Editor-in-Chief
Scott Rogers

Acquisitions Editor
Jane Brownlow

Project Editor
Ron Hull

Acquisitions Coordinator
Tara Davis

Technical Editor
Ariel Silverstone

Copy Editor
Marcia Baker

Proofreader
Stefany Otis

Indexer
Irv Hershman

Computer Designers
Jani Beckwith
Elizabeth Jang

Illustrators
Beth Young
Robert Hansen

Series Design
Peter F. Hancik

This book was composed with Corel VENTURA™ Publisher.

For Vivian Celeste Hallberg, from a loving and proud father.

About the Author

Bruce Hallberg has consulted on many network system implementations for Fortune 1000 companies. He is the author of more than 20 computer books on Windows NT, NetWare, Exchange Server, and other networking technologies.

About the Technical Reviewer

Ariel Silverstone has been involved in the computer industry for over 15 years. He has consulted nationally for Fortune 1000 firms on the implementation of management information systems and networking systems (with emphasis on security). He has designed and set up hundreds of networks over the years, using all versions of NetWare and Windows NT Server. For five years, he has been the Chief Technical Officer for a computer systems integrator in Indiana. While no longer a professional programmer, he is competent in a variety of computer languages, including both low- and high-level languages. He has authored two networking books about routers and connectivity and has reviewed over 25 books on topics including Windows NT, NetWare, Windows 2000, Cisco routers, and firewalls.

CONTENTS

Part I

Networking Ins and Outs

Part II

Hands-On Knowledge

ACKNOWLEDGMENTS

Books such as this are not developed through the efforts of one person, but rather by an entire team of people. I would like to call your attention to the following people for their contributions.

Jane Brownlow was the acquisitions editor for this book. This means that she is responsible for putting together the initial concept and outline, for getting the publisher's approval to more forward with the project, for handling all of the contract issues, and for shepherding the book all the way through to completion. This is the second book I've worked on with Jane, and she is without a doubt the most dedicated, professional, and focused acquisitions editor I've ever worked with. Even in the face of constantly slipping deadlines (which were entirely my fault!) Jane remained focused and was always a pleasure to work with. In many ways, this book is the product of her efforts as much as anyone's.

Tara Davis was the acquisitions coordinator for this book, and was essentially the "Radar O'Reily" for the project. Tara coordinated the process of moving chapters through all of the people that needed to work on them, and always knew where every piece of the book was at any given time. Without Tara's efforts, the project would have become very chaotic. Tara enabled everyone else on the project to do his or her job efficiently.

Ron Hull handled the job of being the project editor for the book. His job involves working with the copy editors and production to manage the book through to completion. In addition, Ron went above the call of duty to provide sound advice on the book's content. Ron was unfailingly competent, professional, and his advice was always right on the money. Marcia Baker, working with Ron, handled most of the copy editing and did a terrific job correcting and improving my mangled approximations of the English language. Also, the entire production team (especially Jean Butterfield, Jani Beckwith, Beth Young, Bob Hansen, Brian Wells, Jim Kussow, and Liz Pauw) put in a lot of hard work getting this book ready and to the printer under very tight deadlines.

Ariel Silverstone was the book's technical editor. He reviewed the entire book for technical accuracy, and made many valuable suggestions throughout.

Finally, I would be seriously remiss if I failed to thank my family, for putting up with my being unavailable for the better part of three months. Most particularly, I would like to thank my wife, Christy. Her support truly made my work on the book possible.

INTRODUCTION

Welcome to *Networking: A Beginner's Guide*!

I've run into many people over the years who have gained good—even impressive—working knowledge of PCs, their operating systems, applications, and common problems and solutions. Many of these people are wizards with desktop computers. Quite a few of them have been unable to make the transition into working with networks, however, and they have had trouble gaining the requisite knowledge to conceptualize, understand, install, administer, and troubleshoot networks. In many cases, this inability limits their career growth because most companies believe networking experience is fundamental to holding higher-level MIS positions. And, in fact, networking experience *is* very important.

Certainly, networks can be complicated beasts to learn about. To add to the difficulty, most companies aren't willing to let people unskilled with networks experiment and learn about them using the company's production network! This leaves the networking beginner in the difficult position of having to learn about networks by:

▼ Reading an endless number of books and articles

■ Attending classes

▲ Building small experimental networks at home, using cobbled-together and/or borrowed parts and software

Fortunately, many good books are available on various aspects of networking; but, unfortunately, the books that introduce networking seem to come up short and don't speak to experienced computer professionals. These introductory books seem to fall into two categories. The first category assumes readers know nothing about computers, but somehow need to learn about networks because they got tapped to administer a small office LAN. The second category assumes readers know something about computers, but presents its information as if readers are learning-impaired. In the first case, the books available barely touch on what serious students need to know. In the second case, the books cover material with all the speed of tectonic plates.

This book is designed for people who understand computers and the rudiments of computer science, but who want to begin an education about networks and networking. I assume you understand and are comfortable with the following topics:

▼ How bits and bytes work.

■ The notion of binary, octal, decimal, and hexadecimal notation.

■ How basic PC hardware works, and how to install and replace PC peripheral components. You should know what IRQs, DMAs, and memory addresses are.

■ Two or three desktop operating systems in detail, such as Windows 9x, Macintosh, OS/2, Windows NT, and maybe even DOS.

▲ Detailed knowledge of a wide variety of application software.

None of these topics is strictly required to read this book, but the basic idea is you're knowledgeable about computers, in general, and about one or two systems in detail. You are comfortable with computer concepts and you want to learn about networking at a rapid clip.

The purpose of this book is both to educate and familiarize. The first part of the book discusses basic networking technology and hardware. Its purpose is to help you understand the basic components of networking, so you can build a conceptual framework into which you can fit knowledge that is more detailed in your chosen area of expertise. The second part of the book is concerned with familiarizing you with three important network operating systems: Windows 2000, NetWare® 5, and Linux. In the second part, you learn the basics of setting up and administering these network operating systems and about additional networking services available for Windows 2000 and NetWare 5. Topics related to other Novell® products such as GroupWise®, Novell Directory Services® (NDS™), and Novell BorderManager™ are also discussed.

This book covers the basics of most networking topics. However, it's intended to provide an *overview* of all these technologies, while still including a useful level of detail. You should seek more detailed knowledge in the areas of networking to which you want to apply yourself. Generally, networking people seem to fall into one of the following categories:

▼ **Small-to-medium network administrator**   If you plan on building and administering networks with 200 or fewer users, you should extend your knowledge by studying the network operating systems you intend to use, server hardware, client PC administration, and network management. You may find more detailed knowledge of network hardware, like routers, bridges, gateways, switches, and the like useful, but these may not be an important focus for you.

■ **Large network administrator**   If you plan on working with networks with more than 200 users, then you need to pursue detailed knowledge about TCP/IP addressing and routing, and network hardware, including routers, bridges, gateways, switches, and firewalls. Also, in large networks, administrators tend to specialize in certain areas, so you should consider several areas of particular specialization, such as e-mail servers like Lotus Notes or Microsoft Exchange, or database servers like Oracle or SQL Server.

▲ **Internet administrator**   Many people these days are pursuing specialization in Internet-based technologies. Depending on what area you want to work in, you should learn more about Web and FTP servers, HTTP and other application-level Internet protocols, CGI and other Web scripting technologies, HTML design, and SMTP mail connections. You may also want to become an expert in TCP/IP and all its related protocols, addressing rules, and routing techniques.

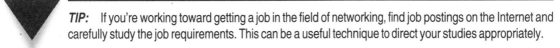

TIP: If you're working toward getting a job in the field of networking, find job postings on the Internet and carefully study the job requirements. This can be a useful technique to direct your studies appropriately.

Networking computers together is one of the most interesting—and fun!—fields in which a person can work. The importance of modern networks to their companies cannot be overstated and the people who design, install, and administer these networks play an important role in any company's success. I sincerely hope this book marks the beginning of a fascinating and educational journey for you!

PART I

Networking Ins and Outs

CHAPTER 1

Understanding Networking

Networking can be a complex subject, but you'll find you can be an extremely effective networking professional without having a Ph.D. in computer science. However, there are *a lot* of aspects to networking, and this tends to make the subject seem more complex than it really is. In this chapter, you learn about the fundamental aspects of networking—laying the groundwork for the more detailed chapters to follow. This chapter discusses some basic and key networking concepts and gives an overview of some of the more detailed networking information in the remainder of the book. You learn about the following in this chapter:

▼ **Knowing network relationships**   Peer-to-peer and client/server are the two main types of network relationships you encounter.

■ **Learning network features**   Just what are the features provided by a network?

■ **Understanding the OSI Model**   The OSI Model provides a conceptual framework that defines how any computer connects to any other computer over any kind of network.

▲ **Learning about network hardware**   This section includes a basic primer on network hardware; much more detail is found in following chapters of this book.

If you're new to networking, getting a good fundamental understanding of the subjects in this chapter will enable you to build a mental framework into which you can fit more detailed knowledge, as it is presented later in the book. In addition, the rest of this book assumes you're comfortable with all the concepts presented in this chapter.

KNOWING NETWORK RELATIONSHIP TYPES

The term *network relationships* refers to two different concepts about how one computer connects to another computer over the network.

Two fundamental types of network relationships exist: Peer-to-peer and client/server. These two types of network relationships (in fact, you may refer to them as *network philosophies*) define the very structure of a network. To understand them better, you might compare them to different business management philosophies. A *peer-to-peer network* is much like a company run by a decentralized management philosophy. A client/server network is more like being in a company that works on centralized management. Circumstances exist where both are appropriate and many networks have aspects of both types within them.

Both peer-to-peer and client/server networks require that certain network layers be common. Both types require a physical network connection between the computers and the same network protocols be used, and so forth. In this respect, no difference exists between the two types of network relationships. The difference comes in whether you spread the shared network resources around to all the computers on the network or use centralized network servers.

Peer-to-Peer Network Relationships

A *peer-to-peer network relationship* defines one in which computers on the network communicate with each other as equals. Each computer is responsible for making its own resources available to other computers on the network. These resources might be files, directories, application programs, or devices like printers, modems, or fax cards, or any combination thereof. Each computer is also responsible for setting up and maintaining its own security for those resources. Finally, each computer is responsible for accessing the network resources it needs from other peer-to-peer computers, and for knowing where those resources are and what security is required to access them. Figure 1-1 illustrates how this works.

NOTE: Even in a pure peer-to-peer network, using a dedicated computer for certain frequently accessed resources is possible. For example, you might host the application and data files for an accounting system on a single workstation to get good performance and not use that computer for typical workstation tasks, like word processing. It's still working in a peer-to-peer fashion, it's just not used for any other purposes.

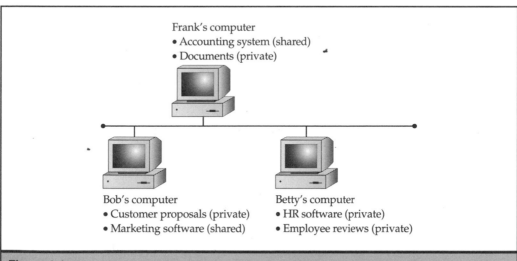

Figure 1-1.   A peer-to-peer network with resources spread across the computers

Client/Server Network Relationships

A *client/server network relationship* is one in which a distinction exists between the computers that make available network resources (the *servers*) and the computers that use the resources (the *clients*, or *workstations*). A pure client/server network is one in which *all* available network resources—like files, directories, applications, and shared devices—are centrally managed and hosted, and then are accessed by the client computers. No client computers share their resources with other client computers or with the servers. Instead, the client computers are pure consumers of these resources.

NOTE: Don't confuse client/server networks with client/server database systems. While the two mean essentially the same thing (conceptually), a client/server database is one where the processing of the database application is divided between the database server and the database clients. The server is responsible for responding to data requests from the clients and supplying them with the appropriate data, while the clients are responsible for formatting, displaying, and printing that data for the user. For instance, Novell NetWare or Windows NT/2000 Server are both client/server network operating systems, while Oracle's database or Microsoft's SQL Server are client/server database systems.

The server computers in a client/server network are responsible for making available and managing appropriate shared resources, and for administering the security of those resources. Figure 1-2 shows how resources would be located in such a network.

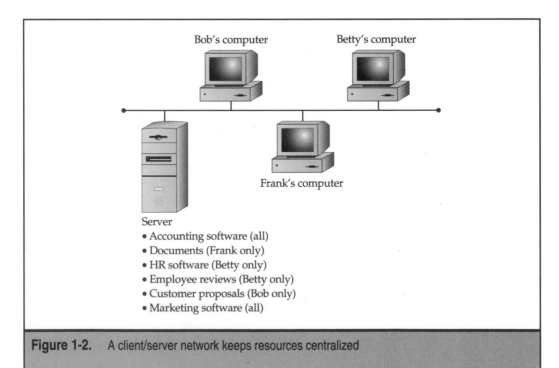

Figure 1-2.   A client/server network keeps resources centralized

Comparing Peer-to-Peer and Client/Server Networks

As mentioned earlier, most networks have aspects of both peer-to-peer and client/server relationships. While it is certainly possible—and even sometimes desirable—to have just one type of relationship or another, the fact is both relationships have their place. Before deciding on setting up a network using one or both types of relationships, you have to examine the pros and cons of each and determine how each meets your needs and the needs of your company. Consider the following pros and cons for exclusively using a peer-to-peer network:

Pros for Peer-to-Peer Networks

There are a number of advantages to peer-to-peer networks, particularly for smaller firms, as follows:

▼   **Uses less expensive computer hardware**   Peer-to-peer networks are the least hardware-intensive. In a pure peer-to-peer network, the resources are distributed over many computers, so there is no need for a high-end server computer. The impact on each workstation is usually (but not always!) relatively minor.

■   **Easy to administer**   Peer-to-peer networks are, overall, easiest to set up and administer. Because each machine performs its own administration—usually for certain limited resources—the effort of administering the network is widely distributed to many different people.

■   **No NOS required**   Peer-to-peer networks do not require a network operating system (NOS). You can build a peer-to-peer network just using Windows 95 or 98 on all the workstations, or all Macintosh computers for that matter. Both of these workstation operating systems include all the features necessary to do this. Similarly, you can do this with all UNIX-based computers (although this is admittedly much more complex to set up and maintain).

▲   **More built-in redundancy**   If you have a small network, with 10-20 workstations and each one with some important data on it, and one fails, you still have most of your shared resources available. A peer-to-peer network design can offer more redundancy than a client/server network because fewer single points of failure can affect the entire network and everyone who uses it.

Cons for Peer-to-Peer Networks

There are also various drawbacks to peer-to-peer networks, particularly for larger networks, or for networks that have more complex or sophisticated requirements, such as the following:

▼   **May hurt user's performance**   If some workstations have frequently used resources on them, the use of these resources across the network may adversely affect the person using the workstation.

■ **Not very secure**   Peer-to-peer networks are not nearly as secure as client/server networks because you cannot guarantee—no matter how good the users of the network are—that they will appropriately administer their machines. In fact, in a network of any size (say, more than ten people) you can almost guarantee at least a few people will not follow good administration practices on their own machines. Moreover, the desktop operating systems on which one runs a peer-to-peer network, like Windows 98 or the Macintosh, are not built to be secure operating systems.

▲ **Hard to back up**   Reliably backing up all the data on all the workstations is difficult and experience has shown that leaving this vital task up to users means it will not get done.

Client/server networks, on the other hand, offer the opportunity for centralized administration, using equipment most suited to managing and offering each resource. Consider the following general pros and cons for client/server networks:

Pros for Client/Server Networks

Client/server networks are the type that you almost always see for networks larger than about ten users, and there are quite a few good reasons for this, as follows:

▼ **Very secure**   A client/server network's security comes from several things. First, because the shared resources are located in a centralized area, they can be administered at that point. Managing a number of resources is much easier if those resources are all located on one or two server computers, as opposed to having to administer resources across ten or hundreds of computers. Second, usually the servers are physically in a secure location, such as a lockable server closet. Physical security is an important aspect of network security and it cannot be achieved with a peer-to-peer network. Third, the operating systems on which one runs a client/server network are designed to be secure. Provided that good security and administration practices are in place, the servers cannot be easily "hacked."

■ **Better performance**   While dedicated server computers are more expensive than standard computer workstations, they also offer considerably better performance and they are optimized to handle the needs of many users simultaneously.

■ **Centralized backup**   Backing up a company's critical data is much easier when it is located on a centralized server. Often such backup jobs can even be run overnight when the server is not being used and the data is static. Aside from being easier, centralized backups are also much faster than decentralized backups.

▲ **Very reliable**   While it is true more built-in redundancy exists with a peer-to-peer network, it is also true a good client/server network can be more reliable, overall. Dedicated servers often have much more built-in redundancy than standard workstations—they can handle the failure of a disk drive, power supply, or processor, and continue to operate until the failed component can be replaced. Also, because a dedicated server only has one relatively simple job to do, its complexity is reduced and its reliability increased. Contrast this with a peer-to-peer network where actions on the part of the users can drastically reduce each workstation's reliability. For example, having to restart a PC with Windows 98 or a Macintosh every few days is not uncommon, whereas dedicated servers often run for months without requiring a restart or crashing.

Cons for Client/Server Networks

Balancing the pros of client/server networks, you also need to realize that there are drawbacks, particularly for companies that don't have their own in-house network administration, or who want to minimize the expense of the network as much as possible, as follows:

▼ **Require professional administration** Client/server networks usually need some level of professional administration, even for small networks. While companies that do this for a living can provide this service, it's important to remember this. Knowing the ins and outs of a network operating system is important and requires experience and training.

▲ **More hardware-intensive** In addition to the client computers, you also need a server computer; this usually needs to be a pretty "beefy" computer with lots of memory and disk space. Plus, you need a network operating system and an appropriate number of client licenses, which adds at least several thousand dollars to the cost of the server. For large networks it adds tens of thousands of dollars.

In a nutshell, choose a peer-to-peer network for smaller networks with fewer than 10-15 users, and choose a client/server network for anything larger. Because most networks are built on a client/server concept, most of this book assumes such a network.

LEARNING NETWORK FEATURES

Now that you understand the two basic ways computers on a network can interact with each other, understanding what types of things you can do with a network is important. What are the benefits of having a network, for example? The following sections discuss common network features and capabilities.

File Sharing

Originally, file sharing was the primary reason to have a network. In fact, small and mid-size companies in the mid-1980s usually installed networks just so they could perform this function. Often this was driven by the need to computerize their accounting systems. Of course, once the network is in place, sharing other types of files becomes easier as well, such as word processing files, spreadsheets, or other types of files to which many people need regular access.

File sharing requires a shared directory or disk drive to which many users can access over the network, along with the logic needed to make sure more than one person doesn't make different changes to a file at the same time (called *file locking*). Additionally, network operating systems that perform file sharing (basically, all of them) also administer the security for these shared files. This security can control, with a fine level of detail, who has access to which files.

Printer Sharing

A close runner-up in importance to file sharing is printer sharing. While it is true laser printers are currently so inexpensive you can afford to put one in every office, if you wish, sharing laser printers among the users on the network is still more economical overall. This enables you to reduce the number of printers you need and also enables you to offer much higher-quality printers. For example, a high-end color printer that uses dye-sublimation costs about $8,000-$10,000; sharing such a printer among many users makes sense.

Printer sharing can be done in several different ways on a network. The most common way is to use *printer queues* on a server, which hold the print jobs until any currently running print jobs are finished and then automatically send the waiting jobs to the printer. This is also the fastest for the workstations because they can quickly print to the printer queue and they don't have to wait for the printer to process their job. Another way to share printers on a network is to let each workstation access the printer directly (most printers can be configured so they are connected to the network just like a network workstation), but each must wait its turn if many users are vying for the printer at once.

Networked printers that use printer queues always have a *print server* that handles the job of sending each print job to the printer in turn. The print server function can be filled in a number of ways:

▼ By a fileserver with the printer connected directly to the fileserver (not usually recommended because of performance impacts to the fileserver).

■ By a computer connected to the network, with the printer connected to that computer. The computer runs special print server software to perform this job.

■ Through the use of a built-in print server on a printer's network interface card (NIC). For example, nearly all Hewlett-Packard LaserJets offer an option to include a network card in the printer. This card also contains the computer necessary to act as a print server. This is far less expensive than the previous option.

▲ Through the use of a dedicated network print server, which is a box about the size of a deck of cards that connects to the printer's parallel port on one end and the network on the other end. It also contains the computer necessary to act as a print server.

Application Services

Just as you can share files on a network, you can often also share applications on a network. For example, you can have a shared copy of Microsoft Office, or some other application, and keep it on the network server, from where it is also run. When a workstation wants to run the program, it loads the files from the network, just like it would from a local disk drive, and runs the program normally. Keeping applications centralized reduces the amount of disk space needed on each workstation and makes it easier to administer the application (for instance, with some applications you only have to upgrade the network copy; with others you also must perform a brief installation for each client).

Another application service you can host on the network is a shared installation point for applications. Instead of having to load a CD-ROM onto each workstation, the contents of the CD-ROM can usually be copied to the server and the installation program run from there for each workstation. This makes installing the applications much faster and more convenient.

CAUTION: Make sure any applications you host on a network server are licensed appropriately. Most software licenses do NOT let you run an application on multiple computers. Even if you only need one copy of the application to set up the files on the server, you still need a license for every user. Different applications have different fine print regarding this (some require one license per user, some require one license per computer, some allow your network users to use a copy at home freely, and so forth). Make sure to carefully read the license agreements for your business software and adhere to their terms and conditions.

E-Mail

An extremely valuable and important network resource these days is e-mail. Not only can it be helpful to communicate within a company, but it is also fast becoming a preferred vehicle to communicate with people outside a company.

E-mail systems are roughly divided into two different types: file-based and client/server. A file-based e-mail system is one where the e-mail system resides in a set of files kept in a shared location on a server. The server doesn't actually do anything beyond providing access to the files. When connections are required from a file-based e-mail system and the outside, say, to the Internet, this is usually accomplished with a stand-alone computer that handles the e-mail interface between the two systems.

A client/server e-mail system is one where an e-mail server contains the messages and handles all the e-mail interconnections, both inside the company and to connections outside the company. Client/server e-mail systems, such as Microsoft Exchange or Lotus Notes, are more secure and far more powerful than their file-based counterparts. They often offer additional features that enable you to use the e-mail system to automate different business processes, such as invoicing or purchasing. Unless a company has at least 100 employees, though, these are usually overkill and too costly for smaller companies.

Remote Access

Another important service for most networks is remote access to the network resources. Users use this feature to access their files and e-mail when they're travelling or working from a remote location, such as their homes. Remote access systems come in many different flavors. Some of the methods used to provide remote access include

▼ Setting up a simple Remote Access Service (RAS) connection on a Windows NT Server, which can range from using a single modem to a bank of modems.

■ Using a dedicated remote access system, which handles many modems and usually includes many computers, each one on its own stand-alone card.

■ Employing a workstation on the network and having users dial in using a remote control program like PCAnywhere.

■ Setting up a Virtual Private Network (VPN) connection to the Internet, through which users can access resources on the company network in a secure fashion through the Internet.

▲ Installing Windows Terminal Server or Citrix WinFrame, both of which allow a single Windows NT Server to host multiple client sessions, each one appearing to the end user as a stand-alone computer.

As you can see, many ways offer remote access services to users of the network. The right solution depends on what the users need to do remotely, how many users exist (both in total and at any given time), and how much you want to spend. See Chapter 7 for more information on remote access.

Wide Area Networks

You should think of a wide area network (WAN) as a sort of "meta network." A *WAN* is simply the connection of multiple local area networks (LANs) together. This can be accomplished in many different ways, depending on how often the LANs need to be connected to one another, how much data capacity (bandwidth) is required, and the distance between the LANs. Solutions range from using full-time leased telephone lines that can carry 56Kbps of data, to dedicated DS1 (T-1) lines carrying 1.544Mbps to DS3 lines carrying 44.736Mbps to other solutions (like private satellites) carrying even higher bandwidths. You can also create a WAN using Virtual Private Networks (VPNs) over the Internet (although this method usually offers inconsistent bandwidth, it's often the least expensive).

WANs are created when the users of one LAN need frequent access to the resources on another LAN. For instance, a company's Enterprise Resource Planning system may be running at the headquarter's location, but the warehouse location needs access to it to use its inventory and shipping functions.

TIP: As a general rule, if you can architect a system where a WAN is *not* required, you're usually better off because WAN links are usually expensive to maintain. However, often the geographic and management structure of a particular company dictates the use of a WAN.

Internet and Intranet

There's no way around it these days: the Internet has become vital to the productivity of most businesses and handling Internet connectivity on a network is often a vital service. Many different types of services are available over the Internet, including e-mail, the Web, and Usenet newsgroups.

An Internet connection for a network consists of a telecommunications network connection to an Internet service provider (ISP), using a connection such as a leased 56K line, an ISDN line, or a fractional or full DS1 (T-1) connection. This line comes into the building and connects to a box called a CSU/DSU (Channel Service Unit/Data Service Unit), which converts the data from the form carried by the local telephone company to one usable on the LAN. The CSU/DSU is, in turn, connected to a router that routes data packets between the local network and the Internet. Security is provided either by filtering the packets going through the router or by the addition of a firewall system, which runs on a computer and offers the highest level of security and administration features.

An *intranet*, as its name suggests, is an internally-focused network that mimics the Internet itself. For example, a company may deploy an intranet that hosts a Web server, and on that Web server they may place documents like employee handbooks, purchasing forms, or other information that people publish for internal use. Intranets may also host other Internet-type services, like FTP servers or Usenet servers, or these services may be provided by other tools that offer the same functionality. Intranets are usually not accessible from outside the LAN (although they can be) and are just a much smaller version of the Internet that a company maintains for itself.

Understanding the technologies, services, and features of the Internet is complex. You can learn much more about these technologies in Chapter 5.

Network Security

Any time you share important and confidential information on a network, you have to carefully consider the security of those resources. Users and management must help set the level of security needed for the network and the different information it stores and they need to participate in deciding who has access to which resources.

Network security is provided by a combination of factors, including features of the NOS, the physical cabling plant, how the network is connected to other networks, the features of the client workstations, the actions of the users, the security policies of management, and how well the security features are implemented and administered. All these things come together into a chain and any single weak link in the chain can cause it to fail.

Depending on the company, any failures of network security can have severe consequences, so network security is usually an extremely important part of any network. For
a more detailed discussion of network security, see Chapter 8.

UNDERSTANDING THE OSI NETWORKING MODEL

The Open Systems Interconnection (OSI) Model defines all the methods and protocols
needed to connect one computer to any other over a network. The OSI Model is a conceptual model, used most often in network design and in engineering network solutions.
Generally, real-world networks conform to the OSI Model, although differences exist between the theory of the OSI Model and actual practice in most networks. Still, the OSI
Model offers an excellent way to understand and visualize how computers network to
each other and it is required knowledge for anyone active in the field of networking.

The OSI Model separates the methods and protocols needed for a network connection
into seven different *layers.* Each higher layer relies on services provided by a lower-level
layer. As an illustration, if you were to think about a desktop computer in this way, its
hardware would be the lowest layer and the operating system drivers—the next higher
layer—would rely on the lowest layer to do their job. The operating system itself, the next
higher layer, would rely on both of the lower layers working properly. This continues all
the way up to the point at which an application presents data to you on the computer
screen. Figure 1-3 shows the seven layers of the OSI Model.

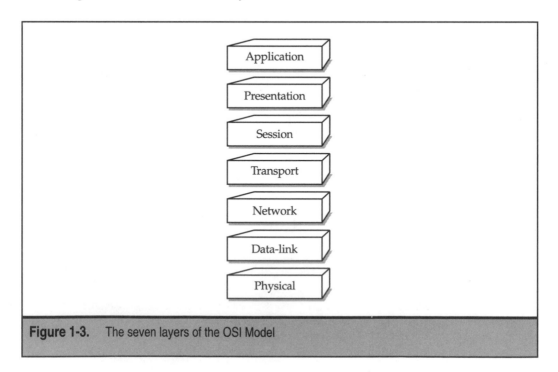

Figure 1-3. The seven layers of the OSI Model

NOTE: The OSI Model is sometimes called "the seven-layer model." It was developed by the International Standards Organization (ISO) in 1983 and is documented as standard 7498.

For a complete network connection, data flows from the top layer on one computer, down through all the lower layers, across the wire, and back up the seven layers on the other computer. The following sections discuss each layer in turn, making comparisons to real networking systems as appropriate.

Physical Layer

The first layer, the *physical layer*, defines the properties of the physical medium used to make a network connection. The physical layer specifications result in a physical medium—a network cable—that can transmit a stream of bits between nodes on the physical network. The physical connection can be either point-to-point or multipoint, and it can consist of either *half-duplex* (one direction at a time) or *full-duplex* (both directions simultaneously) transmissions. Moreover, the bits can be transmitted either in series or in parallel (most networks use a serial stream of bits, but the standard allows for both serial and parallel). The specification for the physical layer also defines the cable used, what voltages are carried on the cable, the timing of the electrical signals, the distance that can be run, and so on. A network interface card (NIC), for example, is part of the physical layer.

Data-Link Layer

The data-link layer, layer 2, defines standards that assign meaning to the bits carried by the physical layer. It establishes a reliable protocol through the physical layer so the network layer (layer 3) can transmit its data. The data-link layer typically includes error detection and correction to ensure a reliable data stream. The data elements carried by the data-link layer are called *frames*. Examples of frame types include X.25 and 802.x (802.x includes both Ethernet and Token Ring networks).

The data-link layer is usually subdivided into two sublayers, called the Logical Link Control (LLC) and Medium Access Control (MAC) sublayers. If used, the LLC sublayer performs tasks like call setup and termination (the OSI Model can be applied to telecommunications networks as well as LANs) and data transfer. The MAC sublayer handles frame assembly and disassembly, error detection and correction, and addressing. The two most common MAC protocols are 802.3 Ethernet and 802.5 Token Ring. Other MAC protocols include 802.11 100BaseVBG, 802.12 Wireless, and 802.7 Broadband.

On most systems, drivers for the NICs perform the work done at the data-link layer.

Network Layer

The *network layer*, layer 3, is where a lot of action goes on for most networks. The network layer defines how data *packets* get from one point to another on a network and what goes into each packet. The network layer defines different packet protocols, such as IP (Internet Protocol) and IPX (Internet Protocol Exchange). These packet protocols include source and destination routing information. The routing information in each packet tells the network where to send the packet to reach its destination and tells the receiving computer from where the packet originated.

The network layer is most important when the network connection passes through one or more *routers*, which are hardware devices that examine each packet and, from their source and destination addresses, send them off to their proper destination. Over a complex network, like the Internet, a packet may go through ten or more routers until it reaches its destination. On a LAN, a packet may not go through any routers to get to its destination or it may go through one or more.

Note that by breaking the network layer (also known as the *packet layer*) into a separate layer from the physical and data-link layers means the protocols defined in this layer can be carried over any variations of the lower layers. So, to put this into real-world terms, it means an IP packet can be sent over an Ethernet network, a Token Ring network, or even a serial cable connecting two computers to one another. The same holds true for an IPX packet.

Transport Layer

The transport layer, layer 4, manages the flow of information from one network node to another. It ensures the packets are decoded in the proper sequence and all packets were received. It also identifies each computer or node on a network uniquely. The transport layer is the first layer that becomes differently implemented on different networking systems. Unique at this layer are Windows NT networks, Novell NetWare networks, or any other networking system. Examples of transport layer protocols include TCP (Transmission Control Protocol) and SPX (Sequenced Packet Exchange). Each is respectively used in concert with IP and IPX.

Session Layer

The session layer, layer 5, defines the connection from a user to a network server, or from a peer on a network to another peer. These virtual connections are referred to as *sessions*. They include negotiation between the client and host, or peer and peer, on matters of flow control, transaction processing, transfer of user information and authentication to the network.

Presentation Layer

The presentation layer, layer 6, takes the data supplied by the lower-level layers and transforms it so it can be presented to the system (as opposed to the presentation to the user, which is handled well outside the OSI Model). The functions that take place at the presentation layer can include data compression and decompression, as well as data encryption and decryption.

Application Layer

The application layer, layer 7, controls how the operating system, and its applications, interact with the network. The applications you use, such as Microsoft Word or Lotus 1-2-3 aren't a part of the application layer, but they certainly benefit from the work that goes on there. An example of software at the application layer is the network client you use, such as Windows 9x's Client for Microsoft, Novell Networks, or Novell's Client 32 software. It also controls how the operating system and applications interact with those clients.

Understanding How Data Travels Through the OSI Layers

As mentioned earlier in this section, data flows from an application program or the operating system, and then goes through the protocols and devices that make up the seven layers of the OSI Model, one by one, until the data arrives at the physical layer and is transmitted over the network connection. The computer at the receiving end reverses this process, with the data coming in at the physical layer, travelling up through all the layers until it emerges from the application layer and is made use of by the operating system and any application programs.

At each stage of the OSI Model, the data is "wrapped" with new control information, which concerns the work done at that particular layer, leaving the previous layers' information intact and wrapped within the new control information. This control information is different for each layer, but it includes *headers*, *trailers*, *preambles*, and *postambles*.

So, for example, when data goes into the networking software and components making up the OSI Model, it starts at the application layer and includes an application header and application data (the real data being sent). Next, at the presentation layer, a presentation header is wrapped around the data and it is passed to the component at the session layer, where a session header is wrapped around all of the data, and so on, until it reaches the physical layer. At the receiving computer, this process is reversed, with each layer unwrapping its appropriate control information, performing whatever work is indicated by that control information, and passing the data onto the next higher layer. (Although this whole process works nicely and is actually a good design, it may appear at first glance to be something so complicated, it's a wonder networks ever get data to where it's supposed to go!)

LEARNING ABOUT NETWORK HARDWARE COMPONENTS

This section overviews the hardware involved in making networks work. Understanding the general types of devices you typically encounter in a network is important, not only for planning a network but also for troubleshooting and maintenance.

Servers

A *server* is any computer that performs network functions for other computers. These functions fall into several categories, including:

▼ File and print servers, which provide file sharing and services to share network-based printers.

■ Application servers, which provide specific application services to an application. An example is a server that runs a database that a distributed application makes use of.

■ E-mail servers, which provide e-mail storage and interconnection services to client computers.

■ Networking servers, which may provide a host of different network services. Examples of these services include the automatic assignment of TCP/IP addresses (DHCP servers), routing of packets from one network to another (routing servers), encryption/decryption and other security services, Virtual Private Network (VPN) servers, and so forth.

■ Internet servers, which provide Web, Usenet News (NNTP), and Internet e-mail services.

▲ Remote access servers, which provide access to a local network for remote users.

Servers typically run some sort of NOS, such as Windows NT Server, Novell NetWare, or UNIX. Depending on the NOS chosen, all the functions previously listed might all be performed on one server or distributed to many servers. Also, not all networks need all the previously listed services.

NOTE: You can learn more about servers in Chapter 7.

Server computers can be nearly any type of computer but, today, they are mostly comprised of high-end PCs using the Intel architecture. You may also see certain types of servers that use a different platform. For instance, many dedicated Web servers run on UNIX-based computers, such as those from Sun Microsystems.

A number of things distinguish a true server-class computer from a more pedestrian client computer. These things include built-in redundancy with multiple power supplies and fans (for instance) to keep the server running if something breaks. They also include special high-performance designs for disk subsystems, memory, and network subsystems to optimize the movement of data to and from the server, the network, and the client computers. Finally, they usually include special monitoring software and hardware that keeps a close eye on the health of the server, warning of failures before they occur. For example, most servers have temperature monitors in them; if the temperature starts getting too high, a warning is issued so the problem can be resolved before it causes failure of any of the hardware components in the server.

Hubs, Routers, and Switches

Hubs, routers, and switches are the most commonly seen pure network hardware. These are the devices to which all the cables of the network are connected and that pass the data along at the physical layer of the OSI Model.

NOTE: Hubs, routers, and switches are discussed in more detail—along with other networking hardware—in Chapter 3.

A *hub*, sometimes called a *concentrator*, is a device that connects a number of network cables coming from client computers to a network. Hubs come in many different sizes, supporting from as few as two computers, up to large hubs that may support 60 computers or more. (The most common hub size supports 24 network connections.) All the network connections on a hub share a single *collision domain*, which is a fancy way of saying all the connections to a hub "talk" over a single logical wire and are subject to interference from other computers connected to the same hub. Figure 1-4 shows an example hub and how it is logically wired.

A *switch* is wired very similarly to a hub, and actually looks just like a hub. However, on a switch all of the network connections are on their own collision domain. The switch makes each network connection a private one, and then collects the data from each of the connections and forwards it to a network backbone, which usually runs at a much higher speed than the individual switch connections. Often, switches will be used to connect many hubs to a single network backbone. Figure 1-5 shows a typical switch and hub wiring arrangement.

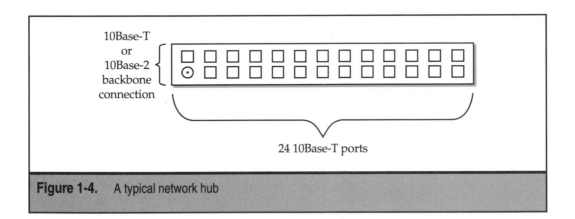

Figure 1-4. A typical network hub

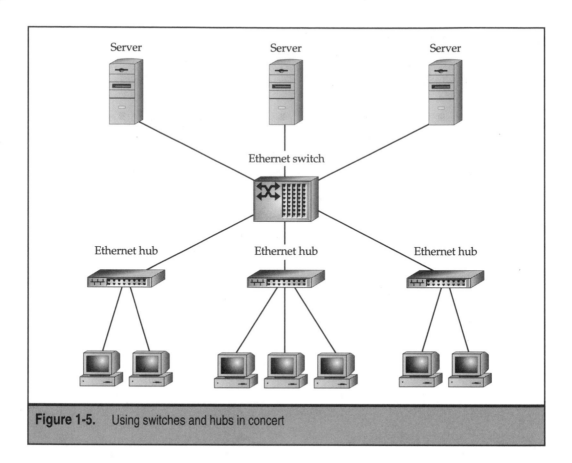

Figure 1-5. Using switches and hubs in concert

A *router* routes data packets from one network to another. The two networks connect to the router using their own wiring type and connection type. For example, a router that connected a 10Base-T network to an ISDN telephone line would have two connections: one leading to the 10Base-T network and one leading to the ISDN line provided by the phone company. Routers also usually have an additional connection that a terminal can be connected to; this connection is just used to program and maintain the router.

Cabling and Cable Plants

Many different types of network cable exist, but only a few are commonly seen that you have to worry about. The most common network cable for LANs is Category 3 (Cat-3) twisted-pair cable. This cable carries the network signal to each point through four wires (two twisted-pairs). Cat-3 cable is used to support 10Base-T Ethernet networks.

NOTE: The twisting of each pair in the cable jacket reduces the chances of the cable picking up electrical interference.

Higher in quality and capability than Cat-3 cable is Category 5 (Cat-5) cable. This is similar cable, made up of sets of twisted-pairs, but it contains twice as many pairs as Cat-3 cable. Cat-5 cable is required for 100Base-T networks. You can also use Cat-5 cable to carry two simultaneous Cat-3 network connections.

Coaxial cable (called *coax*) is not currently used for new cable installations, but you may still come across it in older buildings. Coax cable has a center core of copper (called the *conductor*), surrounded by a plastic wrapper, which is, in turn, wrapped with braided metal, called the *shield*. For instance, the cable that one uses to connect a television to a cable TV network is a type of coax cable. Most coax cable used for networks is a type called RG-58, which is used for 10Base-2 (thin Ethernet) networks. Another is RG-56, used for ARCnet networks. The different types of coax cable refer to the specifications of the cable, which affects whether a particular network type can make use of the cable. You cannot mix different types of coax cable in a single network and you must use the correct type for the network you are building.

NOTE: Read Chapter 2 for more information on network cabling.

The term *cable plant* refers to the entire installation of all your network cable. It includes not only the cable run throughout a building, but also the connectors, wall plates, patch panels, and so forth. It's extremely important that a new installation of a cable plant be performed by a qualified contractor trained to install that type of cable. Despite the apparent simplicity of cable, it is actually quite complex and its installation is also complex.

Workstation Hardware

Any computer on a network that is used by people is usually referred to as a *network workstation*. Usually, this is an Intel-based PC running some version of Windows, which has a NIC installed into it, along with network client software, all of which allow the workstation to participate on the network. Network workstations can also be any other type of computer that includes the necessary network hardware and software, such as an Apple Macintosh or some form of UNIX-based computer.

TIP: Don't confuse a network workstation (a generic term) with workstation-class computers. Workstation-class computers are high-end computers used for computer aided design, engineering, and graphics work.

CHAPTER SUMMARY

This chapter introduced a number of important networking concepts. You learned about how computers on a network relate to one another, how the different parts of a network connection are logically broken down in the OSI network model and how this model is useful in understanding networks. You also learned about a number of basic network features and resources.

The following chapters cover these subjects in more detail, starting with the next chapter, which discusses the often misunderstood world of network wiring.

CHAPTER 2

Understanding Network Cabling

I f you were to compare a computer network to the human body, the network cabling system would be the nervous system. The network cabling system is what actually carries all the data from one point to another and determines how the network works. How a network is cabled is of supreme importance to how the network functions, how fast it functions, how reliable the network will be as a whole, and how easy it is to expand and change the network. With any new network, the first thing you do after assessing the needs for the network is to determine how the network should be wired; all the other components of the network are then built on that foundation.

In this chapter, you learn everything important about network cabling, including:

▼ Network topologies, or how the networks are logically and physically wired

■ Cable types, including specifications and requirements

▲ Cable installation, including how to choose a contractor, how to specify the project, how to maintain a cabling system, and how to end up with a solid cabling system

Many people think network cabling is relatively simple. After all, what could be simpler than running a wire between a number of points? As you will see, though, the topic of network cabling encompasses more than meets the eye and it's an extremely important area to get right.

UNDERSTANDING CABLE TOPOLOGIES

Because the word *topology* basically means *shape*, the term *network topology* refers to the shape of a network. There are several different topologies in which networks are wired, and the choice of a topology is often your most important choice when you plan a network. The different topologies have different costs (both to install and maintain), different performance, and different levels of reliability. In the next several sections, you learn about the main topologies in use today.

Bus Topology

A *bus topology*, more completely called a *Common Bus Multipoint Topology*, is a network where, basically, one single network cable is used from one end of the network to the other, with different network devices (called *nodes*) connected to the cable at different locations. Figure 2-1 illustrates a simple bus topology network.

Different types of bus networks have different specifications, which include the following factors:

▼ How many nodes can be in a single segment

■ How many segments can be used through the use of repeaters

■ How far apart does each node need to be from the nearest other nodes

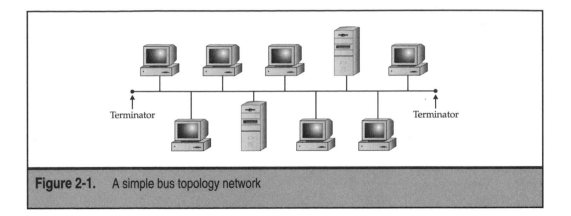

Figure 2-1.   A simple bus topology network

- How long can a segment be
- Which coax cable type is required
- ▲ How must each end of the bus be terminated

New network wiring installations these days rarely use bus topologies, although many older networks do still use it. Bus topology networks use coaxial cable, described in the previous chapter. Each end of each segment of the network has a special cable terminator on it, without which the network will not function. Bus topology networks use BNC connectors to tie all the individual pieces of cable together. Each computer is connected to the network through the use of a BNC *T-connector* (called that because it's shaped like the letter *T*) that allows the network to continue its bus and lets the computer connect to it.

DEFINE IT!—Network Segment

A *network segment* can mean somewhat different things depending on the topology of the network, but the concept is simplest with bus networks and is essentially the same for any topology. A *segment* is a single length of cable to which all the nodes in that segment are connected. In truth, a segment is not a single strand of cable because it is broken at each computer connection point with a connector that lets the node connect to the network cable, but the cable is electrically one single length. In any given segment, all the network traffic is "seen" by all the nodes on that segment. You need to take this into account when planning how many nodes you will connect to any given segment. If you have 20 computers all fully using that segment at the same time, each computer will only achieve approximately $1/20^{th}$ of the available maximum bandwidth. This is simplified; you learn more about how this works later in this chapter and in following chapters.

DEFINE IT!—BNC Connectors

Depending on whom you ask, BNC stands for Bayonet Nut Connector, British Naval Connector, or Bayonet Neill-Concelman (with the latter two words standing for its inventor, Mr. Neill-Concelman). BNC is a bayonet-style connector that quickly attaches and detaches with a quarter-turn. A variety of different parts—T-connectors, barrel connectors, elbow connectors, cable ends that splice onto appropriate cable, and so forth—use BNC connectors, so you can achieve nearly any type of connection needed. The BNC connector is extremely easy to use and makes a secure connection.

Bus network topologies are by far the least expensive to install because they use much less cable than the other two topologies and, accordingly, they use less material and need less installation labor.

But there are some big drawbacks to bus networks. Because all the sub-cables that make up the segment and run from node-to-node must be connected at all times, and because a failure in any part of the segment will cause the entire segment to fail, bus networks are prone to trouble. And even more important, that trouble can take a long time to track down because you must work your way through all the cable connections until you find the one causing the problem. Because of the tendency of bus networks to be unreliable, they aren't installed much for new networks any more.

TIP: If you're setting up a small network with all the computers within a single room or two, then a bus network, such as one using thin Ethernet, is still a good choice. In this situation, you can quickly solve any cabling problems that arise, the installation cost is the lowest, and a bus network will perform on par with any other network topology.

By far the most prevalent bus network in existence today is one called 10Base-2 Ethernet, or more commonly: thin Ethernet. This network type has the following characteristics:

▼ Has a rated maximum speed of 10Mbps.

■ Uses RG-58/AU or RG-58/CU coaxial cable and BNC connectors.

■ Requires a 50 ohm terminating connector at each end of each segment to function.

■ Can handle a maximum of 30 nodes per segment.

■ Can be run up to a maximum segment length of 185 meters (607 feet).

■ Can use extended segments through the use of repeaters. If used, a maximum of three segments may be connected together with repeaters and each segment may each have up to 30 nodes (with the repeater counting as a node). You can also have two additional segments (a total of five) if those extra two are used for distance only and have no nodes on them. In no case can the total, repeated segment exceed 925 meters (3,035 feet). Remember the 5-4-3 rule: five segments, four repeaters, three populated segments.

▲ Requires each node to be at least 1.5 feet (cable distance) from any other node.

NOTE: *Repeaters* electrically boost the signal on a cable so it can be extended further; they do not route any of the data, and, in fact, a repeater is "ignorant" of any of the data it carries. Repeaters are inexpensive and reliable. Remember, however, a cable extended with a repeater means all the network traffic on one side of the repeater is echoed to the cable on the other side of the repeater, regardless of whether it needs to go to a node on that other cable.

Star Topology

A *star topology* is one in which a central unit, called a *hub* or *concentrator*, hosts a set of network cables that radiate out to each node on the network. Technically, the hub is referred to as a Multi-station Access Unit (MAU) but that particular terminology tends only to be used with Token Ring networks, which use a ring topology (see the following section). Each hub usually hosts about 24 nodes, although hubs exist that range in size from two nodes up to 96 nodes. Regardless of the hub size, you can connect multiple hubs together to grow the network in any way that makes sense. See Chapter 3 for more on connecting hubs together in different configurations. Figure 2-2 shows a simple star topology network.

All the network traffic used on any of the network connections to the hub is echoed to all the other connected nodes on that particular hub. Because of this, all the bandwidth of any single node connection is shared with all other node connections. For example, if one of the nodes connected to the hub is using half the available bandwidth, all the other

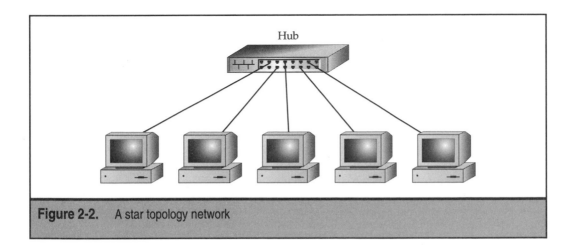

Figure 2-2. A star topology network

nodes must contend with that use for their own. In other words, if you're using a network type with a capacity of 10Mbps, that's the total amount of bandwidth available to all nodes connected to the hub in aggregate.

NOTE: Networks that are physically wired in a star topology are logically either a bus or a ring. This means, despite what the network looks like, it still "behaves" as either a bus or a ring. Ethernet networks wired in a star fashion are logically a bus, while Token Ring networks wired in a star fashion are logically a ring.

Star topology networks can use one of several forms of Ethernet. The most common is 10Base-T Ethernet, which provides 10Mpbs of bandwidth. Becoming more popular is 100Base-T Ethernet, which provides 100Mpbs of bandwidth. 10Base-T requires a type of twisted-pair cable called Category 3 (Cat 3) cable, while 100Base-T requires Category 5 (Cat 5) cable (10Base-T can also use Cat 5, but 100Base-T cannot use Cat 3).

10Base-T networks share the following wiring characteristics:

▼ Require four actual wires (two twisted-pairs in a single sheath); can be either unshielded twisted-pair (UTP) or shielded twisted-pair (STP).

■ Can be run on either Cat 3 or Cat 5 cable (Cat 5 cable provides eight wires—four twisted-pairs—and so can carry two node connections in each cable if desired).

■ Are limited to a length of 100 meters (328 feet) for each node connection.

■ Are not limited in the number of nodes in a single logical segment.

▲ Uses RJ-45 connectors for all connections (this is similar to a modular telephone connector, but it is larger).

DEFINE IT!—Physical Versus Logical

You'll often hear the terms "physical" and "logical" bandied about when discussing networks. These terms are used for quite a few different things. *Physical*, used in the context of networking, means the actual, physical thing; what you can see and feel. *Logical* means how something works, despite its appearance. For example, a Token Ring network is physically wired in a star; each cable radiates out from the MAU to each node. Logically, though, it's a ring, in which the signals travel from node to node. The fact that the signals travel from the node, to the MAU, and back to the next node is usually unimportant when thinking about the logical arrangement of Token Ring.

100Base-T networks are similar to 10Base-T networks and have these characteristics:

▼ Require eight actual wires (four twisted-pairs in a single sheath).

■ Must use Cat-5 cable or better. (Some vendors are supplying cable called Cat-6 and Cat-7. While these cables may be of higher grade than Cat-5, the standards are not yet finalized and these cable categories do not yet officially exist.)

■ Are limited to a length of 100 meters (328 feet) for each node connection.

■ Are not limited in the number of nodes in a single logical segment.

▲ Use RJ-45 connectors for all connections.

Two tradeoffs are involved with star topology networks as compared to bus networks. First, star topology networks cost more. Much more actual wire is required, the labor to install that wire is much greater, and there is an additional cost for the needed hubs. To offset these costs, however, star topologies are far more reliable than bus topologies. With a star topology, if any single network connection goes bad (is cut or damaged in some way) only that one connection is affected. While it is true that hubs echo all the network signals for the connected nodes to all other nodes on the hub, they also have the capability to *partition*, or cut off, any misbehaving node connections automatically—one bad apple won't spoil the whole bunch. In addition, because each cable is run directly from the hub to the node, it is extremely easy to troubleshoot; you don't have to go traipsing over an entire building trying to find the problem.

Ring Topology

A ring topology is actually not a physical arrangement of a network cable as you might guess. Instead, rings are a logical arrangement; the actual cables are wired in a star, with each node connected on its own cable to the MAU. However, electrically the network behaves like a ring, where the network signals travel around the ring to each node in turn. Figure 2-3 shows a sample ring topology network.

Ring topology LANs are based on Token Ring instead of Ethernet. Some may also run Fiber Distributed Data Interface (FDDI)—a 100Mbps fiber-optic network. Rings are also used for some larger telecommunications networks like Synchronous Optical Network (SONET).

Comparing Rings to Stars and Buses

To understand how rings compare to stars and buses, you first need to understand a basic concept of how all Ethernet networks work. Ethernet networks manage all the needed signals on the network using a technique called CSMA/CD, which stands for Carrier Sense Multiple Access/with Collision Detection. CSMA/CD allows each node on a segment to transmit data whenever it likes. If, by chance, two nodes try to transmit at the same time,

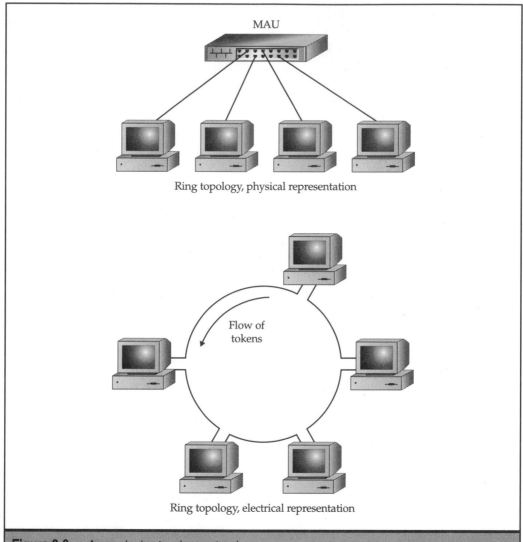

MAU

Ring topology, physical representation

Flow of
tokens

Ring topology, electrical representation

Figure 2-3. A sample ring topology network

they each detect this occurrence with their collision detection, and then both nodes wait a random amount of time (counted in milliseconds) to retry their transmission.

NOTE: All Ethernet networks use CSMA/CD except for a defunct standard proposed by Hewlett-Packard called 100-BaseVG, which used a hybrid of Ethernet and Token Ring collision management techniques.

If you think about how data packets flow on a network using CSMA/CD, you'd probably think that it can quickly become a confusing mess with data and collision retries causing more collisions. And you'd probably think the potential exists for the network to reach a saturation point where virtually nothing gets transmitted because of excessive collisions. You'd be right. For 10Base-T networks, this point occurs somewhere around 3.5Mbps (about a third of the 10Mbps theoretical maximum that one node could achieve sending a stream of data to one other node). However, the reality is that this isn't much of a problem on most networks for two reasons. First, most network traffic is *bursty*, and network nodes rarely consume all the bandwidth on a particular network for any significant length of time. Second, even on a network where excessive collisions are hampering performance, breaking the network segment into smaller pieces and reducing the chances of collisions proportionately is relatively easy. In the real world, CSMA/CD works well and Ethernet is the predominant network standard in the world because it works so well and it is so flexible.

Token Ring networks operate on a different principle than CSMA/CD. Token Ring networks manage their bandwidth with a technique called *token passing*. Electrically, a data entity called a *token* circulates around the logical network ring. The token has two states: free and busy. When a node wants to transmit some data, it waits until the token coming into it is in a free state, and then the node marks the token as busy. Next, the node adds the data to be sent and the destination address to the token packet, and sends it on to the next node. The next node, finding the token set to its busy state, examines the destination address and passes the token on unchanged toward the destination. Once the destination node receives the token, it gets its data, marks the token as free, and sends it along to the next workstation. If, somehow, the token becomes "lost," then a workstation generates a new, open token automatically after a set period of time passes.

The beauty of Token Ring networks is that they have predictable behavior as the bandwidth needs of the nodes increase and collisions (which are impossible in a Token Ring network) never bog them down. However, these benefits of Token Ring networks are offset somewhat by the greater overhead and processing needs to handle the tokens, so Token Ring networks perform, overall, about as fast as similar-bandwidth Ethernet networks.

IBM invented the Token Ring network technology in the late 1960s, and the first Token Ring networks started appearing in 1986. While quite a few Token Ring LANs are installed (running at either 4Mbps or 16Mbps), you tend to see them predominantly in companies that have a strong IBM relationship and, perhaps, also use an IBM mainframe or minicomputer.

If you're designing a new LAN, generally your best bet is to use Ethernet in a star topology. You'll find network equipment for this choice is readily available, inexpensive, and many qualified installers are available for either 10Base-T or 100Base-T. Choose Ethernet in a bus topology (thin Ethernet) for *very* small networks that share a common space.

Choose Token Ring if some external need is driving this, such as connectivity needs to an old IBM mainframe that doesn't support Ethernet.

DEMYSTIFYING NETWORK CABLING

Network cabling can be incredibly confusing. Not only do lots of different types of network cables exist, all with their own names and properties, but you can often use different types of cables with the same type of network. For example, Ethernet networks can use an astonishing number of cables, ranging from coaxial cable, to unshielded or shielded twisted-pair cable, to thick coaxial cable, to fiber-optic cable. To design or support any given network, you need to know what your cable choices are and you need to know how to maintain that particular type of cable.

The focus in this section is to demystify cabling systems for you. You learn primarily about the most common types of network cable, the kinds you'll find in 99 percent of the networks in existence and you'll use for 99 percent of any new networks. When appropriate, passing reference is made to other cable types so you know what they are, but you should focus your attention on only a few ubiquitous cable types—the ones primarily discussed here.

Learning Basic Cable Types

There are many different basic cable types. The most common are unshielded twisted-pair (UTP) and coaxial, with UTP being by far the most common today. Other common types of network cabling are shielded twisted-pair (STP) and fiber-optic cable.

Unshielded twisted-pair cable consists of two or more pairs of plastic-insulated conductors inside a cable sheath (made from either vinyl or Teflon). For each pair, the two conductors are twisted within the cable, helping the cable resist outside electrical interference. Rigid standards exist for how this cable is made, including the proper distance between each twist of the pair. Figure 2-4 shows an example of UTP cable.

STP is similar to UTP, but it has a braided metal shield surrounding the twisted-pairs to reduce further the chance of interference from electrical sources outside the cable.

Coaxial cable consists of a central copper conductor wrapped in a plastic insulation material, which is, in turn, surrounded by a braided wire shield, and, finally, is wrapped in a plastic cable sheath. (The coaxial cable used for televisions is similar in design). Two main types are used for networks. Thin Ethernet (10Base-2) uses RG-58/AU or RG-58/CU cable, while thick Ethernet (10Base-5) uses—you guessed it—a much thicker RG-8 coaxial cable. Figure 2-5 shows an example of coaxial cable.

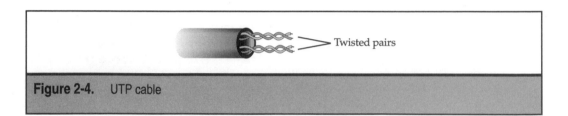

Figure 2-4.   UTP cable

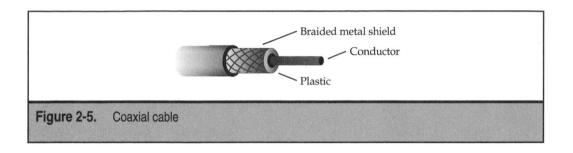

Figure 2-5.   Coaxial cable

Fiber-optic cable uses a glass strand and carries the data signals as light instead of electricity. It used to be that fiber-optic cable was used for higher-speed networks, but this is changing. Even now, there are proposals to carry 1Gbps over copper cable, so the need for fiber-optic cable is being greatly reduced. This is good news, as fiber-optic cable is extremely expensive to purchase, install, and maintain. However, fiber-optic cable can do one thing that copper cables cannot: span extremely long distances. Fiber-optic cable can easily reach two miles at 100Mbps. For this reason, fiber-optic cable is often used to connect buildings in a campus-like setting together. But other than using it in situations when you need to span very long distances, you should avoid using fiber-optic cable.

Twisted-Pair Cabling: The King of Network Cables

For the past several years, virtually all new networks have been built using some form of twisted-pair cabling. Usually Cat-5 twisted-pair is used, although quite a few networks exist in which Cat-3 is installed. UTP is used instead of STP in almost all cases because it's less expensive, easier to install and maintain, and it isn't much affected by electrical interference. Both Ethernet and Token Ring networks use twisted-pair cabling. Note, different Ethernet types require different cables and some higher-speed standards require shielded cable.

When a new twisted-pair network is installed, a number of wiring components form the complete run from the workstation to the hub. As shown in Figure 2-6, the cabling starts at the hub, where a patch cable (usually 6-10 feet long) connects a port on the hub to a patch panel, using RJ-45 connectors on each end. On the other side of the patch panel, the twisted-pair cable is hard-wired to the patch panel connection, and then runs continuously to a wall jack, to which it is also hard-wired. The wall jack contains a RJ-45 connector on its other side, to which another patch cable connects, and then connects to the computer's network interface card (NIC). The distance from the connector on the hub to the connector on the computer's NIC cannot exceed 100 meters of cable length.

Anywhere twisted-pair cabling isn't hard-wired, it uses RJ-45 modular connectors. These are just like the modular connectors you see on telephones, but they are larger and can accommodate up to eight wires. 10Base-T uses four of those wires (two pairs: one for transmit and one for receive), while 100Base-T uses eight of those wires.

10Base-what?

The various Ethernet standards referred to as, for instance, 10Base-2, 10Base-T, 100Base-T, and so on contain in their name all you need to know about what they do. The first portion—the number—can be 10, 100, or 1000, and this is the data rate (in Mbps) the standard carries. The word *Base* means the network is *baseband* rather than *broadband*. The terminating letter or number indicates what sort of cable is used, with *T* denoting twisted-pair, 2 denoting thin coaxial, and 5 denoting thick coaxial. Here's a quick reference guide to the different standards commonly seen:

▼ 10Base-2. 10Mbps, coaxial (RG-58) cable.

■ 10Base-5. 10Mbps, coaxial (RG-8) cable.

■ 10Base-T. 10Mbps, twisted-pair (two pairs, Cat-3 or higher) cable.

■ 100Base-T. 100Mbps, twisted-pair (four pairs, Cat-5) cable. Also called 100Base-T4 to designate four pairs.

■ 100Base-TX. 100Mbps, twisted-pair (two pairs, Cat-5) cable.

■ 100Base-FX. 100Mbps, fiber-optic cable.

▲ 1000Base-T. 1Gbps, twisted-pair (four pairs, Cat-5) cable.

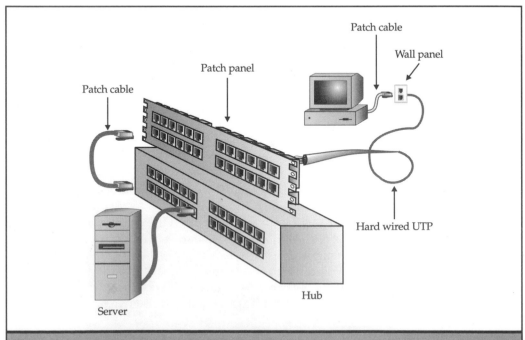

Figure 2-6.   A typical twisted-pair network arrangement

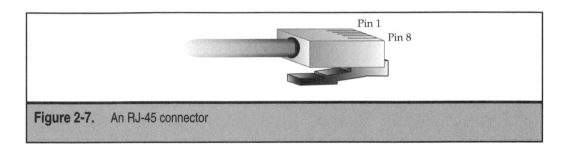

Pin 1

Pin 8

Figure 2-7.   An RJ-45 connector

The eight wires in the RJ-45 connector are numbered from one to eight. If you were to hold the connector in your left hand, with the pins in the connector facing up and pointed forward, pin 1 of the connector is the one furthest away from you (see Figure 2-7). Table 2-1 shows both the colors of standard Cat-5 cable that should be wired to each pin and 10Base-T assignments.

Most communications and network devices, including those designed to use RJ-45 connectors, are either *data communications equipment* (DCE) or *data terminal equipment* (DTE). If you have DTE equipment on one end, you need DCE equipment on the other. The RJ-45 jack on a hub is DCE, while the RJ-45 jack on a computer's NIC is DTE. Note, you cannot communicate between DCE and DCE devices, or DTE and DTE devices using a standard twisted-pair/RJ-45 cable that has been wired as described in Table 2-1. For instance, you cannot use a standard twisted-pair patch cable to connect directly from a network server to a workstation, or between two workstations, because those are all DTE devices. Instead, you must purchase or prepare a *crossover cable* that compensates for having, say, two DTE devices connect directly to each other. For 10Base-T networks, Table 2-2 shows you the wiring needed for a crossover cable.

Pin Number	Wire Base Color	Wire Stripe Color	10Base-T Use
1	White	Orange	Transmit Negative
2	Orange	White	Transmit Positive
3	White	Green	Receive Negative
4	Blue	White	N/A
5	White	Blue	N/A
6	Green	White	Receive Positive
7	White	Brown	N/A
8	Brown	White	N/A

Table 2-1.   10Base-T Wire Assignments

Pin	Wire Base Color	Wire Stripe Color	Pin	Wire Base Color	Wire Stripe Color
1	White	Orange	1	White	Green
2	Orange	White	2	Green	White
3	White	Green	3	White	Orange
6	Green	White	6	Orange	White

Table 2-2. Twisted-Pair/RJ-45 Crossover Cable Wiring

TIP: You can easily purchase all the tools and parts needed to make twisted-pair/RJ-45 cables and you should do so if you manage a network of any appreciable size (more than 50 workstations). Learning to use these tools and parts to make patch cables or to replace a failed cable quickly can be invaluable. This way, you can quickly make cables of any size you need. However, even though you should be able to do this, you're better off purchasing pre-made twisted-pair/RJ-45 cables to use with your network. Professionally made cables are more reliable and should give you fewer problems than the ones you make yourself.

What's All This About Cable Categories?

Twisted-pair network cables are rated in terms of their capability to carry network traffic. These ratings are defined by the Electronics Industry Association (EIA) and are referred to as levels 1 and 2, and categories 3, 4, and 5. The different category levels are simply called Cat-3 through Cat-5. Table 2-3 shows the rated performance for each of these levels.

Level or Category	Rated Performance
Level 1	Not performance rated
Level 2	1Mbps
Category 3	10Mbps
Category 4	16Mbps
Category 5	100Mbps

Table 2-3. Twisted-Pair Performance Designations

Plenum Versus Non-Plenum Cable

In a building, the area between the ceiling of the rooms and the roof of the building is called the *plenum space*. Most buildings use ducts (big, flexible hoses) to provide conditioned air to the rooms in the building and they use the open plenum space for air returned from the rooms. Occasionally, a building uses ducts for the return air, but the standard for office space is simply to use the plenum space. Why is this important in this chapter about cables? Because to run network cable in a building that uses the plenum for return air, you must either install the cable inside conduit (which is extremely expensive) or use plenum-grade cable. The difference between non-plenum cable and plenum cable is the plastics used in plenum cable do not give off toxic fumes in case of a fire. Make sure to check with your cabling contractor for details about the municipality in which you are installing network cable, but virtually all areas in the United States require conduit or plenum-level cable for buildings with plenum air returns. In addition to choosing the right kind of cable, it's also important for the cable installer to be familiar with, and comfortable with, doing any required wall penetrations that cross one-hour fire-rated corridors or building fire zones. Those wall penetrations must be properly sealed to maintain the building's fire ratings.

To achieve a particular performance rating in practice, you not only need cable certified to that performance level, but you must observe other requirements, including using connectors and patch cables that also meet the level of performance you want to achieve. For example, for a Cat-5 installation, you must have Cat-5 cable, connectors, patch panels, and patch cables. The entire circuit, from where the client computer connects to the hub connection at the other end, needs to be tested and certified to the performance level you need to achieve.

TIP: You can use higher-rated cable systems for networks with lower requirements. For example, common practice these days is to use Cat-5 cable for all network wiring, even if the network only uses 10Base-T at 10Mpbs. Doing this makes good sense because cable plants are expensive to replace and using Cat-5 cable means you won't have to replace the network cabling when the network is upgraded eventually to 100Base-T or some higher standard. Also, Cat-5 cabling components are of higher quality than Cat-3 components, so your network cabling is likely to be more reliable.

Coaxial Cable

Many older networks (those built prior to circa 1992) still have coaxial cable installed. Most of this coaxial cable is the thin variety, which is RG-58 and is used with thin Ethernet. A few may also use the thicker RG-8 cable for thick Ethernet, but this is rare.

Thin Ethernet cabling is wired in a bus arrangement, where each network segment starts with a terminator that connects to the end of the cable, runs to each node in turn, and ends with another terminator on the other end. The terminators contain special 50-ohm resistors and the network cable will not work without both being installed.

All the connectors in a thin Ethernet system are BNC connectors, a quick-release bayonet-style connector, both reliable and easy to use. BNC connectors come in a variety of different styles to enable you to make just about any network connection you need along the bus, including T-connectors, which have two female BNC connectors on each side of the crossbar of the *T* and a male BNC connector at the end of the shaft of the *T*. The two female connectors are used for the RG-58 cable coming into and out of a node, while the male connector attaches to a female BNC connector on the node's Ethernet card. There are also barrel connectors, with two female connectors on them; these are used to connect two thin Ethernet wires together. Barrel connectors are also available in different shapes, including an elbow bend and a U-shaped bend, but most of the time the simple straight barrel connector is used. Figure 2-8 shows the various parts of a thin Ethernet BNC cable system.

Coaxial cable has a central *conductor*, which can be either a solid, single copper wire or a stranded set of wires. A white plastic material surrounds the central conductor, which is, in turn, surrounded by a metal foil, and then a braided wire *shield*. The shield is finally wrapped in the final plastic cable sheath.

CAUTION: Cable types must not be mixed in any coaxial network. If the network uses, say, RG-58/AU, then that is what you must always use—not any other coaxial cable. Not mixing RG-58/AU and RG-58/U is also a good idea because they have ever-so-slightly different signaling characteristics. (/AU cable uses a stranded center conductor, while /U—sometimes called /CU—uses a solid center conductor).

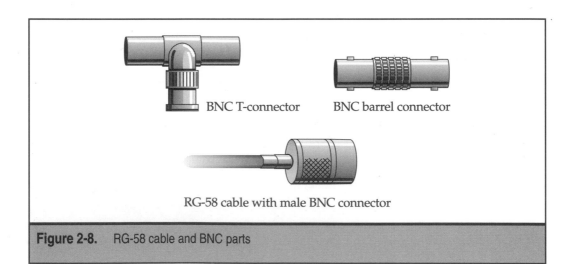

BNC T-connector

BNC barrel connector

RG-58 cable with male BNC connector

Figure 2-8. RG-58 cable and BNC parts

Learning to make coaxial cables with BNC connectors is fairly easy, but you need two special tools to make the job easy. First, you need a wire stripper that will cut the various parts of the cable to the right length. Many good strippers can do this for you automatically; check with your cable supplier to order one. You also need a crimper that can both crimp the central BNC pin onto the central conductor of the cable and the metal sleeve that holds the entire connector onto the wire. Again, you can buy special crimpers that can easily do both jobs. The best crimpers use a ratcheting mechanism to make exerting the proper amount of force easier for a solid, reliable connection.

INSTALLING AND MAINTAINING NETWORK CABLING

Not only is the selection of a type of network cabling important, it's also important it be installed correctly. A proper cable plant installation should include all of the following:

▼ Proper cable and connectors for the type of network, including documentation of what components were selected and used.

■ Complete labeling of all parts of the network, which should include the wall plates, cables, patch panel ports, patch cables, and hub port assignments.

■ An *as-built* drawing of the building showing all the cabling routes and locations.

■ A certification report showing all installed cables operate properly, using one of several test devices.

▲ For bus-type networks, education of the user base that the coaxial cable should not be touched by them for any reason whatsoever. The coaxial cable will cause all other nodes in their segment to fail if the cable is separated. Make sure Facilities personnel also know this.

Making sure a new cable plant installation is properly installed and documented will save you time over the long run, by making the network more reliable and much easier to maintain and repair.

Choosing a Cabling Contractor

When building a new network, choosing a cabling contractor is extremely important. A contractor who does high-quality, well-documented work is desirable and, unfortunately, hard to find.

When choosing a contractor, make sure he or she has a lot of experience installing networks like the one you're installing. In addition, assess the following issues as part of your selection:

▼ How will the contractor document the cable plant? What are his or her standards and do you think those documentation standards meet your needs? (Remember, no such thing exists as too much documentation for cable plants.)

■ Will the contractor provide a set of as-built drawings?

■ How does the contractor install the cable to avoid electrical interference sources in the ceiling and walls?

■ Does the contractor recommend a wiring solution that combines telecom wiring with data wiring? (Generally, keeping these two cable plants separate is best. They have different requirements and respond differently to different building conditions. What works fine for telephones may not work at all for network cable and vice versa.)

■ Are there local installations the contractor has performed that you can go and view?

■ Does the contractor also provide speedy post-installation support for new wiring drops? This is important, as many wiring contractors who specialize in new construction wiring are not good about returning to do the occasional single drop for new node locations. Ask their references about this important information.

■ What equipment does the contractor use to certify the cable plant? What certification documentation will they provide upon completion?

▲ Does the contractor also provide post-installation troubleshooting services?

Make sure to spend time finding the best local cable contractors available to you and perform a careful comparison of them. You may want to contact either other companies like yours or computer user group members in your area to seek recommendations and experiences with different contractors.

Solving Cable Problems

Cable problems can be extremely hard to diagnose and repair. Many cable problems are intermittent or result in reduced network bandwidth for the affected nodes. Tracking down the source of the problem can be difficult. At times, it's hard to know there *is* a problem!

Problems with network cabling exhibit themselves in the following ways:

▼ Abnormally slow network performance, particularly if one node is much slower than other, similar nodes (for star networks) or if all nodes on one segment have slower network performance than nodes on other segments (for bus networks).

■ Sporadic disconnections from the network.

▲ Complete loss of network connectivity. This can also be intermittent.

Star networks are the easiest to troubleshoot. Because each node is on its own network cable leading to the hub, it's easier to isolate the problem down to several lengths of cable. If you're having trouble with a node on a star topology network, first determine if something is wrong with the computer or the cabling. Move the computer to a different location in the building and see if the same problems occur. If they do, then it's a sure bet the problem is in the computer, like a failing NIC. Next, if the computer has normal network performance in a different location, try replacing the patch cable leading from the node to the wall. These cables can often become slightly damaged as furniture or computers are moved around. Next, in the wiring closet you can try connecting the patch panel from the node's location to a different port on the hub using a different patch cable. While wiring closet patch panels are less likely to fail, because they aren't moved around much, they can still have poor connections or wiring that can become problematic over time. Finally, if you eliminated all other factors, you must consider replacing the cable leading from the wiring closet to the node's location. At this point, having a qualified network cabling contractor to assist you can be extremely helpful. The qualified network cabling contractor has equipment to test the cable in the wall and to determine if it's bad before pulling a replacement cable through the building.

Coaxial networks can be much harder to troubleshoot, because many nodes share a single segment of the network. Usually, a problem in one part of the segment affects all nodes on the segment similarly. By far the most common problem on coaxial networks is loss of network connectivity for all the nodes in a segment. Someone disconnecting the network cable so it is not a continuous run invariably causes this loss. To track this problem down, find out who's moving or rearranging offices, or which offices are being painted. The chances are excellent the problem is there. If this fails, then the troubleshooting job becomes much more difficult. There are two ways to track down cable breaks that aren't obvious:

▼ **Use a coaxial cable scanner**   These hand-held instruments can be attached to a coaxial network cable and can tell you how far along the cable any shorts or breaks are occurring. Keep attaching the cable scanner to the network cable in different locations until you can track down the problem.

▲ **Get an extra terminator for the network**   Disconnect the cable in a particular location and attach the terminator. See if the computers on the new, smaller segment can log into a server (a server must be available in the same segment; otherwise, you can use the PING command—if you're using the TCP/IP protocol on your computers—and try to ping another workstation in the complete segment). If they can, then you know the problem is further on along the cable. Move to a new location, attach the extra terminator, and try again. Eventually, you will find two nearby locations where the terminator will allow the network to work in one spot, but not in the next spot. You should find the cable problem somewhere between those two node locations. This approach requires patience, but it works fine in a pinch.

More troublesome still on coaxial networks is some problem that is causing poor network performance, but it is not causing any nodes actually to disconnect from the network. These problems can be tough to find because they are often intermittent and they don't usually lend themselves to finding with a cable scanner. When you have this type of problem, your best approach is to come up with a test that can quickly tell you how fast the nodes are communicating with the network. For example, you can time how long it takes to copy a particular file from the server. Then, use a terminator to close off a large part of the segment and perform the test again. Keep moving the terminator and retrying the test until you discover what part of the cable causes the slow network performance on the segment. Then, either replace all those portions or narrow your search further. This type of problem is usually caused by a poor connection in one of the male cable-end BNC connectors, although a flaky T-connector or barrel connector can also cause it. It's usually fastest—providing you narrowed the problem to a small enough area—simply to replace all the cable and connectors in that location.

> **TIP:** Before going to the trouble of pulling a new section of cable through the wall or replacing various cables and connectors, try simply running an extra cable from one location to another, such as out the door of one room, down the hallway, and into the room of another. Then, test to see if "mapping out" the suspect portion of the segment fixes the problem. If the problem goes away, then go ahead and have new cable run in the walls. If the problem is still there, you need to look further before replacing cable and connectors.

As a general rule, troubleshooting cable problems requires a careful step-by-step approach and a lot of patience. For coaxial cable systems, troubleshooting is made more difficult because you have a lot of network users breathing down your neck while you're trying to concentrate and find the problem. You're lucky if you can find and solve a coaxial network problem and solve it within an hour. Some problems, though, may take several hours (or more) to resolve.

> **TIP:** Having a second person to help you troubleshoot coaxial cable problems helps a lot and finding the problem goes much more quickly if you both have portable radios with which to communicate. One way to take advantage of this is to have one person in a fixed location at one end of the segment with a test computer and the other person moving from location to location with a terminator, alternately mapping out parts of the segment with the terminator, while the stationary person quickly tests to see if the problem is abated each time.

CHAPTER SUMMARY

In this chapter you learned about network cable systems. You learned about the major topologies in which networks are wired, how CSMA/CD and token passing work, what types of cables are commonly used, and how they should be installed. You also learned some tips about selecting cabling contractors and troubleshooting network cable problems.

The next chapter goes hand-in-hand with this chapter. Chapter 3 teaches you about the different types of network devices available and what they do. You learn about hubs, bridges, routers, and the other types of network devices into which the cabling in this chapter connects.

CHAPTER 3

Understanding Network Hardware

If network wiring constitutes the nervous system of a network, then the devices discussed in this chapter represent the various organs. The network devices discussed in this chapter—including repeaters, routers, hubs, and such—are responsible for moving data from one network cable to another. Each device has different properties and uses. A good network design uses the right device for each of the various jobs the network must fulfill.

CONNECTING RS-232 DEVICES WITH SHORT-HAUL MODEMS

While some may not consider a short-haul modem to be a true network device, it is a device you may require in your network to provide point-to-point connectivity between a workstation and another device. Short-haul modems (sometimes called *line drivers*) enable you to connect two distant RS-232C devices to one another. Standard RS-232C cables are limited in distance from 50 to 100 feet. Short-haul modems allow the same connection to run as far as five miles using twisted-pair cabling.

Short-haul modems can often be perfect solutions when a computer needs terminal access to a remote device. For example, an individual may need to access a terminal port on a PBX, which uses an RS-232C port. You have two options to provide this remote access. You can install regular modems on each end and use a telephone connection to connect from the workstation to the PBX or you can use two short-haul modems and run a twisted-pair cable between the two points. Depending on how frequently access is needed and how distant the device actually is, either approach can be good. Generally, short-haul modems are preferred when the two devices often or always need to be connected and running a twisted-pair wire between the locations is not prohibitively expensive or difficult. Short-haul modems are fairly inexpensive, costing about $100 each.

Most short-haul modems operate using two pairs of wire between each short-haul modem, although one pair variants exist. With the two pair variety, one pair is used for transmit data and one for receive data. Most short-haul modems are full-duplex, allowing transmission to take place in both directions simultaneously.

To hook up two devices using short-haul modems, you use a standard RS-232C cable to connect from each device to its short-haul modem. Then, you wire the twisted-pair wire to the short-haul modem, using the instructions that come with the modem. Finally, most short-haul modems require external power, so you need an available power outlet to plug them into. Figure 3-1 shows a sample of a short-haul modem connection.

TIP: If you frequently do RS-232C interfacing, you should invest in a device called a *break-out box*. This is a small device that has two RS-232C connectors on each end. In the box, each of the RS-232C pin signals is represented with an LED. Special patch posts and switches are available that enable you to reconfigure the RS-232C connection on the fly. Break-out boxes can be invaluable for achieving RS-232C communications between two devices that aren't communicating. They can show what is actually happening with the signals and enable you to try different cable cross-overs dynamically.

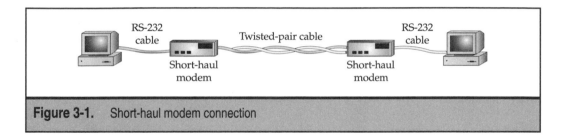

Figure 3-1. Short-haul modem connection

DIRECTING NETWORK TRAFFIC

The critical test of any network design is its capability to direct network traffic from one node to another node. You do this by connecting various network devices in a configuration that accomplishes this in the most efficient manner possible, taking into account the type of network and the different connectivity requirements for the network. Devices you use to do this include

▼ Repeaters, which extend the distance network traffic can travel over a particular type of network media.

■ Hubs, which are used to connect nodes to one another when you use a star topology, such as 10Base-T.

■ Bridges, which are something like intelligent repeaters, but only direct needed traffic from one network segment to another.

■ Routers, which can intelligently route network traffic in a variety of important ways.

▲ Switches, which form fast point-to-point connections for all the devices connected to them as they need the connections, eliminating traffic collisions caused by non-communicating segments.

Putting together all the necessary pieces in the right way is the art of network design. Chapter 11 discusses important aspects of putting these pieces together so they work optimally, but you first have to know what these devices are and what they can do. The following sections discuss these essential network devices.

Repeaters

A *repeater* is a device that extends the distance of a particular network run. You most often see repeaters on thin Ethernet networks, but they are available for virtually any network connection. For instance, if you have to run a 10Base-T cable longer than 100 meters, a repeater enables you to double that distance.

Repeaters operate at the physical layer of the OSI networking model. They have no intelligence to understand the signals being transmitted over them. Repeaters merely amplify the signal coming in either side and repeat it out their other side. (Remember, however, they also amplify any noise on the cable!) Repeaters are only used to connect the same type of media, such as 10Base-2 to 10Base-2, or Token Ring to Token Ring.

Repeaters do have a small amount of intelligence that can be useful. They can segment one of their connections from the other when there is a problem. For example, consider two segments of thin Ethernet that are connected using a repeater. If one of those segments is broken, the repeater still allows the good segment to continue working within itself. Users on the good segment will be unable to connect to resources on the broken segment, but they can continue to use the good segment without trouble. (Remember, though, this capability does you little good if your servers are on the broken segment and your workstations are on the good segment!) Figure 3-2 shows a network extension using repeaters.

Hubs and Concentrators

Intelligent LAN concentrators, more simply called *hubs*, are used to connect network nodes to network backbones. Nodes are connected to hubs in a physical star fashion (cables fan out from the hub to each node), whether they are used for a star topology or a ring topology network. Chapter 2 contains a detailed discussion of bus, ring, and star topologies.

Hubs are available for virtually any network media type, with the higher-end hubs using replaceable modules to support multiple media types. For example, you can purchase a high-end hub chassis that can house both Ethernet and Token Ring modules.

You can purchase hubs in a variety of sizes, ranging from those that support only two workstations to those that support over 100 workstations. Many network designers use

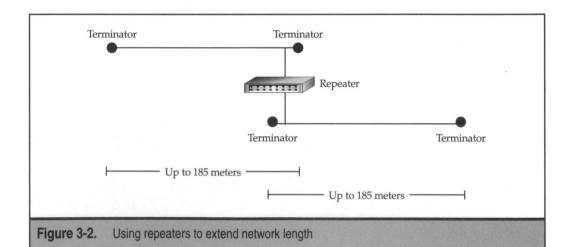

Figure 3-2.   Using repeaters to extend network length

stackable hubs, which usually support 24 node connections each and these are often used in concert with switches, which are discussed in their own section of this chapter.

Hubs have two important properties. The first important property is that hubs echo all data from each node to all the other nodes on the hub. While hubs are wired in a star fashion, they actually perform electrically more like a bus topology segment in this respect. Because of this echoing, no filtering or logic occurs to prevent collisions between the packets of one node on the hub and any other node on the hub. The second important property hubs possess is *automatic partitioning*, where the hub can automatically *partition* any node having trouble from the other nodes, in effect, shutting down that node. This occurs when, for example, a cable short is detected, or if the node is broadcasting excessive packets and is flooding the network.

Hubs are becoming much more sophisticated. They often have a number of advanced features built into them, including the following:

▼   Built-in management, where the hub can be centrally managed over the network, using SNMP or other network management protocols and software.

■   Autosensing of different connection speeds. For example, Ethernet hubs that can automatically detect and run each node at either 10Mbps (10Base-T) or 100Mbps (100Base-TX) are becoming increasingly common.

■   Built-in bridging and routing functions, where separate devices aren't needed to fulfill these functions.

▲   Built-in switching, where nodes on the hub can be switched instead of shared.

When ordering a hub, it's important to know how many nodes you want to connect, how much bandwidth each requires, and what type of network backbone is being used. Backbones can be anything from a shared 10Mbps thin Ethernet backbone, to 100Mbps 100Base-TX backbones, up to and including SONET rings. Your choice of a backbone technology depends on the total amount of bandwidth needed and the various other network design criteria that must be met.

Each hub is a separate *collision domain*, or an area of the network in which collisions can occur. When hubs are connected together in some fashion, you generally end up with a larger collision domain, encompassing all the hubs. The exception to this rule is a configuration where all the separate hubs are connected to a switch, which keeps each hub in its own collision domain. Figure 3-3 shows an example of a network using hubs.

Bridges

A *bridge* is basically a more intelligent repeater. Bridges can connect two network segments together and have the intelligence to pass traffic from one segment to another only when that traffic is destined for the other segment. Bridges are, therefore, used to segment networks into smaller pieces. Some bridges are also available that can span different networking systems and media, such as thin Ethernet to twisted-pair Token Ring.

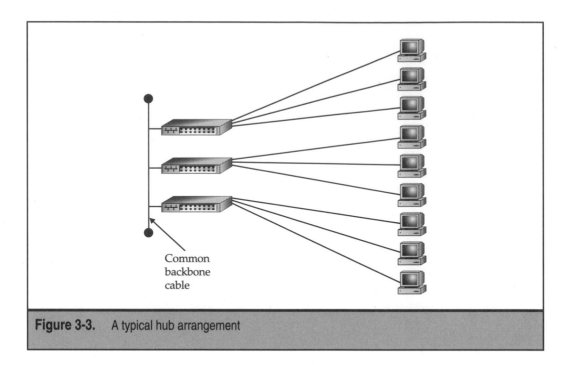

Common
backbone
cable

Figure 3-3. A typical hub arrangement

As you may recall, repeaters operate at the physical layer (layer 1) of the OSI networking model. Bridges operate one layer higher, at the data-link layer (layer 2). Bridges examine the MAC address of each packet they encounter and forward the packet to the other network if its address indicates it should do so. Bridges contain address information about all the devices and subnetworks in your network, through either a static routing table you program or a dynamic, learning-tree system that discovers all the devices and addresses on the network.

Bridges should only be used on smaller networks. Often routers or switches offer better solutions that perform better and create fewer problems.

Routers

Just as bridges are basically more intelligent repeaters, routers are more intelligent bridges. *Routers* operate at the network layer (layer 3) of the OSI Model and are far more intelligent than bridges in sending incoming packets off to their destination. Because routers operate at the network layer, a connection across a router only requires that the protocols used in the higher layers be in common. The router can translate from any of the protocols at layers 1 through 3 to any other protocols at layers 1 through 3 (provided the router has been configured to do so). Routers can connect both similar and dissimilar networks. They are often used for wide area networks (WANs) and links.

Routers actually become a node on a network and they have their own network address. Other nodes send packets to the router, which then examines the contents of the packets and forwards them appropriately. (For this reason routers often have fast microprocessors—usually RISC-based—and lots of memory built into them to perform this job.) Routers can also determine the shortest route to a destination and use it. They can perform other tricks to maximize network bandwidth and dynamically adjust to changing problems or traffic patterns on a network.

Routers form the backbone of the Internet. When you use the TRACERT command to trace the route from a node to a destination, most of the addresses you see appear for the hops are actually different routers, each one forwarding the packet onto the next until it reaches its destination.

Routers must be programmed to function correctly. They need to have the addresses assigned to each of their ports and various network protocol settings must be set. Routers are usually programmed in one of two ways. First, most routers include an RS-232C port. You can connect a terminal or PC with terminal emulation software to this port and program the router in text mode. Second, most routers have network-based software that enables you to program the router, often using graphical tools. The method you use depends on the router and your security needs (you may want to disable network-based router programming so the router can't have its configuration changed by unauthorized people). Figure 3-4 shows an example of a network that uses routers.

Switches

Switches, as their name implies, can switch connections from one port to another and they can switch rapidly. They are connection-oriented and dynamically switch among their

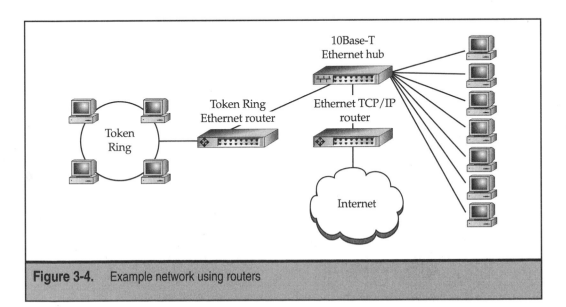

Figure 3-4.   Example network using routers

various ports to create these connections. Think of a train yard—with many trains coming in on some tracks and leaving on other tracks—with the switch being the yard manager who orders all the track "switches" to take place so the trains get to their destination. A network switch is like this; just replace trains with packets and train tracks with Ethernet cabling.

Because switches form one-to-one connections between any two ports, all the ports coming into a switch are not part of a single collision domain. In this sense, the switch acts as a sort of super-bridge. Switches are often used to connect a number of hubs to a much faster backbone. For example, say you have ten hubs, each with 24 workstation nodes connected. If you simply connect all the hubs together on a common backbone, all 240 workstations would share a single collision domain, which could hurt performance quite badly. Instead, a much better approach is to install a 12-port switch and to connect each hub to one of the ports on the switch. The switch, in turn, connects to a common backbone, usually running at a faster rate than the hubs. For instance, it is common (and makes good sense) to use 10Base-T Ethernet for the workstation connections, but 100Base-T (or some other fast network connection) for the backbone. This further allows all the traffic being generated by each of the ten hubs to continue to run at about 10Mbps net connection speed to the servers, even though all the hubs are sharing the backbone. Figure 3-5 illustrates this approach.

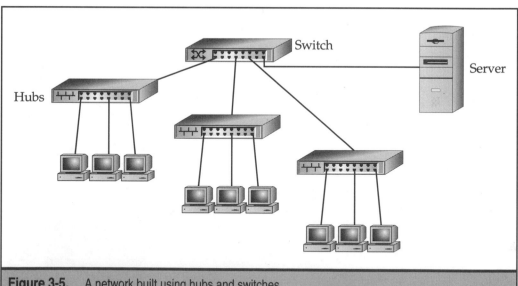

Figure 3-5.   A network built using hubs and switches

Switches have become inexpensive and they are blazingly fast. For LAN connections, switches make more sense than routers, partly because of their cost and the reduced complexity of a switch. In fact, it has currently become difficult even to purchase bridges any more because switches achieve the same benefits at a much lower cost and complexity.

MAKING HIGH-LEVEL CONNECTIONS WITH GATEWAYS

Gateways are application-specific interfaces that link all seven layers of the OSI Model when they are dissimilar at any or all levels. For instance, if you need to connect a network that uses one of the OSI networking models to one using IBM's SNA model, a gateway would perform this task admirably. Gateways can also translate from, say, Ethernet to Token Ring, although simpler solutions exist if this is your need. Also, because gateways have to translate so much, they tend to be slower than other solutions, particularly under heavy loads.

PROTECTING A NETWORK WITH FIREWALLS

Firewalls, also discussed in Chapter 8, are hardware devices that enforce your network security policies. They are mentioned here because they often are installed hand-in-hand with routers—for instance, for internetwork connections.

A firewall is a hardware device (which may be a computer set up for the task) that sits between two networks and enforces network security policies. Generally, firewalls sit between a company LAN and the Internet, but they can also be used between LANs when appropriate.

There are basically two different types of firewalls: network-based and application-based. A network-based firewall operates at the packet level, and usually implements a technique called *packet filtering*, where packets between networks are compared against a set of rules programmed into the firewall before they are allowed to cross the boundary between the two networks. Packet filtering rules can allow or deny packets based on source or destination address, and by TCP/IP port. Application-based firewalls, on the other hand, usually act in a proxy role between the two networks, such that no network traffic actually passes *directly* between the two networks. Instead, the firewall (usually called a *proxy firewall*) acts as a proxy for the users of one network to interact with services on the other network. This is usually done using a technique called *address translation* where the network addresses on the internal network are not directly exposed to the external network. The proxy firewall takes care of translating the addresses so that the connections can take place in this model.

TIP: Firewalls do not provide a network security panacea. The best firewall in the world won't protect you from other security threats, such as some discussed in Chapter 8. However, they are an important part of network security, particularly for LANs connected to the Internet.

Firewalls come in all shapes and sizes, and range in cost from as little as a few thousand dollars to tens of thousands of dollars. Different firewall devices have different features, and may encompass both network-based and application-based techniques to protect the network. Firewalls also usually serve as an audit point for the traffic between the two networks, using logging and reporting tools to help the administrator detect and deal with inappropriate network traffic.

CHAPTER SUMMARY

In this chapter, you learned about the key pieces of hardware that make up most networks. It is important for you to be familiar with the capabilities of all these types of network hardware, which should form the basis of any network design or performance-tuning efforts. While the hardware you learned about here is extensive, it's not the end of the types of network hardware about which you need to know. Additional important network hardware is discussed in other chapters in this book. In particular, you should also know about remote access hardware, about hardware that supports WAN links, and about certain network functions that are carried out on different types of network servers.

Chapter 4 discusses the different technologies used to connect networks to other networks, usually over greater distances. WAN connections are used to connect to the Internet and also to form part-time or full-time connections between LANs, such as from one company location to another.

CHAPTER 4

Making WAN Connections

Many companies have multiple locations and these locations need to share network resources. For example, maybe the company's accounting system runs at the headquarters building where the accounting and MIS staff are located. But the warehouse may be across town and it still needs access to the accounting system for inventory pick tickets, data entry, and other order fulfillment and inventory tasks.

Or, perhaps the company uses a groupware system like Lotus Notes that requires regular updates of information and messages from one site to another. In the real world, the situation can become even more complex. Some companies have offices all around the world and each office has different requirements both to access and update data in other locations.

All these are situations in which a *wide area network* (WAN) can be useful. Certainly, in a pinch multiple offices can send data to and receive data from each other by using FedEx and identical tape machines, Zip drives, JAZ drives, or other media, and simply send them back and forth (assuming the application supports this). But this sort of arrangement has some drawbacks, such as being relatively slow.

There are many ways to connect LANs in one location to LANs in another location, and that's the subject of this chapter. First, you learn about basic concepts involved in linking LANs over a WAN. Then, different WAN technologies are discussed, along with the relative tradeoffs involved in each one.

DETERMINING WAN NEEDS

Except in rare cases, WAN links are almost always expensive to maintain, particularly because bandwidth needs increase over time. Moreover, WAN links are generally much more prone to trouble than LANs because many additional possible points of failure exist. For these reasons, it's important to assess the need for a WAN carefully and then study the different options available, their costs, and the tradeoffs involved before making a choice. Costs can vary wildly between different technologies, speeds, and other factors (including where you're located) so you have to rely closely on cost and availability data from local providers for your own WAN analysis. Plus, prices and availability are changing almost on a weekly basis, so make sure to get current data from your local providers before committing to a particular WAN technology.

Analyzing Requirements

Before beginning to look into different WAN technologies, you need to have a firm grasp of the need for a WAN. Because of their cost and the time required to implement and maintain them, you usually do not want to pursue a WAN until the need is strong.

A company's first WAN is usually driven by a particular application, like an accounting system, and then once the WAN is operational, it is often used by other applications. For example, a company may be transferring e-mail from one location to another using dial-up lines, but once the WAN that supports the accounting system is installed, you find it's easier to route the e-mail over the WAN link rather than maintain two separate connection schemes. Other applications emerge this way, too, so it's important to analyze the primary application fully and then consider what other uses could be made of the WAN.

You need to answer a number of questions before you consider different WAN approaches. These questions are

▼   What are the locations that will participate in the WAN and what kind of WAN services are available to them? A sales office in Tahiti, for instance, is unlikely to be able to purchase the latest xDSL line.

■   How much data needs to be transferred from each site to each other site?

■   How quickly does the data need to be transferred?

■   Does the data transfer need to be synchronous or can it be asynchronous? For example, a warehouse clerk who is entering records directly into an accounting system located at another site requires a synchronous (real-time) connection, while a restaurant that only needs to upload sales data at some time each night needs an asynchronous connection.

■   When do the data transfers need to be accomplished? Do they need to occur all the time? Do they need to occur once every 30 minutes, or some other schedule?

▲   What are the budget constraints?

Once you have the answers to these questions, you can then answer the questions that can guide you to a particular WAN technology. These issues are discussed in the following sections.

Switched or Dedicated?

A *switched* WAN link is one that is not active all the time. For instance, a modem connection from one location to another would be a switched connection. Another example is an ISDN connection from one location to another. These are examples of connections that are only formed when you need them and you usually pay for the time the connection is open, rather than the amount of data you're able to transmit over the connection. Figure 4-1 is an example of a switched WAN link.

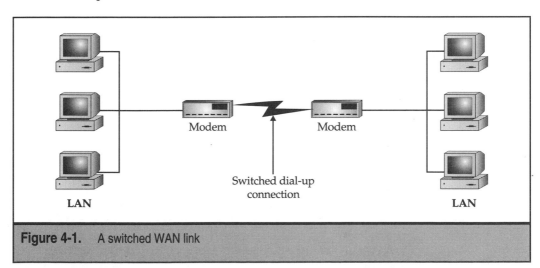

Figure 4-1.   A switched WAN link

Switched links can be either connection-based or packet-based. A *connection-based switched link* is one where a connection is formed as needed and a fixed amount of bandwidth is made available over that link. A *packet-based switched link* is one in which data packets are sent into a network cloud and they can follow a number of paths to their destination, where they then emerge from the cloud. Packet-switched networks can be more reliable because the data can take many different paths, but you are not guaranteed each packet will arrive in a certain amount of time. A connection-based switch just gives you one "pipe" from your source to your destination, but you can completely control what goes into the pipe and how long it will take to get to its destination.

A *dedicated* WAN link is one that is always up and running. Examples of dedicated WAN connections are DS1 (T-1) lines, xDSL lines, or leased telephone lines. You use a dedicated connection when you need the connection to be up all the time or when the overall economics show it's cheaper than a switched link. Figure 4-2 illustrates a dedicated WAN link.

Private or Public?

A *private network* is one that is exclusive to a particular company. No other company's data is sent over the private network. The advantages are the data is secure, you can control how the network is used, and you can predict how much bandwidth you have available. A public network, like the Internet, is a network through which many companies' data passes. Public networks are less secure than private networks, but the advantages are they are less expensive to use and you don't have to maintain the external network yourself.

Use a public network when:

▼ You don't care if data occasionally takes longer to reach its destination or if this is relatively unpredictable

■ You want the minimum cost network connection possible

▲ The data does not need to be secure or you have the ability to make it secure over the public network (technologies exist that can do this, such as virtual private networks)

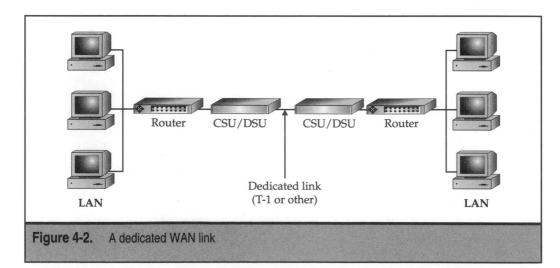

Figure 4-2. A dedicated WAN link

Use a private network when:

▼ Data security is of utmost concern

■ You have a large, experienced staff to set up and maintain the public network

■ Cost is relatively unimportant relative to the benefits the network brings

▲ You must be able to rely on being able to control the bandwidth use of the network fully

UNDERSTANDING WAN CONNECTIONS

Now that you understand some basics of WAN links, the remainder of this chapter overviews different available WAN technologies and offers tips and advice on each type of link.

POTS

Plain Old Telephone Service (POTS) is the telephone service everyone knows. While not technically qualifying as a WAN connection (at least as most people think of WANs), it can still serve to link two or more sites together for certain low-bandwidth uses. While it's true using POTS is among the slowest methods of establishing a network connection, POTS is ubiquitous and easily used throughout the entire world. POTS is also generally (but not always!) the least expensive way to connect.

POTS is carried over one set of twisted-pair wires (in other words, just two wires). In some cases two sets of twisted-pair wires will be used, but the telephone signal and ring signals are only carried over the two main wires. The other two wires can be used for other features, such as backlighting a keypad on a phone or providing a message-waiting light with some PBX systems. POTS connections currently use simple RJ-11 telephone jacks, which simply snap into place.

The maximum theoretical speed of basic analog POTS is 33.6Kbps. Many factors can decrease this speed; chief among them is line quality. Telephone lines with static typically do not connect at the top speed of 33.6Kbps, may lose their connections unexpectedly, may lose data being transmitted, or may pause for excessive periods of time as bursts of static inhibit the ability to transfer data.

When using POTS to establish a network connection, having matched modems at both ends is optimal. Matched modems from the same manufacturer more easily negotiate the highest possible data transmission rates and often can support "step-down" modes, where a slower speed is used automatically when line noise unexpectedly becomes a problem.

Signals sent over POTS are analog signals, not digital ones. The data sent between systems is converted from digital data to analog data using a modem. The word *modem* is actually an acronym and comes from their function—modulator/demodulator. At each end of the connection, the sending system's modem modulates the digital data into an analog signal and sends it over the telephone line as a series of audible sounds. Then, at the receiving end, the modem demodulates the audible analog signal back into a digital signal for use with the computer.

Integrated Services Digital Network (ISDN)

The technology for Integrated Services Digital Network (ISDN), a high-speed digital communications network based on existing telephone services, has been around for ten years. Because of extensive upgrades required at telephone company central offices (COs), however, ISDN has not become widely available until now and, even now, it is only really available in major metropolitan areas.

ISDN is available in two primary forms: the Basic Rate Interface (BRI) and the Primary Rate Interface (PRI). The ISDN-BRI connection is made up of three channels. Two channels are called *bearer channels* and carry data at speeds of 64Kbps per channel or voice calls (one voice call per bearer channel is possible). The third channel, called a *data channel*, carries call setup information and other overhead communications necessary to manage the two bearer channels. The data channel carries 16Kbps of data. Bearer channels are abbreviated as *B-channels*, while the data channel is abbreviated as a *D-channel*. Thus, an ISDN-BRI connection is often called a 2B+D connection, which reflects the number and the type of channels it contains.

ISDN-PRI is made up of 24 B-channels and one D-channel. A PRI connection can carry a total of 1.544Mbps, just like a T-1 line.

NOTE: Different flavors of PRI configurations are in different parts of the world. 24B+D is common and you may also see variations like 22B channels with a 64Kbps D-channel, 24 56Kbps B-channels, or even 30 standard B-channels (totaling 1.92Mbps).

ISDN connections are usually formed as needed. To use ISDN for a WAN link, you use on-demand ISDN routers at each end, which have the capability to "dial-up" the other router when data is pending. Because ISDN has extremely fast call setup times, the connection is formed much more quickly than POTS connections; usually within a second.

ISDN is still fairly new in terms of widespread adoption. Pricing changes occur regularly. ISDN prices also vary considerably in different parts of the country. Getting full pricing information from your own Regional Bell Operating Company (RBOC) before choosing ISDN is important. Then, using your projected usage data, you should be able to calculate the cost to use ISDN.

Generally, the installation of an ISDN-BRI line, assuming no wiring changes are necessary, carries an installation charge of about $250. In some cases, the installation charge may be waived if an agreement is signed to keep the ISDN line for one to two years.

NOTE: In some parts of the country, especially now in Northern California, having an ISDN line installed takes a considerable amount of time—up to two months in some cases. Before choosing ISDN, get an accurate, written estimate from your RBOC on when they can complete the installation and prepare for them not to meet their initial target date.

Monthly ISDN use charges are similar to POTS charges. Long-distance ISDN call charges are similar to POTS charges. Remember, though, connecting with two B-channels is equivalent to making two separate calls and whatever charge exists for a single call will be doubled when both B-channels are used.

xDSL

A relatively new connection type becoming available is called a Digital Subscriber Line (DSL). A number of different flavors of DSL exist, such as:

▼ **ADSL** Asymmetric DSL allows for up to 8Mbps of data to be received and up to 1Mbps of data to be sent. Many RBOCs are only offering up to 1.5Mbps to be received (called *downstream*) and 256Kbps to be sent (called *upstream*), however, and distance from the CO may affect what speeds are available at any particular location.

■ **HDSL** High-speed DSL allows between 768Kbps and 2.048Mbps connections between two sites.

■ **RADSL** Rate Adaptive DSL allows for 600Kbps to 12Mbps of data to be received and 128Kbps to 1Mbps of data to be sent.

■ **SDSL** Symmetric DSL allows bidirectional rates varying from 160Kbps to 2.048Mbps.

▲ **VDSL** Very-high-speed DSL allows up to 51Mbps of data downstream and up to 2Mbps upstream.

In this section you learn about how xDSL works and about when you might be able to implement its extremely high bandwidth capabilities. For these discussions, I focus on ADSL because it is the most prevalent and the least expensive. For WAN links, however, you should focus on SDSL if your WAN data needs are similar in both directions.

How xDSL Works

The twisted-pair copper wire that carries POTS service is capable of carrying signals with up to a 1 MHz spread of frequencies. However, POTS service only uses 8 KHz worth of the frequency bandwidth. The reason is, in the RBOCs CO switch, a card exists that interfaces the analog signal coming in through the twisted-pair wire onto the phone company's digital network. This interface card only allows 4 KHz worth of signaling frequencies in each direction, even though the wire itself is capable of carrying a far broader frequency range.

xDSL works by opening up that 1 MHz maximum capability through the use of new xDSL interface cards that the RBOC can install in their CO switch. For lines that connect to those cards, the new frequency range is capable of carrying much more data than otherwise. The data rate is limited by the distance from the computer equipment to the CO switch, however. Most xDSL implementations function optimally at only 12,000 feet (about two miles). In particular, the 8Mbps receive and 1Mbps send data rates of ADSL are only possible within the 12,000 foot distance to the CO. Longer distances are possible, but not at the full possible data rate. For instance, running an ADSL connection at 18,000 feet—the distance at which 95 percent of locations exist in relation to their CO switch—degrades the performance to about 1.5Mbps in the receive direction. Only an estimated 50 percent of U.S. locations are within 12,000 feet of an RBOC CO switch. The good news is some newer implementations of xDSL may be able to overcome the distance limitation. The situation is still developing and solutions probably won't be available along these lines until well into the year 2000.

ADSL

As mentioned, ADSL can support up to 8Mbps of received data (also called *downstream* data) and up to 1Mbps of sent data (also called *upstream* data). In addition to these two data channels, ADSL also carves out an 8 KHz channel for normal POTS service, which can coexist with the ADSL data channels.

Specific implementations of ADSL varies in their data rate. Some of the slower implementations only function at 1.5Mbps downstream and 256Kbps upstream. In some cases, this may even be dropped to 384Kbps downstream and 64Mbps upstream.

A lot of interest surrounds xDSL, particularly ADSL. The cost/megabyte of data transmitted is far less than POTS and is even considerably less expensive than ISDN. Even with all that interest, it will be, at best, several years before xDSL is more widely available. Right now, a number of RBOCs are rolling out xDSL, but still in limited markets.

No one knows yet how rapidly xDSL will catch on. The main limitation is in the implementation curve of the RBOCs and the investment they need to make is considerable. Each xDSL line card (one required for each connection) is estimated to cost at least $1,000. Each CO switch may also need to be upgraded, at an estimated cost of between $250,000 and $500,000. While these costs can reasonably be recouped in a relatively short period of time, a great deal of capital will be required to make these changes.

Why Asymmetric DSL?

Many data access needs are asymmetrical. In other words, more data needs to be received than needs to be sent (or vice versa). Most remote access connections meet this criteria, particularly Internet connections. The emphasis is on being able to receive data rapidly, rather than sending data rapidly.

Because of this, ADSL is receiving the most interest among the xDSL implementations, simply because it offers more benefit within the same amount of frequency bandwidth. Most applications will work far better with the data rate being faster downstream than upstream.

Some xDSL implementations are symmetric, such as Symmetric DSL and Highspeed DSL. These xDSL connection types are more suited to applications where data is exchanged in roughly equal directions, such as when connecting two remote LANs to one another.

Cynics note that ISDN has been possible for over 12 years, but it is only now being more widely used. Will xDSL suffer the same fate? The jury is still out, but it should be clearer by the year 2000.

T-1/T-3 (DS1/DS3) Connections

Over 40 years ago, Bell Labs developed a hierarchy of systems that can carry digital voice signals. At the lowest level in their hierarchy, is a connection called a *DS0* connection, which carries 64Kbps bandwidth. 24 DS0 channels aggregated together is called a *DS1*, which can carry up to 1.544Mbps when all channels are in use. The next common level is called a *DS3*, which carries 672 DS0 channels, for an aggregate total of 44.736Mbps. The DS1 connection is commonly called a *T-1 connection*, which actually refers to the system of repeaters that can carry the DS1 traffic over a four-wire twisted-pair connection. (Many people are surprised by this, but a DS1 only requires two twisted-pairs, and not fiber-optic cable or anything exotic. To understand how much data can be carried over simply telephone wire, see the preceding section on xDSL.)

DS1 connections are commonly used as digital connections between a company's PBX and a Point of Presence (POP) for a long-distance telephone carrier and they are also commonly used to connect LANs to the Internet. Over a DS1, up to 24 voice calls can be handled simultaneously. Or, up to 24 data connections can be handled simultaneously. Or, one big 1.544Mbps connection can be formed through the use of a multiplexer.

A popular technology called *Fractional T-1* also exists, where a full DS1 is installed, but only the number of channels you pay for are turned on and available for use. Fractional T-1 is great because you can buy just the bandwidth you need and increasing the bandwidth (up to the maximum for a DS1) is just a phone call away.

NOTE: DS0, DS1, and DS3 WAN connections make use of *frame relay* signaling technology on the RBOC's side of the CSU/DSU. Understanding the ins and outs of frame relay isn't especially important, although you should understand that when you install a Fractional T-1 connection to the Internet for your LAN, you are using frame relay services.

At each end of a DS1 connection are two key pieces of equipment: a CSU/DSU that converts the DS1 signals into network signals and a router that allows packets to be routed from and to the DS1 from the LAN.

X.25

X.25 connections have been available for a long time, but they are not typically used for WAN connections both because of the overhead involved and the tradeoff between price and bandwidth is not competitive with other solutions. Some older networks may still have X.25 connections in place, however, and they are commonly used in Europe. X.25 is a packet-switched WAN connection, in which data travels through a X.25 cloud, similar to the Internet, but through a private/public X.25 network. X.25 connections are typically relatively slow (56Kbps), but in some cases may be faster.

X.25 was originally developed by the U.S. military for voice traffic and was specifically designed to enable military voice traffic to be available even after a nuclear strike. As you might guess, X.25 is an extremely reliable, secure protocol over which data can be sent. All frames (similar to a packet) sent over X.25 networks are completely verified from one end of the connection to the other.

CHAPTER SUMMARY

In this chapter you learned about concepts and technologies relating to wide area network links, including different types of links and different types of connections, as well as how to specify a particular type of WAN technology for a given application. While the number of choices may make this area confusing, it becomes easier when you break the problem down into smaller chunks. Basically, make sure you do a careful and thorough job of identifying your WAN needs and then work with various WAN providers in your area to analyze how their different solutions may meet your needs.

The next chapter moves into network protocols, like TCP/IP, and IPX/SPX. You learn how these network protocols work, how their packets are constructed, and various characteristics of each type of network protocol. You also learn about some of the other common protocols, particularly those associated with TCP/IP, such as SMTP, HTTP, and WINS.

CHAPTER 5

Understanding Networking Protocols

A network *protocol* is a set of rules that nodes on a network follow to complete network transactions. For example, TCP/IP defines a protocol used to send data from one node on a network to another node. Simple Mail Transfer Protocol (SMTP) is a set of rules and standards used to transfer e-mail and attachments from one node to another. Dynamic Host Configuration Protocol (DHCP) is a set of rules and standards used to allocate IP addresses dynamically for a network, so they needn't be fixed for each workstation.

Many protocols are used in networking. In fact, in a sense, *everything is a protocol* of one sort or another. Some protocols function at a low level in the OSI network model, others operate at a high level, and still others operate in between.

In this chapter, you learn about the essential networking protocols used to transmit and receive data across a network.

UNDERSTANDING TCP/IP AND UDP

As its name suggests, TCP/IP is actually two protocols used in concert with one another. *Internet Protocol* (IP) is one that defines how network data is addressed from a source to a destination and in what sequence the data should be reassembled at the other end. IP *datagrams* (another term for *packets*) are then "wrapped" inside a TCP datagram, which contains information that ensures the accuracy of the IP datagram, such as checksums. TCP provides the handshaking necessary between two nodes, so any packets damaged or lost during transmission can be resent.

User Datagram Protocol (UDP) serves the same role as TCP, but it offers fewer features. Although UDP packets carry IP packets, the only reliability feature UDP supports is the resending of any packets not received at the destination. The chief advantage to UDP is that it is much faster for trivial network communications, such as sending a Web page to a client computer. On the other hand, UDP would be totally unsuitable for a bank to send banking transactions.

TCP and UDP Ports

Both TCP and UDP support the concept of *ports,* or application-specific addresses, to which packets are directed on any given receiving machine. For example, most Web servers run on a server machine and receive and send data through port number 80. Any packets sent to that machine, which are intended for the Web server (such as a request to serve up a Web page), are directed to that port. Hundreds of different ports have standardized uses and defining your own ports on a server for specific applications is easy. A text file called SERVICES defines the ports on a computer. An example of a portion of Windows NT's SERVICES file follows (only selected entries are shown due to space constraints; the following is not a complete SERVICES file, but it illustrates what the file contains).

```
# Copyright (c) 1993-1999 Microsoft Corp.
#
# This file contains port numbers for well-known
# services as defined by
# RFC 1700 (Assigned Numbers).
#
# Format:
#
# <service name><port number>/<protocol>[aliases...][#<comment>]
#
echo              7/tcp
echo              7/udp
discard           9/tcp     sink null
discard           9/udp     sink null
systat            11/tcp    users              #Active users
daytime           13/tcp
daytime           13/udp
chargen           19/tcp    ttytst source      #Character generator
chargen           19/udp    ttytst source      #Character generator
ftp-data          20/tcp                       #FTP, data
ftp               21/tcp                        #FTP. control
telnet            23/tcp
smtp              25/tcp    mail               #SMTP
time              37/tcp    timserver
time              37/udp    timserver
tftp              69/udp                       #Trivial File Transfer
gopher            70/tcp
finger            79/tcp
http              80/tcp    www www-http       #World Wide Web
kerberos-sec      88/tcp    krb5               #Kerberos
kerberos-sec     ·88/udp    krb5               #Kerberos
rtelnet           107/tcp                      #Remote Telnet Service
pop2              109/tcp   postoffice         #POP-V2
pop3              110/tcp                       #POP v3-
nntp              119/tcp   usenet             #NNTP
ntp               123/udp                      #Network Time Protocol
snmp              161/udp                       #SNMP
snmptrap          162/udp   snmp-trap          #SNMP trap
print-srv         170/tcp                      #Network PostScript
irc               194/tcp                       #Relay Chat Prot
ipx               213/udp                       #IPX over IP
ldap              389/tcp                       #Lightweight DAP
https             443/tcp   MCom
https             443/udp   MCom
who               513/udp   whod
```

```
cmd            514/tcp     shell
syslog         514/udp
printer        515/tcp     spooler
router         520/udp     route routed
netnews        532/tcp     readnews
uucp           540/tcp     uucpd
wins           1512/tcp                    #Windows Name Service
```

As you can see, most of the Internet services that you may be familiar with actually work through the use of TCP/UDP ports, such as HTTP for the Web, SMTP for e-mail, NNTP for Usenet, and so forth. The use of ports ensures that network communications intended for a particular purpose are not confused with others that may also be arriving at the same machine.

IP Addressing

Internet Protocol packets include addresses that uniquely define every computer connected to the Internet (see Figure 5-1). These addresses are used to route packets from a sending node to a receiving node. Because all the routers on the Internet know the network addresses to which they are connected, they can accurately forward packets destined for a remote network.

In addition to the data they carry, IP packets each contain a number of fields. These fields, in the order they occur, are

▼ **Version** This is the version of the IP protocol being used. This indicates, for instance, whether IP version 4 or version 6 is being used.

■ **Header length** This field indicates the length of the header information before the data begins in the packet.

■ **Type of service** This field is used for different things by different vendors. It can be used for such features as requesting high-priority routing, requesting highest possible reliability, and so forth.

■ **Total length** This field indicates the total length of the packet.

■ **Identification, flags, and fragment offset** These three fields are used to reassemble an IP packet that was disassembled at some point during transmission. These fields include all the information necessary for the correct reassembly of the packet at the receiving end.

■ **Time to live** This field defines how many network hops the packet can traverse before it is declared dead and the routers stop forwarding it to other routers. This number is set when the packet is sent and each router that handles the packet decrements the value by one. When the number reaches 0, the packet is dead and is no longer transmitted.

■ **Protocol** This field indicates whether the IP packet is contained within a TCP or a UDP packet.

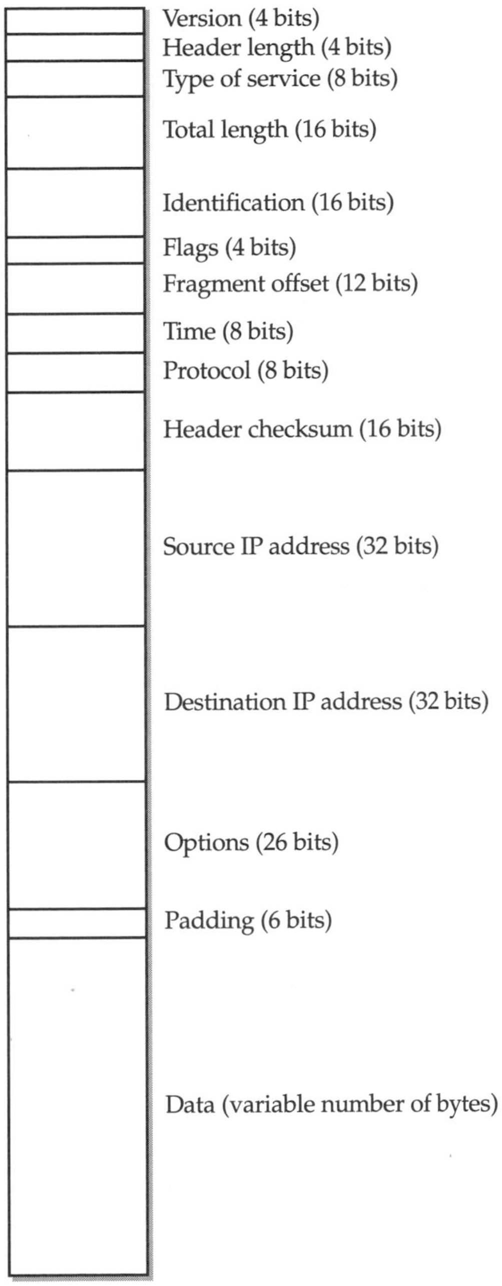

Version (4 bits)
Header length (4 bits)
Type of service (8 bits)

Total length (16 bits)

Identification (16 bits)

Flags (4 bits)
Fragment offset (12 bits)

Time (8 bits)
Protocol (8 bits)

Header checksum (16 bits)

Source IP address (32 bits)

Destination IP address (32 bits)

Options (26 bits)

Padding (6 bits)

Data (variable number of bytes)

Figure 5-1.   IP packet structure

- ■ **Header checksum**   The header checksum is used to help ensure that none of the packet's header data (the fields being discussed here) is damaged.

- ■ **Source IP address**   This field contains the address of the sending computer. It is needed in case retransmission of a packet is required, in which case the receiving node (or, in some cases, a router) knows from which node retransmission should be requested.

- ■ **Destination IP address**   This field contains the address of the receiving node.

- ■ **Options and padding**   These final two fields of the header of the IP packet are used in case specific routing instructions must be requested or to contain time information of when the packet was sent.

- ▲ **Data**   The final field of an IP packet is the actual data being sent.

IP addresses are 32 bits long, allowing for a theoretical maximum number of addresses of 2^{32}, or about 4.3 billion addresses. To make them easier to work with and to help route them more efficiently, they are broken up into four *octets*, which are each one byte long. Thus, in decimal notation, IP addresses are expressed as *xxx.xxx.xxx.xxx*, where each *xxx* represents a number from 0 to 255. The numbers 0 and 255 are usually reserved for special purposes, which typically leaves those numbers unavailable to assign to nodes and leaves 254 available unique addresses in each octet.

Addresses on the Internet are guaranteed to be unique through the use of an address registration service, presently administered by the Internet Corporation for Assigned Names and Numbers (ICANN).

ICANN assigns three major classes of addresses, called Class A, B, and C. A Class A address means the owner is assigned a number in the first octet and is then free to use all possible combinations in the remaining three octets. For example, a Class A address might be 57.*xxx.xxx.xxx*. Class A addresses give the capability to address up to 16.5M unique nodes. Class B addresses define the first two octets, leaving the remaining two open to be used by the owner of the address. For instance, 123.55.*xxx.xxx* would be a valid Class B address assignment. Class B addresses give the holder the capability to have 65K unique nodes. Class C follows this progression, with the first three octets defined and

Help! We're Almost Out of Addresses!

The current implementation of IP, called IP version 4 (IPv4) is approaching the point where running out of addresses is becoming a real possibility. In 1994, a proposal was issued to address this limitation. Called IP Next Generation (IPng and now IPv6), the new version of IP takes care of the addressing limitation by bumping up the address length from 32 bits to 128 bits. This allows 3.4×10^{38} (34 followed by 37 zeroes) unique addresses, which should have plenty of room for all anticipated Internet addresses, even allowing for having things like refrigerators, toasters, and cars with their own IP addresses!

only the last octet available for the Class C owner to assign, giving them the capability to assign up to 255 unique nodes.

An Internet service provider (ISP) may own either a Class A or a Class B address, and then can handle a number of Class C addresses within its own address structure. Changing ISPs, even for a company that has a valid Class C address, means changing its address from a Class C available through the first ISP, to a Class C available from the second ISP.

As mentioned earlier, the addresses 0 and 255 are reserved. Usually, address 0, as in 123.65.101.0, is used to refer to the network itself, and the router that connects the network to other networks handles this address. The address 255 is used to refer to all computers on the network, so a broadcast message to address 123.65.101.255 would go to all addresses within 123.65.101.*xxx*.

OTHER INTERNET PROTOCOLS

Quite a few other protocols are used on the Internet that either rely on, or make use of, TCP/IP. In this section, you learn about these different protocols, what they do, and, when appropriate, how they work in detail.

Domain Name System

If all you had to use to address computers over the Internet was their IP address number, trying to keep track of them and trying to use their correct addresses might make you a little crazy. To solve this, a system called the Domain Name System (DNS) was developed whereby domain names can be registered with ICANN and can then be used to access a particular node over the Internet. This is how you can open a Web browser and type **http://www.yahoo.com** and end up making a connection to a particular computer over the Internet. In this case, **yahoo.com** is the full domain name.

> **TIP:**   Domain names are given out on a first-come, first-served basis. However, a holder of a valid registered trademark is given preference if a conflict develops. ICANN, upon being presented with valid trademark information and notice of the domain name that infringes on that trademark, goes through a process to assess the truth of the claim and, if necessary, takes a domain name away from its present holder and transfers the name to its rightful owner.

Domain names are organized at their top level into domain types. The most common is the **.com** domain type, usually used with for-profit commercial entities. Other common domain types include

- ▼ **.edu** for educational institutions
- ■ **.gov** for governmental entities
- ■ **.mil** for military entities
- ■ **.net** for Internet-related entities
- ■ **.org** for non-profit entities
- ▲ *.xx* for different countries. For instance, **.it** would be for Italy, **.de** for Germany (Deutschland) and so forth.

Within a domain name, entities are free to add other names to the beginning of the domain name. For example, if you had the domain **bedrock.gov**, you would be free to create additional names, like **quarry.bedrock.gov**, or **flintstone.bedrock.gov**.

As a matter of standards, the first portion of a domain name, preceding the actual domain name, indicates what type of service is being connected. For instance, **www.bedrock.gov** would be used for a World Wide Web server for **bedrock.gov**, while **ftp.bedrock.gov** would be used for an FTP server, and so forth. The standards for service types within the domain name are usually followed, but not always, and the owner of the domain name is free to invent its own service types, which meets some need of theirs. As an example of this, some domain name holders refer to their e-mail servers as **smtp.domain.org**, while others may prefer to use **mail.domain.org**. They could also use anything else they wanted.

Domain names are resolved to IP addresses through the use of *name servers*, or servers that accept the typed domain name, perform a database query, and then return the actual address that should be used for that domain name. Generally, each ISP maintains its own DNS servers (and many larger companies do, too) and any changes are propagated throughout all the Internet's DNS servers within a few days.

Dynamic Host Configuration Protocol (DHCP)

In the early days of TCP/IP-based networks, each node had its address set by defining it in a file or dialog box. From then on, the address was fixed unless someone changed it. The problem was that, occasionally, conflicting addresses would get put into other nodes on the network by mistake, causing a network's version of pandemonium. To resolve this and to make the assignment of TCP/IP addresses easier, a service called Dynamic Host Configuration Protocol (DHCP) was invented. DHCP services run on a DHCP server, where they control a range of IP addresses called a *scope*. Nodes on the network, when they connect to the network, contact the DHCP server to get an assigned address and then they use that address. Addresses from a DHCP server are said to be *leased* to the client that uses them, meaning they remain assigned to a particular node for a set period of time before they expire and become available for another node to use. Often, lease periods are for just a few days.

Knowing DHCP should not be used for nodes that provide network services is important, particularly to those that provide services over the Internet. This is because a changing TCP/IP address would make reliably connecting to those computers impossible. Instead, DHCP is used to support client workstations that do not need to host services for other nodes.

DEFINE IT!—Host

You may think a *host* is a server and, in some networking contexts, you'd be right. When discussing Internet names and addresses, however, every computer that has an address is called a *host*. Thus the name, Dynamic Host Configuration Protocol.

Hypertext Transfer Protocol (HTTP)

The World Wide Web is made up of documents that use a formatting language called *HTML,* which stands for Hypertext Markup Language. These documents are composed of text to be displayed, graphic images, formatting commands, and hyperlinks to other documents located somewhere on the Web. HTML documents are displayed most often using Web browsers, like Netscape Navigator or Microsoft Internet Explorer.

A protocol called *Hypertext Transfer Protocol* (HTTP) controls the transactions between a Web client and a Web server. HTTP is an application-layer protocol. The HTTP protocol transparently makes use of DNS and other Internet protocols to form connections between the Web client and the Web server, so the user is only aware of the Web site's domain name and the name of the document itself.

HTTP is fundamentally an insecure protocol. Text-based information is sent "in the clear" between the client and the server. To address the need for secure Web networking, alternatives are available, such as Secure HTTP (S-HTTP) or Secure Sockets Layer (SSL).

Connections from a Web client to Web server are connection-oriented, but they are not persistent. Once the contents of an HTML page are sent to the client, the connection is no longer active. Clicking a hyperlink in the HTML document reactivates the link, either to the original server (if that is where the hyperlink points) or to another server somewhere else.

File Transfer Protocol (FTP)

The acronym FTP stands for two things: File Transfer Protocol and File Transfer Program (which makes use of the File Transfer Protocol). Sort of like, "it's a dessert topping and a floor polish" from the old *Saturday Night Live* TV show. Because FTP (the program) makes use of FTP (the protocol), it can become confusing to know which is being discussed. In this case, we're talking about the protocol. If I'm referring to the program, I'll say so.

FTP is an application-layer protocol used to send and receive files between an FTP client and an FTP server. This is done, usually, by using the FTP program, or another program that can also use the protocol. FTP transfers can be either text-based or binary-based, and they can handle files of any size. When you connect to an FTP server to transfer a file, you log into the FTP server using a valid user name and password. Many sites are set up, however, to allow something called *anonymous FTP*—where you enter the user name *anonymous* and then enter your e-mail address as the password. For example, Microsoft maintains an FTP site you can use to download updates to their products. Located at **ftp.microsoft.com**, it is an example of a site that allows anonymous FTP.

To use the FTP program, on most platforms you type the command **ftp** followed by the address to which you want to connect. So, to use the Microsoft example, you would type **ftp ftp.microsoft.com** and then press the ENTER key. You then log in and you can use all of the FTP commands—**PUT**, **GET**, **MGET**, and so forth. Most FTP program implementations have online help to assist you with the various commands. Type **?** or **HELP** to access this feature.

NetNews Transfer Protocol

Usenet (NetNews) is a set of discussion groups devoted to an extremely wide variety of topics. Over 35,000 such groups are currently in existence and the number seems to keep increasing by leaps and bounds. Usenet conversations are posted to Usenet servers, which then echo their messages to all other Usenet servers around the world. A posted message can travel to all the Usenet servers in a matter of hours and then be available to users accessing that particular Usenet server.

Usenet discussion groups are loosely organized into the branches of a tree. The following are some of the main branches:

▼ Alt, used for discussions about alternative lifestyles and other miscellaneous topics

■ Comp, used for computer-oriented discussions

■ Gov, for government-oriented discussions

■ Rec, devoted to recreational topics

▲ Sci, for science-based discussions

Usenet groups can either be public, which are echoed to other Usenet servers, or private, which are usually hosted by a particular organization and require appropriate login credentials to read and post messages.

The NNTP protocol is what makes Usenet possible. It allows for a connection between a Usenet reader (also called a *news reader*) and a Usenet server. It also provides for message formatting, so messages can be text-based or can also contain binary attachments. Binary attachments in Usenet postings are usually encoded using Multipurpose Internet Message Encoding (MIME), which is also used for most e-mail attachments. Some older systems use different methods to encode attachments, however, including one called UUEncode/UUDecode and, on the Macintosh, one called BinHex.

Telnet

Telnet defines a protocol that allows a remote terminal session to be established with an Internet host, so remote users have access similar to if they were sitting at a terminal connected directly to the host computer. Using Telnet, users can control the remote host, performing such tasks as managing files, running applications, or even (with appropriate permissions) administering the remote system.

For Telnet to work, Telnet software must be running on both the host and client computer. You run the program Telnet on a client computer and Telnetd on the host computer to allow the connection. Telnet is specific to the TCP protocol and, typically, runs on port 23 (although it can run on any port that has been enabled on the host system). Once users connect using Telnet, they must log into the remote system using the same credentials they would use if they were using a directly connected terminal.

Simple Mail Transfer Protocol

E-mail had a somewhat rocky start on the Internet, with early e-mail programs sharing few standards with other e-mail programs, particularly in the handling of attached binary data. The good news is the situation is now much improved and most current e-mail software supports all the widely accepted standards.

The Simple Mail Transfer Protocol (SMTP) is used to send and receive e-mail messages from one e-mail server to another. Details on SMTP can be found in RFC 821. The SMTP protocol defines a dialogue between a sending system and a receiving system.

An SMTP dialogue starts when a sending system connects to port 25 of a receiving system. After the connection is established, the sending system sends a HELO command, followed by its address. The receiving system acknowledges the HELO along with its own address. The dialogue then continues, with the sending system sending a command indicating it wants to send a message and for what recipient the message is intended. If the receiving system knows of the recipient, it acknowledges the request, and then the body of the message is sent, along with any attachments. Finally, the connection between the two systems is terminated once the receiving system acknowledges it has received the entire message. Figure 5-2 illustrates this process.

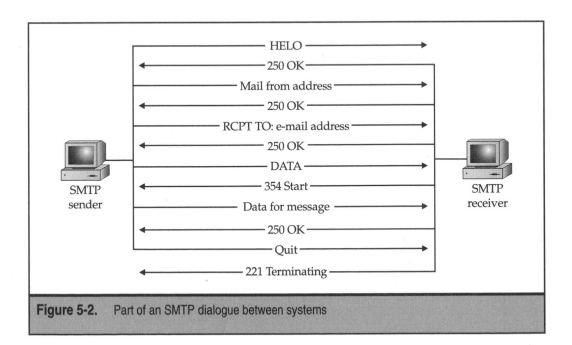

Figure 5-2. Part of an SMTP dialogue between systems

OTHER IMPORTANT PROTOCOLS

While Microsoft-based, Novell-based, and Apple-based networks can fully work with TCP/IP and all the previously listed protocols, each got its start supporting somewhat proprietary protocols unique to each company and each is still in wide use. All these companies have embraced TCP/IP and support it fully, both for servers and network clients. In the case of Microsoft and Novell networks, they can be easily deployed using only TCP/IP (at least with Windows NT 4 and Novell NetWare 5). In theory, you could do the same thing with an Apple-based network, but you would lose a good deal of the Macintosh's network functionality if you did so. Because of this, an Apple-based network should support both AppleTalk (Apple's proprietary protocol) and TCP/IP.

Novell networks, until just recently, predominantly used the Internetwork Packet Exchange/Sequenced Packet Exchange (IPX/SPX) protocols. These are derivatives of the Xerox XNS protocol. While different from TCP/IP, IPX/SPX can be compared to it; IPX is analogous to IP, and SPX is analogous to TCP.

Microsoft networks were originally based on an IBM-developed protocol called NetBIOS, short for Network Basic Input/Output System. NetBIOS is a relatively high-level protocol that, in essence, extends the functionality of DOS to a network. Microsoft also used IBM's NetBEUI (NetBIOS Extended User Interface), an enhancement to NetBIOS.

Apple Macintosh computer networks originally only supported AppleTalk. The protocol was originally designed expressly for the purpose of sharing expensive Apple LaserWriter printers within small workgroups, using a low-bandwidth (230Kbps originally) network media called LocalTalk. Over time AppleTalk was extended somewhat to enable file sharing and other network functions, but it is still an extremely inefficient network protocol that, even over Ethernet (called EtherTalk in Apple's implementation), works slowly. Still, if you have an Apple-based network, you have to live with the AppleTalk protocol.

Novell's IPX/SPX

Novell's IPX protocol was originally a derivative of the Xerox Network Systems architecture (XNS) and closely resembles it. While IPX can be used on any of the popular network medias (Ethernet, Token Ring, and so forth) it was originally designed for Ethernet networks and works best with that media. In fact, the IPX protocol depends on Ethernet MAC addresses for its own, although the addresses are dynamic and are automatically negotiated with the server at login, rather than being statically set, as is the case with TCP/IP without DHCP services. An IPX network address is comprised of both a 32-bit network address and a 48-bit node address. In addition, another 16 bits are used for a connection ID, which allows up to 65 thousand unique client/server connections between a client and a server. The address design of IPX theoretically allows for about 281 trillion nodes on each of 16 million networks.

IPX was originally designed only for LANs, but it has been enhanced to support WAN connections. While typically considered a "chatty" protocol that requires a lot of send/acknowledgement transactions, IPX has been enhanced with burst-mode capabilities, which increase the size of packets destined for a WAN and decrease the number of back-and-forth communications required. IPX can be routed, but requires an IPX-capable router to do so.

NetBIOS and NetBEUI Protocols

NetBIOS and NetBEUI were originally developed by IBM to support small networks and were adopted by Microsoft as part of LAN Manager, a network operating system built on top of early versions of the OS/2 operating system.

Neither protocol is routable; they are only suitable for small LANs that do not rely on routers between different LAN segments. However, NetBIOS can be encapsulated within TCP/IP packets on Windows NT networks using a service called NetBIOS over TCP/IP (NBT).

Microsoft LANs (prior to Windows 2000) rely on a NetBIOS service called NetBIOS names to identify each workstation uniquely.

In a simple NetBIOS implementation, names are registered with all workstations through the use of a broadcast message. If no computer has already registered a particular name, the name registration succeeds. In a more complex Windows NT-based network that also uses TCP/IP, however, the NetBIOS names resolve to TCP/IP addresses through the use of a Windows Internet Name Service (WINS). Because many networking applications still make use of NetBIOS names, this service allows such applications to continue to function in a TCP/IP-only network. As far as the application is concerned, it is still working with NetBIOS, while "behind the scenes," the actual work is being carried out using TCP/IP.

AppleTalk

AppleTalk has been extended in recent years into AppleTalk Phase II, which now allows routing of AppleTalk packets (assuming an AppleTalk Phase II-capable router). The Phase II variant can run over Ethernet, Token Ring, or Apple's LocalTalk media. Under Ethernet, AppleTalk uses a variant of the 802.2 frame type called Ethernet SNAP (SubNetwork Access Point).

While Apple Macintosh computers can use both TCP/IP and IPX/SPX through the addition of special software, the Macintosh operating system is dependent on AppleTalk, so both TCP/IP and IPX/SPX are translated at each node into AppleTalk messages before being passed to the operating system. This is one of the reasons Apple Macintosh computers tend to be slower than other types of computers over network connections. Still, the approach works and is relatively easy to set up and maintain.

CHAPTER SUMMARY

This chapter is built on the knowledge you gained in earlier chapters, delving into various important protocols involved in virtually all networks, including the Internet. You learned primarily about the TCP/IP protocol, which is fast displacing older protocols like IPX/SPX and NetBIOS/NetBEUI (although both are still widely used). You also learned about some specific application-layer Internet protocols, like SMTP, DHCP, and HTTP. These are all vital protocols to understand for any networking professional.

It would be nice if the protocols discussed in this chapter were all you had to contend with but, unfortunately, many more protocols exist. Some are specific to certain functions, like remote access to a network, and are discussed in appropriate chapters within this book. Others are still being developed and are not a factor now, but may be in the near future. As always, staying current with network technology if you work in the field is important and staying up-to-date with emerging protocols that may become important to any networks you manage or support is valuable.

CHAPTER 6

Learning About Directory Services

In the early days of LANs, finding server resources was pretty simple. Most organizations started with just a file and a print server or two, so knowing what files, printers, and other services were in which locations in the LAN was easy.

These days, the situation is considerably more complex. Even relatively small organizations may have multiple servers, each one performing different services, storing different sets of files, providing different Internet or intranet services, hosting different printers, and so forth.

Directory services work to bring organization to this far-flung network clutter. In this chapter, you learn about what directory services do and how they work. You also learn about directory services in use today and slated for the near future. With directory services becoming more and more central to the administration of networks, learning this information becomes an increasingly important part of designing, deploying, and managing networks.

WHAT IS A DIRECTORY SERVICE?

In most networks. you optimize the function of different services by hosting them on different computers. Doing so makes sense. Placing all your services on one computer is a bit like placing all your eggs in one basket. Drop the basket and all your eggs break. Moreover, optimal performance, more reliability, and higher security can be achieved by segregating network services in various ways. Most networks have quite a few services that need to be provided and often these different services are run on different servers. Even a relatively simple network has the following services now:

▼ File storage and sharing

■ Printer sharing

■ E-mail services

■ Web hosting, both for the Internet and an intranet

■ Database server services

■ Specific application servers

■ Internet connectivity

■ Dial-in and dial-out services

■ Fax services

■ DNS, WINS, and DHCP services

■ Centralized virus detection services

▲ Backup and restore services

This is only a short list. Larger organizations have multiple servers sharing in each of these functions—with different services available through different means in each building or location—and may have additional services beyond those discussed here.

All of this complexity quickly makes a network chaotic to manage. If you imagine each one of the individual servers requires separate administration (with, for instance, separate lists of users, groups, printers, network configurations, and so on) then you can easily see how the job becomes virtually impossible in no time.

Directory services were invented to bring organization to networks. Basically, directory services work just like a phone book. Instead of knowing a name to look up an address and phone number in a phone book, you query the directory service for a service name (like the name of a network folder or a printer) and it tells you where it is located. Directory services can also be queried by property. For instance, query the directory service for all items that are "printers" and it can return a complete list, no matter where the printers are located in the organization. Even better, directory services enable you to browse all the resources on a network easily, in one unified list organized in a tree structure.

One important property of directory services is they eliminate the need to manage duplicates of anything on the network. For example, you don't have to maintain separate user lists on each server. Instead, you manage a single set of user accounts that exists in the directory service and then assign them various rights to particular resources on any of the servers. Other resources work the same way and become centralized in the directory service.

NOTE: In this chapter, when you see the term *network resource*, it refers to things like user accounts, security group definitions, e-mail distribution lists, storage volumes, folders, files, and any other discrete resource on a network.

To provide redundancy, directory services usually run on multiple servers in an organization, each of the servers having a complete copy of the entire directory service database. The separate databases are kept in synch through a process called *replication*, in which changes to any of the individual directory databases are transparently updated to all the other directory service databases. Because a directory service becomes central to the functioning of a network, this approach lets the network as a whole continue to operate if a server with directory services on it crashes.

You should know about five directory services:

▼ Novell Directory Services (NDS) is the network directory service that has been popular for the longest time. NDS runs on Netware 4.x and greater servers, and is also available for other server operating systems (like Windows NT) enabling you to use it as a single directory service for managing a multivendor network.

■ Windows NT domains are not a complete directory service, per se, but they provide some of the features and advantages of directory services.

■ Microsoft's Active Directory debuts with its Windows 2000 line of products (previously known as Windows NT 5). This is a true directory service and it promises to bring the full features of a directory service to a network predominantly built using Windows NT.

■ *X.500 directory access protocol* (DAP) is an international standard directory service that is extremely full-featured. However, X.500 is so full-featured, its overhead makes deploying and managing it prohibitive. Consequently, X.500 is in an interesting position: It is an important standard, yet, paradoxically, it is not actually used.

▲ To answer the problem with the complexity of X.500, a consortium of vendors came up with a subset of X.500 called the Lightweight Directory Access Protocol (LDAP). LDAP is in wide use for e-mail directories and is suitable for other directory service tasks. The most recent versions of NDS—and also Active Directory—are compatible with LDAP.

Forests, Trees, Roots, and Leaves

One thing common to all directory services is a tree-based organization, somewhat similar to the organization of directories on a hard disk. At the top of the directory tree is the *root* entry, which contains other entries. These other entries can be containers or leaves. A *container object* is one that contains other objects, which can also include more containers and leaves. A *leaf object* represents an actual resource on the network, such as a workstation, printer, shared directory, file, or user account. Figure 6-1 shows a typical directory tree.

All the objects in a directory tree have *attributes* (sometimes called *properties*), which vary depending on to which type of object the attribute is attached.

For example, a printer leaf object may contain attributes that describe the printer, who can administer the printer, what the printer's name is on the network, and so forth. A *user account leaf object* may contain attributes that include the full name of the user account, its password, and resources the user can access. The details of what attributes attach to what leaf or container objects vary among all the directory services, although they generally use similar attributes.

Department of Redundancy Department

Directory services are essential to using any network that makes use of them. Because the directory service contains all details about accounts, resources, and security, its absence means the network won't work—at all! Because the directory service becomes so important to a network, it must be protected with some degree of redundancy. Keeping duplicate copies of the directory on multiple servers does this. This is done in two ways: primary/backup (master/slave) and multimaster. In the *primary/backup model,* a single primary database contains the directory and one or more backup copies on different servers. If the primary copy stops working for some reason, the backups can continue to provide directory services to the network and they do so without the user even knowing the

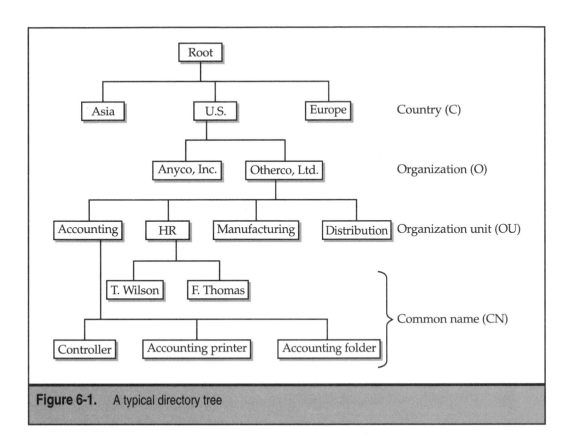

Figure 6-1. A typical directory tree

primary isn't available. In the *multimaster model,* multiple directory servers exist, but they are all peer to one another. If one goes down, the other peers continue to operate normally. The advantage to the multimaster model is each directory server can fully participate in doing the work of the directory service.

Directory servers, whether they use the primary/backup or multimaster approach, must keep in synch with changes on the network. This is handled using a process called *replication,* which updates any changes to the directory to all the other directory servers automatically.

A potential problem exists with any replication process, though. If two changes are made to the same leaf object on two different directory servers and the changes are different, what does the system do when the changes "collide" during replication? Different directory services handle this in slightly different ways. In the case of NDS, the time stamp of the change drives which of two conflicting changes will win. (Because of this, servers running NDS must carefully keep their time synchronized; this is also handled during replication.) Active Directory doesn't use time stamps but, instead, uses sequence numbers in a clever scheme that avoids the potential problems with a time-stamp approach.

(Even though NDS servers synch their time, it can still become out of synch in-between synchronizations.)

Some directory services also allow a concept called *partitioning*, in which different directory servers keep different parts of the entire directory tree. In this case, a controlling directory server usually has the entire tree (called the *global catalog* in Active Directory) and then other directory servers can manage smaller pieces of the total tree. Partitioning is important for networks with multiple LANs connected by a WAN. In cases like this, you want to host a partition that relates to a particular LAN locally and yet still allow access to the entire tree for resources accessed over the WAN. Each LAN hosts its own partition, but can still access the total tree when needed. You arrange the partitions to make the best use of the WAN's usually slower performance.

LEARNING ABOUT SPECIFIC DIRECTORY SERVICES

Quite a few different directory services are available. Choosing one usually goes hand-in-hand with choosing a main network operating system, although this isn't always the case. Both NDS and Active Directory can handle non-Novell and non-Microsoft servers, respectively. Consequently, even in a network that presently uses mostly Windows NT servers, you may still rely on NDS for directory services through the use of Novell's NDS for Windows NT product. This often happens because an organization starts out favoring a particular network operating system and then becomes forced to support more than one, but it still wants to maintain a coherent directory service.

Earlier in the chapter, the main directory services were listed. Here they are again:

▼ Novell Directory Services (NDS)

■ Microsoft's Windows NT Domains

■ Microsoft's Active Directory

■ X.500 Directory Access Protocol (DAP)

▲ Lightweight Directory Access Protocol (LDAP)

These are the predominant directory services you will encounter, although you should be aware others exist. While this isn't discussed in detail here, you should also be aware of a product called StreetTalk, from a company called Banyan. StreetTalk has been in existence for a long time as part of the Banyan Vines network operating system (which is essentially a UNIX-based NOS). StreetTalk is available for Novell servers as well as Vines servers. Seeing Banyan-based networks is extremely rare now, though, and you're unlikely to encounter this product.

NDS

Novell Directory Services (NDS) has been available for over four years now, being introduced as part of NetWare 4.x. With many organizations having tens or hundreds of

NetWare servers, this product was a real boon and was rapidly implemented, particularly in larger organizations that desperately needed its capabilities. NDS is a reliable, robust directory service that has continued to evolve from its introduction. Version 8 is now available and it incorporates the latest directory service features. NDS uses a Master/Slave approach to directory servers and also allows partitioning of the tree. In addition to running on Novell network operating systems, NDS is also available for Windows NT and UNIX systems, making it a good choice to manage all these platforms under a single directory structure.

The NDS tree is managed from a client computer logged into the network with administrative privileges. You can either use a graphical tool designed to manage the tree called *NWAdmin*, or a text-based tool called *NETADMIN*. Both allow full management of the tree, although the graphical product is much easier to use.

The NDS tree contains a number of different object types. The standard directory service types are included—countries, organizations, and organizational unit. The system also has objects to represent NetWare security groups, NetWare servers, and NetWare server volumes.

Windows NT Domains

Windows NT 4 introduced a directory service feature organized around the use of domains. The Windows NT domain model breaks the organization into chunks called *domains,* all of which are part of an organization. The domains are usually organized geographically, which helps minimize domain-to-domain communication requirements across WAN links, although you're free to organize domains as you wish. Each domain is controlled by a *Primary Domain Controller* (PDC), which may have one or more Backup Domain Controllers (BDCs) to kick in if it fails.

Windows NT domains can be organized into one of four domain models. You choose an appropriate domain model depending on the physical layout of the network, the number of users to be served, and other factors. (If you're planning a domain model, you should review the detailed white papers on Microsoft's Web site for details on planning large domains because it can be complex and difficult.)

The four domain models are:

▼ **Single domain model**   In this model, only one domain contains all network resources.

■ **Master domain model**   The master model usually puts users at the top-level domain and then places network resources, like shares or printers, in sub-level domains (called *resource domains*). In this model, the resource domains trust the master domain.

■ **Multiple master domain model**   This is a slight variation on the master domain model, in which users may exist in multiple master domains, all of which trust one another and then resources are located in resource domains, all of which trust all the master domains.

▲   **Complete trust model**   This is a variation of the single domain model, in which users and resources are spread across all domains and all the domains trust each other.

NOTE: A good white paper on designing Windows NT 4 domains, while keeping Windows 2000 in mind, can be found at: http://technet.microsoft.com/cdonline/Content/Complete/boes/bo/Winntas/technote/Planning/nt4tont5.htm

Explicit trust relationships must be maintained between domains using the master or multiple master domain models, and must be managed on each domain separately. This is one of the biggest difficulties in the Windows NT domain structure approach, at least for larger organizations; if you have 100 domains, you must manage the 99 possible trust relationships for each domain within each domain. If you had 100 domains in an organization, you would have to manage 99 trust entries per domain or a total of 9,900 trust relationships. For smaller numbers of domains (say, several domains) this doesn't become much of a problem, although it can still cause difficulties.

Active Directory

Windows NT domains work relatively well for smaller networks, but they can become difficult to manage for larger networks. Moreover, the system is not nearly as comprehensive as, for example, NDS. Microsoft recognized this problem and has been developing a new directory service for several years now called *Active Directory*, which is a comprehensive directory service that Microsoft will be working hard to put into use at client sites. Active Directory is fully compatible with LDAP (versions 2 and 3) and also with the Domain Name System (DNS) used on the Internet.

Active Directory uses a peer approach to domain controllers; all domain controllers are full participants at all times.

Active Directory is built on a structure that allows "trees of trees," which is called a *forest*. Each tree is its own domain and has its own domain controllers. Within a domain, separate organization units are allowed to make administration easier and more logical. Trees are then aggregated together into a larger tree structure. According to Microsoft, Active Directory can handle millions of objects through this approach.

Active Directory does not require the management of trust relationships, except when connected to Windows NT 4.x servers that are not using Active Directory. Otherwise, all domains within a tree have automatic trust relationships.

X.500

The X.500 standard was developed jointly by the International Telecommunications Union (ITU) and the ISO. It defines a directory service that can be used for the entire Internet. Because of this, the X.500 specification is overly complex for most organizations to implement. Also, because of its design, it is intended to publish specific organizational directory entries across the Internet, which is something most companies would not want to do. Just the same, the X.500 standard is an extremely important standard and most directory services mimic or subset it in some fashion.

The X.500 directory tree starts with a root, just like the other directory trees, and then breaks down into country (C), organization (O), organizational unit (OU), and common name (CN). To specify an X.500 address fully, you provide five fields, as in the following:

CN=user name, OU=department, OU=division, O=organization, C=country

Or, for example:

CN=Bruce Hallberg, OU=Networking Books, OU=Computer Books,
O=McGraw-Hill, C=USA

LDAP

To combat the complexity problems involved with full X.500 DAP, a consortium of companies came up with a subset of X.500, called the Lightweight Directory Access Protocol (LDAP). LDAP runs over TCP/IP and uses a client/server model. Its organization is much the same as X.500, but with fewer fields and fewer functions.

LDAP starts with a root, which then contains entries. Each entry can have one or more *attributes.* Each of these attributes has both a *type* and *values* associated with it. One example is the CommonName entry (CN), which contains at least two attributes: FirstName and Surname. All attributes in LDAP use the text string data type.

Entries are broken up into a tree and managed geographically and then within each organization.

One nice feature of LDAP is an organization can build a global directory structure using a feature called *referral*, where LDAP directory queries that are managed by a different LDAP server are transparently routed to that server. Because each LDAP server knows its parent LDAP server and its child servers, any user anywhere in the network can access the entire LDAP tree. In fact, the user won't even know he or she is running on different servers in different locales.

CHAPTER SUMMARY

In this chapter, you learned about both the importance of directory services and the factors driving that importance. You also learned how directory services work, what they accomplish, and those common features found in almost all directory services. Finally, the most important directory services were each reviewed, including Novell's NDS, and Microsoft's domain directory service and new Active Directory service.

The next chapter continues the discussions about essential network technologies and services by teaching you about remote access services, in which far-flung users can access LANs from anywhere in the world. Implementing a good remote access system that everyone is happy with is one of the most difficult things to do—especially for larger organizations with many different needs—so a variety of approaches are discussed.

CHAPTER 7

Connections from Afar: Remote Network Access

In preceding chapters, you learned about networking systems together through a LAN and through a WAN, and about the technologies that go into both. You also need to know about another important type of network connection: remote access to a network. With today's travel-happy corporate cultures and with companies needing to support such things as working from home and small remote offices, remote access has become more important than ever. Unfortunately, it's also one of the most difficult parts of a network to get right, as you see in this chapter.

In this chapter, you learn about:

▼ Different classes of remote access users

■ Determining remote access needs for different users

▲ Technologies that support remote access, ranging from single-modem remote-access solutions to solutions that can support tens or hundreds of simultaneous users

One of the big problems with remote access is it can seem as though all the remote users have different needs and all the different solutions available speak to different needs, and none of those solutions take care of all the needs. Spending some time analyzing your company's needs and finding solid solutions that meet those needs is usually nontrivial and requires a fair amount of time and effort.

CLASSIFYING REMOTE USERS

Users who require remote access fall into one of a number of different categories. Each category may have different needs, and different technologies and remote access solutions are often needed to satisfy these different needs completely. Most important to remember is you need to know what categories of remote users *you* have to support. Every company has a different mix of remote users, who have different needs from company to company. Moreover, even when needs are identical, the solutions you employ may change based on other criteria. For instance, access to an accounting system from a remote location can be handled differently, depending on whether it's a client/server or a monolithic application.

The most common type of remote access user is called the *broad traveler*. This is someone normally based in a main office who usually has LAN access, but who occasionally or frequently travels on business. Travel takes this person to virtually any place in the world, so the traveler must contend with different telephone systems, long distance carriers, and other geographic challenges (see Figure 7-1). Often, this type of user mostly needs e-mail access, but also needs occasional access to stored or e-mailed files. This type of user may or may not have a dedicated portable computer. The user might normally use a desktop on the LAN (but have a portable for traveling), might use a single portable both on the LAN and when traveling, might check out portable computers from a shared pool when travel needs arise, or might even rent portable computers for an occasional travel need.

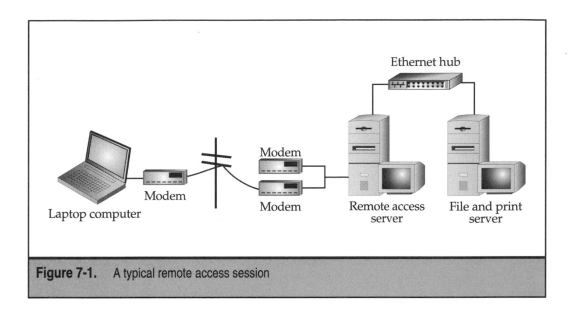

Figure 7-1.   A typical remote access session

Another common type of remote access user is called a *narrow traveler*. This is someone who travels to relatively few locations, such as from corporate headquarters to the company's manufacturing plants or distribution centers. The nice thing about this type of user is you can predict from which sites the user may need to access data, and local support can be available to help. For instance, you may have a way for the user to log into the distribution center's LAN and access e-mail and files at the headquarters location through an existing WAN link shown in Figure 7-2. This type of user needs e-mail, file access and, often, access to a centralized application, like an accounting system.

The third common type of remote access user is the *remote office user.* This user is in a single location and needs access to the corporate LAN for e-mail and, possibly, application access (see Figure 7-3). This person usually does not need file access, except to have files sent through the e-mail system, because this person maintains local file storage. This user is in a single location, so you can pursue certain high-speed links that aren't feasible for the travelers. By the way, a person telecommuting from home would fall into the category of remote office user.

The fourth type of remote access user is something of a hybrid. Sometimes you have a small group (two to five people), who are in a remote location and need certain services from the corporate LAN. These services aren't cost-effective for them to have locally, yet they have a small local LAN for printer and file sharing, as seen in Figure 7-4. This becomes a mix between a WAN-linked LAN and a remote user, and usually requires a mixture of both types of solutions for proper support.

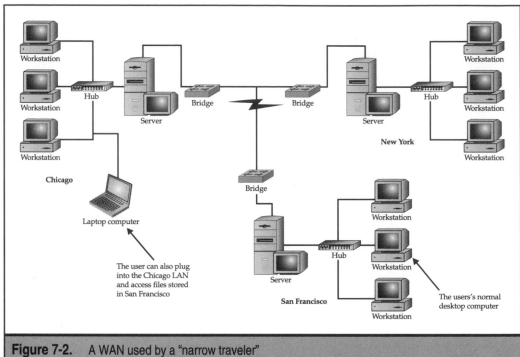

Figure 7-2. A WAN used by a "narrow traveler"

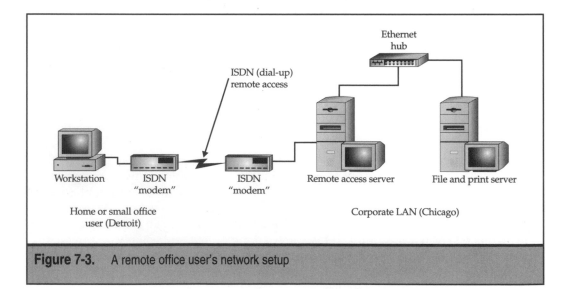

Figure 7-3. A remote office user's network setup

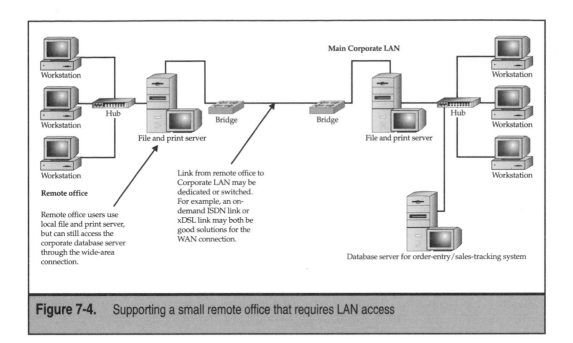

Figure 7-4.   Supporting a small remote office that requires LAN access

UNDERSTANDING REMOTE ACCESS NEEDS

Before implementing any remote access system, you need to define clearly what the different types of remote users in the company need. Examples of needs you should meet include:

▼ Easy remote access to e-mail and files stored in e-mail

■ Remote access to stored private or shared files on the LAN

■ Remote access to a centralized application, like an accounting system or a sales order system

■ Remote access to groupware programs or custom applications

■ Remote access to any of the previous from a fixed location, such as a remote sales office

▲ Remote access to any of the previous from anywhere in the world

To understand your specific remote access support needs, it's important to interview all the potential users and find out if you can categorize them. Chances are, you must support remote access through more than one mechanism. How the users and their needs break down will suggest which mechanisms make sense.

To interview the users, make sure you carefully probe all possible needs. For example, if you ask them if they need remote access to the files stored in their LAN directories and they reply "not really," that's not an adequate answer. You need to pin them down by asking such questions as: "Will you *ever* need remote access to files? What if you only had e-mail access? Could your assistant e-mail you any needed files?" You also might want to consider taking this tack: Once you have come up with different remote access needs in your company, try to survey the users in writing to inquire about their specific needs. Not only should you get less ambiguous answers, but you can also have important documentation to justify the required expenses and effort.

When examining remote access needs, you need to estimate bandwidth requirements and tolerances for the different users. This is important for planning and also for appropriately setting up expectations. For example, if salespeople want minute-to-minute access to a sales tracking system and also frequently want to download 4MB file packages to use for quotations, you have to explain about the limitations of modem speeds and telephone connections to reduce their expectations. Or, you can find different solutions to meet their needs that are consistent with the amount of bandwidth you can offer.

 You can estimate a particular application program's bandwidth requirements in a few good ways. The first involves measuring its bandwidth needs. On the LAN, you can monitor the amount of data being sent to a particular node that uses the application in the way it would be used remotely. The measurement can be done in a number of ways. For a Windows 9x PC, you can run System Monitor on the client and look at the network traffic the PC is using (see Figure 7-5). You can also measure it from the server. For a Windows NT server, you can use Performance Monitor to measure bytes transmitted to the client. For a Novell server, you can use the console Monitor application and watch the amount of data being used by the client's server connection.

If the bandwidth requirements of an application are simply too great to be handled over the type of remote connection you have to use (such as a 33.6Kbps modem connection), you need to explore other alternatives. These include using a remote control solution (more on this soon) or using the application in a different way. For example, you might load the application in question onto the remote computer rather than use it across the LAN. Also, perhaps the data needs of the user don't need to be up-to-date, minute-to-minute, and you can set up a procedure whereby weekly data updates are sent to them on a CD-ROM or through some other mechanism.

The ways you can satisfy remote access needs are virtually limitless, but the key information to remember in this section is this: You need to assess the needs carefully and you need to work creatively, given your remote access technology, to find ways to satisfy the remote user's needs.

LEARNING REMOTE ACCESS TECHNOLOGIES

A variety of different ways exist to accomplish remote access connections for users. Sometimes these different technologies are appropriate for some users, but not for others. Sometimes the choices you have are restricted by how the remote user needs to access the

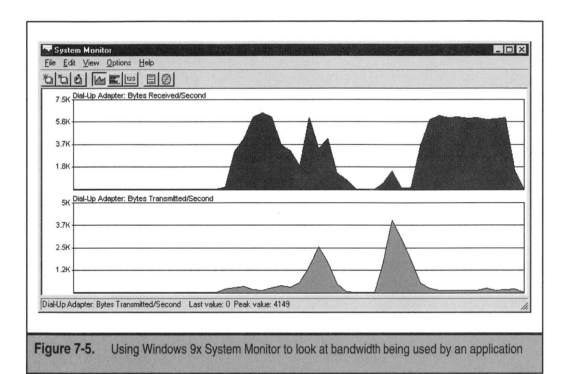

Figure 7-5.   Using Windows 9x System Monitor to look at bandwidth being used by an application

data. For example, a remote user at a single location can, fairly easily, set up a high-speed link to the corporate LAN, while a travelling remote user may be limited to using modems and dial-up telephone connections.

In the following sections, different techniques and technologies are discussed, along with the pros and cons of each. The ones you implement depend on the needs you've identified, your budget, and the existing infrastructure of your network.

Remote Node Versus Remote Control

Remote users can connect to a network in two basic ways: Remote node and remote control. A *remote node connection* is one in which the remote computer becomes a node on the network. Data flows between the remote node and the network much as it would for a LAN-connected user, albeit usually at much slower rates. When you connect to an ISP to access the Internet, you are using a remote node type of connection.

A *remote control connection* is one in which a remote user takes control of another computer directly connected to the LAN, with only the screen, keyboard, and mouse information being transmitted through the connection. Because the remote control computer is directly connected to the LAN, its network performance is just as fast as any other LAN workstation. The information actually transmitted—the screen information, keyboard data, and mouse data—usually doesn't require much bandwidth. Remote control connections also have ways to transfer files back and forth from the remote computer to the controlled computer, so files can still be downloaded from the LAN to the remote computer and vice-versa.

Remote control is accomplished using special applications designed for this purpose. Examples of remote control software includes PCAnywhere, Carbon Copy, and ReachOut, as well as Windows NT Terminal Server and Citrix WinFrame. You run the remote control software on both the LAN-connected computer and the remote computer. The connection is established over some sort of dial-up line or through the Internet.

Two types of remote control applications are available. The first runs on a single computer and supports a single remote computer at a time. PCAnwhere and Carbon Copy are examples of this type. Another type allows multiple sessions to run on a single computer, so you can have more than one user making use of a single computer connected to the LAN. Windows NT Terminal Server and Citrix WinFrame are examples of this type. The multiuser solutions use the LAN computer's multitasking capabilities to construct multiple virtual PCs, windows, and desktops, sort of like a mainframe with multiple terminal sessions.

Remote control is the best bet when the remote users need to access applications that don't work well over slow-bandwidth connections. And, because most applications don't run well over slow-bandwidth connections, it's generally true that any time a remote user needs to use a LAN-connected application, it will probably work best with remote control, instead of remote node.

Any of the remote connection technologies can work with both remote node and remote control. You can connect to a remote control system through modems connected directly to the remote control computer, through ISDN lines, over the Internet, or even over a LAN or WAN link.

How do you know whether to choose remote node or remote control connections? Consider these points:

▼   When a remote user only needs LAN file access and e-mail access, remote node can meet these needs and is often simpler to set up and maintain on both sides of the connection.

■   If a remote user needs to run an application that is LAN-connected, choose remote control. A few applications may be able to run reasonably well over a remote node connection, provided the application itself is already installed on the remote computer and only relatively small amounts of data must be accessed by the application through the remote link. For example, accessing e-mail through Microsoft Outlook works fine over a remote node connection, provided the remote users already have Outlook installed on their local computer.

■   Many applications now are being Web-enabled, so a remote user can use a Web browser to access and use the application. These types of applications run—more or less—equally well over a remote node or remote control connection. For example, Microsoft Exchange Server supports a number of connection types, including Web access to people's mailboxes and calendars. Many client/server accounting systems now are also starting to implement Web access.

▲ If you need to maintain an application directly for the users, remote control may be the way to go because it leaves the application on the LAN-connected machine, where you can easily get to it to make configuration changes or perform other maintenance. The remote user only runs the remote control software and instantly benefits from any work you do on the LAN-connected machine. This can be a real advantage with users who aren't comfortable doing their own maintenance or troubleshooting on the software and it's easier for you to take care of any needs that arise without having to travel to some remote location or have the user ship their computer to you for repair or maintenance.

Whether you choose remote node or remote control, you then have to determine how the users will connect to the LAN. A variety of different ways exist to do this, as discussed in the following sections.

To Modem or Not to Modem, That Is the Question . . .

Remote users can connect to your network in two ways: by connecting to devices connected to the network in some fashion or by connecting to an ISP, and then coming into the network over the LAN's Internet connection. For example, users can use a modem to dial a modem connected to the LAN you maintain or they can use a modem to connect to a modem managed by an ISP, and then make use of the LAN's high-speed link to the Internet to reach the LAN.

Managing Your Own Modems

For small networks, it can often be easiest simply to add a modem or two to a computer set up to accept remote connections and let the users use those modems to connect. You can set up the modems on individual PCs that run remote control software, on PCs that run remote node software (such as Windows NT's RAS), or on special LAN-connected interfaces built for the purpose of providing remote node connections. You can also build your own "modem farms" with tens or hundreds of modems, using special hardware that supports such uses.

Taking Advantage of Someone Else's Modems

Usually, it's a real hassle to manage your own modems because not only do you have to manage the modems themselves, but also the remote node software and hardware, the telephone lines used, and all the problems that can occur at any time. If a LAN already has a high-speed link to the Internet, such as through a fractional T-1 or full T-1, it can be easier to let the remote users dial into a local ISP and then connect to the LAN through the Internet. This has many advantages:

▼ **No need to support modems directly** You don't have to worry about managing the modems. If users can't connect, they can call the ISP for connection help. Larger ISPs have round-the-clock support staff in place for this, which beats getting beeped at 2:00 A.M. because a user in Europe can't connect.

- **No long-distance tolls**   The user usually only has to make a local call to connect to the ISP, saving money on long-distance charges compared to dialing the LAN directly.

- **Minimal impact on LAN performance**   Using the LAN's Internet connection usually doesn't affect the LAN users who also use that connection for two reasons. First, many remote users connect to the LAN outside normal working hours when the Internet connection probably isn't being used much. Second, because the remote user is connected to the ISP through, usually, a slow 33.6 or 56Kbps modem connection, the total impact to your high-speed Internet link is minimal, even during working hours.

- **High-speed connections**   Your users can take advantage of whatever high-speed Internet links are available to them and you don't have to worry about having to implement matching technology on the LAN side. A user can use a xDSL line, or a cable modem, or an ISDN line, and then connect to an ISP that supports that high-speed connection. On the LAN side, the high-speed connection (for example, a T-1) remains the same.

- **Better global access**   For users travelling internationally, they will have better luck making connections to a local ISP than over an international telephone connection. Using a modem internationally is problematic at best; connection speeds are slow, the quality of the line is usually not good, and delays added by satellite connections (most international telephone traffic goes through a satellite) cause additional problems. And, of course, the cost can be prohibitive. I once spent hundreds of dollars just checking e-mail from Singapore to the U.S. several times in one week. Because Singapore telephone rates are much higher than U.S. rates, originating calls from Singapore cost $2 to $3 per minute (although even the standard U.S. rate of $0.75 per minute to Singapore would have been expensive).

When you allow remote users to access the LAN through the Internet, you usually do this using a technology called Virtual Private Network (VNP). This is a network link formed between the remote user dialed into an ISP and the company LAN, through the Internet. VPNs use sophisticated packet encryption and other technologies so the link from the user to the LAN is secure, even thought it is being carried over a public network. VPN solutions range from simple solutions that can be implemented on Windows NT Server essentially free (using the RRAS service, included with the latest versions of Windows NT Server) to stand-alone specialized VPN routers that can support hundreds of users. Figure 7-6 shows how a VPN connection works.

TIP: Windows 98 includes built-in support for client-side VPN connections. You can also get support for Windows 95 by downloading the latest version of Windows 95's Dial-Up Networking software, version 1.3. Also, many makers of stand-alone VPN routers enable you to license VPN software for the remote users. Some charge a per-license fee for the software, while others include a license for unlimited remote users as part of their VPN router.

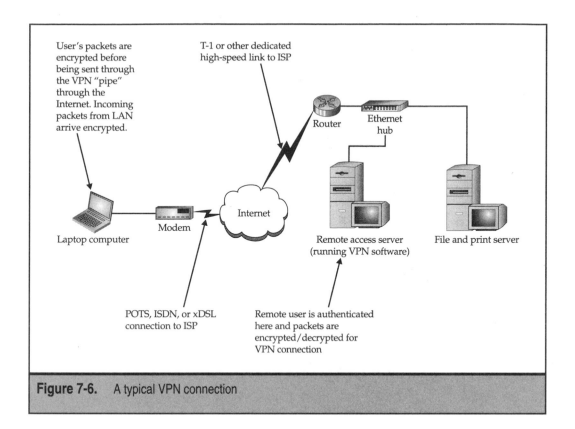

User's packets are encrypted before being sent through the VPN "pipe" through the Internet. Incoming packets from LAN arrive encrypted.

T-1 or other dedicated high-speed link to ISP

Router

Ethernet hub

Internet

Laptop computer

Modem

Remote access server (running VPN software)

File and print server

POTS, ISDN, or xDSL connection to ISP

Remote user is authenticated here and packets are encrypted/decrypted for VPN connection

Figure 7-6.   A typical VPN connection

Higher Speed Remote Links

Modem connections are fairly slow, usually only running at up to 33.6 Kbps. While many applications can be made to work reasonably well over this speed connection, the trend isthat this speed is becoming more and more inadequate, even for just transferring files (application files seem to keep growing with each new version of an application). Modems are still the lowest common denominator for remote access, however, because standards POTS (Plain Old Telephone Service) connections are available virtually everywhere and modems work reasonably well, all things considered.

In a nutshell, users who travel to different locations need to rely on modem connections. No standard high-bandwidth connection exists yet that is ubiquitous enough to find in most hotels. For remote users who are at a single location, however, higher-speed connections become feasible. Home users in many metropolitan areas can now get high-speed DSL and cable modem connections to the Internet. And using a VPN, they can benefit from these higher speeds when connecting to the corporate LAN. Even for users who don't have DSL or cable modems available in their area, ISDN is usually an option from the local telephone company.

Remote users using DSL or cable modems are "hard-wired" to a particular ISP for their connection, so they have to use a VPN approach to connecting to the LAN. ISDN users, on the other hand, have the choice of either connecting to an ISDN-capable ISP or to ISDN "modems" hosted on the LAN. Through a process called *bonding*, ISDN users can achieve speeds up to 128Kbps, although this consumes two B-channels (and doubles the call charges!). Still, it's better than the 33.6Kbps you can otherwise achieve through a modem.

NOTE: ISDN and DSL technology are discussed in more detail in Chapter 4.

CHAPTER SUMMARY

Most network administrators would agree that supporting remote access is one of the trickiest parts of managing any network. Many factors come together to make this so. You can support remote connections in a number of ways: Most remote connection speeds have lower bandwidth than remote users would like, many remote users are often important people in the company, and various problems are introduced with any connection made over a distance. Still, remote access is an important network service and its benefits to the company justify most levels of effort to make it reliable and work right.

Use the information you learned in this chapter to assess your own company's remote access needs, to learn what your users actually need, and to start searching for different possible solutions for the ones that make the most sense for your situation. You should also plan on having to support more than one type of solution. For example, most networks support both modems hosted by the company and other types of connections that come in through a VPN link.

The next chapter talks about technologies and techniques that can keep a network's information safe and from falling into the wrong hands. Network security, when done right, shouldn't require much of your time to maintain. You need to spend enough time and effort when you set up a network to ensure the network's security is strong from the beginning.

CHAPTER 8

Securing Your Network

Most things you learn about networking are relatively straightforward and can be accomplished. Do you want a new file and print server? You install it and set it up, and it either works or it doesn't. If it doesn't work, you proceed to troubleshoot it, fix any issues, and, ultimately, you complete the task. Network security, on the other hand, is a horse of a different color. You can never finish the project of securing a network and you can't ever be completely certain a network is secure. How much money you invest in securing a network, how much time you devote to the job, or how much fancy security hardware and software you install doesn't matter: No network is ever completely secure. (Amusingly, there's a corollary to this: the only secure network is the one nobody can use.)

Having said this, network security is one of the most important jobs facing any network administrator. Good network security helps prevent all the following:

▼ Company secrets, such as proprietary designs or processes, from falling into the wrong hands (both internally and externally)

■ Personal information about employees from falling into the wrong hands

■ Loss of important information and software

■ Loss of use of the network itself

▲ Inappropriate corruption or modification of important data

. . . and those are just some of the more important things. If you spend any time thinking about all the information that is stored and flows through networks with which you work (and you *should* spend time thinking about this), you'll probably come up with additional dangers to avoid.

This chapter overviews the subject of network security. Its aim is to familiarize you with important network security ideas and concepts, and also various technologies involved in network security. If you are responsible for a network's security, you should pursue more detailed information and you should also seriously consider hiring a specialist on this subject to help you secure your network. Even if you don't have primary responsibility to keep your network secure, the security of the network is everyone's job and, as an IS professional, it's an even more important part of yours.

DEFINE IT!—Important Network Security Devices

Here are some important security devices with which you should be familiar:

▼ **Firewall** A system that enforces a security policy between two networks, such as between a LAN and the Internet. Firewalls can use many different techniques to enforce security policies.

■ **Proxy server** A server that acts as a proxy, usually for users of a network. For example, it may stand in as a proxy for browsing Web pages, so that the user's computer isn't connected to the remote system, except through the proxy server. In the process of doing this, a proxy server may speed Web access by caching Web pages, and may provide some firewall protection into the LAN.

▲ **Packet filter** Usually built into a router, a packet filter enables you to set criteria for allowed and disallowed packets, source and destination IP addresses, and IP ports.

INTERNAL SECURITY

Internal security is the process of securing your network from internal threats, which are generally much more common (greater than 75 percent) than external threats. Examples of internal threats include the following:

▼ Internal users inappropriately accessing information to which they should not have access, such as payroll records, accounting records, or business development information

■ Internal users accessing other users' files to which they should not have access

■ Internal users impersonating other users and causing mischief, such as sending e-mails under another person's name

■ Internal users accessing systems to carry out criminal activities, such as embezzling funds

- ■ Internal users compromising the security of the network, such as by accidentally (or deliberately) introducing viruses to the network (viruses are discussed in their own section later in this chapter)

- ▲ Internal users "sniffing" packets on the network to discover user accounts and passwords

To deal with threats such as these, you need to manage the network's security diligently. You should assume that, in the population of internal users, at least some exist who have the requisite sophistication to explore security holes in the network and at least a few of those may, at some point, have reason to do so.

NOTE: One of the more unpleasant parts of managing security is you need to expect the worst of people and then you must take steps to prevent those things you expect. It's not a happy mindset, but it is required to do a good job in the security arena. Remember, too, you're likely to get better results if you hire an outside firm to help manage the network's security. Not only should the outside firm have a higher skill level in this area, but they will be used to thinking like security people and they will have invaluable experience gained from solving security problems at other companies.

Account Security

Account security refers to the process of managing the user accounts enabled on the network. A number of tasks are required to manage user accounts properly and the accounts should be periodically audited (preferably by a different person than the one who manages them daily) to ensure no holes exist. Following are a number of general steps you should take to manage general account security:

- ▼ Most NOSs start up with a user account called "Guest." This account should be removed immediately because it is the frequent target of crackers.

- ▲ Most NOSs start up with a default name for the administrative account. Under Windows NT, it is called Administrator; under NetWare, it is called either Supervisor or Admin (depending on which version you are using). You should immediately rename this account to avoid directed attacks against the account. (Under NetWare 3.*x*, you cannot rename the Supervisor account to something else.)

TIP: As a safety measure, also create a new account to be a backup of your administrative account. Call it whatever you like (although less obvious names are better), give the account security equivalence to the administrative account, and safely store the password. Should something happen that locks you out of the real administrative account, you can use the backup account to regain access and correct the problem.

■ You should know the steps required to remove access to network resources quickly from any account and be sure to explore *all* network resources that might contain their own security systems. For example, accounts will be managed on the NOS (and possibly on each server) and also in specific applications, like database servers or accounting systems. Make sure you find out how the system handles removed or inactivated accounts. Some don't actually deny access to resources if the account is removed until the user logs out (or is logged out in some fashion).

■ Work closely with the Human Resources department so it is comfortable working with you on handling security issues related to employee departures. The HR department may not be able to give you much—if any—advance notice, but it needs to understand you need to know about any terminations *immediately*, so you can take proper steps. Along the same lines, you want to work out a set of procedures on how you handle accumulated e-mails, files, and other user access both for friendly departures and terminations. Your relationship with the appropriate people in the HR department is crucial in being able to handle security well, so make sure mutual trust is established and maintained.

▲ Consider setting up a program whereby new users on the network have their assigned permissions reviewed and signed-off by their supervisor. This way, you won't mistakenly give someone access to things he or she shouldn't have.

Another important aspect of account security is account password security. Most NOSs enable you to set policies related to password security. These policies control how often the system forces users to change their passwords, how long their passwords must be, whether users can re-use previously used passwords, and so forth. At a minimum, consider these suggestions for password policies:

▼ You should cause users to change their main network password every 90 to 180 days (30 days is a common recommendation, but this may be too frequent in most environments).

■ You should set the reuse policy so passwords cannot be reused for at least a year.

■ You should require passwords that are *at least* six characters long. This yields, on a random basis, 36^6 possible permutations, or a bit over 2 billion possibilities. Eight characters yields 36^8, or almost 3 trillion possibilities. And if the NOS uses case-sensitive passwords, then the possibilities are much larger: 62^6 (57 billion) and 62^8 (218 trillion), respectively. By the way, even 2 billion possibilities is a lot. If someone were able to try one password a second, it would take up to 63 years to try that many permutations.

TIP: Many password-cracking programs rely on dictionaries of common words and names to reduce dramatically the number of possibilities they have to try. Because of this, encourage users to create passwords that are not words in any language or, if they are words, that they have numbers and other non-alphanumeric characters inserted somewhere in the word so a "dictionary attack" won't work. Also, for networks that support mixed-case passwords, encourage users to use mixed-case characters.

■ Make sure you turn on any policies that monitor for and deal with people entering in wrong passwords. Often called *intruder detection,* this type of policy watches incorrect password attempts. If too many attempts occur within a set period of time, the system locks the user account, preventing further attempts. I like to set this type of feature to lock an account any time five incorrect passwords are entered within an hour and then to lock the account for either a number of days, or forever (until it's reset by the administrator). This way, if someone is entering in a large number of incorrect passwords, he or she will have to talk with you to get the account re-opened, and you can find out why this situation developed and correct it.

▲ Novell NetWare and Windows NT enable you to establish limits on when and where a user can log onto the network. You can establish times of day a user is allowed to log on and you can also restrict a user account to a particular network node. Doing so for all users on the network is usually overkill, but you may want to consider restricting the administrative account to several different workstations, so someone at a different workstation (or coming in through a WAN connection) cannot log in to the account, even if that person somehow knows the password.

There's an interesting catch-22 concerning network security policies: If you make them *too* strict, you can actually *reduce* the security of your network. For example, say you set the network to force a password change once a week and to disallow the re-use of passwords. Most users will be unable to remember from week to week what password they're using and they will naturally resort to writing down their password somewhere in their office. Of course, this is much less secure than a remembered password. The trick with network security is to strike a balance between strict security and usability.

File and Directory Permissions

The second thing to keep information on your network secure is the security you set for files and directories users access. These are actually a bit tougher to manage than user accounts because you usually have at least 20 directories and several hundred files for every user you have on the network. The sheer volume of directories and files makes this a more difficult job. The solution is to establish regular procedures and follow them, and then periodically spot-audit parts of the directory tree, particularly areas that contain sensitive files. Also, structure the overall network directories so you can, for the most part, simply assign permissions at the top levels. These permissions will "flow down" to subdirectories automatically and this makes it much easier to review who has access to which directories.

NOSs allow considerable flexibility to the permissions they let you set on files and directories. Using the built-in permissions, you can enable users for different roles in any given directory. These *roles* control what the user can and cannot do within that directory. Examples of generic directory roles include

▼ **Create only** This type of role enables users to add a new file to a directory, but they cannot see, edit, or delete existing files, including any they've created. This type of role is perfect to enable a person to add new information to a directory to which they shouldn't otherwise have access. The directory almost becomes like a mailbox on a street corner: you can only put new things in it. Of course, another user will have full access to the directory to retrieve and work with the files.

■ **Read only** This role enables users to see the files in a directory and they can even pull up the files for viewing on their computer. However, they cannot edit or change the stored files in any way. This type of role is good for material published to users who need to view the information, but that should not be changed by them. By the way, you should know users with read privileges can copy a file from a read-only directory to another directory and they can then do whatever they like with the copy they made. They simply cannot change the copy stored in the read-only directory itself.

■ **Change** This role lets users do whatever they like with the files in a directory, *except* they cannot give other users access to the directory.

▲ **Full control** Usually reserved for the "owner" of a directory, this role enables the person(s) to do whatever they like with the files in a directory and, further, they have the ability to grant other users access to the directory.

These roles are created in different ways on different NOSs. More detail on how Windows 2000/NT and NetWare handle directory permissions is discussed in Chapters 14 and 17.

Just as you can set permissions for directories, you can also set security for specific files. File permissions work similarly to directory permissions. For specific files, you can control a user's ability to read, change, or delete a file. File permissions usually override directory permissions. For example, if users had change access to a directory, but you set their permission to access a particular file in that directory to read-only, they would only have read-only access to that file.

Practices and User Education

The third important area in achieving good internal security concerns the most insecure part of any network: the people. You should be concerned about two things here. First, you need to establish good security practices and habits. It's not enough to come up with a great security design and implementation if it's not well managed on a daily basis. Coming up with good practices means you need to document what the security-related procedures are and then set up some sort of process to make sure they're followed regularly. In fact, you're far better off having a rudimentary security design that is followed to the letter, than having an excellent security design that is poorly followed. For this reason, keep the overall network security design as simple as possible consistent with the needs of the company.

You also need to make sure—to the maximum extent possible—the users are following prudent procedures. Some of these you can easily enforce through settings on the NOS, but others must be handled through education. Some tips to make this easier are:

▼ Spell out for users what is expected of them in terms of security. Provide a document for them that describes the security of the network and what they need to do to preserve it. Examples of things the users do include choosing secure passwords, not giving their passwords to anyone else, not leaving their computers unattended for long periods of time while they are logged in to the network, not installing software from outside the company, and so forth.

■ When new employees join the company and are oriented on using the network, make sure you discuss security issues with them.

■ Depending on the culture of the company, consider having users sign a form acknowledging their understanding of important security procedures the company expects them to follow.

■ Periodically audit users' security actions. If they have full control access to directories, examine how they've assigned permissions to other users.

▲ Make sure you review the security logs of the NOS you use. Investigate and follow up on any problems reported.

TIP: It's a good idea to document any security-related issues you investigate. While most are benign, occasionally you may find one in which someone had inappropriate intent. In such cases, your documentation of what you find and what actions you take may become important.

While it's important to plan for the worst when designing and administering network security, you also need to realize that most of the time security issues that arise are based on ignorance or other innocent causes and not on malicious intent.

EXTERNAL SECURITY

External security is the process of securing the network from external threats. Before the Internet, this wasn't difficult. Most networks only had external modems for users to dial in to the network and it was easy to keep those access points secure. With the advent of the Internet and given that nearly all networks are connected to the Internet, however, external security becomes much more important.

Earlier in this chapter, you read that no network is ever totally secure. This is especially true when dealing with external security for a network connected to the Internet. Almost daily, new techniques are discovered by hackers that they can use to breach the security of a network through an Internet connection. Even if you were to find a book that discusses all the threats to a specific type of network, the book would be out-of-date soon after it was printed.

Three basic types of external security threats exist:

▼   **Front-door threats**   This is where someone, from outside the company, somehow finds, guesses, or cracks a user password and then logs on to the network. The person doing this may be someone who, at some point, had an association with the company or this could be someone totally unrelated to the company.

■   **Back-door threats**   These are threats where software or hardware bugs in the network's OS and hardware enable an outsider to crack the network's security. Once accomplished, the outsider often finds a way to log in to the administrative account, and then can do anything he or she likes.

▲   **Denial of service**   These are attacks that deny service to the network. Examples include specific actions that are known to crash different types of servers or flooding the company's Internet connection with useless traffic (such as a flood of PING requests).

NOTE: A fourth type of external threat exists: computer viruses, Trojan horses, worms, and other malicious software from outside the company. These threats are covered in their own section later in the chapter.

Fortunately, you can do a number of things to implement strong external security measures. They probably won't keep out a determined and extremely skilled hacker, but they can make it difficult enough so even the best hacker will probably give up and go elsewhere.

Front-Door Threats

Front-door threats, where someone from outside the company is able to gain access to a user account, is probably the most likely threat you need to protect against. These threats can take many forms. Chief among them is the disgruntled or terminated employee, who once had access to the network. Another example is someone guessing or finding out a password to a valid account on the network, or somehow getting a valid password from the owner of the password.

Insiders, whether current or ex-employees, are potentially the most dangerous overall. People like this have many advantages some random hacker won't have. They know the important user names on the network already, so they know what accounts to go after. They may know other users' passwords from when they were associated with the company. They also know the structure of the network, what the server names are, and other information that makes cracking the network's security much easier.

Protecting against a front-door threat revolves around strong internal security protection because, in this case, internal and external security are closely linked. This is the type of threat where all the policies and practices discussed in the section on internal security can help to prevent problems. You can also take additional steps to stymie front-door threats:

▼   Keep network resources that should be accessed from the LAN separate from resources that should be accessed from outside the LAN, whenever possible. Here's an example: Maybe you're lucky enough that you never need to provide access to the company's accounting server to external users. You can then make it nearly impossible to access that system from outside the LAN, through a number of measures. You can set up the firewall router to decline any access through the router to that server's IP or IPX address. If the server doesn't require IP, you can remove that protocol. You can set up the server to disallow access outside normal working hours. Depending on the NOS running on the server, you can restrict access to Ethernet MAC addresses for machines on the LAN that should be able to access the server. You can also set the server only to allow each user one login to the server at a time. The specific steps you can take depend on the server in question and the NOS it is running, but the principle holds true: segregate internal resources from external resources whenever possible.

■   Control which users can access the LAN from outside the LAN. For example, you may be running VPN software for your travelling or home-based users to access the LAN remotely through the Internet. You should only enable this access for users who need it and not for everyone who is likely to need it.

■   For remote users, consider setting up a separate remote access account for them to use, which is more restrictive than their normal LAN account. This may not be practicable in all cases, but it's a strategy that can help, particularly for users who normally have broad LAN security clearances.

■   For modems that users dial into from a fixed location, such as from their homes, set up their accounts to use dial-back. *Dial-back* is a feature whereby you securely enter the phone number of the system from which users are calling (like their home phone numbers). When they want to connect, they dial the system, request access, and then the remote access system terminates the connection and dials the pre-programmed phone number to make the real connection. Their computer answers the call and then proceeds to connect them normally. Someone trying to access the system from another phone number won't be able to get in if you have dial-back enabled.

▲   If an employee with broad access leaves the company, review user accounts where he or she may have known the password. Consider forcing an immediate password change to such accounts once the employee is gone.

NOTE: An important aspect of both internal and external security is physical security. Make sure the room in which your servers are located is physically locked and secure.

People trying to access the network, who have not been associated with the company at some point, often try a technique euphemistically called *social engineering,* which is where they use nontechnological methods to learn user accounts and passwords inside the company. These techniques are most dangerous in larger companies, where everyone in the company doesn't know each other. An example of a social engineering technique is calling an employee and posing as a network administrator who is trying to track down a problem and who needs their password temporarily. Another example would be sorting through a company's trash looking for records that may help them crack a password. Make sure your employees are carefully instructed to never give out their password to anyone over the telephone and also that bona-fide IS people usually never need to ask anyone's password.

Back-Door Threats

Back-door threats are often directed at problems in the NOS itself or, at some other point in the network infrastructure, like its routers. Make no mistake about it, all NOSs and most network components have security holes. The best thing you can do to prevent these problems is to stay current with your NOS software and any security-related patches that are released. You should also periodically review new information about security holes discovered in the NOS software you use (and don't rely on the vendor's Web site for the best information on this!). A good Web site to use to stay current on security holes is the one maintained by the Computer Emergency Response Team (CERT) located at http://www.cert.org. Aside from advisories on security holes, you can also find much valuable security information on their site.

Web servers are a frequent target for hackers. Consider the following tips to help protect against threats to Web servers:

▼   You're better off if you can host the company's Web site on an external server (such as an ISP's system) than on your own network. Not only is an ISP better able to provide 24 × 7 service to the server, it also has better security. Also, you needn't worry about allowing Web server access to your LAN from outside the company, which can sometimes leave open other holes.

■   Make sure you implement a strong firewall router for your network. Firewall routers are discussed in more detail in Chapter 3. You should also have someone knowledgeable of the specific firewall and Web server you implement test your configuration or help with the configuration. Remember, firewalls also need to have their software kept current.

■ Make absolutely certain that you've carefully reviewed the security settings appropriate for your Web server and have implemented all of them, and that you audit this occasionally.

▲ Consider placing a Web server designed for people outside the company outside of your firewall. (In other words, between the firewall and the router that connects you to the Internet.) This way, even if someone is able to break into the Web server, they won't have an easier time of getting to the rest of your network.

Denial of Service Threats

Denial of Service (DoS) attacks are those that deny service to a network resource to legitimate users. These are often targeted at e-mail servers and Web servers, but they can affect an entire network. DoS attacks usually take one of two forms: they either deny service by flooding the network with useless traffic or they take advantage of bugs in network software that can be used to crash servers. DoS attacks against e-mail servers usually flood an e-mail server with mail, until the e-mail server either denies service to legitimate users or crashes under the load placed on it.

Flooding an E-Mail System

I once witnessed an innocent problem that resulted in a denial of service to a multinational company's entire e-mail system. The situation that caused this went like this: A user at Company A had set the e-mail system to always send mail with a return receipt requested. When this user went out of town, he created a rule in his e-mail Inbox that replied to all messages with a message saying he was out of the office. While he was gone, a user at Company B sent him a message, to which the automatic reply was issued. However, because the user at Company A had his default set to always request delivery receipts (which are often generated by the receiving server for Internet e-mail, and not by the user reading the message), the mail server at Company B dutifully sent back a receipt that the message had been received. Of course, the user at Company A's Inbox rule then replied automatically to the receipt message, which generated another return receipt, and so forth. Before anybody noticed what was going on, some 50,000 messages had flooded Company B's e-mail system, which crashed under the load. Because they had a somewhat fragile configuration, it affected about 30,000 employees around the world, who went without e-mail for a couple of hours because of this.

This was an innocent mistake by the user at Company A. If he had instead used the e-mail system's "Out of Office" feature, only one automatic message would have been sent to any given sender and the problem would not have occurred. Though the problem was caused by user error in this case, this sort of sequence can easily be exploited by someone who actually wants to cause trouble.

To help prevent DoS attacks, again make sure your various network software is kept current. Also, use settings on your firewall to disallow ICMP traffic service (which handles PING requests) into the network and deny access servers from outside the LAN that needn't be accessed from outside the LAN. For example, probably the company's accounting system server doesn't need to be accessed from outside the LAN. In such a case, you would configure the firewall or packet-filtering router to deny all outside traffic to or from that server's IP address.

VIRUSES AND OTHER MALICIOUS SOFTWARE

Unfortunately, an increasing array of malicious software is circulating around the world. Many different types of this software exist, including the following:

▼ **Viruses**   A computer *virus* is a program that spreads by infecting other files with a copy of itself. Files that can be infected by viruses include program files (.COM, .EXE, and .DLL) and document files for applications that support macro languages sophisticated enough to allow virus behavior (Microsoft Word and Excel are common targets of macro-based viruses).

■ **Worms**   A *worm* is a program that propagates by sending copies of itself to other computers that run the worm and then send copies to other computers. Recently, worms have spread through e-mail systems like wildfire. One way this happens is when an attachment is e-mailed to users, along with a message that entices them to open the attachment. The attachment contains the worm, which then sends out copies of itself to other people defined in the user's e-mail address book, without the user knowing this is happening. Those recipients then have the same thing happen to them. A worm like this can rapidly spread through the Internet in a matter of hours.

■ **Trojan horses**   A *Trojan horse* is a program that purports to do something interesting or useful and then performs malicious actions in the background, while the user is interacting with the main program.

▲ **Logic bombs**   *Logic bombs* are malicious pieces of programming code inserted into an otherwise normal program. They are often included by the program's original author or by someone else who participated in the source code. Logic bombs can be timed to execute at a certain time, erasing key files or performing other actions.

Over 20,000 known viruses are in existence today, with more being written and discovered daily. These viruses are a major threat to any network and an important aspect of your network administration is protecting against them.

To protect a network from virus attacks, you need to implement some sort of antivirus software. Antivirus software runs on computers on the network and "watches" for known viruses or virus-like activity. The antivirus software then either removes the virus, leaving the original file intact, quarantines the file so it can be checked by an administrator, or locks access to the file in some other fashion.

Antivirus software can be run on most network computers, such as file and print servers, e-mail servers, desktop computers, and even computerized firewalls. Antivirus software is available from a number of different vendors, with two of the most notable being Symantec (Norton Anti-Virus) and Network Associates (McAfee VirusScan). Your best bet is to make sure you run antivirus software on all your servers and set up the software so it is frequently updated (every few days). (Most server-based antivirus software can be set up to securely update its list of known viruses over an Internet connection automatically.) Also, because e-mail is the chief mechanism of transmission for computer viruses these days, make especially sure that you run antivirus software on your e-mail server.

You may also want to run antivirus software on your workstations, but you shouldn't rely on this as your primary means of prevention. Users can and will disable such software on occasion, and workstation-based antivirus software can cause other support problems, such as interacting with other desktop software (or the desktop OS) in ways that cause problems. Instead of relying on such software as your primary protection, consider desktop antivirus software as a supplement to your server-based software.

CHAPTER SUMMARY

Even in an entire book devoted to the subject of network security, you can't learn all you need to know to make a network as secure as possible. New threats are discovered constantly and the changing software landscape makes such information quickly obsolete. Instead, in this chapter you learned about common security threats and read advice that can help you formulate and implement good security practices. You should especially consider retaining an outside security consultant to help you set up your security plans and to review and audit them on a regular basis.

Finally, if you're responsible for network security, you should know it's a job that never sleeps and you can never know enough about it. You need to spend time learning more of the ins and outs of network security, particularly for the NOSs you use on your network. The following books can help further your network security education:

▼ *Hacking Exposed: Network Security Secrets and Solutions,* by Joel Scambray and Stuart McClure (ISBN: 0-07-212127-0, Osborne/McGraw-Hill, 1999)

■ *Windows NT Security Handbook,* by Tom Sheldon (ISBN: 0-07-882240-8, Osborne/McGraw-Hill, 1998)

▲ *Windows 2000 Security,* by Tom Sheldon and Phil Cox (ISBN: 0-07-212433-4, Osborne/McGraw-Hill, forthcoming, spring 2000)

CHAPTER 9

Network Servers: Everything You Wanted to Know, But Were Afraid to Ask

Lots of different *types* of servers exist—file and print servers, application servers, Web servers, communications servers, and more. What all servers have in common, though, is they are relied upon by multiple people and they are usually integral to some sort of network service. Because servers may be used by tens or hundreds (or thousands!) of people, the computers you use for servers need to be a cut—or two—above just any old workstation. Servers need to be much more reliable and serviceable than workstations. Plus, they need to perform in different ways from workstations.

In this chapter you learn about network server hardware. You learn what distinguishes a server from a workstation, about different server hardware configurations, and about preparing a server for use in your network.

WHAT DISTINGUISHES A SERVER FROM A WORKSTATION

With high-performance desktop computers selling for $2-3K, it can be hard to see how a computer with the same processor can cost in excess of $10K, just because it is designed as a "server." Server computers truly are different from workstations, however, and they incorporate a number of important features not found in workstations. These features are important to a server's job, which is serving up data or services to large numbers of users.

Server Processors

Much of the performance of a server derives from its *central processing unit*, or CPU. While servers are also sensitive to the performance of other components (more so than a workstation), the processor is still important in determining how fast the server will be.

Servers can run using one processor or using many. How many processors you choose for a server depends on many factors. The first is the network operating system (NOS) you use. If you plan to use Novell NetWare 3.x or 4.x, you only need one processor because that's as many as those versions of NetWare support. NetWare 5.x now supports multiple processors (up to 32) and is said to make good use of them.

If you plan to use Windows NT Server, you may choose up to eight processors, although you may need a custom version of Windows NT available from the maker of the system because most multiprocessor systems have certain custom features that must be supported by the operating system. If you plan to use UNIX, then it depends: some versions of UNIX support multiple processors, while others do not. Another factor to consider is the job the server does and whether it is presently bottlenecked at the processor. File and print servers tend not to need multiple processors. While they benefit from fast processors, it's not by as much as you may think. It's far more important for a file and a print server to have lots of RAM and a fast disk subsystem. Database servers, on the other hand, are processor-hungry and definitely benefit from as many processors as possible, running at the fastest possible speed. (Of course, it's also important for the database server software to be built in such a way that it can make use of multiple processors.) Web servers tend to be modest in their processor requirements—they rely on fast busses, fast network connections, lots of RAM, fast disks, and that's about it. A fast processor (or multiple processors) is nice on a Web server, but it may be overkill.

Managing more than one processor requires a lot of overhead work on the part of the system. Because of this, having two processors in a computer doesn't result in doubling the server's processing capability; instead, it's more like 50 percent faster. The same rule of thumb holds true if you use four processors instead of two processors: the system with four processors will be about 50 percent faster than the system with two processors, not 100 percent faster. Depending on the operating system being used, there is also a point of diminishing returns, past which additional processors won't give you much additional performance. Part of this has to do with how the operating system handles multiple processors. Another part has to do with the number of threads doing work in the operating system (threads cannot be shared between processors, so if only two main threads are doing all the work, three processors won't improve your performance).

DEFINE IT!—What's a Thread?

Operating systems that multitask often do so using a mechanism called a thread. In fact, all modern operating systems today use threads, including Windows 9x, Windows NT, OS/2, NetWare, and many versions of UNIX. In operating systems that make use of threads, each running program runs as a *process*, which has its own memory resources and is kept separate in the computer from other processes. However, the process is divided up into different units of work, called threads. These *threads* have access to all the resources of the process in which they run and they are the actual "agent of work" within the process. For example, a word processor like Microsoft Word may have a main thread that accepts typed input from the user and displays it on the screen, another that handles any printing chores, and others that constantly check spelling and grammar in the background as the user works.

To determine the number of processors you should use for any given task, you should consult with the maker of both the network operating system you plan to use and the primary applications you plan to run on the server. You may also want to discuss this with other users who are performing similar work. For instance, for a database server for an accounting system that supports hundreds of users, you should talk to other sites that use the same software and have roughly the same number of users to learn about their experiences and suggestions.

Intel Pentium Family

Intel's Pentium family has a variety of different processors, ranging from the basic Pentium, all the way up to the Pentium III Xeon processor. Current server-class computers are shipping with Pentium II Xeon, Pentium III, or Pentium III Xeon processors. The Xeon series of processors are optimized for server-type duties and are more amenable to running in a multiprocessor system.

Pentium II Xeon and III Xeon processors are available in speeds ranging from 400 MHz up to, presently, 550 MHz. Intel plans to increase the speed of the Pentium III Xeon up to 700 MHz, and possibly slightly beyond. The design of the Xeon processor allows for up to four processors in a Pentium II Xeon system and eight processors in a Pentium III Xeon system. For certain applications, this many processors can be an advantage. The Xeon processor family is packaged in a Single Edge Contact Cartridge, which is much larger than the packaging used for the Pentium II and III non-Xeon processors. The Xeon processors also generate quite a bit more heat than their non-Xeon brethren, mostly due to the much larger cache memory and other features that boost Xeon processor performance in a server. (It's a good thing most servers can monitor their in-case heat levels!)

Few differences exist between the Pentium II and III families, aside from these two: First, Pentium III processors operate at a higher clock speed. Second, Pentium III processors have support for a feature called Streaming Extensions (SIMD) which can provide additional performance in certain circumstances, provided the operating system supports these extensions (SIMD mostly enhances multimedia performance).

Intel Clones

Two companies make processors that are essentially clones of Intel's processors. Advanced Micro Devices (AMD) makes the K6 series of processors, which perform on par with Intel Pentium II and III processors. A company called Cyrix also makes a line of Intel-compatible processors, called the 6086MX and M II series.

The problem with Intel clone chips is, despite their manufacturers' protestations to the contrary, they won't ever be 100 percent compatible with Intel's processors. Because software vendors *usually* only certify their software against Intel processors, they are certain to be slow to respond to any problems that crop up with the clones. Because of this issue, clone chips are not typically used in server-class machines, where reliability and serviceability are of paramount importance.

DEC Alpha

The DEC Alpha is a fast RISC processor that can run Windows NT and DEC UNIX. Unfortunately, its future is uncertain. Intel now owns DEC's Alpha processor and Compaq now owns DEC's server division. While Alpha-based machines are still available, their use is dwindling. Except for some special application or when you already have a large investment in Alpha-based servers, the purchase of new Alpha-based servers should probably be avoided.

HP PA-RISC

Hewlett-Packard's Precision Architecture-Reduced Instruction Set Computing (PA-RISC) processor is extremely fast and runs HP's HP-UX (UNIX) operating system. The PA-RISC architecture can be scaled to use many processors (hundreds!) in a symmetric multiprocessing (SMP) arrangement. For extremely high-end computing needs, the PA-RISC architecture can make a lot of sense and HP's equipment tends to be among the most reliable available.

PowerPC

Originally, Motorola, IBM, and Apple teamed up to design and use the PowerPC processor, a RISC-based processor that is actually manufactured by Motorola. Today, the PowerPC is used in Apple Macintosh computers, and some UNIX-based servers from IBM and Motorola. If you're running a Macintosh-based network, you are almost certainly using the PowerPC processor in both your desktop computers and any Apple- or IBM-built servers.

Bus Capabilities

For most servers, the name of the game is moving data around and it's usually *lots* of data. File and print servers may need to serve up hundreds of files simultaneously to hundreds of users, and to coordinate and handle the data needs of all those users. Database servers may manage databases that are many gigabytes or terabytes large, and they must be able to retrieve large chunks of data from their databases and provide it to users within milliseconds. Application servers may perform both processor-intensive and disk-intensive operations while providing application services to end users.

Just as networks often have fast backbone segments connecting many slower segments together, a computer relies on its bus to do the same sort of work. A bus is the data transfer "backbone" of a computer system, to which the processor, memory, and all installed devices connect. At any given time, a server may be moving megabytes of data from its disks to the network cards, to the processor, to the system's memory, and back to the disks as it performs its task. All these components are connected together by the system's bus, so optimizing that portion of the computer as much as possible makes sense. The bus, in fact, may handle about five times more data than any single component in the system and it needs to do so quickly. While it's true a modern PCI bus can handle 33 MHz at 32 bits, this just isn't enough in a high-end server. Many servers must handle multiple NICs (each running at speeds up to 100Mbps) and multiple disk controllers running at speeds up to 40Mbps. If those devices are busy at the same time, even a PCI bus will quickly get saturated.

Because of this, there are many ways for server manufacturers to get around bus speed limitations. One way is by using multiple busses in a single system. For example, Micron's NetFrame servers use three PCI busses that can all run at full speed simultaneously. Just by using a little planning in placing certain peripherals on the different busses, the system's overall speed can be greatly increased through this mechanism.

A consortium of hardware vendors is also working on enhancements to PCI. This consortium, which includes Compaq, HP, IBM, Dell, and many others, is working on an improvement to PCI called PCI-X. PCI-X offers a 133 MHz bus at 64 bits, or up to 1066MBps throughput (yes, that's mega*bytes* per second). PCI-X systems should start appearing in the second half of 1999.

NOTE: PCI-X is being designed to be backward compatible with standard PCI, but using a slower PCI card on the PCI-X bus will "throttle down" the bus to run at the slower speed. Instead, such systems are expected to support both a standard PCI bus for PCI cards and the PCI-X bus for PCI-X cards.

Other bus enhancements are also in the works. Some vendors are working on an initiative called Future I/O, which promises speeds of 1GBps and the capability to use more than one channel (called a *link*) to go even higher. Intel is also working on a competing specification called Next Generation I/O (NGIO) with speeds of around 2.5GBps.

RAM

Another important part of any server is its installed memory. Servers rely heavily on caching data from the network and from the server's disks to achieve the best possible performance and they rely heavily on their random access memory (RAM) to do this. For example, most network operating systems cache the entire directory of files they store for quick access. They also keep requested files in cache for an extended period of time, in case the data from the file is needed again. They also buffer writes to the system's disk through write-caches in RAM and perform the actual disk writes asynchronously, so the disks are not as much of a bottleneck as they otherwise would be. For most servers, 256MB of RAM should be considered a practical minimum. For heavy-duty database servers supporting hundreds of users, you might install more than 1GB of RAM to achieve the best possible performance.

TIP: How much RAM do you really need for your server? This is hard to say because a lot depends on how the server is used. The good news is both Windows NT Server and Novell NetWare provide statistics showing how the memory in the system is used. You can use this information to help determine when more memory would be beneficial. For Windows NT, use Performance Monitor to see how memory and the system swap file are being used. For Novell NetWare, use the cache statistics in the console's MONITOR program

RAM comes in three varieties: non-parity, parity, and Error Checking and Correcting (ECC). Parity RAM uses an extra bit for every byte to store a checksum of the byte's contents. If the checksum doesn't match when the memory is read, the system stops and reports a memory error. Non-parity memory eliminates the parity bit and, of course, can't detect any memory errors because of it. Inexpensive workstations sometimes use non-parity RAM, although you should avoid its use whenever possible, even on workstations.

There are two problems with parity-based memory. First, the system can only detect memory errors; it can't correct them. Second, because only one bit is used to store the parity, it is possible to "fool" the parity mechanism with a more severe error. For instance, if two bits simultaneously changed polarities, the parity system wouldn't detect the problem. ECC memory is designed to address these problems. Systems using ECC memory can detect up to two bits of errors and can automatically correct one bit of error. Most servers these days use ECC memory because of the added protection it offers.

Disk Subsystems

The third crucial performance subsystem for a server is its disk drives. Hard disk drives are usually the slowest component of any system, yet because most of the server's work involves the hard disks, this is the area most likely to bottleneck the system. Also, the data stored on a server is usually critically important to the company, so it's also important to have the most reliable disk configuration you can afford.

Disk Interfaces: SCSI vs. EIDE

Two types of disk interfaces are in widespread use today: Enhanced Integrated Drive Electronics (EIDE) and Small Computer Systems Interface (SCSI). For a workstation using Windows 9x, EIDE performs on par with a SCSI-based disk system. For a server running Windows NT or Novell NetWare, however, SCSI offers clear performance advantages.

NOTE: SCSI is pronounced "scuzzy." For a while, Macintosh users tried to adopt the pronunciation "sexy," but it never took hold. (SCSI first saw widespread use on the Macintosh, at least in the personal computing world.)

Many varieties of SCSI-based disk systems are available, as follows:

▼   **SCSI-1**   The basic SCSI specification can transfer data to and from the disks at approximately 5MBps using an 8-bit transfer width. Advances in SCSI technology have made SCSI-1 obsolete and it is not used on current systems. (This is good because most SCSI-1 implementations weren't compatible with one another.)

■   **SCSI-2**   This is the basic SCSI interface in use today. It extends the SCSI specification and adds many features to SCSI, and it also allows for much faster SCSI connections. In addition, SCSI-2 greatly improved the SCSI compatibility between different SCSI device manufacturers.

■   **Fast-SCSI**   With Fast-SCSI, the basic SCSI-2 specification increases the SCSI bus speed from 5 MHz to 10 MHz and the throughput from 5MBps to 10MBps. Fast-SCSI is also called *Fast Narrow-SCSI*.

■   **Wide-SCSI**   Also based on SCSI-2, Wide-SCSI increases the SCSI-2 data path from 8 bits to either 16 or 32 bits. Using 16 bits, Wide-SCSI can handle up to 20MBps.

■   **Ultra-SCSI**   Also called SCSI-3, this specification increases the SCSI bus speed even higher—to 20 MHz. Using a narrow, 8-bit bus, Ultra-SCSI can handle 20MBps. It can also run with a 16-bit bus, increasing the speed further to 40MBps.

■   **Ultra2 SCSI**   Yet another furthering of the SCSI standard, Ultra2 SCSI doubles (yet again) the performance of Ultra-SCSI. Ultra2 SCSI subsystems can scale up to 80MBps using a 16-bit bus.

▲ **Ultra3 SCSI**   By now you should know the story: another doubling of the performance available from Ultra2 SCSI. Ultra3 SCSI is not yet available, but devices using this standard should appear sometime in the year 2000. Speeds of up to 160MBps are possible.

NOTE: A new storage connection technology should start emerging over the next few years. Fibre Channel, which can use either fiber-optic or copper cable, is a much more flexible connection scheme than SCSI, and promises throughput many times faster than even Ultra3 SCSI. Based loosely on a network paradigm, Fibre Channel will initially be expensive to implement, but large data centers will benefit greatly from its advances over SCSI.

As you can see from the preceding list, there is a dizzying array of SCSI choices on the market today. Because of all the different standards, it's a good idea to make sure you purchase matched components when building a SCSI disk subsystem or when purchasing one as part of a server. Make sure the controller card you plan to use is compatible with the drives you will use, uses the appropriate cables, and is compatible with both the server computer and the network operating system you will use. The good news is, once you get a SCSI disk subsystem up and running, it runs reliably and with excellent performance.

Disk Topologies: It's a RAID!

The acronym *RAID* stands for Redundant Array of Inexpensive Disks. RAID is a technique of using many disks to do the work of one disk and it offers many advantages compared to using fewer, larger disks.

The basic idea behind RAID is to spread a server's data across many disks, seamlessly. For example, a single file may have portions of itself spread across four or five disks. The RAID system manages all those parts so you never know they're actually spread across all the disks. You open that file, the RAID system accesses all the appropriate disks and "reassembles" the file, and provides the entire thing to you.

The immediate benefit you get is the multiple disks perform much more quickly than a single disk would perform. This is because all the disks can independently work on finding their own data and sending it to the controller to be assembled. A single disk drive would be limited by a single disk head and would take much longer to gather the same amount of data. Amazingly, the performance of a RAID system *increases* as you add more disks, because of the benefit of having all those disk heads independently working toward retrieving the needed data.

If you think about a simple RAID array with data spread across many disks, you'll probably notice that, while it improves performance, it also increases the chance of having disk failure. Using five disks to do the work of one means five times more chances exist for a disk failure. Because the data is spread among all the disks, if one fails, you might as well throw away all the data on all the remaining disks because it's useless if a big chunk is missing. Fortunately, different RAID schemes address this problem, as you see in the following discussion.

There are many different ways to use multiple disks together in some sort of RAID scheme and, accordingly, a number of *RAID levels* are defined, each of which describes a different technique, as follows:

▼ **RAID 0** This scheme is a configuration whereby data is spread (*striped*) across multiple disks, although *with no redundancy*. Losing one drive in a RAID 0 array results in the data on all the disks being lost. RAID 0 is only appropriate for improving performance and should only be used with nonessential data. RAID 0 arrays can stripe data across two or more disks, as shown in Figure 9-1.

■ **RAID 1** This type of array doesn't stripe data across multiple disks. Instead, it defines a standard whereby data is mirrored between disks. Two disks are used instead of one and the data is kept synchronized between the two disks. If one of the disks fails, the remaining disk continues working just fine, until the failed drive can be replaced. RAID 1 is often simply referred to as *mirroring*. An enhancement to RAID 1 is called *duplexing*; the data is still duplicated between two disks, but each disk has its own disk controller, adding another level of redundancy (because you can lose either a disk, or a controller, and still keep operating). Duplexing can also improve performance somewhat, compared to straight mirroring. Some RAID 1 implementations are also intelligent enough to read data from either disk in such a way that whichever disk has its drive head closest to the data performs the read request, while the other one sits idle. However, all writes must occur simultaneously for both disks. Figure 9-2 shows a typical RAID 1 array layout.

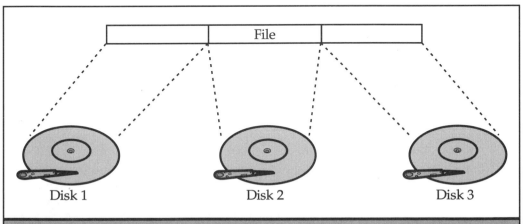

Figure 9-1.   A RAID 0 array stripes data across multiple disks

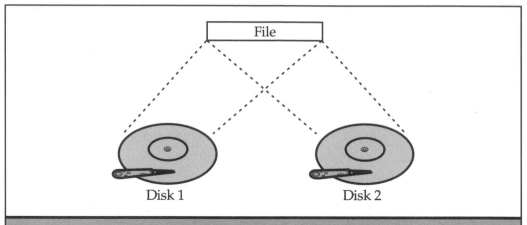

Figure 9-2.   A RAID 1 array mirrors data between two disks

TIP: RAID levels 0 and 1 can be combined to offer the performance benefit of RAID 0, with the high level of redundancy of RAID 1. Imagine a RAID 0 array with five disks, with the data striped across all five disks. With another five disks, you can have two RAID 0 arrays, mirrored to each other using RAID 1. This technique is often known as RAID 10 ("10" meaning a combination of RAID 1 and 0).

■ **RAID 2**   You won't see RAID 2 implemented in the real world. RAID 2 is a technical specification that stripes data across multiple disks and then uses a Hamming Code ECC that is written to a set of ECC disks. The ratio of data disks to ECC disks is quite high with RAID 2, 4 data: 3 ECC. RAID 2 isn't used because of its inefficiencies.

■ **RAID 3**   This is where RAID starts to get interesting; RAID 3 implementations used to be fairly common, although these days you see RAID 5 used much more often than RAID 3. RAID 3 stripes data across multiple data disks and then uses an exclusive OR (XOR) bit-wise operation against all the stored data on each data disk to come up with ECC data, which is written to a single ECC drive. So, for example, you can have four data drives and one ECC drive to back them up. Figure 9-3 shows a RAID 3 array. The XOR data has an interesting mathematical property. If you remove one of the data drives, you can take the remaining data, plus the data on the ECC drive, and reconstruct what is missing from the failed drive. RAID disk controllers do this automatically if a drive fails, although the drives operate at a much slower rate than normal because of the overhead of having to reconstruct the data on the fly. More useful is to replace the failed drive and to use the ECC data to rebuild the lost data.

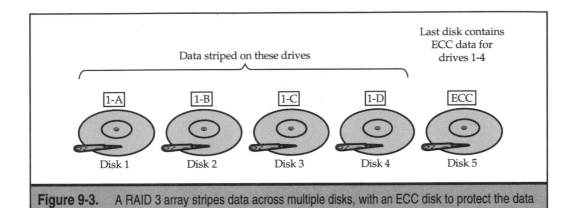

Data striped on these drives

Last disk contains ECC data for drives 1-4

1-A   1-B   1-C   1-D   ECC

Disk 1   Disk 2   Disk 3   Disk 4   Disk 5

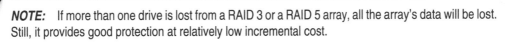

Figure 9-3.   A RAID 3 array stripes data across multiple disks, with an ECC disk to protect the data

NOTE: If more than one drive is lost from a RAID 3 or a RAID 5 array, all the array's data will be lost. Still, it provides good protection at relatively low incremental cost.

■ **RAID 4**   This is another of the RAID standards that isn't used in the real world. RAID 4 is similar to RAID 3, except data is not striped between the different data drives. Instead, each block of data is written whole to a single data drive, with the next block being written to the next data drive, and so forth. RAID 4 still uses a single ECC disk for all the data drives but, otherwise, it is too inefficient to be of much benefit, particularly when compared to RAID 3.

▲ **RAID 5**   RAID 5, depicted in Figure 9-4, is the current standard for RAID systems (except for RAID 1, which has different applications). Recall how RAID 3 worked, with data striped to a set of data disks, and the ECC code written to a single ECC disk. RAID 5 improves on this scheme by interleaving the data and ECC information across all the disks. The big benefit to this approach over RAID 3 is you aren't relying on a single ECC drive for all write operations, which became a bottleneck on RAID 3 systems. Because all the drives share the ECC work, performance with RAID 5 is slightly better than with RAID 3. There is a small drawback to this, though, that most commentators miss. In RAID 3, if you lost a data drive, the system slowed down (usually dramatically) as the data was reconstructed on the fly. If you lost the ECC drive, however, the system would still run just as fast as if no drive were lost. With RAID 5, if you lose a drive, you're always losing part of your ECC drive (because its job is spread among all the disks) and you get a slowdown no matter what.

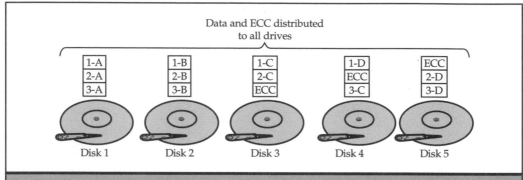

Data and ECC distributed
to all drives

| Disk 1 | Disk 2 | Disk 3 | Disk 4 | Disk 5 |

Figure 9-4.   A RAID 5 array stripes data across multiple disks, and alternately uses all disks for
ECC data

TIP: Server manufacturers make a big to-do about how the design of a RAID 5 system will allow a
system to continue running if a drive fails. While this is technically true, however, the performance of
the server in that condition is poorer than otherwise—possibly so poor no one would want to use it.
What RAID 5 excels at, however, is rebuilding the missing data once the failed drive is replaced. While
this process may take several hours to complete, it gives you added peace of mind. This process may
keep you from losing data and having to restore from a recent tape backup, which you might otherwise
have to do if you didn't have some level of RAID protection on your server.

Which level of RAID should you use on your network server? Most network administrators favor RAID 5 because it only takes away from 20 to 25 percent of the total disk
capacity for the redundancy function. Yet it performs well and offers a measure of
safety. However, I have seen RAID 3 and RAID 5 arrays fail to recover data properly
and, for this reason, I always use either RAID 1 or RAID 10 for network servers that store
important data.

You must make your own decision based on the importance of the data, the required
levels of performance, the capabilities of the server, and the budget available to you. One
thing you should *never* do, though, is think any RAID level replaces regular, tested, reliable tape backups of network data!

I2O

Short for Intelligent I/O, I2O (often written I_2O) is an emerging standard that moves the
I/O processing from the computer's processor to the disk controller. I2O promises to improve the performance of disk subsystems somewhat, although not as much as many of
the proponents would suggest. At the end of the day, the I/O processing still must be

done; it's just done on the disk controller with I2O. Where I2O does benefit systems is by relieving some of the load on the computer's central processor, freeing it to do other tasks.

Server State Monitoring

An important feature of most servers is the capability to monitor its own internal components and to notify you proactively if any problems develop or appear to be developing. Higher-end servers can typically monitor the following:

▼ Proper fan operation

■ System voltage

■ Memory errors, even if corrected by ECC memory

■ Disk errors, even if corrected automatically

■ In-case temperature

■ Operating system hangs

▲ Computer case opening

Any of these errors may indicate a current problem with the server or an impending problem. For example, a 1-bit memory error that is corrected by the system's ECC memory may not cause a problem for the server because it was corrected, but it may indicate a RAM chip or bank of RAM is starting to experience trouble. Similarly, climbing temperatures in a case may not cause an immediate problem, but may indicate a fan isn't operating properly, has a blocked intake, or something else, and, ultimately, temperatures higher than those allowed for in the server design will cause a failure.

Server state monitoring solutions can alert you to problems either via an e-mail or through a pager, so you can resolve them. Many high-end servers also offer "pre-failure" warranties, where the warranty will replace any components reporting even minor errors, so you can replace them proactively before trouble actually strikes. For those servers you depend on to be the most reliable possible, monitoring features such as these can be a real lifesaver.

Hot-Swap Components

Most servers these days include hot-swap components that can be replaced while the system continues to operate. Usually, hot-swap components are limited to disks, power supplies, and fans, all of which are running in a redundant configuration. For example, a system may have two power supplies. If one fails, the system still operates normally and you can replace the failed power supply without having to turn off the server. Similarly, most RAID disk configurations enable you to replace a failed drive without shutting down the server, provided the disks are installed in a hot-swap configuration.

TIP: Many RAID disk systems enable you to install a stand-by disk and the system itself uses that stand-by disk to replace any failed drive automatically. Of course, you would then replace the actual failed disk as soon as possible, where it then becomes the stand-by disk for the disk array.

CHOOSING SERVERS FOR WINDOWS NT AND NETWARE

There's more to choosing a server than simply finding the fastest possible computer on which to base your server. Because servers are usually important to a company, their selection requires some thought and research. You need to define your needs properly, know how you want to use the server, and know what software you plan to run on the server.

NOTE: Throughout this chapter and most of this book, Windows NT Server means both Windows NT Server 4 and Windows 2000 Server. When important differences exist between these two products, those differences will be clearly noted.

In this section you learn about the basics of defining server needs, selecting a server, and purchasing a server.

Defining Needs

Before looking at different server models, you need to understand clearly the needs the server has to meet. Otherwise, you risk either under- or over-purchasing hardware, both of which can cause problems and may lead you to spend more than you needed to spend. Under-purchasing leads to additional, unplanned for purchases, which may include needing more disks, more memory, or even having to replace the server much too soon. Over-purchasing means you spent more for a server than you needed to and may even cause your request for a particular server to be denied. Instead, you need to find the "sweet spot" for specifying just the right server for your needs; then you can defend your required configuration and its cost. You can't do any of this unless you have clearly defined your needs.

To specify the needs for a server clearly, you must be able to answer all the following questions:

▼ *What is the useful life of the server?* How long do you expect to use the server? Will you replace it in two, three, or four years? (Most servers are used for two or three years before being replaced.) Everyone should agree on this timeframe because if you plan to replace it in two years, you can get by with a smaller server than if you need one to last three or four years. If you specified a server capable of meeting two year's needs, however, you don't want to get to the end of two years and then find out a replacement won't be approved.

■ *What job will the server perform?* Will it be a file and print server, a Web server, a database server, or some other kind of server?

- *How many users does the server have to support and what are the needs of those users?* For example, with a file and print server, you must estimate the storage and bandwidth requirements needed to satisfy all the planned users' requests. For a database server, you must know how quickly the server needs to respond to various database operations.

- *How reliable must the server be?* What are the consequences (costs and impacts) if the server crashes for one or more hours, or for a day or two?

- *How safe must the data on the server be from loss?* This is different from the preceding question because you may have cases where a server must never lose data, even if it isn't a big deal if it goes down for a few hours. In such a situation, you would use a RAID-1 or RAID-10 configuration, but you may not care too much about, say, redundant power supplies. You might also explore some kind of hierarchical storage scheme, where data is automatically copied to tape or optical disk in real-time, or where you make several live incremental backups of files during each day.

- *If the planned-for server fails, what are your backup plans?* Do you plan to keep a hot-spare server available or do you plan simply to rely on the server manufacturer's service capabilities? Also, sometimes if a server fails, other existing servers may temporarily meet some of its needs. For example, in a Windows NT network, if your Primary Domain Controller fails, you can have Backup Domain Controllers that can pick up the slack while the PDC is down. Or, you may have redundant printer queues defined on another server, ready to be made available if the primary print server fails.

- *How do you plan to back up the server?* Do you plan to have a tape drive on the server itself or do you plan to back it up over the network to some other server's backup device? Do you plan to make backups while the server is being used or overnight when it's not being used? These are important questions to answer because if you host the backup device on the server, this also means you need to have backup software on the server. If you plan to back up a server while it's being used, you need a fast backup system connected to a fast server bus to minimize the impact to the users during the day. If you plan to back up a server over a network connection, you need a fast enough network connection to handle the amount of data on the server. Think carefully about your backup plans when specifying a server.

- *How could the demands placed on the server change over time?* Is the company aggressively hiring more employees, so the server may have to support twice as many users a year from now and four times as many users two years from now? Make sure you understand the company's overall plans and factor them into your server needs definition. Also, even in companies where the number of users is relatively static, the amount of storage required by each user will still grow rapidly. Estimate that current storage requirements could double every 18 months, everything else being equal. If you have historical data for how much storage users consume, this is even more accurate than the rule-of-thumb guess just given. (And don't forget to anticipate any new network services that could more rapidly increase your storage needs!)

▲ *Does the new server need to work with any existing hardware?* If you have to re-use a network backup device, for instance, you should make sure the new server can properly support it (and vice versa).

Once you answer these questions and any others that may crop up, you're ready to start looking at different servers that can meet the needs you defined.

Selecting the Server

Aside from choosing the types of equipment you need for a server, you must remember three basic prerequisites that should be met for all server purchases: Compatibility, compatibility, and compatibility. Times can occur when your network operating system starts giving you error messages on a particular server and you'll need fast responses to these types of problems. If you built a server yourself by buying a motherboard, a disk controller, a video card, and so forth, you're not going to get effective support, either for the hardware or for any compatibility problems that crop up with the software. For both Novell and Microsoft network operating systems, make sure each part of the server—as well as the entire system collectively—is certified by Novell or Microsoft for their respective network operating systems. For Novell, go to the following URL and check that any planned hardware is certified through Novell's YES! program:

http://developer.novell.com/npp/advanced.htm

For Microsoft operating systems, go to the following URL and look at Microsoft's Hardware Compatibility List (HCL) and make certain the hardware you like is certified:

http://www.microsoft.com/hcl

When selecting servers, you often select a manufacturer first and then select the actual model you need. This is because, everything being equal, you're slightly better off if all your servers are from the same maker. Managing servers from one manufacturer is much easier than managing servers from many manufacturers. You can do a better job of stocking spare parts that may fit into all of your servers and you can build a better relationship, which may hold additional benefits, with the manufacturer. For example, Dell lets companies certify their in-house technicians on Dell hardware (including servers) and then lets them order parts more directly, bypass the first level of support (which wastes time if you know what you're doing and have already performed basic troubleshooting), and also provides other benefits.

My advice is to be conservative in selecting servers and server brands. This means you should stick with the top names in the industry. For servers, the best makers are Compaq,

Dell, HP, and IBM. Micron's NetFrame servers are well thought of, too. You should stick with the "majors" when you select a server for many reasons, including these:

▼ They have much more established service organizations and practices

■ They are likely to offer higher quality support

■ Because so many other networks are based on their equipment, their technical support databases probably already contain any problems you encounter and they probably have fixes available

■ The NOS vendor is also more likely to have data on any problems concerning one of the top servers

▲ They have much better in-house engineering, and their servers are likely to perform better and to be more reliable

These are just the biggest reasons. You may remember a time when the mantra in MIS departments was "Nobody ever got fired for buying IBM." A similar type of thinking actually makes sense when buying servers, not only because it's more defensible, but because it does make better sense because of the previous reasons.

Remember these general differences when you select a server for either NetWare or Windows NT Server: First, while any server is RAM-hungry, Windows NT Server works better with more RAM than an equivalent NetWare server. If everything else is equal, plan on giving Windows NT 50 to 100 percent more RAM than a NetWare server. Also, database servers are RAM-hungry and for databases of any appreciable size (10GB or larger), plan on using at least 512MB of RAM (1GB isn't out of the question for the best possible performance).

You need to remember NetWare 3.x and 4.x are uniprocessor NOSs, while Windows NT Server can operate with up to eight processors. NetWare 5.x can support up to 32 processors. Still, for a NetWare server, you probably want the fastest Pentium Xeon processor you can find, while a Windows NT Server may make due with two or four slower processors. Also remember, with single-processor servers, NetWare tends to perform better than Windows NT Server. Depending on the actual application, NetWare outperforms Windows NT Server by 15 to 30 percent, even if you've already added more RAM to the Windows NT Server configuration.

Both Windows NT Server and NetWare can implement certain RAID levels themselves. For best performance, however, you should select a disk controller that can take this burden off the NOS. High-throughput disk controllers also often have a significant amount of RAM on them for caching disk data and they usually have their own processor to help handle their chores. Moreover, you always want to use SCSI-based disk subsystems on a server. A workstation running Windows 98 performs equally with either EIDE or SCSI, but a server can take advantage of SCSI's features to improve performance significantly over EIDE disk interfaces.

Choosing your actual disk configuration is relatively straightforward. You start by knowing your current and planned space requirements, and then you consider your performance and reliability needs to choose a particular RAID level that makes sense (see the earlier section on RAID levels for more information on this). Once you know these things, you can choose the amount of disk space you need and ensure the server you want can handle your current and planned disk space needs. One tip to remember in this area: you're better off knowing what your disk needs will be over time and planning to purchase additional disk space as the need arises. This is because the capacity of disk drives is increasing at a rapid rate, while prices are falling at a rapid rate. Buying, say, a 20GB drive a year from now will be much less expensive than purchasing the same drive today. Just make sure the server you select can handle all the drives you'll need and plan on purchasing and installing those drives as needed to save your company money. Also remember, for NetWare servers, the optimal amount of RAM is dependent on the amount of disk space in the server, so you want to plan on purchasing more RAM when you add any significant amount of disk space. But, happily, the same rule of thumb for disks holds true for RAM: prices are spiraling downward and tomorrow's RAM will almost certainly be much less expensive than today's RAM.

If you plan to purchase a server for Windows NT Server or NetWare 5.x, you may also want to consider selecting a system that accepts additional processors. This way, if you find the system is becoming bottlenecked at the processor level, you can install additional processors to reduce or remove that bottleneck.

Purchasing the System

Once you decide on the server you want, purchasing it is relatively straightforward—shop around and get the best price on the system you want, provided the suppliers you approach include the level of support you need, both pre-sales selection assistance, and post-sales support.

TIP: Remember, it's not really "cricket" to rely on the expertise of a particular supplier to help you select a server and answer any pre-sales questions you have, and then to purchase the server from some mail-order supplier with the best price. Try to be fair in your dealings. Vendors with higher support capabilities shouldn't be abused in this fashion or they won't be around to help you with after-sales issues that arise, or to help you with future purchases! I'm not saying you should pay a lot more for a piece of hardware from such vendors—just take into account the vendor's level of service when you evaluate different price quotes and, remember, price isn't everything.

Depending on your company's financial practices, you may want to consider leasing a server. Doing so brings you several benefits. First, leasing conserves your company's cash: instead of shelling out $20K all at once, you can pay it off over time. Also, the annual impact of a lease is much lower than with a purchase and leasing may make it easier to fit a particular server within your budget. There is also a hidden benefit to leases: They force you to consider whether to replace a server at the end of the lease term (usually three years), and they usually make it easy to return the server to the leasing company, and to lease a new server going forward. In the end, you pay about as much for leasing as buying (all things considered) and leases can help a company be disciplined about keeping its computer equipment relatively current. The only drawback to this is that you must have enough time to replace the server at the end of the lease, when you may prefer to do it several months before or after the lease is up. Still, in some companies, the benefits of leasing far outweigh the disadvantages. Discuss leasing with your financial department before ordering a server.

Installing Servers

The actual practice of setting up a server is mostly specific to the server itself and the NOS you plan to use. Later in this book, basic installations of NetWare, Windows 2000 Server, and Linux are shown.

When you set up a new server, remember to plan on extensively testing its hardware prior to implementing it. While most servers are reliable right out of the box, the fact is, if some part of the server is going to fail, it almost always fails shortly after being set up and used. I prefer to test servers for at least a week, even before installing the NOS onto the server. Most servers come with diagnostic software that can be configured to operate continuously, testing the system's processor, video subsystem, disk surfaces, and RAM, and log any errors that crop up. Right after pulling a server from its box and installing any components you need to install, plan on putting the server into a diagnostic loop using its diagnostic software and letting it run those tests for as long as possible. In no case should you test the server for less than several days (try to shoot for a week of testing).

After finishing the testing, you can install the NOS. During this phase, pay careful attention to any peculiarities of the server and to any error messages reported by the NOS or the server during the installation process. These must be fully resolved prior to going live with the server. In particular, watch out for any intermittent messages, like a message that there was a parity error in the system's RAM or an unexpected lockup of the server during installation. Even if those problems only occur once and don't recur, consult with the maker of the server and get advice on the problem. (Be sure you carefully write down any messages or other things you notice if this happens.) Servers have a tendency to fail at the most inopportune times, so make sure you have complete confidence in it before making it available to users.

Most server manufacturers have made the process of installing their server and installing the NOS onto the server easy. Companies like Compaq even ship their servers with special CD-ROMs that mostly automate the process of installing various NOSs onto the server and also install any needed support files the NOS needs to work optimally with the server hardware. Prior to installing a NOS onto a server, make sure to read the server's documentation carefully and to take advantage of any automated tools provided by the server manufacturer.

TIP: The top-tier server makers (Compaq, HP, and Dell, for example) maintain e-mail notification systems that let you know about any new patches they release or any serious problems they have with a particular model. These e-mail services are extremely useful and you should plan on signing up for them immediately on receipt of any new server.

Here's something else to think about: sometimes servers are built and then sit around in inventory for several months before being sold. Consequently, the server may not come with the most current software. Before installing the server, check the maker's Web site for any updates that aren't in your package and consider whether to install those updates during your implementation process.

MAINTAINING AND TROUBLESHOOTING SERVERS

To do the best job of maintaining and troubleshooting servers, you need to take steps to do two things: decrease the chance of failure and improve your chance of rapidly resolving any failures that do occur. Problems are inevitable, but you can greatly decrease your odds of having them and you can greatly improve your chances of resolving them by taking steps *before* you actually have any problems.

To decrease the chance of failure, make sure to follow all the advice previously given: use reliable, tested servers and components. You should also take these additional steps:

▼   Whenever possible, try to reduce the number of jobs a server must do. While building a single server that will be a file and print server, a database server, an e-mail server, and a Web server is certainly possible, you're much better off (from a reliability standpoint) segregating these duties onto smaller, separate servers.

■   Set up a practice of frequently viewing the server's error logs. If the server NOS supports notification of errors (such as to a pager), implement it. Many failures start with error messages that may precede the actual failure by a few hours, so getting an early heads-up may help you keep the server running or at least let you resolve the problem at the best possible time.

■   If a server supports management software that monitors the server's condition, make sure to install it.

■   Most RAID arrays that support hot-swap of failed drives also require special software to be installed on the NOS to support this feature fully. Make sure you install this software before any failures occur.

▲   NOS software is among the most bug-free available, but it's still a truism that there is no such thing as completely bug-free software. Over time, any NOS will eventually fail. While many servers run for up to a year without trouble, you're better off establishing a practice of periodically shutting down the server and bringing it back up again. This eliminates small errors that may be cropping up, like memory leaks in the NOS. Monthly restarts are the best frequency.

CAUTION: Make sure you do a backup *before* shutting down the server and restarting it. The greatest chance of hardware failure occurs when the system is powered back up again.

You can also do some general things to improve your ability to resolve any server failures rapidly. The most important is to maintain an extensive binder for each server, which I call a "rebuild kit." This binder should contain the following:

▼ All purchase data for the server, including your purchase order and a copy of the supplier's invoice.

■ A printout of the server's configuration. Most server's setup programs can generate a detailed list with all components and versions.

■ All software needed to rebuild the server completely from scratch. This includes the setup software for the server, the NOS software, device driver disks, and any patch disks you need or have applied.

■ Contact information for service on the server, including any extended warranty contract numbers or other information you need to get service.

■ Note paper, for documenting all changes to the server's configuration and any error messages that appear. Write all the information clearly, noting the date and time, and any other details you (or someone else) may need to fix the server if it fails.

▲ A printout, or document, noting anything special about the server or how you configured the disk drives, including NOS settings. You need these if you have to rebuild from scratch. Knowing these settings may enable you to recover the data on the server's disks rather than being forced to restore from backup tape.

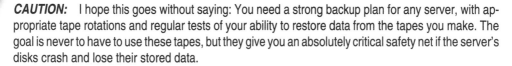

CAUTION: I hope this goes without saying: You need a strong backup plan for any server, with appropriate tape rotations and regular tests of your ability to restore data from the tapes you make. The goal is never to have to use these tapes, but they give you an absolutely critical safety net if the server's disks crash and lose their stored data.

Even if you're the best computer troubleshooter in the world, you should plan on working with the service department of your server's manufacturer to troubleshoot any problems. Doing so can save you because they have extensive databases available to them of the problems others have experienced. They also are familiar with the steps needed to help prevent data loss as you work to troubleshoot the problem. Troubleshooting a server on your own, no matter how experienced and knowledgeable you are, is usually a mistake.

CHAPTER SUMMARY

When building a network, the one component you should pay the most attention to is the server. While other parts of the network, like the wiring, network architecture, or workstations are also significant, the server is the most likely component to experience trouble over time. The server is the single component you must spend the most time managing. Because of this, take extra care when selecting, implementing, and maintaining your servers. If you take care of your server, your servers will take care of you.

The following chapter concerns network workstation computers and discusses the different requirements desktop computers have, how you should buy and manage them, and how to support them.

CHAPTER 10

All About Client Computers

Desktop computers are really where the "rubber meets the road" when it comes to networks. They are the users' primary interface to the network and the resource on which users most rely to get their jobs done. In a way, the network is designed to support the desktop computers' work, rather than the other way around. Desktop computers are also where you often spend the most time in managing a network, so their purchase, implementation, and management is important. You can have the best network in the world, but if your desktop computers aren't up to the task, the network's users won't be productive.

This chapter focuses on the management of desktop computers. Chances are, if you're reading this book, you already know about the bits and bytes that make up desktop computers and desktop operating systems. You're probably already a wizard with Windows 9x or the Macintosh, and you're comfortable installing new computer hardware and repairing problems on desktop computers. If you don't know about these things yet, many good books exist that cover the technologies in desktop computers in more detail than this book can. Here, the major concern is how desktop computers integrate with the network and how you can get the most out of them when you're managing or setting up a network.

CHOOSING DESKTOP COMPUTERS

Choosing desktop computers involves many things. Making good choices here will pay big dividends over time. When purchasing new desktop computers, you have the opportunity to select machines to reduce your support burden, improve end-user productivity, and—overall—conserve your company's cash. The following sections explore the different factors that go into choosing desktop computers.

Desktop Platforms

You need to know what desktop computer platform you will use. Generally, companies tend to gravitate toward either PC-based desktop computers or Macintosh-based desktop computers. A few companies also tend toward UNIX-based desktop computers, like Sun SPARCstations or Silicon Graphics computers, although this is rare. You'll usually choose between PCs and Macintoshes.

Advantages and disadvantages exist for each platform. Regardless of the specific pros and cons, you're *much* better off if you can keep the company standardized on a single desktop computer platform. Companies that have allowed their population of desktop computers to follow user preferences end up with real support headaches, which arise from many different sources. Supporting two desktop platforms is more than twice as difficult as supporting one platform. Why? Consider:

▼ You need to maintain expertise in two platforms, and in their applications and platform-specific peculiarities. In a small company, you need more people to keep the requisite levels of expertise on both platforms than you would if you only had to support one platform.

■ You need to stock more spare parts and expansion hardware. Generally, components that work in a PC won't work in a Macintosh and vice versa.

■ You need to license and inventory more software titles (on average, twice as many).

■ Problems that would never occur with one platform or another occur when you have to support both, even in the network itself. Supporting two platforms is more complex than supporting one and so servers must run additional software, must allow for the different ways each platform works, and so forth. All this increases the complexity of the network and increased complexity means less reliability for everyone.

■ Inter-platform incompatibilities cause problems for users who have to work together. Even if you use the same application on both PCs and Macintoshes (like Microsoft Word), platform differences still exist. For example, even Adobe fonts with the same name look and paginate differently on Macs and PCs. People might painstakingly format a document in Word, Excel, FrameMaker, or other applications available on both platforms, only to find the other platform doesn't represent their work in exactly the same way. When users need to interact frequently with their files like this, it becomes a real problem.

■ In some cases, you may be unable to find software titles with matching versions available for both platforms. This usually means users who are using a particular application won't be able to interact with users who are using the other platform's functionally equivalent application.

▲ You will be limited in the programs you can develop for widespread use. For example, try developing a Microsoft Access-based application and then having Macintosh users use it. They can't, because Microsoft Access doesn't exist on the Macintosh and there's no real way to use the same database application on both platforms in cases like this. You can probably exchange data, but not the program written in Access. The same situation exists for virtually all programming languages: They are almost universally platform-specific, despite the efforts of their makers to make them platform-neutral. Examples of this kind of problem are much more common than not. (One exception would be a SQL-based application that makes use of something like an Oracle database server, but this doesn't make sense for simple applications.)

I hope you're convinced that you're better off running the *wrong* desktop platform than running *two* desktop platforms. If you're in a company where two desktop platforms are in use, you should work to change it. This is a difficult process and takes a long time, but this is important both for increasing overall company productivity and keeping IS costs at a reasonable level. If you're setting up a network from scratch, make sure you have an agreement to standardize on a single platform. Make sure this support goes all the way to the CEO; otherwise, the company may hire some VP who insists on Macs (or vice versa). If you don't have this support worked out in advance, you may have trouble with this situation.

Your next platform decision concerns which one to choose. Most often, a company has a history with a particular platform and sticking with this is usually easiest, unless a good reason exists for a change. If you're lucky enough to be setting up a company network for the first time, then you get to help choose a platform. This choice should always be driven by what the users need to accomplish, what applications they need to run, and what platform best supports those applications. You need to consider the full range of applications the company is likely to need, but this should be the primary driver. For most companies, this means you'll strongly lean toward PCs as the standard but, for some companies, Macs are still a good idea. Generally, Macs make sense in companies that have a strong artistic or graphic bent to their makeup, like a Web design firm, a graphic design house, and so forth.

NOTE: As you have probably already noticed, many people want to make a platform decision based on which platform they like the best. With some people, the issue almost rises to the level of importance of a religion. Many people happily call themselves "PC fanatics" or "Mac fanatics." While this is a poor way to make a smart business decision, this also means you must tread carefully with this topic!

If no need exists that strongly suggests a particular platform, then, for many reasons, you should lean toward choosing PCs. PCs are the most price-competitive, are in the widest use, attract the largest assortment of software and hardware developers, and have much more infrastructure to support them. Also, there are certain important business application software categories for which good solutions exist on the PC platform, which do not exist (or exist minimally) on the Mac platform.

NOTE: While this book aims to be platform-neutral, the fact is over 90 percent of networked desktop computers are PCs. While this book is just as applicable to Macs as PCs, for the remainder of this chapter a PC environment is assumed.

Reliability and Serviceability

The most important feature to look for in any desktop computer is its reliability—and closely related—its serviceability. Studies have shown that the actual cost of a desktop computer is a small percentage of its lifetime cost, which includes software costs, training costs, and support costs. Anything you can do to minimize support costs will pay a hefty (although not easily measured) premium over the lifetime of your desktop computers. And, not only should you consider the cost of support and repair, but you should also consider the cost to the company that occurs when users lose work because of computer crashes or when they lose work time because their primary work tool isn't available for any amount of time.

When assessing reliability, you need to look at the entire picture. Reliability comes from several things. First, reliability means the computer uses tested, high-quality components. Second, reliability means those components are engineered to work well together. You can make a cake with the best ingredients available, but if your recipe isn't

Author's Note

I once joined a company that had been purchasing "no-name" clones for its desktop computers. In my first week, I set up five brand new units still in boxes, only to find three of them were dead on arrival (DOA). That same week, the company's CFO, who was working on an important financing activity, had his computer crash repeatedly (losing unsaved work each time) until I finally swapped his entire computer for one of the new ones that actually worked. Was the money saved on those computers (about $400 per unit) worth it? What was the cost to the company for all these mishaps? The answer is simple: far more than the company saved. I immediately changed their brand to a more reliable one (the CFO was sympathetic!) and got rid of the existing machines as quickly as possible. Don't be penny-wise and pound-foolish when you purchase computers!

good, you still get a bad cake. Computers are no different. Even the best components don't always work well together. Top-tier manufacturers test all the components that go into their systems and assure they're compatible with one another. Third, reliability means you use a reliable combination of software on the unit and you use software that has been certified on the computers whenever possible.

Serviceability is closely related to reliability. Serviceability simply means working on or repairing a particular computer is easy. Features that enhance serviceability are easy-opening cases requiring no tools, quickly replaceable internal components—such as hard disks, memory, or video cards that require simple or no tools—and other features, such as easily updateable Basic Input Output Software (BIOS) in the computer. Serviceability is also strongly influenced by the services available from the computer's maker. Does the computer manufacturer stay current in offering updates to its computers? Is technical information about its systems readily available or does the company tend to gloss over any discovered problems? How quickly can you get replacement parts? Does the manufacturer include on-site service for a period of time that reduces your support burden? What is the warranty on any given computer? Is the vendor of sufficient size to be around for the entire useful life of the unit? What other value-added services are offered if problems occur?

TIP: PC Magazine performs an annual survey of reliability and serviceability for the major computer and printer manufacturers, based on survey responses from thousands of readers. This information is *extremely* valuable when selecting a computer manufacturer and you should pay close attention to the results.

Another factor that strongly influences serviceability is often overlooked. How many computers does the maker sell and is the model you are buying in widespread use? This is important because a widely used computer is more likely to be supported when new software or hardware comes out because companies that make software and hardware know they must ensure their products work properly with these computers. If you use computers from a small, local company (or, even worse, build the computers yourself) and some software package or operating system that comes out in a year or two doesn't work properly, the maker of the software or hardware may say something like, "Well, we haven't tested on that computer, so we don't know why our product isn't working right." While they may act in good faith to resolve the problem, the problem may take much longer to resolve and it may never be resolved. On the other hand, if you're using a top-tier computer, such as one from IBM, Compaq, Dell, HP, or even Gateway, the vendor of the new product probably knows how to resolve any problems that arise and has already done so before the product was shipped.

TIP: If your company runs an application that is vital to its business, but is not in widespread use, it sometimes pays to find out what computers the application maker uses. This can reduce your risk of having trouble with that application.

Serviceability is also improved if you standardize on a particular manufacturer because you can focus your resources on supporting that line of computers. Those people who support the desktop computers in the company are more able to stay up-to-date with the peculiarities of that manufacturer, are more comfortable working with those computers, and can solve a problem once—and then apply the result to many computers—rather than having to troubleshoot many different types of problems on many different types of computers.

Price and Performance

Once the preceding priorities are satisfied, you can then strike the appropriate balance between performance and price. You need to take into account the useful life you plan for new purchases and make certain to purchase systems that will be productive over that useful life. In determining this, don't look at how well a particular configuration can handle today's needs, but how well it can handle tomorrow's needs.

Some people may disagree, but price should be your last priority when you purchase computers. I'm not suggesting price isn't important, only that you first need to determine what you need and then work on optimizing the price you pay. Different strategies exist for getting the best price, ranging from straightforward bargaining and competitive bids, to slightly underpurchasing on the performance side, but planning to upgrade the existing computers when needed (at least in terms of RAM and hard disk space, both of which decrease pretty rapidly in price over time).

Estimate the demands placed on a desktop computer will double every 24 months or so and then take into account your planned useful life. Set your performance levels to meet that need. (People used to assume performance requirements doubled every 18 months, but this seems to be slowing a bit in recent years.) For example, say you've determined today's user requires 5GB of disk space, 64MB of RAM, and a Pentium II 300 MHz processor. In 24 months, your users are likely to be clamoring for 10GB of disk space, 128MB of RAM, and a Pentium III 600 MHz processor. In another 24 months (about four years from purchase), this will double again, to 20GB of disk space, 256MB of RAM, and the equivalent of a Pentium IV 1200 MHz processor (whatever that turns out to be). While this may seem unreasonable to you that this actually happens (who can imagine a processor running at an equivalent 1200 MHz?), when you look back four years, you'll see it's true: Today's 5GB, 64MB, Pentium II 300 MHz processor would calculate out to be a 1GB, 16MB, 80486-based computer at about 75–100 MHz, which is what people were purchasing four years ago.

NOTE: I once worked out the "18–24 month doubling rule" back to the dawn of PCs (not to date myself too much!), with machines containing 64K of RAM, 8088 or 6502 processors, and—if they were lucky—a 5MB hard disk, and this rule-of-thumb turns out to be extremely accurate!

Using this way of estimating performance needs, you should be able to find a "sweet spot" between price, performance, and useful life that minimizes your costs and maximizes the benefits your users will receive.

UNDERSTANDING NETWORK WORKSTATION REQUIREMENTS

Computers connected to a LAN differ slightly from computers that are stand-alone. They have additional hardware installed in them and they run additional network software. In this section, these differences are explored.

Network Workstation Hardware

All network computers need an installed network interface to connect to the network. These usually take the form of a network interface card (NIC) but some computers have the NIC integrated onto the system's motherboard. Each NIC is specific to the type of network it supports. NICs are available for Ethernet networks, Token Ring networks, and even other networks. NICs are also usually specific to the cable media you have installed. For example, Ethernet NICs are available for 10Base-2 media, 10Base-T media, or 100Base-T media, with 1000Base-T NICs now beginning to appear. Some NICs also support multiple media types, which can be a blessing if you're in the middle of migrating from one media type to another. For example, some Ethernet NICs support both 10Base-2, 10Base-T, and 100Base-T on a single NIC.

Network Workstation Software

Network workstations also need networking hardware to work with the network. This consists of several components: A driver for the NIC, driver software for the protocols being used, and a network requestor. Workstations acting in a peer-to-peer fashion also have peer software that provides network services to other workstations. Additionally, network service software may be needed, such as to use a particular network directory service.

For Windows 9x-based computers, you can choose to use included Microsoft software to connect to both Novell networks or to Windows NT-based networks. You can also use Novell's network software for Novell-based networks. Both sets of network software work well, although differences exist.

For Novell-based networks, Microsoft's networking software consumes less memory than Novell's, but it doesn't offer as many features and doesn't integrate with the Novell servers quite as nicely. Still, it's reliable and performs well. Novell's client software (called Client 32) works well and makes good use of the Novell server's features.

When using the Microsoft software with NetWare 4.x or greater servers, you must also run service software to access Novell Directory Services (NDS). This software is included both with Windows 9x and Client 32, if you are using it.

Under Windows 9x, the network software is managed through the properties dialog box for Network Neighborhood or through the Network object in the Control Panel (both methods access the same dialog box). Figure 10-1 shows an example of this dialog box.

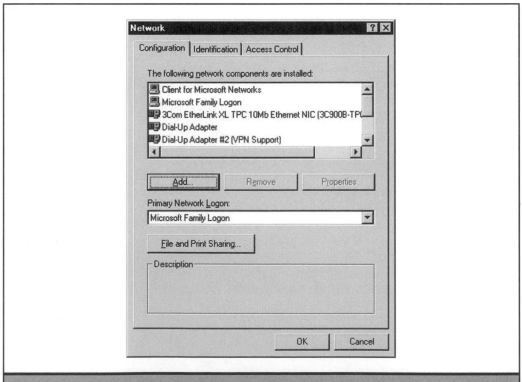

Figure 10-1. The Network Properties dialog box in Windows 98

The Network Properties dialog box contains a number of entries, including the following main categories:

▼ **Client**   You may have client software installed for Novell networks or Microsoft networks. This client software interacts with the servers to request network services.

■ **Network interface**   This software represents the driver software for any installed NICs or for "virtual NICs" used to connect to a network through a modem.

■ **Protocols**   This software adds support for any needed networking protocols, such as TCP/IP, IPX/SPX, or NetBEUI.

▲ **Services**   Any additional network service software, such as that used for NDS, also appears in the Network Properties dialog box.

You add new entries, whether they be clients, protocols, or services, by clicking the Add button on the dialog box. This accesses the Select Network Component Type dialog box, shown in Figure 10-2. You choose which type of component you want to install and click the Add button.

After choosing which type of component you wish to install, you then see a Select dialog box that lists the available software of that type. Figure 10-3 shows this dialog box if you are installing an additional network protocol. Choose the protocol to be installed and click the OK button.

NOTE: When using Novell Client 32 software, you instead use the Client 32 setup program. The results will appear in—and can be managed in—the Network Properties dialog box, but they are installed separately.

After choosing the software to be added, you are returned to the Network Properties dialog box, from which you can choose to install additional network software. After you

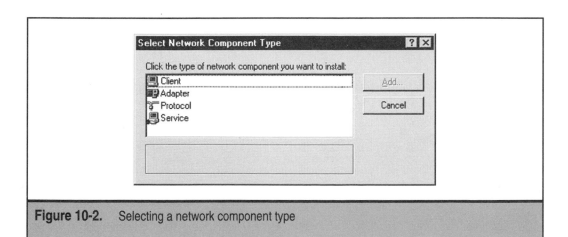

Figure 10-2.   Selecting a network component type

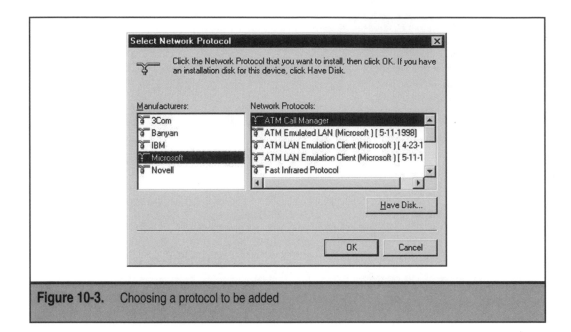

Figure 10-3.   Choosing a protocol to be added

have completed all your choices, you click OK in the Network Properties dialog box to save the settings and actually install the software into the operating system. You will be prompted for any needed installation diskettes or CD-ROMs at this time. After the installation completes, you need to restart the computer to begin using the software.

TIP: First install the client software you wish to use, either the one for Novell networks or that for Microsoft networks. Doing so automatically loads the protocols on which the requestor relies, which saves time if you are using the default protocols.

In the Network Properties dialog box, entries are *bound* to other entries, enabling them to work together. For example, protocols are bound to NICs, which enables the protocol to send and receive that type of packet through the NIC. Clients are bound to protocols, enabling that network requestor to use a particular protocol. By default, this is done for you automatically when you install the components. If combinations of protocols exist, NICs, and requestors that you do not use, you can delete those particular bindings.

TIP: Only install the network components you actually need in the Network Properties dialog box. Adding unnecessary components only unnecessarily reduces the performance of the network workstation.

CHAPTER SUMMARY

Managing network workstation computers can be a daunting task. Many of them must be managed frequently, each user may have different needs, and because of how they are used, network workstation computers are the most likely to experience trouble. In this chapter, you learned general information about network client computers, along with how to select appropriate network computers. You also learned about the components network computers have in common, which separate them from stand-alone desktop computers.

PART II

Hands-On Knowledge

CHAPTER 11

Designing a Network

Networking professionals rarely have the opportunity to walk into a company and design a new network from the ground up, but those who do are certainly lucky. In exchange for long hours, stress, deadlines, and the nagging worry that maybe they're forgetting something, they get to shape the computing environment of a large number of users and set the tone for—in many companies—how efficiently the company can function in coming years. In some companies that rely heavily on information technology, a smoothly running network may even determine if the company will be successful. It's an enormous responsibility, but also one of the most rewarding jobs you can have.

Of course, designing a network from the ground up is more the exception than the rule. Mostly, networks start small and simply grow over time. Networks are almost like skin cells, where you're sure to replace each one of them every few years, but only a few at a time. Networks do the same thing: They grow over time and, if you measure them now and then again in a few years, an entirely new network will appear to have been built. But the process is usually evolutionary rather than revolutionary. Exceptions exist to this rule, though. The company that moves to a new building, decides to scrap the old network during the process, and puts in a new one at the new location, or the well-funded start-up company that goes from 5 to 500 employees in six months.

Regardless of whether you're building a brand new network from scratch or evolving an existing network, the tools you use are much the same and the process of designing the network is also much the same. The concept is actually simple: you assess the needs the network must meet and then you meet those needs. In practice, this is much more complex, but the idea is straightforward. Even in an evolving network, using network planning to formulate a long-term plan to evolve the network makes sense, so understanding what you must examine when you build a network is important.

NOTE: Network design is not really an exact science. Getting it right immediately is nearly impossible, even with the best design tools and resources available. This is because every network has different demands placed on it and these demands often interact in surprising ways. Moreover, predicting what new demands will be placed on the network over time, how users will use the network resources, or what other changes you may have to make is almost impossible. The entire situation is both fluid and chaotic. The trick is to do a good job of estimating needs and then do the best job possible to create a design to meet those needs. Having fallback plans is also important, in case some part of the network doesn't perform the way you intended. For instance, you may find once the network is up and running that the distribution of bandwidth across segments is poor. You want to know in advance how you can measure and address these events. You may also find storage requirements are much higher or lower than you expected. You need to know what to do if this happens. The real point is this: network design is a process and often an iterative process.

A lot of the network design process is what you decide to make of it. There are simple network design processes, and there are horrendously complex processes that involve dozens of people, complex statistical modeling, and even network simulation software to test a planned design and see if it holds together. In this chapter, you learn a relatively comprehensive process that is straightforward and simple. Using the information in this chapter, along with a good dose of experience, will yield a flexible network that should easily meet the needs of hundreds of users.

NOTE: You can't design a network of any size without plenty of experience running similar networks. You can manage the overall process by understanding the methodology, but you can't create a good design without strong experience. If you're new to networking and you have to design a network, make sure you get experienced people on the team—either as consultants or as part of a supplier-led team—and listen carefully to their experiences and knowledge. Listening well pays off with a design that will work, rather than one that may look good on paper, but won't hold up to actual use.

This chapter relies on all the information you learned in the preceding chapters. Think of this chapter as the one that takes all the information you already learned and brings it together into a coherent whole. Preceding chapters have focused on the bits and bytes of networks, while this chapter is the view from 30,000 feet where you start to see how everything works together.

ASSESSING NETWORK NEEDS

The importance of doing a good job in assessing the needs that a network must meet cannot be overstated. Many adages exist concerning the importance of knowing your goals. "Measure twice and cut once" is one carpenters use. "Ready, Fire, Aim" is one that pokes fun at people who don't properly set goals. And hundreds of others exist. The point is this: Before worrying about what network topology to use, what NOS platform to use, how to structure your hubs, bridges, and routers, and what grade of wiring to install, you must know what the network needs to accomplish. Doing a proper job of this can be tedious, but assessing needs is where you should place the most emphasis during a design process. Failing to do so almost certainly will result in a network that isn't productive for its users.

NOTE: Many IS professionals are, at heart, technologists who love to play with the latest technologies. Be careful to avoid giving in to the temptation to design the network around the "hot" technologies and then finding out how the needs fit into those technologies (many people try to do this). Instead, start with the needs and then find out what technologies support those needs.

When assessing needs, you are trying to come up with detailed answers to the following questions:

▼ How much storage space is required?

■ How much bandwidth is required?

▲ What network services are required?

These basic considerations are fairly easy to create as a whole, but you need to break them down further to make sure no holes in the network design could lead to problems.

For example, it may be easy to determine the network must be able to support up to 100Mbps of bandwidth, but you need to know how and when that bandwidth is used. If 90 percent of the bandwidth is being used by, say, the accounting department when communicating to its accounting server, then naturally you want to put that server and its users on their own network segment. You won't be able to know these things unless your assessment leads you to determine how these resources will be used with some degree of detail.

The following sections discuss what you should examine as you learn what a given network must be able to do. No particular order exists in which you should examine these topics and you may find you must cycle through the list several times to get a complete picture. You also may find a particular company's needs require more or less analysis in each category. Common sense is required when you design a network. The following suggestions are guidelines to start you on the right path.

Applications

A good place to start with a network design is to list and understand the applications that will run on the network. Ultimately, a network is only as good as the work it helps people accomplish and people do their work most directly through the application software they use. If the applications don't work right, then the users won't work right, so the network has to support the planned applications properly.

Most networks have both common applications and department- and user-specific applications. In most companies, the common application needs are usually met through a suite of desktop applications, like Microsoft Office or Lotus SmartSuite. The following is a listing of applications most companies simply install for all users, whether or not each user needs each one:

▼ Word processor

■ Spreadsheet

■ End-user database

■ Presentation graphics

■ E-mail

■ Personal information manager (calendar, contact list, and so forth)

▲ Virus-scanning software

Your first order of business is to determine a number of things about the common applications. You need to know whether all users need to have the entire suite installed, how often different users plan to use the different applications, how many files they will create and store, how large those files may be, and how those files will be shared among users. For example, in a 1,000 user population, you may determine that 90 percent will use word processing to generate an average of ten documents a month—each document being an average of 100KB in size—and they probably will want to keep two years' worth of documents on hand at any given time. Yes, these will be educated guesses, but it's important to come up with reasonable estimates. Experience with similar user populations and companies pays off handsomely in determining these estimates. With this information alone, you know immediately you need about 24MB of storage per user, or 21.6GB for the word processing population of 900 users, just for word processing documents. For applications where files will frequently be shared among users, you may have to factor in that most users keep personal copies of some files they share with others.

TIP: Establishing shared directories that different groups of people can access and into which they can store those shared files they work on, will help reduce overall network storage requirements.

Then you come up with the same estimates for the other applications, taking into account their expected size, frequency of creation, and long-term storage requirements.

TIP: Don't worry if you can scientifically prove whether your estimates are accurate and don't get bogged down in "analysis paralysis." Instead, make sure the estimates are reasonable to other network professionals. At a certain point, you need to justify the network design and cost, and, to do this, having these estimates is necessary.

After determining the common applications, move on to department-specific applications. This gets trickier for new networks in new companies because you may not know what applications will be used. For existing companies, you have the advantage of already knowing what department applications you need to support. Different departmental applications can have wildly different impacts on the network, which can create a problem if you don't know what these applications will be for a new company. For example, an accounting system designed around shared database files needs a different network design than a client/server accounting system. The former relies more on fileserver performance and is more likely to be bandwidth-sensitive than an efficient client-server application that runs on a dedicated server. If a departmental application is not yet selected, talk with the managers of that department to get their best estimates and then proceed.

Following are common departmental applications you should consider:

▼   Accounting

■   Distribution and inventory control

■   Manufacturing

■   Electronic commerce

■   Human resources

■   Payroll and stock administration

■   Legal

▲   Other line-of-business applications specific to the company's industry

For each one of the departmental applications you identify, you need to know how much storage they will consume, from where the applications will be run (local computers with data on a server or completely centralized), whether they will have their own dedicated servers, how much network bandwidth the application needs, and how all these things will change as the company grows.

Finally, while you may not formally include this in your plan, consider user-specific applications that may be run. For example, you may estimate that people in the company's R&D group are all likely to run two or three unknown applications as part of their job. If you decide that user-specific applications will have a significant impact on the network, then you should estimate their needs just as you have the other types of applications. If you decide they will have minimal impact, then you may decide either to include a small allowance for them or none at all.

Users

Once you know what applications the network must support, you can estimate how many users need to be supported and what applications each user will use. Estimating total users will likely be easier because the company should already have a business plan or long-range budget from which you can derive these estimates. Your user estimates should be reasonably granular: know the number of users in each department in the company as well as in total.

You should estimate how many users will need to be supported immediately, in one year, in three years, and in five years. Even though five years is a distant horizon to use for an estimate, this is important information to know during the design process. Different growth rates suggest different network designs, even at the inception of the network. A company estimating it will have 100 users immediately, 115 users in one year, 130 users in three years, and 150 users in five years needs a different network design than a company estimating 100 users immediately, 115 users in one year, 300 users in three years, and 1,000 users in five years. In the latter case, you must invest more in a design that is more quickly scaleable and you are likely to spend much more at inception to build the network, even though you have the same number of users in the first two years.

Knowing the number of users isn't enough, though. You need to know more about the users. At a minimum, consider the following questions to determine if any of the following will be important factors for the users generally or for subgroups of the users:

▼ **Bandwidth requirements** Aside from the bandwidth required to save and retrieve files, send and receive e-mail, and perform an average amount of browsing on the Internet, do any users need significant amounts of bandwidth? For example, will scientists download a fresh copy of the human genome from the Internet once a week? Will groups of users need to exchange large quantities of data among different sites? Will any users be running video conferencing software over your LAN and WAN/Internet connection? How much Web browsing do you expect your users to do? Will people be sending large attachments frequently through Internet e-mail?

■ **Storage requirements**   Will any group of users need significantly more storage capacity than the overall average you already determined? For instance, will an electronic imaging group catalog millions of documents into image files on a server? If so, how many people need access to that data? Will the accounting group need to keep the previous ten years financial information online? Will the company use or install an executive information system where all the managers have query capability into the company's accounting, distribution, and manufacturing systems, and, if so, how much additional bandwidth or server performance could that require?

▲ **Service requirements**   Will any groups of users need additional network services not needed by most users? For example, does part of the company do work of such sensitivity that they should be firewalled from the rest of the LAN? Will a subset of users need direct inward fax capability?

When examining user bandwidth requirements, remember to look at the timeliness of the bandwidth needs. If certain known activities require a lot of bandwidth and must be carried out during the normal workday, that high-bandwidth use may interfere with the performance of the rest of the network. Therefore, make sure to estimate both average and peak bandwidth needs.

Network Services

The next area you should look at concerns the services that the network must provide. These can vary widely in different companies. A very basic network might only need file and print services, plus perhaps Internet connectivity. A more complex network will need many additional services. Consider which of the following types of services the network you are designing will need to provide, as well as any others that are specific to the company:

▼ File and print services

■ Backup and restore services

■ Internet Web browsing

■ FTP and Telnet

■ Internet or external e-mail

■ Internet security services

■ Dial-out from LAN through a modem pool

■ Dial-in to LAN through a modem pool

■ Fax into LAN (manually distributed or automatically distributed)

■ Dynamic Host Configuration Protocol (DHCP) services

■ Centralized virus protection services

■ WAN services to other locations

■ Streaming Internet radio and other media

▲ Voice over IP (VoIP)

For each service, you must answer a number of questions. First, you need to know the storage and bandwidth requirements for each service, and any other impacts they will make. For instance, a fax-in service may itself require a small amount of storage space, but all the fax bitmaps users will end up storing may have a large impact on total storage needs. Second, you need to know how the service is to be provided. Usually, this means what server will host the service. Some services require such little overhead, you can easily host them on a server that does other jobs. A DHCP server, which requires minimal resources, is a good example of this. On the other hand, an e-mail system may require such high resources that you must plan to host it on its own dedicated server. Third, you need to know what users or groups of users need which services. This is because you may need to break the network down into smaller segments and you want to locate frequently used services for a particular user population on the same segment as they use to minimize backbone traffic.

Security and Safety

The preceding considerations are all related to the bits and bytes required by different parts of the network. Security and safety concern the company's need to keep information secure—both inside and outside a company—and to keep its data safe from loss. You need to know how important these two issues are before attempting to set down a network design on paper.

For both these considerations, a tradeoff exists between cost and effectiveness. As mentioned in earlier chapters, no network is ever totally secure and no data is ever totally safe from loss. However, different companies and departments have different sensitivities to these issues, indicating more or less money should be spent on these areas. Some applications may be perfectly well suited to keeping their data on a striped RAID 0 array of disks, where the risk of loss is high, because the data may be static and easy to restore from tape if the disk array is lost. Other applications may require the highest level of data-loss safety possible, with fail-over servers each having mirrored RAID 1 or RAID 10 arrays and online tape backup systems updating a backup tape every hour or for every transaction. Similarly, some companies may work with data of such sensitive nature that the best firewalls must be installed, perhaps with two levels of firewalls, and full-time professionals dedicated to keeping the data secure. Other companies may not care if their data is seen.

The point is you must determine how important these issues are to the company for which you are designing the network. Then you can propose different solutions to address these needs and factor these needs into the rest of your design.

Growth and Capacity Planning

The final area to consider is the expected growth of the network, particularly if this growth is expected to be substantial. As mentioned earlier in this chapter, a network designed for a rapidly growing company looks different from one for a slowly growing company. In the former case, you want a design that can be quickly and easily expanded without having to replace much of the existing hardware and software. In the latter case, you can get by with a simpler network design.

You want to consider the impact of growth on the different parts of the network you've already examined (applications, users, and services), because linear growth does not always mean a matching linear impact to the network. Assuming a linear growth curve, the impact to the network may be much lower, or much higher, than the curve.

For example, you saw in Chapter 4 how Ethernet uses a collision-detection mechanism to manage network traffic. In that chapter, you also learned Ethernet scales linearly, but only up to a point. Once the network starts to become saturated, performance starts to drop rapidly because of the chaotic nature of collision-detection schemes. Consider a 10Mbps Ethernet network over which 3Mbps of traffic is transmitted. This traffic probably flows smoothly, with few collisions and few retransmissions required. Push the network demand up to 4 or 5Mbps, however, and its performance grinds to a halt as the network becomes saturated and you end up with as many collisions and retransmissions as real data. In fact, the amount of good data flowing over a saturated Ethernet network will actually be less than the amount flowing over a less-saturated network.

You can also find examples where an increase in demand doesn't cause a corresponding increase in network or server load. For example, the server load for a complex e-mail system may only increase by a small amount if you doubled the number of users because most of the load is generated by the system's overhead. Or, the storage requirements for an accounting system may not double just because you keep twice as much data in it because the overhead may consume most of the existing space. Alternately, that same accounting system may consume four times as much storage space if you double the data storage, because its indexing scheme is relatively inefficient. The point is that you need to know how different applications scale with increased use. The vendors of the main applications you will use should be able to provide useful data in this regard.

MEETING NETWORK NEEDS

Once you complete your assessment (by this point, you're probably sick of the assessment process!) you can then start working on finding ways to meet all the needs you've identified. This is largely a holistic process and is not worked through by following a series of steps and ending up with a single answer, like an equation. Instead, you should start by mapping out the various parts of the network, considering the three main topics discussed next, and "build a picture" of the network design. The design you create will incorporate all you learned during the assessment process, taking into account your experience and the advice you get to devise a concrete design that results in an equipment list, specifications, and a configuration.

Seeking criticism of your design from other network professionals, who may have valuable experience that you can then factor into your design, is important. No single networking professional exists who has seen and had to cope with all possible design needs, so you want to combine the advice of as many seasoned people as you can.

Choosing Network Type

You probably want to start the design by choosing a network type. This should be a relatively straightforward decision, based on the overall bandwidth requirements for the network. For most new networks, you almost certainly will decide to use one of the flavors of Ethernet. By far, Ethernet is the most common type of network installed today and it's an easy default choice.

You also need to decide what level of Ethernet you need. For wiring to the desktop, you should choose either 10Base-T or 100Base-T. Seriously consider planning 100Base-T to the desktop. This is reliable, doesn't cost much more than 10Base-T, and provides plenty of capacity increase over time.

Choosing Network Structure

Next, decide how you plan to structure the network. In other words, how will you arrange and wire the various hubs, switches, and routers the network needs? This is probably the trickiest thing to determine because it's hard to predict how much data must flow from any given set of nodes to any other set of nodes. Still, you should have estimates based on your assessment work that will help. If you can identify expected heavy traffic patterns, you should also draw the network with these patterns indicated to help you sort it out. Remember the following tips:

▼   Ethernet's CDMA/CD collision handling means an Ethernet network will only handle about one third of its rated speed. In other words, a 10Base-T segment, which is rated at 10Mbps, will handle about 3.3Mbps in practice. The same holds true for 100Base-T, which will handle about 33Mbps of actual data before starting to degrade.

■   Whenever possible, use "home run" wiring for all nodes to a single wiring closet or server room. Doing so enables you to change the network structure more easily (for example, break segments into smaller segments) as needs change.

■   Except in the smallest networks, plan on a network backbone to which the hubs connect. An Ethernet switch rather than a nonswitching hub should handle the backbone, so each hub constitutes a single segment or collision domain. You still must plan to keep each segment's traffic below the Ethernet saturation point, but this structure will give you plenty of flexibility to meet this goal.

■   These days, Ethernet switches are becoming inexpensive enough that you can actually use them as hubs. It's not at all unreasonable using current hardware to wire everything at 100Base-T using only switches, and it's not much more expensive than using a combination of hubs and switches.

■   The physical building may dictate how you structure your network. For example, a building larger than 200 meters in any dimension probably means you won't be able to employ a home-run wiring scheme for all your nodes because twisted-pair Ethernet usually only reaches 100 meters (that includes having to route around building obstructions, patch cables, and other things that make the actual cable distance longer than you might measure on a map of the building).

■ For multifloor buildings that are too big for a home-run wiring scheme, consider running the backbone vertically from floor to floor and then have a wiring closet on each floor that contains the hubs to service that floor's nodes. The wiring from the closet on each floor then fans out to each of the nodes on that floor.

■ Consider running the backbone speed at ten times the hub/desktop network speed. If you're using 10Base-T hubs to connect to the desktop computers, plan on a 100Base-T backbone. If you're using 100Base-T to the desktop, consider one of the emerging gigabit Ethernet solutions for the backbone.

■ Most of the time, most nodes do the majority of their communication to one or two servers on the network. If you are planning department-specific servers or if you can identify patterns like this, make sure each server is on the same segment as the nodes it primarily serves.

■ If your servers tend not to be assigned to support departments and, instead, support the entire company, make sure the servers are directly connected to the backbone's Ethernet switch.

■ If you have any high bandwidth users, keep them on a separate segment from the rest of the network and consider upgrading the speed of that segment to 100Mbps or 1,000Mbps if they need it.

▲ As you start to implement the network, carefully watch the ratio of collision packets to data packets. If the number of collisions on any segment climb to 5 to 7 percent of the total number of packets, performance is starting to suffer; you need to investigate the cause and find a way to get this ratio down. This is usually done by breaking the segment into smaller pieces, assuming a way doesn't exist to reduce the amount of traffic by another means.

Choosing Servers

When choosing servers for a network, start by knowing what network operating system you will use. For PC-centric networks, the decision is usually between Novell NetWare 5 and Windows 2000 Server. Whenever possible, avoid using both, because supporting two NOS systems makes the management of the servers much more difficult. You're better off compromising on a single NOS platform than supporting both.

Next, list the various network services your servers must provide. You need to look for efficient ways to host these various services on your servers, balancing a number of factors:

▼ All else being equal, using more small servers to host fewer services each is more reliable (individually) than using fewer large servers to host many services.

■ Conversely, having more small servers increases your chance of having a server fail at any given time.

■ Using more small servers is more expensive and requires more maintenance than using fewer large servers.

▲ If you plan to use more than one server, consider which services should be redundant on another server or how you plan to deal with the failure of any server.

Using your assessment information, you can easily determine how much storage capacity your servers will need. However, it's much harder to know how capable each server should be in terms of processor power, installed RAM, and other features, such as bus configuration. For these specifications, you need to rely on the advice of the NOS vendor and the manufacturer of the servers you are considering. Fortunately, both Microsoft and Novell have published tests and recommendations for sizing servers given different service and user loads. Many first-tier server manufacturers also have such data to help you choose an actual server model and its specifications.

CHAPTER SUMMARY

Designing an entire network can be extremely complex. Even in an entire book devoted to network design, no way exists to cover the subject in sufficient depth to make you an expert on network design. If you are in the enviable position of designing a network, your best bet is to start with the framework described in this chapter and to use other resources to answer specific questions. Many resources exist to help you do this, ranging from books devoted to network design, server management, network performance tuning, and specific NOS management, to consultants experienced with similar networks, and the various vendors you are working with on any planned purchases. In fact, so many resources exist to help you accomplish this job, you may have trouble deciding which advice to follow!

Always remember to leave some escape hatches in any network design, so you can respond quickly to new or changed requirements, many of which will occur while you're finalizing the design. The good news is, if you follow the advice in this chapter and the rest of the book, along with the other resources mentioned, it's a safe bet you'll end up with a solid, expandable, maintainable network design that meets the needs of the company and of which you can be proud.

CHAPTER 12

Installing and Setting Up NetWare 5

NetWare is perhaps the most mature network operating system (NOS) available today. While it is surpassed in some areas by Windows 2000 Server, overall it is a superior file and print server. Moreover, many add-ons are available that allow NetWare 5 to meet virtually all network server needs. The maturity of the NetWare product line ensures it will meet your NOS needs and that many additional resources are available to support and extend the functionality of NetWare.

In this chapter, you learn how to install NetWare 5 in a basic configuration. Installing NetWare 5 consists of preparing for the installation with a variety of pre-installation checks. Then, you perform the actual installation, providing necessary information that the installation process needs. Finally, you test the installation by having a client computer log into the server properly and perform some basic network duties. All these steps are described in detail in this chapter.

NOTE: Novell sells a special three-user demonstration version of NetWare 5 for a nominal fee that covers the media and shipping. Purchasing this demonstration version is an excellent idea to practice setting up NetWare 5 and learning how to administer it. Details about purchasing a demonstration copy can be found at www.novell.com.

UNDERSTANDING NETWARE 5

NetWare 5 is a dedicated NOS, as opposed to a nondedicated NOS like Windows 2000 Server. The difference is that you can't do actual work on a NetWare server; it exists purely to do the jobs it was designed to do. Windows 2000, on the other hand, enables you to perform end-user tasks like running Microsoft Word or running other applications. If you are building a peer-to-peer network, you would not use NetWare 5 because various versions of Windows 2000 would be better suited to building a secure peer-to-peer network.

The upshot of using a dedicated NOS is that it is dedicated to being a server, and it will be more reliable overall than a nondedicated NOS, all else being equal. While NetWare 5 has not been available long enough for long-term experience, it is not uncommon to find NetWare 3.x or 4.x servers that run for many months at a time (even years) without requiring a restart or experiencing any hangs or other problems.

NetWare 5 is itself an operating system, one dedicated to network server tasks. It does not run "on top of" another OS. Because NetWare 5 only performs server duties, it is better optimized to provide the best possible performance in this role. In fact, on equivalent hardware, NetWare 5 will outperform Windows 2000 Server for most server tasks. Possibly more important (for some networks), is that NetWare 5 performs nicely on hardware you would not want to use with Windows 2000 Server. Its RAM and disk requirements are lower and it will squeeze more performance out of any given processor than its competitors.

NetWare 5 includes a powerful directory service called *Novell Directory Services* (NDS). NDS is analogous to Microsoft's Active Directory, but it has been available for a much longer time and its maturity shows. Because the benefits of a directory service emerge when it can interact with different network services, NDS is available on many platforms, including UNIX and Windows NT. (Presumably a version of NDS for Windows 2000 will be available when Windows 2000 ships.)

Historically, NetWare has been based on the IPX network protocol originally developed by Novell and loosely based on the Xerox XNS protocol. (Chapter 5 contains more information on various network protocols.) With NetWare 5, however, Novell has designed the NOS to support TCP/IP fully, which has become the predominant network protocol standard. NetWare 5 still supports IPX, but you can easily deploy a TCP/IP-only network using NetWare 5.

Another new feature of NetWare 5 (relative to earlier NetWare releases) is the new Novell Storage Services (NSS), which dramatically improves NetWare's capability to handle large and numerous disk volumes. NSS supports billions (yes, *billions*) of files, any of which can be up to 8TB in size. (8TB is 8 million megabytes.) More important, NSS volumes mount much faster than volumes in earlier versions of NetWare. NSS volumes mount in seconds, rather than minutes. Older versions of NetWare used to take 15–30 minutes to mount large volumes. Novell demonstrated a 1TB NSS volume containing a billion files mounting in under ten seconds. The improvements embodied in NSS dramatically improve the availability and recoverability of NetWare servers.

PREPARING FOR INSTALLATION

Before installing any NOS, getting your ducks in a row before you begin is vital. This entails ensuring the computer on which you will run the NOS is fully compatible with it, making sure the computer meets the minimum requirements, testing the computer, and surveying the appropriate settings for the server. The following sections discuss these steps.

Checking Hardware Compatibility

While you can typically install a NOS on just about any computer that meets the minimum requirements, making sure the hardware you want to use has been certified to be used with your NOS is important. Failing to do this can cause many problems, ranging from occasional incompatibilities, being unable to complete the NOS installation, or even loss of data due to corruption of NOS data (both on-disk and in network packets). In short, it pays to make sure your hardware is compatible and you should always do so.

Two sources of information exist for compatibility with NetWare 5: Novell and the maker of the hardware you plan to use. Generally, check Novell's hardware compatibility list first. If the hardware you want to use is not yet listed, check with its manufacturer, who typically can tell you what stage of testing the hardware has completed.

You can view Novell's "Yes, Tested and Approved" bulletins at http://developer. novell.com/infosys/bulletn.htm. Once the page loads, click NetWare 5 and then click specific hardware categories.

Checking Hardware Configuration

Sizing server hardware correctly is important. Too much and you're wasting money. Too little and you're again wasting money because you have to replace or add capability to meet your needs. Chapter 9 discusses different approaches to sizing servers. In any case, however, you need to make sure the server meets the minimum requirements for the NOS you will use. For NetWare 5, these are the minimum requirements:

▼ Pentium 100 MHz or greater processor

■ 64MB of RAM

■ 50MB primary partition to boot DOS and the NetWare kernel

■ 550MB space for a SYS partition to hold the rest of the NetWare NOS and its tools

■ Additional disk space for user and application files

■ Network card certified for NetWare 5

■ CD-ROM from which to install NetWare. If you want to use the bootable CD-ROM feature of NetWare to perform the initial setup, the CD-ROM must comply with the El Torito specification.

▲ MS-DOS version 3.3 or greater (but not the MS-DOS included with Windows 9x) or Caldera DOS. (DOS is needed to boot the server initially, after which NetWare takes over the system.)

The previous are the minimums specified by Novell. They are reasonable minimums, with the possible exception of RAM requirements. All NOS systems run better with more RAM and NetWare 5 is no exception. Consider installing 128MB or 256MB of RAM, particularly if the server will host more than 5 to 10GB of disk storage. Also, as with any NOS, faster processors and disk subsystems can benefit overall performance.

Testing the Server Hardware

You've found all your server hardware listed as Novell Yes, Tested and Approved, you've made sure your server is adequately sized, you've purchased it, and you have your shiny new NetWare 5 CD-ROM sitting there, all ready to be installed. Time to start yet? Not quite. Before installing any NOS, particularly on a server that will be used for production, make sure you carry out hardware testing (also called *burn-in*) on the server before installing NetWare 5. Computer hardware tends to be most reliable after it has been running for a while. In other words, failures tend to happen when equipment is new and the chance of hardware failure decreases rapidly during the first 90 days. Because of this, testing new servers for at least a week (two weeks is better) is a good idea before proceeding to install the NOS. Doing so can help provoke any early failures in the equipment during a time when they're easy to fix and won't affect any users or the network.

You test the hardware using diagnostic software that should have come with the server or is available from the maker of the server. Most such diagnostics software enable you to choose which components of the system are tested and enable you to test them in an endless loop, logging any discovered errors to a floppy disk or to the screen. You should focus the tests on the following components:

▼ Processor(s)

■ System board components (interrupt controllers, DMA controllers, and other motherboard support circuitry)

■ RAM

▲ Disk surfaces

TIP: Server testing software often enables you to choose between nondestructive and destructive testing of the disks. (*Destructive* means any data on the disks is erased during the testing.) Destructive testing is best to discover any errors on the disks and this is one reason you want to carry out this testing before you install your NOS.

If the diagnostic software lets you do so, you can usually safely skip testing components like the keyboard or the display. Your primary concern is that the unit continues to run properly when it is under load for an extended period of time. You also want to make sure the RAM is working properly and no bad sectors show up on the disks during testing.

Surveying the Server

Before beginning the installation of NetWare 5, make sure you have all the information you need during the installation. Nothing is more frustrating than getting half-way through an installation, only to discover you need to cancel the installation because you forgot to gather some important data. In particular, make sure you know the following before starting:

▼ The disk controller model and its settings for IRQ, DMA, and I/O port. You should also know what slot number it occupies.

■ The configuration of the disks, including their sizes, addresses (if SCSI-based), and whether any hardware RAID has already been set up with the controller.

■ The network interface card model and its settings for IRQ, DMA, I/O port, and what slot number it occupies.

■ Models and settings for any other installed cards in the server. For each one, make sure you have its IRQ, DMA, I/O port, and slot number settings.

▲ For a multiprocessor server, the maker of the motherboard.

For all the previous, you should also have the newest versions of their NetWare 5 drivers. Some of these may be found posted on Novell's Web site and some may only be found on the manufacturer's Web site. In any case, don't rely on the drivers packaged with NetWare because newer versions may correct problems discovered in the interim. Similarly, you should examine any available patches from Novell for NetWare 5 prior to installing the NOS and you may want to apply those patches immediately following the installation of NetWare 5.

INSTALLING NETWARE 5

You can run the installation for NetWare 5 several ways. You can set up the computer to boot DOS (with CD-ROM support) and then run the installation program from the CD-ROM. You can also install NetWare 5 over an existing network by copying the CD-ROM contents to another server. You then install the NetWare client for DOS onto the server you're setting up and then map a drive to the location of the CD-ROM files and run the installation from that location. Finally, if the computer supports it, you can boot the NetWare 5 CD-ROM and proceed from there. For this example, the first option will be shown.

Your first step is to set up a primary boot partition on the boot hard disk, which is approximately 50MB large. The remaining disk space needn't be partitioned; it will be partitioned during the installation process and use NetWare partitions rather than DOS partitions. Set up the 50MB boot partition so it boots DOS, along with CD-ROM support for the CD-ROM drive.

After booting the server to DOS, change directories to the CD-ROM drive letter and run the INSTALL.BAT file found in the root of the NetWare 5 CD-ROM. Installation proceeds from there and walks you through various steps required to complete the setup process.

NOTE: If you installed earlier versions of NetWare, you'll be impressed with the improvements Novell has made to the NetWare 5 installation process. It has been simplified considerably and now most common hardware is automatically detected.

As the installation begins, you first select the language you plan to install and then you must read and agree to the license agreement. Pressing F10 at the license screen acknowledges your acceptance of the license.

Next, you are prompted to choose whether you are setting up a new server or upgrading an existing server. For this example, a new server is selected. You are also prompted for the directory from which the basic NetWare files will load, with the default set to C:\NWSERVER. Accept the default directory and choose Continue to proceed.

Next, you choose regional settings for the server, including the appropriate country code, code page, and keyboard type. Generally, the defaults here will be correct but, if they aren't, you can easily change them. Choose Continue to proceed. You are then prompted to select the mouse type and video type for the server. Make the appropriate selections and choose Continue.

Next, you are prompted to choose some important modules for the installation. The first of these is called the Platform Support Module. These modules are used to add support for multiprocessing systems. If you are setting up NetWare 5 on a multiprocessor server, check with the maker of the server for the Platform Support Module you should use. You also will be prompted to select a HotPlug Support Module. This adds support for HotPlug devices, such as removable hard disks. If your server is configured with such devices, make sure to check the server's documentation for how support for those devices should be installed. Finally, on this same setup screen, you are also prompted to choose the drivers for the storage adapters. Generally, these will be automatically detected but, in some cases, you may have to choose additional drivers. For example, on the system used for prototyping this chapter, the built-in IDE hard disk drivers were selected, but not the SCSI driver for the CD-ROM. Adding the necessary support was easy, however, and the drivers for the Adaptec card in question were available as part of the setup process. In any event, you should carefully check the storage adapter device drivers to ensure all appropriate adapters are shown and have drivers selected for them. Choosing Continue moves to the next screen.

The next screen in the installation prompts you to choose storage devices, which are the devices connected to the storage adapters. All storage devices need appropriate drivers loaded. Included are drivers for IDE drives, SCSI drives, CD-ROM drives, and even many tape drives. You are also prompted to choose a network board, which should be automatically detected and shown. If not, change this selection and choose from the available boards listed. After choosing the storage device drivers and the network board drivers, choose Continue to proceed.

Next, you will be prompted to create a NetWare volume into which NetWare 5 will be installed. (Remember, only the files needed to begin booting NetWare are located on the 50MB boot partition. Another 350-750MB will be located on the first NetWare partition.) By default, the system will offer to create a SYS volume that will use up the remainder of the disk space on the primary drive. You may wish to select a smaller SYS partition size, leaving other space available for other volumes. Many NetWare administrators keep their SYS volumes relatively small and prefer to load only NetWare to the SYS volume. Other applications and data files get loaded onto other partitions. At any rate, the SYS volume should be at least 550MB in size. I recommend 1-2GB to allow plenty of room for growth and to allow enough room to add additional Novell products to NetWare, if you wish. Make the appropriate selections and choose Continue to proceed.

Once the preceding selections have been made, NetWare 5 is copied to the hard disk. This process may take from five to ten minutes. Afterwards, the installation process continues in graphical mode and you need to make some additional choices.

The first question to answer once the installation starts in graphical mode is the name for the server. Choose a name 2 to 47 characters long. I recommend a short name because it simplifies things. In this example, the server name OMH is used (short for Osborne/McGraw-Hill).

TIP: You may want to number your server names because you will typically add more servers as time goes by. Having server names like OMH-1, OMH-2, and so forth keeps the server names consistent. Or, you can choose some other scheme that fits the environment at your company. Some people name their servers after cartoon characters, Greek mythology characters, whatever. My main recommendation is to keep the name as short as possible because, as the administrator, you'll have to type the name quite frequently.

Next, you have the opportunity to create additional NetWare volumes, if you wish, using the remaining free disk space on the system. Created volumes can either be traditional NetWare volumes or the new NSS volumes. NSS volumes have significant advantages; however, they also have some limitations. NSS volumes cannot be used by NetWare 5 for disk duplexing, disk mirroring, disk striping, transaction tracking, or hosting FTP data. In many cases, most of these features will be set up on your disk controller anyway and performed by hardware, so these limitations may not matter to you.

After creating any additional required volumes, you are then prompted to select the network protocols the server will support. You can choose TCP/IP, IPX, or both. If you select TCP/IP, you need to provide the server's IP address, subnet mask, and the address for the network router.

Finally, the installation will prompt you either to set up the server so it joins an existing NDS tree on the network or to create a new NDS tree on the network. Because you're probably installing NetWare 5 as the first and primary server, you would choose to create a new tree. You will be prompted to assign a name for the NDS tree, the context for the tree, and to set an Administrator login name and password. The context for the tree defines the organization for the tree, as well as an organizational unit for the tree (only the organization name is required). For a single-server network, these values are not important. You can simply use a variation of your company name. For more complicated networks, you should consult a book that discusses planning an NDS tree.

After completing the preceding steps, the server is restarted, at which point it is functional and ready to accept a connection from the Administrator account.

CONFIGURING A NETWARE 5 CLIENT

For Windows 9*x* or NT clients, you have two choices for what network client software you can use to connect to the NetWare server: the NetWare software included with Windows 9*x* and NT, or the Novell client software. In this section, setting up the NetWare client software is shown.

Choosing which client software to use is not a trivial decision because whatever you choose will most likely be used by all computers on your network. The Novell software is far more powerful than the Microsoft client software, at the cost of memory and disk space requirements. The chief advantages to the Microsoft client software is it doesn't use as much memory and it's contained on the Windows CD-ROM.

Installing the Novell client software is straightforward. Inserting the Novell client CD-ROM into a Windows 9*x* machine's CD-ROM drive starts the installation process. You will see the splash screen shown in Figure 12-1. Click the language you want to install.

You are then prompted for the operating system for which you want to install the client software. Choose the one appropriate for the client computer (such as Windows 95/98) and click it. Then, choose the Install Novell Client option and click it.

You are then prompted to choose either a Typical or Custom installation, as shown in Figure 12-2. Choose Typical and click Install to continue.

The installation then proceeds. You may be prompted for your operating system CD-ROM during the process. Once the copying of the necessary files completes, you are offered the opportunity to enter in the default Preferred Tree and Context. You should do so, entering the appropriate information from the completion of the server setup in the preceding section. Figure 12-3 illustrates the dialog box you should complete.

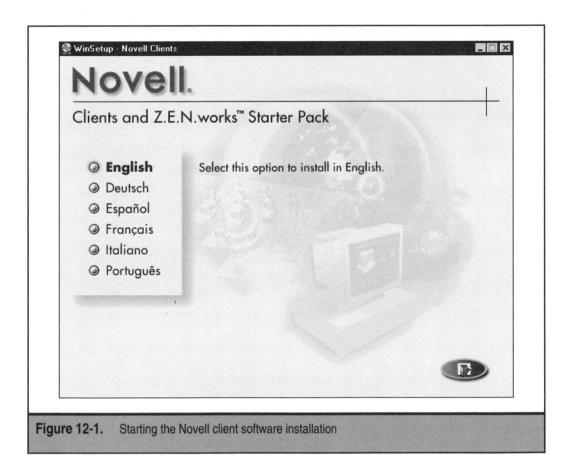

Figure 12-1.   Starting the Novell client software installation

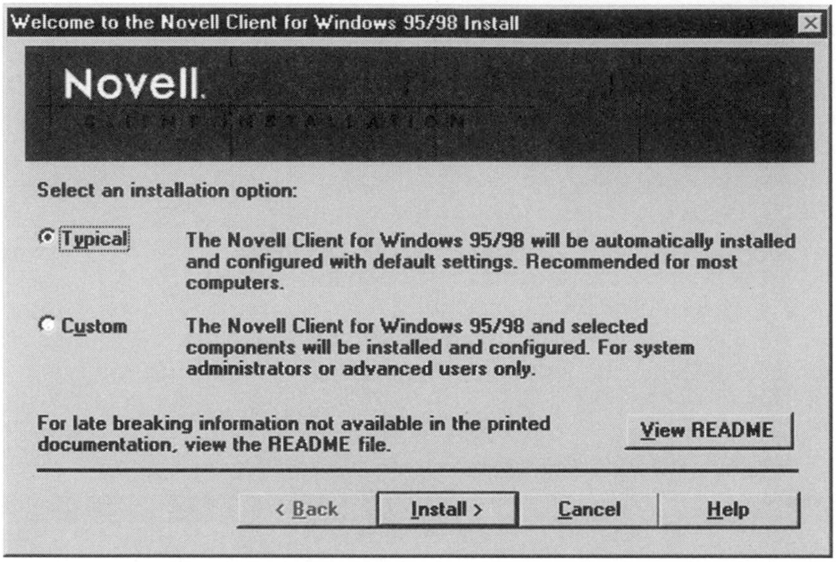

Figure 12-2. Choosing a Typical installation

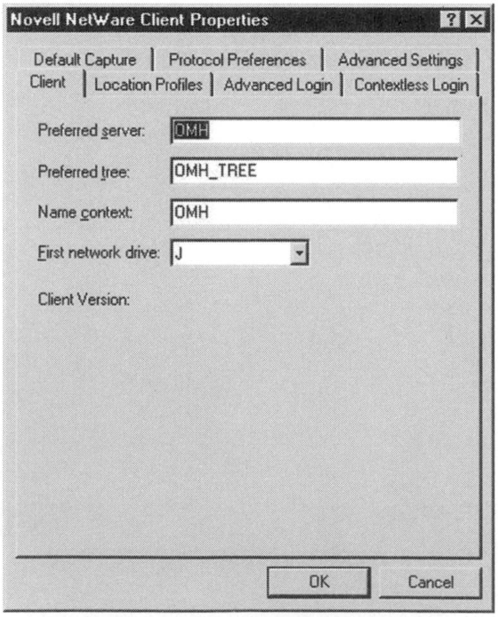

Figure 12-3. Entering a default server, tree, and context

After entering in the default login information, some additional files are copied to your computer, after which you are prompted to reboot the system. You need to do so before you can log into the server. After restarting, you will see a Novell login prompt. Supply the administrative login name and password you set during the initial installation.

After logging in, confirm connectivity to the server by opening Windows Explorer. You should see the SYS volume on the server mapped to drive Z:. Alternately, you can open Network Neighborhood and you should see the NetWare resources appear. You can browse the server and you should see all the default folders located on the SYS partition, such as ETC, PUBLIC, and SYS. Figure 12-4 shows Windows Explorer with the Z: drive selected, as well as Network Neighborhood expanded.

CHAPTER SUMMARY

As you have seen in this chapter, setting up a NetWare 5 server is a relatively straightforward task, at least for simple servers within simple networks. For more complex needs, you definitely want to consult a book dedicated to NetWare 5, which will contain many

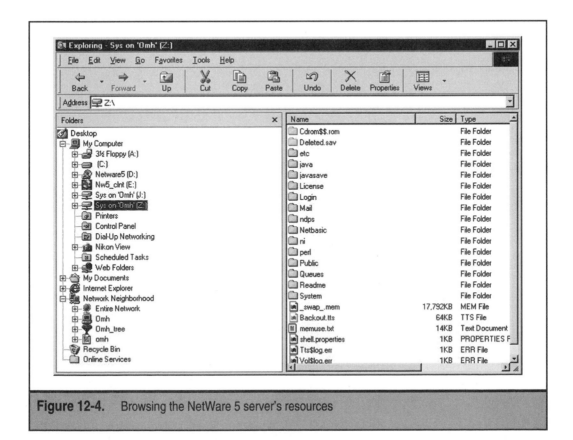

Figure 12-4.   Browsing the NetWare 5 server's resources

more details about different installation options, hardware configurations, and planning for NDS trees in a complex network.

The next chapter shows you how basic administrative tasks are performed on a NetWare 5 server, most of which can be run from either the server console or from a connected client computer logged in with administrative privileges.

CHAPTER 13

Administering NetWare: The Basics

etting up a server with NetWare 5 is easy. While many advanced configurations can certainly become difficult and you should always carefully plan any server setup, the process is straightforward. Any mistakes you make can be corrected later, before the server is brought online. In any case, performing the setup is fairly easy and, at most, you usually only have to set up a particular NOS a few times. Where you spend most of your time with an NOS like NetWare 5 is in the administration. This chapter covers basic administration, including the following:

▼ User accounts

■ Security groups

■ Drive mappings

▲ NetWare volume permissions

You accomplish all these tasks using an application called *NetWare Administrator*, which is not installed with NetWare by default. To install NetWare Administrator, use the Novell Client Software CD-ROM and install the Z.E.N. Works starter pack, which installs the NetWare Administrator (for the client type you are installing) onto the NetWare server. For Win32 clients like Windows 9*x* or Windows NT, you can find NetWare Administrator in the \PUBLIC\WIN32 folder on the SYS: volume after installing the Z.E.N. Works starter pack. The program name is NWADMIN32.EXE.

WORKING WITH USER ACCOUNTS

Usually the first thing you need to do with a freshly installed copy of NetWare 5 is to establish security accounts for the network's users. This is usually done using NetWare Administrator. Figure 13-1 shows NetWare Administrator open.

TIP: Some administrative tasks you normally do in NetWare Administrator can also be done using the new ConsoleOne Java-based administration tool. One benefit to ConsoleOne is it can be run on the NetWare server using the server's Java graphical interface and it can also be run on a Java-capable client, like Windows 98. ConsoleOne is still being enhanced, however, and it does not yet support all the features found in NetWare Administrator. For this reason, you should generally use NetWare Administrator, even if you want to use ConsoleOne occasionally. (At some point in the future, ConsoleOne may come to replace NetWare Administrator, so learning its capabilities is a good idea.)

NetWare Administrator is a comprehensive tool that enables you to administer nearly any object that can exist in an NDS tree. In Figure 13-1, you see a tree view of the current NDS tree showing all the objects that exist in the tree. Each different type of object has its own icon representing the type of object. The objects shown in this figure are the standard objects created with a basic NetWare 5 installation and you needn't modify most of the default objects.

To become proficient at administering computer networks, you need to develop the ability to visualize what a network is doing at any given time. This kind of visualization is essential in network administration.

For example, the concept of Ethernet's CSMA/CD technology can be visualized as a nugget (actually a packet) of data that enters the cable, travels along the wire, and then is received at the other end. In reality, the electrical signal reaches the server at the speed of light and reception begins at the destination before the originating workstation finishes transmission. Nevertheless, visualizing "nuggets" of information can be essential to understanding what happens when, for example, two workstations send packets that collide. Visualization gives you useful analogies with which to understand networks and troubleshoot network problems. In fact, the best network professionals visualize concepts intuitively.

The following blueprints illustrate some basic network topologies. You can use these blueprints as a starting point to build your own visual images of how networks operate. As you read through the book, think about other ways to visualize networking concepts such as hardware configurations.

Bus Topology

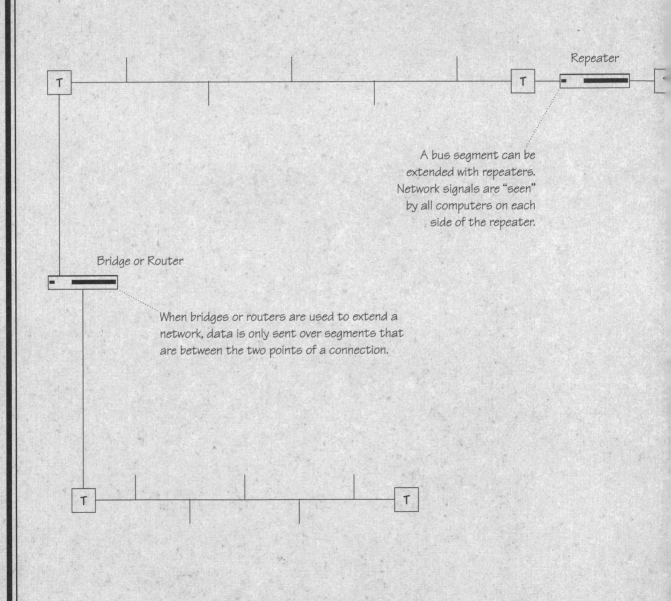

Repeater

A bus segment can be extended with repeaters. Network signals are "seen" by all computers on each side of the repeater.

Bridge or Router

When bridges or routers are used to extend a network, data is only sent over segments that are between the two points of a connection.

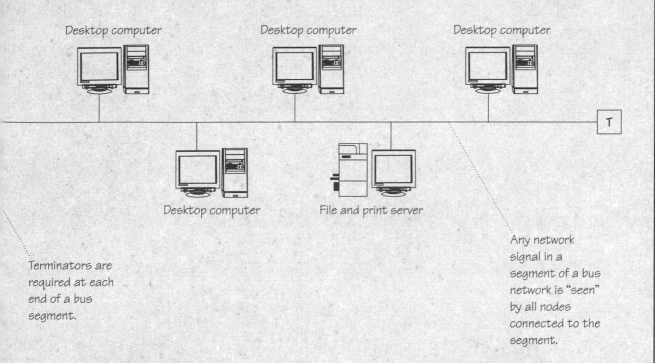

Desktop computer

Desktop computer

Desktop computer

T

Desktop computer

File and print server

Terminators are required at each end of a bus segment.

Any network signal in a segment of a bus network is "seen" by all nodes connected to the segment.

The bus topology used to be the mainstay for wiring LANs, and has been around for many years. Its chief advantages are the low cost for initial wiring and its generally good performance. Its chief drawbacks are low reliability (because a break anywhere in a segment takes down at least an entire segment) and greater difficulty in balancing network traffic on the different segments.

Ring Topology: Logical View

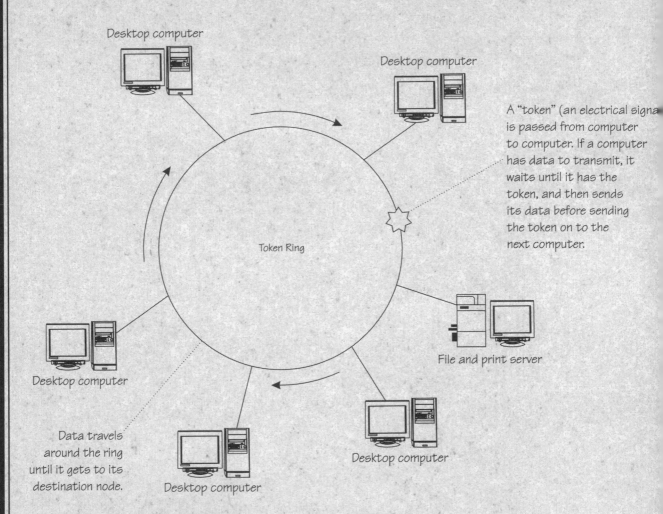

Desktop computer

Desktop computer

A "token" (an electrical signal) is passed from computer to computer. If a computer has data to transmit, it waits until it has the token, and then sends its data before sending the token on to the next computer.

Token Ring

File and print server

Desktop computer

Data travels around the ring until it gets to its destination node.

Desktop computer

Desktop computer

Desktop computer

The ring topology is commonly used for Token Ring networks. Its chief advantages are improved reliability compared to bus topology networks, and a greater ability to predict and handle varying network traffic loads. Its chief disadvantage is that it is generally slower than Ethernet-based bus and ring topologies.

Ring Topology: Physical View

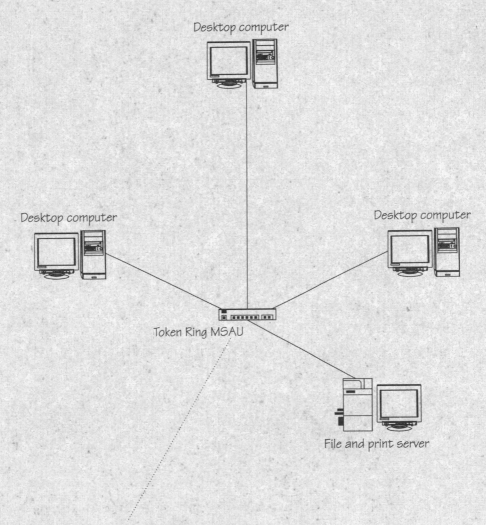

Desktop computer

Desktop computer

Desktop computer

Token Ring MSAU

File and print server

While ring topologies are electrically a ring, physically they're wired like a star, with each computer's network cable running into a central MSAU unit.

Star Topology

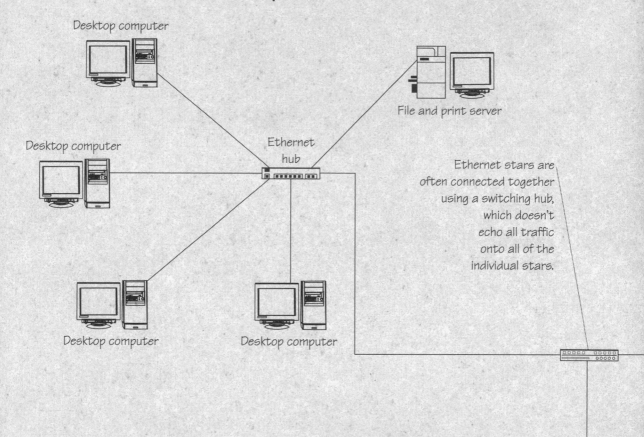

Desktop computer

Desktop computer

File and print server

Ethernet hub

Desktop computer

Desktop computer

Ethernet stars are often connected together using a switching hub, which doesn't echo all traffic onto all of the individual stars.

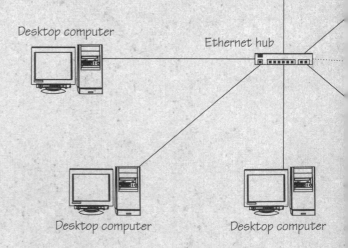

Desktop computer

Ethernet hub

Desktop computer

Desktop computer

The star topology is the standard for wiring LANs today. While a star is electrically the same as a bus, the hubs and switches used on a star eliminate the reliability problems seen with bus networks. The only disadvantage is that, compared to a pure bus topology, a star topology is more expensive to wire and requires more support hardware. Still, the advantages of the star topology far outweigh the additional cost.

Desktop computer

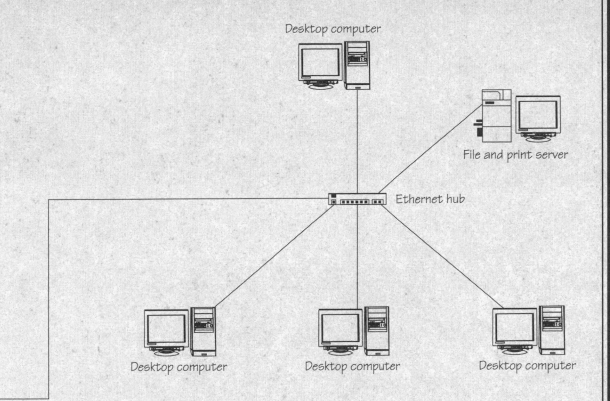

File and print server

Ethernet hub

Desktop computer   Desktop computer   Desktop computer

ile and print server

Desktop computer

In a standard star topology Ethernet network using standard
Ethernet hubs, each hub and its nodes acts like a bus topology
electrically, where the signals sent by one node are "seen" by
all other nodes connected to the hub. However, hubs are smart
enough to disconnect any misbehaving nodes so that other nodes
can continue working normally.

The OSI Networking Model

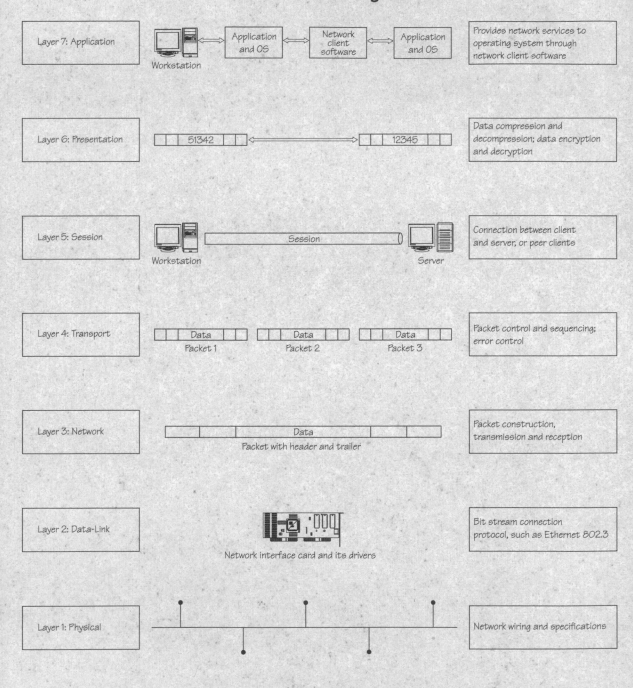

Layer 7: Application		Provides network services to operating system through network client software
Layer 6: Presentation		Data compression and decompression; data encryption and decryption
Layer 5: Session		Connection between client and server, or peer clients
Layer 4: Transport		Packet control and sequencing; error control
Layer 3: Network		Packet construction, transmission and reception
Layer 2: Data-Link		Bit stream connection protocol, such as Ethernet 802.3
Layer 1: Physical		Network wiring and specifications

Layer 7: Application — Workstation, Application and OS, Network client software, Application and OS

Layer 6: Presentation — 51342 ⟷ 12345

Layer 5: Session — Workstation, Session, Server

Layer 4: Transport — Data Packet 1, Data Packet 2, Data Packet 3

Layer 3: Network — Data, Packet with header and trailer

Layer 2: Data-Link — Network interface card and its drivers

Layer 1: Physical

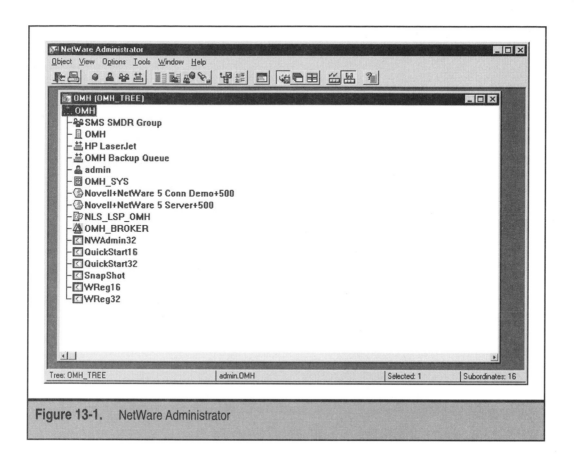

Figure 13-1. NetWare Administrator

To create a new user account, access the Object menu and choose Create. You see the New Object dialog box, shown here, which prompts you to choose a type of object to create:

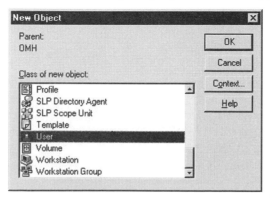

Scroll down the list until you see User, select it, and then click OK.

> *TIP:*   The toolbar in NetWare Administrator has a Create New User button that quickly gets you to the
> Create New User dialog box.

In the Create User dialog box, shown next, you establish the basic facts for the new user
account, including whether you want to define additional properties for the new user.

For now, to keep things simple, just create the user by completing the following fields:

▼ **Login Name**   Enter the name the user will use to log in to the network.
Usually, this is the user's first name, followed by the first initial of his or her
last name (for smaller networks), or the user's last name followed by the first
initial of his or her first name (for larger networks).

■ **Last Name**   Enter the user's real last name. This field must be filled to create
the account.

▲ **Create Home Directory**   Choosing this option causes a directory to be
created on the server that will be designated as the user's home directory on
the network and into which the user can save personal files on the network.
When you select this option, you then need to designate a location in which
the user's home directory will be created. Do this by clicking the button, which
looks like a small directory tree, beneath the Create Home Directory checkbox.
Then select the network location in which the home directory will be created.
Most often, administrators set up a directory on the server called \Homedirs
and then place all the users' home directories into that top-level directory
(otherwise, the root directory of whatever volume you use gets too cluttered).

In the example shown here, a directory called \Homedirs has already been established on the SYS: volume and this directory has been selected in the dialog box. Keeping users' home directories named the same as their user name is a good idea. Not only does this make it much easier to keep track of which users own which home directories, but you can take advantage of advanced login script commands to map the user's home directories automatically to a particular drive letter.

Once you have completed the previous fields, click the Create button to create the user account and you will return to the main NetWare Administrator screen. Now you should be able to see the new user object in the tree.

Modifying User Accounts

Obviously, the steps shown in the preceding section don't fully cover all the important settings you need for your user accounts. Nothing has been done, for example, to set the user's initial password, their password policies, or any of a host of other important settings you need to maintain for user accounts. You can access all these additional settings in the Create User dialog box by selecting the Define Additional Properties check box before clicking the Create button or you can access these settings directly for any user account.

To access the detailed settings for a user account, first select the account with which you want to work in the NDS tree display in NetWare Administrator. Then right-click the user name and choose Details from the pop-up menu. You see the User dialog box, as shown in Figure 13-2.

Along the right side of the dialog box, you can click the different buttons to access different types of settings for the account. Myriad settings and fields are available in this dialog box. This section discusses the most important and commonly needed settings.

NOTE: The different sections of the User dialog box are not really tabs like the tabs you see in Windows dialog boxes, but they work the same. To keep things simple, this chapter refers to these dialog box sections as *tabs*.

The first dialog box tab, Identification (shown in Figure 13-2), is where you can define additional information about the user, such as his or her full name, telephone number, address, and so forth. These settings do not impact the operation of the network at all, but they can be important to document the user account properly. These fields are primarily intended for your convenience; use them if you wish.

The second dialog box tab, Environment, shown in Figure 13-3, enables you to define what language the user will use. The available languages depend on which languages you have installed on the server and this language setting controls what language is presented to the user for network-specific dialog boxes. Another important field on the Environment tab is the Default Server field. For a single-server network, you needn't set this field. For a multiserver network, this should be the server the user primarily uses. When the user makes ambiguous network requests, such as requesting access to the SYS:

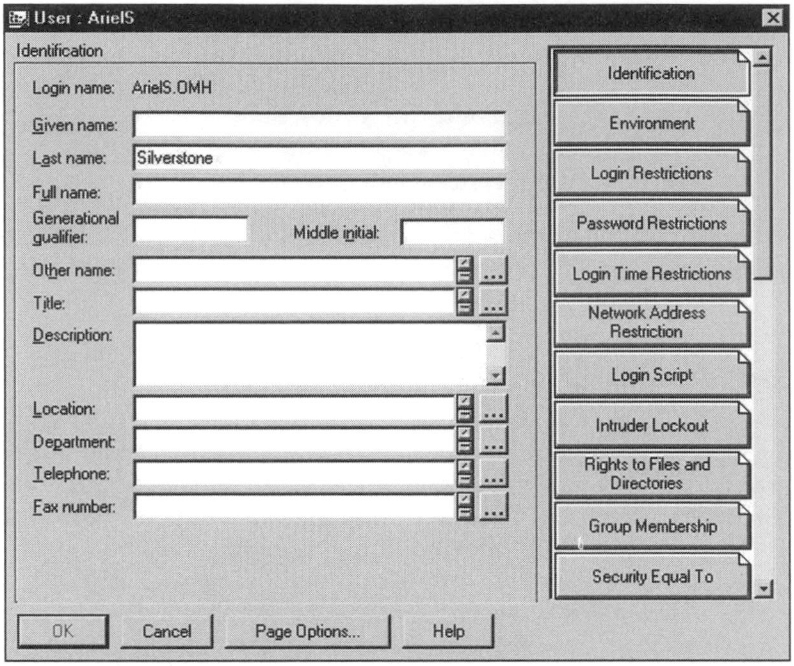

Figure 13-2. Using the User dialog box to set additional user settings

volume (most NetWare servers have SYS: volumes) the Default Server field is used to determine to which server the user is referring. Also on the Environment tab is the location for the user's home directory, which you can change if needed.

The Login Restrictions tab (see Figure 13-4) contains some important settings. The first of these is the Account Disabled setting, which enables you immediately to inactivate the account. Next, the Account Has Expiration Date check box enables you to define an expiration date, after which time the account will not function. Also, you can use the Limit Concurrent Connections field if you want the account only to be able to log into a certain number of computers at the same time.

One of the most important tabs for modifying a user account is the Password Restrictions tab, shown in Figure 13-5. On this tab, you can change a user's password and also set various policies regarding how the system enforces aspects of his or her password. The settings in this dialog box are as follows:

▼ **Allow User to Change Password**   Selecting this option allows users the right to change their password when they wish. Generally, you select this option for most users, although certain accounts should have this option disabled. For example, an account set up for a shared, centralized computer should have this cleared, so a user doesn't inadvertently change the password used.

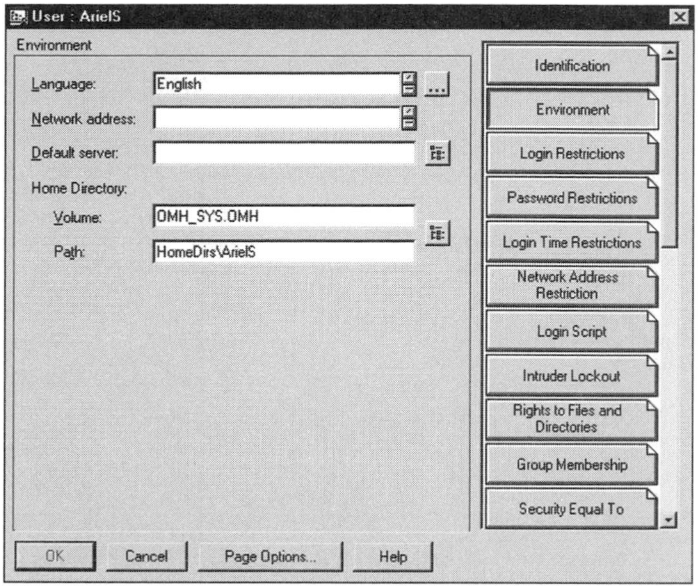

Figure 13-3. The Environment tab of the User dialog box

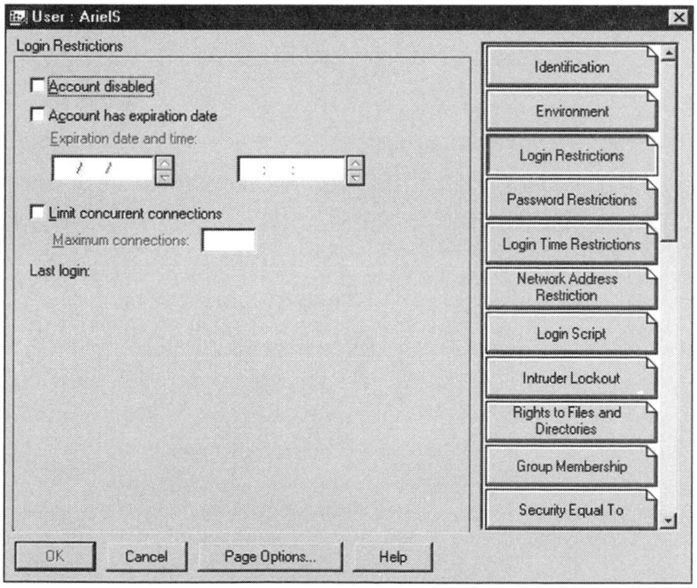

Figure 13-4. The Login Restrictions tab of the User dialog box

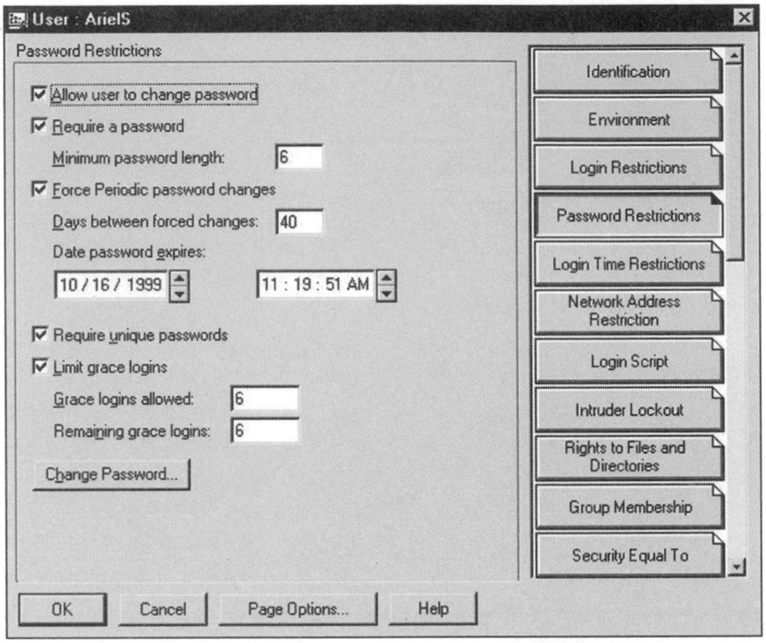

Figure 13-5. The Password Restrictions tab of the User dialog box

■ **Require a Password** While clearing this check box and setting up accounts that do not require passwords is possible, generally, this check box should always be selected so all accounts have at least rudimentary security on them.

■ **Minimum Password Length** If Require a Password is selected, then you can further set the minimum password length. The default password length in NetWare 5 is five characters. Most administrators increase this length to at least six or seven characters, however.

■ **Force Periodic Password Changes** Selecting this option causes the system to force the password on the account to be changed at intervals you specify, using the Days Between Forced Changes field. Requiring passwords to change periodically is a good idea, but the timeframe you choose depends on your security needs and the needs of the users. Choose a period that is too long and you increase the chance another user may inappropriately learn someone else's password. Set a period that is too short and your users may complain about always having to change their passwords. For general purposes, setting the number of days between 40 (NetWare 5's default) and 90 days is a good compromise between these two considerations.

■ **Date Password Expires** The date and time set in this box is normally determined by when the user last changed his or her password, and by how many days you have set for forced periodic changes. If necessary, you can override the date calculated and enter one of your own.

■ **Require Unique Passwords** Selecting this check box, which is recommended, causes the system to remember the last eight passwords used by the user and to deny them the ability to reuse any of those passwords. This keeps someone from reusing two alternate passwords—or even a single password—and so helps enforce periodic password changes.

▲ **Limit Grace Logins** When a password expires on the system, users are warned by the system and they are typically allowed some logins before their accounts become inactivated by the system. This is a helpful policy, as sometimes users aren't in a position to choose a new password at one particular login. Instead, setting the Grace Logins Allowed field to a reasonable number, like six, enables users to choose the best time to select a new password.

You can use the Login Time Restrictions tab either to allow or disallow certain login times. The Login Time Restrictions tab has a grid that enables you to choose times in half-hour increments for any day of the week. A grayed box in the grid means the user cannot be logged into the network during that time interval.

You can also restrict access by using the Network Address Restriction tab. By default, with no entries shown, the user account can log in from any network node. If you add nodes, however, the user can only log in from the defined nodes. Restricting access by network node is useful when you want to control certain user accounts carefully, which otherwise have broad access to the network. For example, you may have a computer you use for making backups of the network, which needs access to everything on the network to do its job. By restricting this account to the computer node that actually performs the backup, you can help ensure someone doesn't inappropriately gain access to the network using this account.

Login scripts are special programs, similar to DOS batch files, which execute whenever the user logs in. You can define a user-specific login script with the Login Script tab of the User dialog box. Login scripts can be set at various points in the network: By user, organization, user template, and default. You can use login script commands to perform startup tasks automatically for users, such as map network drives, display network information, or start programs. The details of login scripts are beyond the scope of this book, but they are an important topic, nonetheless. Login scripts are key to setting up a NetWare 5 server fully and to making administration as easy as possible. You can learn more about login scripts by consulting NetWare Administrator's help or with a book dedicated to NetWare 5 administration.

NetWare supports a security policy called *Intruder Detection*. How Intruder Detection works is, if someone tries to log into an account too many times in too short a time period using the wrong password, the system will lock out the account. Intruder Detection helps protect against someone trying to gain access to a valid account by guessing the password. Often valid users trip the Intruder Detection feature, however, usually after recently changing their password and trying to guess their own password. If this happens, you can use the Intruder Lockout tab to reactivate the account, to see when it was locked, and from what network address the last bad password attempt was tried.

Of all the remaining tabs, four are important for most administrative duties. These are the Rights to Files and Directories tab, the Group Membership tab, the Security Equal To tab, and the Security Equal to Me tab. The Rights to Files and Directories tab enables you to see and modify the rights the user account has to folders on specific volumes. By viewing this information in the User dialog box, you can see all the explicitly granted permissions in one place. The Group Membership tab is where you can add the user to a security group. (Security groups are discussed in more detail in the following section.) The last two tabs—the Security Equal To tab and the Security Equal to Me tab—enable you quickly to set a user's security to be equal to another, existing user's security or to grant another user security equivalent to the user being modified.

TIP: Keep an eye on the Security Equal to Me tab for the administrative account for the network. Someone hacking into a network will often circumvent security on a permanent basis by setting up an innocuous user account and then setting that account to have equal security to the administrative account. By periodically making sure that Security Equal to Me for the administrative account is blank, you can ensure this has not happened.

Many other available tabs are on the User dialog box, but most of these are unimportant to daily administration of a NetWare 5 network. Still, I urge you to explore these other tabs so you understand what other settings are available and could prove useful to you.

Deleting User Accounts

To delete a user account, right-click the user object in NetWare Administrator and choose Delete from the pop-up menu. The user and any security privileges they have been granted on the network will be removed.

TIP: Certain network sites with high-security requirements do not delete user accounts. Instead, they disable user accounts when a person leaves the company. The reason high-security sites do not delete user accounts is because they have a requirement never to confuse an audit trail by reusing a particular user name. While reusing a user name doesn't give the new user the same permissions as the old one, it does make auditing user activities more difficult. For most sites, deleting user accounts once you're sure they're no longer needed is perfectly adequate.

WORKING WITH SECURITY GROUPS

Most network operating systems support the concept of *security groups*, which are logical groupings of users for making security administration on the network easier. To use security groups, you first create the user accounts. Next, you can create groups of users that correspond to different security permissions on the network and you can make those users members of the groups, as appropriate. Then, you grant network permissions to the group, rather than to all the users in question.

For example, a collection of directories may exist that everyone who works in the Accounting department needs to access. Instead of having to grant permission to access all those directories to each user individually (in some cases, hundreds of users and hundreds of directories may exist!), you only have to grant permission to the group and then maintain the group's membership.

One of the powerful advantages to groups is, to give a new person the same permissions as the group, you only have to make the new person a member. To remove those permissions, just remove them from the group. Especially on larger networks, administrating group permissions makes your job *a lot* easier.

Creating Groups

Creating new groups in NetWare Administrator is easy. Start by selecting the organization container at the top of the tree, and then either click the Create a New Group Object icon on the toolbar or pull down the Object menu, choose Create, and then select Group in the New Object dialog box. Both methods result in the Create Group dialog box shown here:

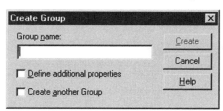

To create the group, all you must do is supply the name of the group and click the Create button. The group then appears in the NDS tree display in NetWare Administrator.

Maintaining Group Membership

Group membership can be maintained in either of two ways. You can either open the group object in NetWare Administrator and use its Members tab to add or remove members, or you can open an individual account's dialog box and use the Group Membership tab. Both methods are important to use.

When creating a new user in an existing network, you will often use that user's Group Membership tab to assign her or him to appropriate groups. Doing so with the user object makes sense because you can make all the group assignments at once. Figure 13-6 shows a user's Group Membership dialog box.

When creating a new group or when checking overall membership in a particular group, opening the group object and using its Members tab is usually much easier. You can add or remove multiple users using that one dialog box. Figure 13-7 shows a group's Members dialog box.

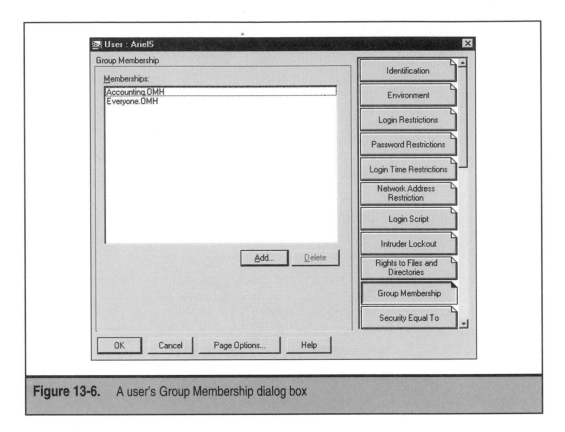

Figure 13-6. A user's Group Membership dialog box

MANAGING FILE SYSTEM ACCESS

Unlike Windows NT or Windows 2000, no need exists to set NetWare volumes as being shared for users to access them. All volumes on a NetWare server are shared, provided they are mounted on the server. The question is whether a particular user or group has access to a volume or any of its contents. If they have the requisite permissions, they can browse volumes and folders to which they have access and they can also map frequently used network volumes or folders to appear as local drive letters.

For Windows-based clients running the NetWare Client software, there are two ways to administer volume and folder security. First, as Administrator, using either Network Neighborhood or My Computer (for mapped drives), you can right-click a folder and enter its Properties dialog box. Some NetWare-specific tabs will be available. You can use the NetWare Rights tab to view and assign specific permissions for the folder in question, as shown in Figure 13-8.

The second method—the one primarily shown in this chapter—uses NetWare Administrator. The advantage to using NetWare Administrator is you can use it for permission assignment, regardless of whether the client computer you are using is running the

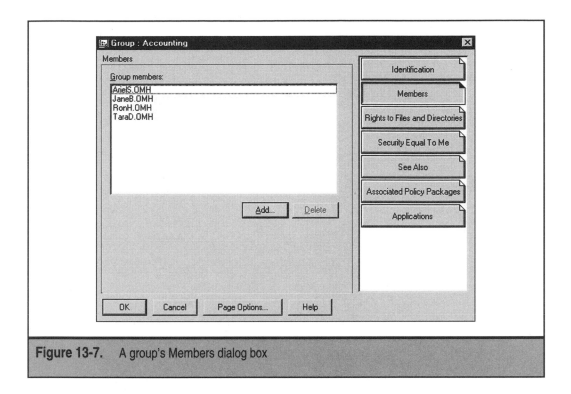

Figure 13-7. A group's Members dialog box

NetWare Client software or Microsoft's NetWare-compatible client software. Figure 13-9 shows a folder's Trustees dialog box in which permissions are managed.

Before learning how to assign folder permissions, you should first review some key NetWare permission concepts discussed in the following section.

Understanding NetWare Folder Permissions

One of the strengths of NetWare is its maturity in managing folder and file permissions for the network. While Windows 2000 Server has made improvements relative to Windows NT 4, NetWare 5 still offers slightly better functionality in this area.

Under NetWare, you can manage permissions both to folders and to individual files. Generally, permission management is handled at the folder level although, occasionally, users give you a set of security requirements that also needs file-specific settings. Both folder and file permissions use the same rights (types of permission) under NetWare. These basic "building-blocks" of file system security are comprised of the following basic rights:

▼ **Supervisor** This right grants all possible rights.

■ **Read** Enables users to read files in folders in which they have this right. Unless they also have the File Scan right, however, they must know the specific filenames in the folder to access them.

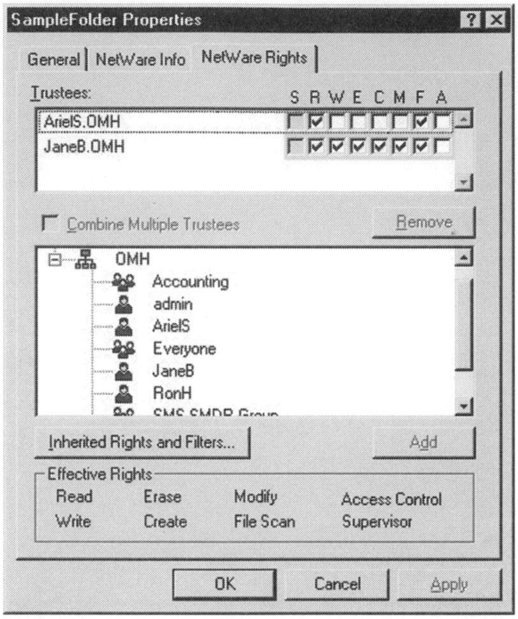

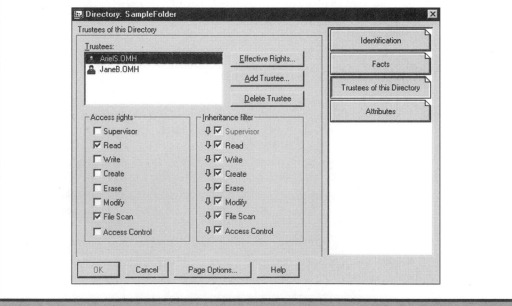

Figure 13-8. With NetWare Client installed, you can use a folder's Properties dialog box to manage permissions

Figure 13-9. NetWare Administrator's Trustees tab for folder permission management

- ■ **Write**   Enables users to open and write to files in a folder. It implies the Read right.
- ■ **Create**   Enables users to create new files within a folder.
- ■ **Erase**   Enables users to erase files within a folder.
- ■ **Modify**   Enables users to rename files or subfolders within a folder.
- ■ **File Scan**   Enables users to see files and subfolders within a folder.
- ▲ **Access Control**   Enables the trustee (the person who holds this right) the ability to control permissions on the folder for anyone on the network. For example, you may give a user the Access Control right for his or her own home directory. The user is then free to grant other people on the network, such as an assistant, access to folders within his or her home directory, as the user sees fit.

Rights to NetWare folders automatically apply to subfolders and files below the level at which they are granted. This behavior can be changed, however, using a feature called the *Inherited Rights Mask.* Changing the Inherited Rights Mask can "block" the masked rights from applying to subfolders and the files within the subfolders. Generally, you needn't use this feature except in rare situations. From an administrative standpoint, organizing folders so a user's rights are free to apply to subfolders is simpler.

When working with rights, understanding some basic rules of thumb and tips is important:

- ▼ To enable a user to have read-only access to a folder, make sure to grant Read and File Scan rights. This enables users to view files in a folder (browse the folder) and to open files for viewing, but they are unable to save changes to the opened files, to rename the files, to delete them, or to do anything other than view them on their screen or to copy them to another location where they have more rights.

- ■ Many document-based applications, like Microsoft Word or Excel, don't actually write changes to the files the user has opened when she or he uses the Save command. Instead, when a user saves a file, the application writes the data to a temporary file and then it quickly deletes the original file and renames the temporary file to the original's name. For this reason, setting up rights so a user can open and modify existing files, but cannot create new files, is difficult. Note, this behavior is application-specific. A database program, for instance, *does* usually write directly to the database file, rather than use the method described for document-based applications.

- ■ You can create folders that are similar to a secure in-box for some needs by granting just the Create right. This can be useful if, say, a manager wants to set up a folder into which employees can deposit (copy) files without being able to see existing files. The user can simply drag-and-drop a file into the folder but, as far as the user is concerned, the folder is a "black hole."

■ File system rights are cumulative. If you grant a user Read and File Scan rights, but this user is a member of a group that also has Create and Write rights, the user will get the full set of rights granted to both.

▲ Be careful and consider the capabilities you are granting a user with rights. For example, just because you limited a user to only Read and File Scan rights—so he or she cannot change the stored files—this doesn't mean the user can't copy the files to another location and make any changes wanted in the copy made. A clever user, for instance, could produce a doctored printout of a file in this way, even if the user isn't able to change the actual secured file.

Assigning Rights

To assign folder rights with NetWare Administrator, first navigate to the folder in question. You do this by first locating the volume with which you want to work in the displayed NDS tree. Volumes appear in NetWare Administrator as *servername_volumename*. So, the volume SYS: on server OMH appears as OMH_SYS. If you double-click this object in NetWare Administrator, it opens and displays the subfolders and files within the volume. You can continue double-clicking to open the subfolders until you locate the folder with which you want to work. Once you have done so, right-click the folder and choose Details from the pop-up menu. You then see the folder's properties dialog box and you can choose the Trustees of This Directory tab, shown in Figure 13-10.

Click the Add Trustee button to add a new user to the list of trustees. In the resulting dialog box, choose the user (or group) from the list and click OK. This adds the user or group as a trustee and gives them default rights of Read and File Scan. You use the check boxes in the Access Rights portion of the Trustees of This Directory tab to assign the rights, making sure to first select the appropriate trustee in the list. In Figure 13-10, for example, the user ArielS is selected and you can see the Read and File Scan rights are the only ones selected.

To remove a trustee, select that person in the list and click the Delete Trustee button.

CHAPTER SUMMARY

NetWare 5 is a mature, powerful network operating system that amply fills file and print server duties on a network. In fact, for file and print server duties, no more capable NOS exists.

While NetWare 5 is predictable and well designed, it is also a complex, powerful product that meets many different needs and incorporates the many years of experience Novell has had in providing file and print servers. If you plan to administer a NetWare 5 server, you need much more training than this overview chapter can provide. The goal of this chapter was to familiarize you with some basic NetWare concepts and to give you a sense of how NetWare is administered using NetWare Administrator. With this information to get you started, you're equipped to set up a small server for learning purposes and to pursue more detailed knowledge and gain practice with the product. In doing so, you

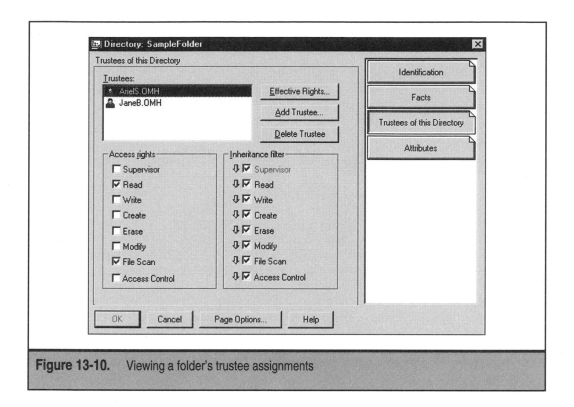

Figure 13-10.   Viewing a folder's trustee assignments

should make full use of the documentation that comes with NetWare 5 and you should purchase a book dedicated to NetWare 5 installation and maintenance. One good book to help you is *NetWare 5: The Complete Reference,* by Bill Payne and Tom Sheldon (ISBN: 0-07-211882-2, Osborne/McGraw-Hill).

The next chapter rounds out this overview of NetWare by discussing the many add-on products available from Novell, which dramatically expand NetWare 5's scope.

CHAPTER 14

Understanding Other NetWare Services

The NetWare family of products is presently the most mature server family available for the Intel-based hardware platform. While NetWare is not generally effective as an application server, it powerfully fills most other server roles, including the following:

- ▼ Network-wide directory services
- ■ Remote Access (both dial-up and VPN)
- ■ Firewall and proxy services
- ■ DNS
- ■ DHCP
- ■ Fault-tolerant services
- ▲ Web and other Internet-related services

This chapter provides an overview of these other services. Some of them are included with NetWare 5, while others are add-on products available from Novell.

NDS

NetWare's file and print-serving features used to be the lynchpin of Novell's network offerings. Today, though, Novell Directory Services (NDS) is central to nearly everything Novell is doing and is an important product in its own right.

NDS originated as a way to manage large numbers of Novell servers from a single point and to allow such features as single login for an entire network's servers. Within a single NDS tree, the administrator could manage all the accounts on the network, as well as all the servers and their resources on the network. A user account only has to be created once and, using NDS, the user account can be assigned privileges for any server's resources. Users only had to log in to the network once—to the NDS tree itself—and then the network as a whole would take care of making the appropriate resources available to them.

For people who used to manage multiple NetWare 2.x or 3.x servers, where each server had its own user lists and rights to folders and files, NDS was a breakthrough feature.

In more recent years, Novell has enhanced the NetWare family through the addition of many other products, including Web servers, firewall software, remote access software, and so forth. Central to all these products is that they are manageable through NDS. This means, as you add new features to your network, you can still administer all of them from a single point and you needn't duplicate administrative efforts each time you add a new network service.

The preceding benefits are all well and good for Novell-only networks, but what about networks that also must support Windows NT Servers or Sun Solaris servers? The truth is, Windows NT is arguably a better application server than any version of NetWare, and Sun Solaris servers are probably the best Web and Internet servers available. Any medium-to-large network will certainly have to support these other types of servers and therein lies the rub—it's much more difficult and requires more effort to support two or three different administrative models.

Imagine you have a network that uses a mix of NetWare, Windows NT, and Solaris servers. This means, among other things, the administrator must manage three separate sets of users and three separate sets of access permissions, and train users how to use the correct logins and passwords for each of the different servers. In reality, this is even harder than it sounds because managing three distinctly different server systems causes all kinds of problems. Administration is only one of the headaches with which you will have to contend.

Because of the problems created when a company runs multiple network operating systems, most companies eventually realize they must choose a single platform for all their servers, even though no single platform is "best in class" for all different server roles.

Fortunately, Novell offers a solution with NDS for Windows NT and NDS for Solaris. These two products enable you to integrate the management of Windows NT servers and Solaris servers into the organization's NDS tree. You can then use NetWare Administrator to administer accounts on all three platforms, easily and seamlessly. From a single console, you can manage single-user objects that represent user accounts on NetWare servers, Windows NT servers, and Solaris servers.

NDS keeps all passwords automatically synchronized between the different systems. Moreover, you can create users and change passwords on any of the systems and the changes are automatically updated into the NDS directory tree. (Of course, you can also create users in NetWare Administrator. Those users will also be created for NDS for NT and NDS for Solaris servers.) What's more, NDS for NT and NDS for Solaris enable you to store a replica of the NDS directory tree on those types of servers, making administration easier for locations where, for example, only a single Windows NT server exists. Finally, you can use NetWare Administrator to administer resources on non-Novell servers that are running NDS.

NOVELL BORDERMANAGER

Novell's *BorderManager* product is a veritable Swiss Army knife of communication services. With BorderManager, you can accomplish the following objectives:

▼ Firewall services for the LAN

■ Virtual Private Network (VPN) connections

■ Proxy caching

▲ Log, alert, and report on Internet traffic

Because BorderManager is fully integrated with NDS, you can easily administer these services through the NDS directory tree using NetWare Administrator, which makes administration easy.

BorderManager is actually a suite of products that all work together. You can purchase them together as BorderManager Enterprise Edition or individually to suit your needs. The individual BorderManager products are as follows:

▼ BorderManager Firewall Services

■ BorderManager VPN Services

■ BorderManager Authentication Services

▲ BorderManager FastCache Services

BorderManager Firewall Services (BFS) is the main security component of Border-Manager. With it, you can implement security policies that protect one network from intrusions from a connected network, such as between a LAN and the Internet, between two LANs, or between two connected WANs. BFS provides TCP/IP packet filtering, IP address masking, and control over access to IP ports, IP addresses, and network files. BFS can follow security policies that you set to protect access through a variety of different protocols, such as HTTP, Telnet, FTP, DNS, UDP, and, of course, TCP and IP.

BorderManager Authentication Services (BMAS) provides a service that authenticates remote access to the network. It makes use of the *Remote Authentication Dial-In User Service (RADIUS)* and integrates with NDS for management. BMAS can work with any RADIUS-compatible remote-access solution to provide authorization for network access. BMAS can be run on either NetWare 4.11 or greater, or Windows NT 4 or greater servers.

BorderManager VPN Services (BMVS) enables virtual private networks to be formed over public networks, like the Internet. Using the services of BMVS, you can set up several types of network links between sites. You can create site-to-site networks, client-server networks, and extranet services where you link your network with the networks of important business partners. Because you can make use of public network links to form these virtual networks securely, the cost of operating the network connections is much lower than otherwise. BMVS supports all the standard encryption, tunneling, and virtual connection methods, including DES and IPSec.

Finally, *BorderManager FastCache Services* provides super-fast caching of static Web site data, such as HTML pages, and GIF and JPEG images for visitors to a Web site you manage. Using FastCache Services can increase the speed of most Web servers by an order of magnitude, and usually at a much lower cost than would be involved with installing ten times as much actual Web server hardware.

NETWARE CONNECT

While many companies have found the benefits of VPN access to the company LAN compelling, many applications still exist for dial-up access using standard modems. NetWare Connect enables you to set up secure dial-in access to your network using standard modems. NetWare Connect also supports dial-out access over the LAN, letting the company leverage a common pool of modems and phone lines to support dial-out needs for multiple users.

IMPROVING SERVER RELIABILITY

Novell offers three products that can dramatically improve the reliability of NetWare servers. Two of these products are available for NetWare 4.2 and 4.11, while the third is available for NetWare 5.

SFT III for NetWare 4 enables you to achieve top levels of reliability through the implementation of identical mirrored servers. To use *SFT III (System Fault Tolerance, level III)* you must have two servers with identical hardware configurations. Each server requires a *Mirrored Server Link (MSL)* adapter, which allows fast communication between the servers to keep them properly mirrored. Aside from the reliability benefits of SFT III, you also can perform staggered upgrades of the servers, even during normal business hours. You just take one server offline, upgrade it, bring it back online, and re-mirror the servers. Then, follow the same steps with the remaining server.

Another Novell product that can improve server reliability is *Novell High Availability Server for NetWare 4.2 (NHAS)*. NHAS is closer to other clustering systems available, such as Microsoft's Windows Cluster Services, where two similar (but not necessarily identical) servers share a single set of disks. (Each server also has its own private disk for its SYS: volume.) The two servers each control different areas on the shared disk set. If one server fails, the remaining server can assume its disk areas and provide its services. In fact, you can even set up the two servers to start each other's NLMs automatically if the other fails. The advantage to NHAS over SFT III is, while both servers are running, you achieve approximately twice the processing power. SFT III, on the other hand, is a true server mirror where only one server is actually doing work; the other one is simply kept updated to take over if the primary server fails. The downside to NHAS is, if something causes the shared disk cabinet to fail, then both servers are unable to function. This trade-off requires careful consideration. While disk cabinets are generally more reliable than the servers that use them, they can still experience failures. On the other hand, the benefits of being able to use both servers productively and simultaneously are strong.

A more advanced product compared to NHAS is *Novell Cluster Services (NCS)* for NetWare 5. NCS builds on the capabilities of NHAS by allowing multiple servers (up to eight) to participate in a cluster, with the capability to shift services dynamically between the servers in the cluster. NCS makes use of Shared SCSI and Fibre Channel disk controllers to share the disks assigned to the cluster.

DNS AND DHCP

Unlike the other services described in this chapter, DNS and DHCP services are included with NetWare 5, although you must choose to install them when you set up NetWare 5 to access them.

Domain Name System (DNS) services, as you know from other chapters in this book, resolve domain names like www.novell.com into their associated TCP/IP addresses. DNS makes working with TCP/IP-based networks much easier for users and administrators. NetWare 5's DNS services can be used to provide DNS services for LAN-based

TCP/IP servers and nodes. They can also download DNS information from other DNS servers to provide LAN speeds for DNS searches.

Dynamic Host Configuration Protocol (DHCP) enables you to set up a bank of TCP/IP addresses that client computers can use on your network. The client computers, when they start up, query the DHCP server for a TCP/IP address, which it *leases* to the client computer for a set period of time. Because DHCP services manage the workstation TCP/IP addresses, the chance of a TCP/IP address conflict on the network is greatly reduced. Moreover, as the administrator, you needn't manually set each client computer's TCP/IP address by visiting each machine.

DNS and DHCP services are managed on NetWare 5 servers using the same utility, called the *DNS/DHCP Management Console,* a Java-based application that can run either on the server's graphical Java desktop or from a Java-compatible client computer. You usually launch the DNS/DHCP Management Console from NetWare Administrator's Tools menu.

CHAPTER SUMMARY

Novell offers a wide range of products, many more than have been discussed here, that can meet virtually any network server need. Aside from the products overviewed in this chapter, you may also be interested in pursuing information on the following NetWare-based and compatible products from Novell:

▼ *Netscape Enterprise Server* for NetWare 4 and 5 provides NDS-managed Web servers on NetWare servers.

■ *Netscape Messaging Server (NMS)* for NetWare provides a simple Internet-type e-mail system for NetWare servers. NMS supports both *Post Office Protocol (POP)* and IMAP client connections, so a wide range of e-mail clients can connect to it.

■ *Novell GroupWise 5.5* is an integrated messaging (e-mail) system compatible with a wide variety of different client and server platforms. GroupWise is a good e-mail system alternative for companies that don't want the administrative or implementation overhead that comes with Lotus Notes or Microsoft Exchange, but do want a reliable, capable e-mail system.

▲ *NetWare 5 NFS Services* enable you to share NetWare 5 volumes and printers with UNIX-based systems.

Today, both Novell and Microsoft offer capable networking solutions to meet the needs of many different types of companies, ranging from small offices to Fortune 500 companies. Both NOS platforms (NetWare and Windows NT/2000) are capable and proven.

CHAPTER 15

Installing and Setting Up Windows 2000 Server

In this chapter, first you learn how to install Windows 2000 Server. Installing Windows 2000 Server consists of preparing for the installation with a variety of preinstallation checks. Next, you perform the actual installation, providing necessary information the installation process needs. Finally, you test the installation by having a client computer log into the server properly and perform some basic network duties. All these steps are described in detail in this chapter.

NOTE: This chapter, along with the two following chapters, is meant as part of an overall introduction to Windows 2000 Server. Certain advanced installation scenarios and techniques are not described here. To learn about other features and choices available when installing, administering, or using Windows 2000 Server, consult a dedicated Windows 2000 Server book, such as *Windows 2000 Administration*, by George Spalding (ISBN: 0-07-212582-2, Osborne/McGraw-Hill).

UNDERSTANDING WINDOWS 2000 VERSIONS

Windows 2000 is an entire family of products, all built on essentially the same programming code, but with significant feature and tuning differences. Windows 2000 is an upgrade from the Windows NT line of products, which end with Windows NT 4.

The desktop version of the product family is called *Windows 2000 Professional*. Windows 2000 Professional is intended to be run on business desktop computers and is not an upgrade for Windows 9x. (A consumer/home-oriented version of Windows 2000 will be available some time in the year 2000.) Windows 2000 Professional supports the following broad features:

▼ Runs on systems with 64MB of RAM (Microsoft claims that Windows 2000 Professional runs faster overall than Windows 9x on systems with 64MB of RAM. An impressive claim you should verify for your own applications).

■ Supports up to 4GB of installed RAM.

■ Supports one or two processors.

■ Works with Windows 2000 Server to take advantage of Active Directory and Intellimirror.

■ Includes support for plug and play (PnP) devices (PnP is not really supported in Windows NT).

■ Includes all Windows NT's features, including a preemptive, protected, multiprocessing operating system.

▲ Supports mobile computers, including power management features.

Windows 2000 Server Standard Edition is the mainstream server version of Windows 2000. It includes all the power of Active Directory, as well as the following features:

▼ New (compared to Windows NT) management tools based on the Microsoft Management Console (MMC).

■ Windows Terminal Services, which allows graphical applications to be hosted on Windows 2000 Server, much like a mainframe hosts applications for dumb terminals.

■ Internet and Web services (DHCP, DNS, Internet Information Server, and Index Server).

■ RAS and VPN services.

■ Transaction and Messaging services.

■ Supports up to two processors, unless upgrading from Windows NT Server, in which case it supports four processors.

▲ Support for the latest network protocols.

NOTE: With Windows 2000, Microsoft is changing the number of processors supported by the different versions of Windows 2000 relative to what they supported with Windows NT. However, if you are running a version of Windows NT that supports four processors and upgrade it with a version of Windows 2000 that supports two processors, the installation program will automatically install the full four-processor support.

Windows 2000 Advanced Server is the mid-range offering of Windows 2000 Server products. It enhances the features of Windows 2000 Server by adding the following:

▼ Supports up to 8GB of installed RAM.

■ Performs network load balancing (for example, can share a heavy TCP/IP load among a number of servers and balances their loads).

■ Includes Windows 2000 clustering.

▲ Supports up to four processors, except when upgrading from Windows NT Server Enterprise Edition, in which case it supports up to eight processors.

The most powerful version of Windows 2000 Server is the Datacenter Server version. Datacenter Server is used when extremely large databases need to be hosted for thousands of users or when other extremely heavy demands need to be placed on a Windows 2000 Server. Datacenter Server includes all the features of the other versions of Windows 2000 Server, plus the following:

▼ Supports up to 64GB of installed RAM.

■ Supports up to 32 processors (16 processors "in the box" and up to 32 processors with special OEM support).

▲ Improvements to clustering.

Windows 2000 is expected to ship by the end of 1999. Because most organizations have a somewhat conservative bent when it comes to implementing new operating systems (particularly network operating systems), widescale deployment of the Windows 2000 family is likely to begin in earnest around the middle of the year 2000, once some experience is gained with the product and the most serious bugs are worked out. Before implementing it in your own organization, you should closely follow reports of its early implementation and any problems experienced. Only deploy once you're comfortable that you'll have a relatively trouble-free implementation.

PREPARING FOR INSTALLATION

Before installing Windows 2000 Server, you first must prepare the server computer you will use and make important decisions about the installation. This consists of a number of tasks, as follows:

▼ Make sure the server hardware is certified for use with Windows 2000 Server.

■ Make sure the server is properly configured to support Windows 2000 Server.

■ Carry out any needed preinstallation testing on the server hardware.

■ Survey the hardware prior to performing the installation.

■ Decide how you will install Windows 2000 Server, including gathering all configuration information you will need during the installation.

▲ Perform a backup of the system prior to an upgrade.

These steps are discussed in the following sections.

Checking Hardware Compatibility

Microsoft maintains an extensive Hardware Compatibility List (HCL) that lists different hardware components and their testing status on various Microsoft products, such as Windows 2000 server. To avoid problems with your server, it is important you make sure the server itself and any installed peripherals have been tested with Windows 2000 Server and work properly. The latest version of the HCL can be found at http://www.microsoft.com/hcl. You can also find a text-based copy on the Windows 2000 Server CD-ROM's \Support folder. Using the Web HCL is preferred, however, because it may have more current data than the file included on the installation CD-ROM.

What If My Hardware Isn't Listed on the HCL?

If a particular hardware component in your planned server isn't listed on the HCL, all is not lost. For one thing, the HCL may not have the most current data and the hardware you wish to use may be certified, but not yet listed. Because the maker of the hardware will know the current status of its certification, it's best to check with them. Also, products not listed in the HCL may work fine with Windows 2000. If you are deploying a server for testing purposes or that will support limited services and you are comfortable doing so, you can still proceed to install Windows 2000 Server and begin working with it. You should not do this for production servers that many people will depend on, however. Not only does a chance exist that an undiscovered incompatibility may cause serious problems with the server, but you will be unable to get the highest level of support from Microsoft for hardware that is not yet certified. For this reason, you should avoid deploying important servers not yet listed in the HCL.

Checking Hardware Configuration

Purchasing a computer for use as a server can be a complex task. You have to contend with the myriad details of installed RAM, processor configuration, disk configuration, and so forth, as well as factor in your anticipated needs to come up with a reasonable server configuration.

NOTE: Chapter 9 contains information about different server technologies and about specifying a server for general use.

Windows 2000 Server requires the following *minimum* hardware configuration:

▼ One 133MHz Pentium class processor or greater

■ 256MB of RAM

■ About 1GB of free disk space for the installation process

▲ CD-ROM or network connection from which Windows 2000 Server is installed. If using a CD-ROM drive, Microsoft recommends one that is 12x or faster.

The previous are the minimums specified by Microsoft. You should carefully consider using more capable hardware than that specified, particularly for any kind of server (even one that will only support a few users!).

Instead, follow this advice when configuring a server for Windows 2000:

▼ Start with at least a single fast Pentium II or III processor running at 400MHz or greater. Pentium Xeon processors are a benefit in a server and you should carefully consider the price of such systems relative to the expected performance improvement (all else being equal, a Pentium II or III Xeon family processor will perform about 15 to 20 percent faster than an equivalent Pentium II or III processor). Also, consider using a system that either has two or more processors or that has the capability to add additional processors later if your needs grow faster than expected.

■ Windows 2000 Server runs best on systems that have plenty of RAM. For a server, make sure you have at least 256MB of RAM. If you plan on supporting all the different services available with Windows 2000 Server (such as Terminal Services, RAS, DHCP, DNS, and so forth) then 512MB of RAM may be a better choice than 256MB of RAM. Using 1GB of RAM is not even an unreasonable amount, particularly for servers that will experience heavy loads. (Don't forget, you can start with 256MB of RAM and install more if or when needed and, possibly, at a less expensive price than when you first purchase the server). Do NOT attempt to run Windows 2000 Server on a system with less than 256MB.

■ A fast SCSI-based disk subsystem is important, particularly for servers that will store a lot of data. See Chapter 9 for more information on choosing SCSI systems, using different RAID levels, and other important disk information.

▲ Windows 2000 Server requires a lot of disk space for its initial setup. The formula to determine the amount of disk space is: 850MB + (RAM in MB * 2). In other words, you need 850MB, plus another 2MB of disk space for each MB of installed RAM in the server. This is a minimum amount required for installation. Installing onto a system that will use FAT (File Allocation Table) formatted disks requires an additional 150MB or so because FAT stores files less efficiently than NTFS. Installing Windows 2000 Server from a network installation point also requires more disk space: figure about 150 MB of additional disk space if you will be installing over a network connection rather than from CD-ROM.

Use the information in Chapter 9 to help you size your server, but remember this rule of thumb: Get the most capable server you can afford and make sure it is expandable to meet your future needs, through the addition of more RAM, more processors, and more disk space.

Testing the Server Hardware

You found all your server hardware in the Windows 2000 Server HCL, you made sure your server is adequately sized, you purchased it, and you have your shiny new Windows 2000 Server CD-ROMs sitting there, all ready to be installed. Time to start yet? Well, not quite. Before installing any NOS, particularly on a server that will be used for production, make sure you carry out hardware testing (also called *burn-in*) on the server before installing Windows 2000 Server. Computer hardware tends to be most reliable after it has been running for a while. In other words, failures tend to happen when equipment is new and the chance of hardware failure decreases rapidly after the hardware has been up and running for 30 to 90 days. Because of this, a good idea is to test new servers for at least a week (testing for two weeks is even better) before proceeding to install the NOS. Doing this can help provoke any early failures in the equipment, during a time when they're easy to fix and they won't affect any users or the network.

You test the hardware using diagnostic software that should have come with the server or is available from the maker of the server. Most such diagnostics software enables you to choose which components of the system are tested and enables you to test them in an endless loop, logging any discovered errors to a floppy disk or to the screen. You should focus the tests on the following components:

▼   Processor(s)

■   System board components (interrupt controllers, DMA controllers, and other motherboard support circuitry)

■   RAM

▲   Disk surfaces

TIP: Server testing software often enables you to choose between nondestructive and destructive testing of the disks. (*Destructive* means any data on the disks is erased during the testing.) Destructive testing is best to discover any errors on the disks. This is one reason you want to carry out this testing before you install your NOS.

If the diagnostic software allows you to do so, you can usually safely skip testing components like the keyboard or the display. Your primary concern is that the unit continues running properly when it is under load for an extended period of time. You also want to make sure the RAM is working properly and that no bad sectors show up on the disks during testing.

Survey the Server

The Windows 2000 family of products takes advantage of PnP hardware, and can detect and automatically configure any PnP devices to work with Windows 2000 Server during the installation. PnP is not perfect, though. For one thing, you may have installed components that are not PnP devices and Windows 2000 will be unable to configure those devices. Also, sometimes PnP devices can conflict with other devices or the drivers for a specific device may not allow proper configuration for some reason. Because of this, it's important to survey the components installed in the server before installing Windows 2000 Server when installing as an upgrade.

For the survey, write down all the installed devices, along with what resources each one uses in the server. The resources include the IRQ channel, DMA channel, and memory I/O addresses used by each device. Then, if a device isn't working properly after you install Windows 2000 Server, you may be able to configure the device manually to known settings that work.

Making Preinstallation Decisions

Once you have your hardware configured, checked, prepared, and tested, you can actually begin the installation of Windows 2000 Server. During this process, you first spend time making a number of important preinstallation decisions you must know during the installation. The following sections discuss these factors.

Upgrade or Install?

You can upgrade a server running Windows NT Server 3.51 or 4.0 to Windows 2000 Server and maintain all your existing settings, user accounts, file permissions, and so forth. You can also perform a full installation where you wipe out any existing NOS on the server. You must perform a full installation to a new server or to one running any other NOS. If you are running an upgradeable version of Windows NT Server, however, pros and cons exist to both approaches.

NOTE: If you are running Windows NT Server 4 Enterprise Edition, you can only upgrade to Windows 2000 Advanced Server.

The main benefit to upgrading is all your existing settings under Windows NT Server will be maintained and automatically carried forward into your Windows 2000 Server installation. This includes networking details, like TCP/IP configuration information, as well as security settings you may have tediously set up over time. In fact, if the server can be upgraded, you should plan on doing so, unless you need to change something fundamental in the server, such as changing from FAT to NTFS.

FAT or NTFS?

Windows 2000 Server supports hard disks formatted using either File Allocation Table (FAT16 and FAT32) or NT File System (NTFS). Important advantages exist to using NTFS under Windows 2000 and, in some cases, it is required. The only time you would want to install Windows 2000 Server onto a disk that uses the FAT file system is when the system must be used in a dual-boot setup, where it retains the capability to boot another operating system, such as Windows 98. Even in cases where you need to maintain dual-boot capability, though, you're better off maintaining a primary FAT partition for the other operating system and setting up an extended partition with NTFS to hold Windows 2000 Server. In such cases, Windows 2000 automatically installs dual-boot support that enables you to choose which operating system to use when the system is started.

> **TIP:** If you are installing Windows 2000 Server onto a system that only has a single FAT partition and you want to dual-boot Windows 2000 Server with that other operating system, but you want to establish a new NTFS partition for Windows 2000 without having to destroy the existing FAT partition, you can use PartitionMagic from PowerQuest to accomplish this. PartitionMagic enables you to resize an existing FAT partition without losing any of its data and it also fully supports FAT and NTFS partitions. Without a product like PartitionMagic, you, instead, have to back up the FAT partition, destroy it as you repartition the hard disk, and then restore the other operating system (and all applications and files) to the new, smaller FAT partition.

NTFS is required for any Windows 2000 servers that will function as domain controllers and also is the only file system that enables you to take advantage of Windows 2000's security features fully. Moreover, NTFS is optimized for server performance and performs better than FAT under almost all circumstances.

Domain Controller, Member Server, or Stand-Alone Server

Before deciding this question, you need to understand about two important concepts in Windows 2000 networks: domains and workgroups. A *domain* is a sophisticated administrative grouping of computers on a Windows 2000 network, such that the network's resources can be administered from a single point and in which strong security can be implemented. Domains enable you to manage many Windows 2000 or Windows NT servers more easily. A *workgroup* is a simple collection of computers on a network and is only suited to pure peer-to-peer networks.

Windows 2000 Servers can be configured in one of three modes to support either domains or workgroups, as follows:

▼ Domain Controllers hold the domain's Active Directory information and authenticate users and access to resources. Most Windows 2000 networks will consist of at least one domain and, therefore, need at least one Domain Controller.

■ Member servers are part of a domain, but do not hold a copy of the Active Directory information.

▲ Stand-alone servers do not participate in a domain but, instead, participate in a workgroup.

Prior to Windows 2000, Windows NT servers that were Domain Controllers had to be designated as either Primary Domain Controllers (PDCs) or Backup Domain Controllers (BDCs). Windows 2000 with Active Directory significantly improves this, so all Windows 2000 Domain Controllers are simply that: Domain Controllers. Each Domain Controller holds a copy of the Active Directory data and can perform all the functions of the other Domain Controllers. Previously, all administrative tasks were performed on the PDC and the BDCs simply kept read-only copies of the domain information to continue authenticating security on the network should the PDC fail. Windows 2000 Server, on the other hand, uses the concept of *multimaster domain controllers*, which all seamlessly operate the same way as the other Domain Controllers.

Per Seat or Per Server?

Another important choice to make when installing Windows NT Server is how the server will manage its Client Access Licenses (CALs). Windows 2000 Server supports two different ways of doing this: Per Server and Per Seat. *Per Server licensing* means the CALs are assigned to the server and the server will only allow as many connections from computers as there are installed CALs on that server. *Per Seat licensing* means you have chosen to purchase a CAL for each of your client computers, which gives them the right to access as many Windows 2000 servers as they wish and the servers don't monitor the number of connections. Generally, Microsoft recommends you use Per Server licensing when running a single server and Per Seat licensing when running multiple servers. Microsoft recommends that, if you are unsure of which mode to use, you choose Per Server because they let you change to Per Seat mode once, at no cost (whereas the reverse is not true). Carefully review licensing options with your Windows 2000 reseller to determine the most economical way to license your network servers properly.

Wait! Back Up Before Upgrading!

If you are installing Windows 2000 Server as an upgrade to another NOS, such as Windows NT Server, it's vital that you fully back up the server prior to installing Windows 2000 Server. You should use whatever backup software you normally use for your existing NOS, making sure the software can properly restore the previous NOS in case you need to "unwind" the upgrade process and revert to your starting point. Even when you are performing an upgrade to Windows NT and you will not reformat any of the disks, making a preinstall backup is good insurance in case of trouble.

INSTALLING WINDOWS 2000 SERVER

There are a number of ways to begin the installation of Windows 2000 Server. You can:

▼ Configure the server computer to boot from the Windows 2000 Server CD-ROM.

■ Begin the installation while running Windows NT Server.

■ Begin the installation while running Windows 95 or 98.

■ Prepare boot diskettes and use them to begin the installation process.

▲ Install from a network installation point that has been previously set up.

When setting up a new server, you only have two real choices to begin the installation: boot from the Windows 2000 Server CD-ROM or prepare boot diskettes. Most servers have the capability to boot from their CD-ROM drives and this is the best way to perform the installation. If, for some reason, you find that you instead need to prepare boot diskettes, you can do so by running the MAKEBOOT.EXE program found in the \Bootdisk folder of the Windows 2000 Server CD-ROM. The example installation in this chapter assumes you are booting the installation process from the Windows 2000 Server CD-ROM.

Running the Windows 2000 Server Setup Program

When you boot from the Windows 2000 Server CD-ROM, you will first be presented with a character-mode screen that walks you through the early installation choices you will make. You first press ENTER to confirm you wish to install Windows 2000 Server or F3 to exit the installation program.

You are then prompted to choose whether you wish to install Windows 2000 Server or to repair an existing Windows 2000 Server installation. You press ENTER to choose to install Windows 2000 Server.

Next, you are required to agree to the Windows 2000 Server license agreement. Press F8 to agree to the license and proceed.

The next screen begins the meat of the installation process. You see a screen listing all available disk partitions to which you can install Windows 2000 Server. You can perform the following actions at this point:

▼   Use the arrow keys and press ENTER to select an existing disk partition.

■   Press the letter C on the keyboard to create a new disk partition (you usually must do this with a new server installation).

▲   Press the letter D on the keyboard to delete an existing partition (you usually must do this only when removing all vestiges of a previous operating system, after which you will create the installation partition you need).

When you press the letter C to create a partition, you are prompted for the size of the partition you wish to create. By default, the maximum size partition will be offered. To accept this choice, simply press ENTER, at which point the new partition will be created. You then return to the screen listing all partitions and the new partition you created is shown as "New (Unformatted)." Choose this partition and press ENTER to proceed.

After selecting the new partition, you are prompted to choose a disk format: either FAT or NTFS. For most servers, you use only NTFS partitions, so choose NTFS and press ENTER to continue. The partition is then formatted for you.

NOTE: A brief discussion about choosing between FAT and NTFS appears earlier in this chapter.

After the format completes, files necessary to continue the installation of Windows 2000 Server are automatically copied to the new partition. After the files are copied, the system is automatically restarted and the graphical portion of the installation starts automatically.

The graphical setup program walks you through various installation choices you must make during the setup process. While most of these choices can be modified later, it's best if you can make the correct choices the first time during the initial installation of Windows 2000 Server. The remainder of this section continues the installation process and discusses the choices that occur.

The graphical setup program first attempts to detect and set up all the basic devices installed in the computer. This process takes five to ten minutes.

Once the basic devices are installed and set up, you are prompted to choose the locale and keyboard settings you wish. These choices default to English (United States) and U.S. Keyboard Layout (if you're using a copy of Windows NT Server purchased for the United States), so you can usually just click the Next button to continue.

Next, you are prompted to enter your name and organization name. Most companies prefer you NOT personalize the operating system to a particular individual. Instead, use a name like "MIS Department" and then enter your company's name in the field provided. Click Next to continue.

You then are prompted to choose either Per Server or Per Seat licensing. Refer to the discussion earlier in this chapter concerning this choice. Then choose the appropriate option button and, if you chose Per Server, select the number of licenses you own and click Next to continue.

The next dialog box is important. You enter the name of the computer to which you are installing Windows 2000 Server; you also enter the initial Administrator password. The computer name you choose will be the name of the server and the name seen by users when they browse the servers on the network. You should choose a name you won't need to change later, if possible. For the Administrator password, choose a good, strong password that could not easily be guessed. The Administrator password is the key to doing anything you need to do with the server and you need to choose one that will be secure. As a rule of thumb, choose an Administrator password with eight or more characters that has both letters and numbers. Make sure it's also a password you will remember! After completing the fields, click Next to continue.

Next, you are shown a dialog box that lists all the different components you can optionally install with Windows 2000 Server. For this example, only basic choices related to setting up a file and print server will be selected. However, following is a list of all the choices (you can choose to add these components after the main installation is complete, if you wish):

▼ **Certificate Services (1.5MB)** Certificate Services are used to enable public-key applications. You do not need to install this option unless you have an application that requires these services.

■ **Cluster Services (2.2MB)** Windows 2000 Cluster Services enable two or more servers to share a common workload and to provide fail-over support in case one of the servers experiences a hardware failure. You do not need to install this option unless you are building a high-availability server cluster.

■ **Internet Information Server (28.7MB)** IIS allows a Windows 2000 Server to operate as a Web and FTP server. Choosing this option installs IIS along with a number of support features related to IIS. You do not need to install IIS for a file and print server.

- **Management and Monitoring Tools (15.7MB)** Choosing this option installs supplemental management tools including:

  - Connection Manager components for managing RAS and dial-up connections

  - Directory Service Migration Tool for migrating from NetWare Directory Services (NDS) to Windows 2000 Active Directory

  - Network Monitor Tools, which can be used to perform rudimentary network packet analysis and decoding

  - Simple Network Management Protocol, which lets the Windows 2000 Server report management information to an SNMP management computer on the network

  For a basic file and print server, you may choose to install the Network Monitor Tools portion of this option, which you can select separately by clicking the Details button and then choosing just that option.

- **Message Queuing Services (2.4MB)** These services queue network messages used with certain client/server applications. Unless required to do so by such an application, you needn't install this option.

- **Microsoft Script Debugger (1.6MB)** This option adds tools that enable you to debug scripts written in VBScript and JScript. Because you may occasionally need to access the Internet through a Web browser on the server (to download driver updates, for example) and because you may develop server-based scripts written in VBScript or JScript, you should choose to install this option.

- **Networking Services (3.6MB)** This installation choice is a catch-all for a wide variety of network services that you may choose to install on your server. In particular, you should consider selecting several of these options for a file and print server. First, consider installing Dynamic Host Configuration Protocol (DHCP), which allows the server to manage a range of IP addresses and to assign addresses automatically to client computers. Second, consider installing Windows Internet Name Service (WINS), which provides name resolution and browsing support to client computers that are running pre-Windows 2000 operating systems (such as Windows NT and Windows 9x) and are only using the TCP/IP protocol. Neither of these options is required for a basic file and print server, however.

- **Other Network File and Print Services** This option enables you to install the additional support required to share the server's files and printers with Macintosh computers and UNIX-based computers. You needn't select this if all your client computers are running some version of Windows.

- **Remote Installation Services (1.4MB)** With RIS, you can remotely install Windows 2000 Professional onto network computers that support a feature called *Remote Boot.* You need a dedicated partition on the server to host the Windows 2000 Professional disk images. You do not need this option for a basic file and print server.

■ **Remote Storage (3.5MB)** This feature enables you to configure a Windows 2000 Server disk to move rarely-accessed files automatically onto an available tape drive or writable CD. The operating system can automatically recall these files if they are needed. This feature is not needed for most servers.

▲ **Terminal Services (14.3MB) and Terminal Services Licensing (0.4MB)** These two options let a Windows 2000 Server host multiple Windows sessions for remote computers, in which the applications execute on the server and the client computer handles only the display and keyboard/mouse input for the application. Windows Terminal Services work somewhat the same as mainframes, where all the work is performed on the mainframe and the client acts only as a terminal to the mainframe. You do not need these options for file and print servers.

After choosing the previous options, click Next to continue. You are then prompted for information about a modem attached to the server, if one exists. You can provide your area code, any number you need to dial to get an outside line, and whether the phone line supports tone dialing or pulse dialing. Complete the requested fields and click Next to continue.

Next, you are prompted to enter the correct date and time, as well as the time zone in which the server resides. Update these fields if necessary and click Next to continue.

You are next prompted to select your network settings. You can choose between Typical settings or Custom settings. For a small network, you can usually safely choose the Typical settings option. Choosing Custom settings enables you to define details, such as exactly what networking components will be installed and how each is configured. For this example, Typical settings is chosen.

Next, you are prompted to choose between setting up Windows 2000 Server as a member of a workgroup or a domain. A discussion about the differences between these two choices appeared earlier in this chapter. You cannot join the new server to a domain, however, unless the domain already exists and a domain controller is available to validate the new server into the domain. For a new server, even one that will be a domain controller, therefore, choose workgroup and click Next to proceed.

The setup program then completes its portion of the installation of Windows 2000 Server, using the information you provided.

Completing Windows 2000 Server Setup

After the main setup program completes, the system restarts to the Windows 2000 Server login prompt. You press Ctrl-Alt-Del to log into the server. You log in as Administrator, using the password you defined as part of the setup process in the preceding section. After doing this, the Windows 2000 Server desktop appears, along with the Windows 2000 Configure Your Server program (called the Server Configuration program for the remainder of this section), which walks you through the remaining steps required to get the server operational. Figure 15-1 shows the Server Configuration program running on the Windows 2000 desktop.

If you are setting up a single server for a small network—the assumption made for the example in this chapter—you can choose the option marked This is the only server in my network, shown in Figure 15-1. For more complicated Windows 2000 installations, choose There are already one or more servers operating in my network, which requires more detailed setup knowledge.

You then see a confirmation screen (shown in Figure 15-2) that confirms you want to set up the server with Active Directory, DHCP, and DNS services, which are standard for a single server in a network. If you like, you can read more about these services by clicking the links shown in the Server Configuration dialog box. Once you are done, click Next to proceed.

Next, you are prompted for the name of the domain you will create and any Internet domain of which the server needs to be aware. The domain name cannot have spaces and you should choose a simple name, one you can work with easily. Many companies

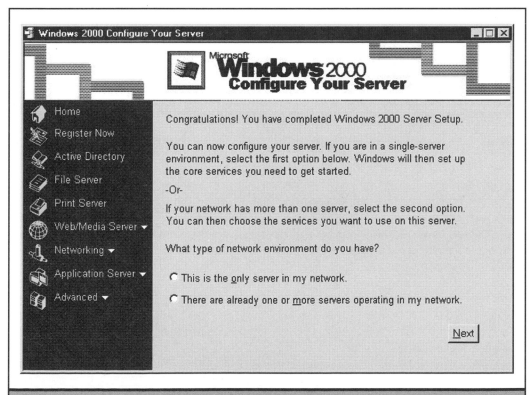

Figure 15-1. The Windows 2000 Server Configuration program

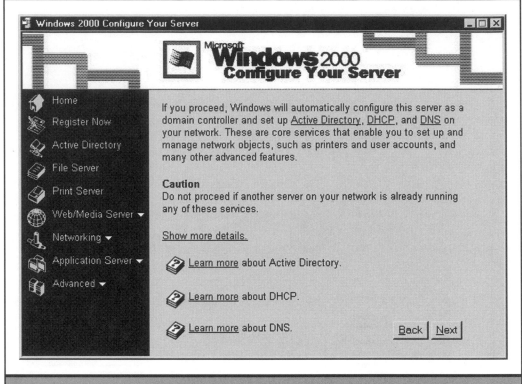

Figure 15-2.   Confirming the installation of core network services

choose the name of their company, or some abbreviation thereof, for their domain name. You also enter any Internet domain name that exists for your network. The Internet do-main name is one owned by your company. For example, if you work for a company called Acme Corporation, you can call your Windows 2000 domain ACME, and your Internet domain would probably be acme.com. (If your company doesn't have an Internet domain name registered, enter **local** in the field instead.) For this example, the Windows 2000 domain name will be OMH and the Internet domain name will be **local**. Enter your information and click Next to continue. After a pause, you will be warned the choices you have made will now be installed and the server will be restarted. Click Next a second time to do this. Note, you may be prompted for a Windows 2000 Server CD-ROM during this process.

After the system installs the components needed and restarts, you need to complete some final steps in the Server Configuration program, after which you will be done with installing the server. Follow these steps:

1. Right-click the desktop object My Network Places and choose Properties from the pop-up menu.

2. Right-click the Local Area Connection object and choose Properties from the pop-up menu. This opens the Local Area Connection Properties dialog box, shown in Figure 15-3.

3. Choose the Internet Protocol entry and click the Properties button.

4. Click the Use The Following IP Address option button.

5. Enter the correct IP number for this server to use as its IP address. If you don't have an existing range of numbers and your network isn't directly connected to the Internet, use 10.10.1.1.

6. Enter the correct subnet mask. If your network hasn't used subnet masks before, choose 255.0.0.0.

7. In the Preferred DNS Server field, enter the IP address you just assigned to the server. In this example, 10.10.1.1 is used. At this point, the Internet Protocol (TCP/IP) Properties should look like the one shown in Figure 15-4. Click OK to close the various Properties dialog boxes already opened.

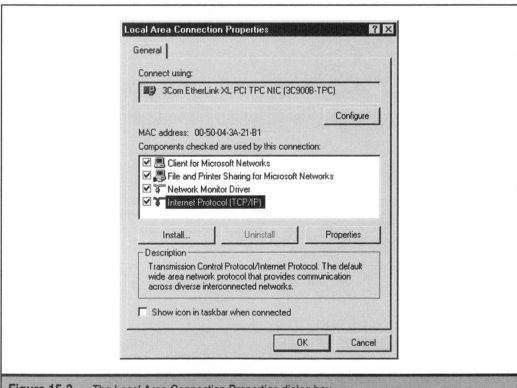

Figure 15-3. The Local Area Connection Properties dialog box

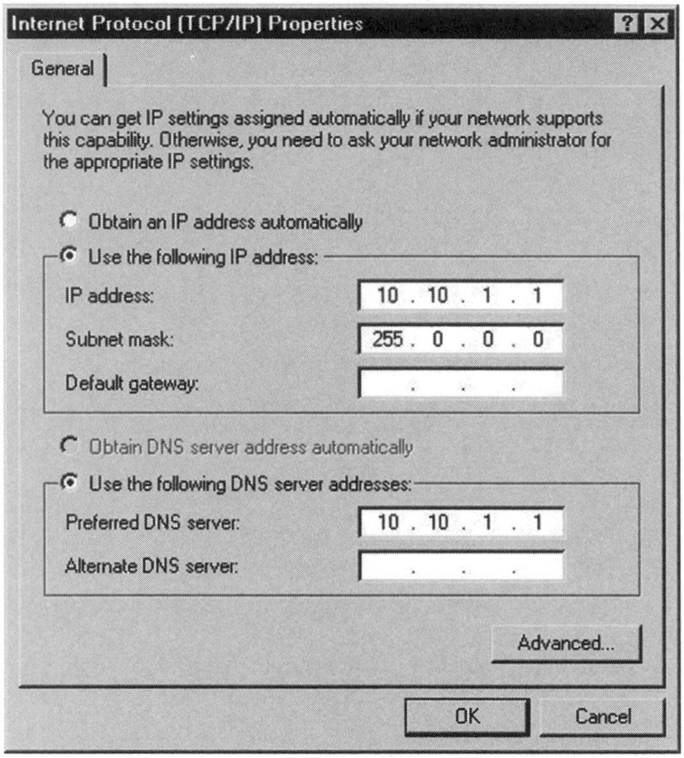

Figure 15-4. The Internet Protocol (TCP/IP) Properties dialog box with sample choices

8. You now need to authorize DHCP services. Open the Start menu, choose Programs, Administrative Tools, and then DHCP. You see the DHCP Manager, as shown in Figure 15-5.

9. Expand the tree in the left-hand pane. Then, right-click the server shown in the pane, choose All Tasks, and then Authorize. This authorizes the server to fulfill DHCP requests and to be able to parcel out IP addresses to client computers on the network.

10. Shut down and restart the server for the preceding changes to take effect.

Congratulations! If you followed this example, you just finished installing a Windows 2000 Server, capable of serving the needs of many users and of performing a number of useful tasks.

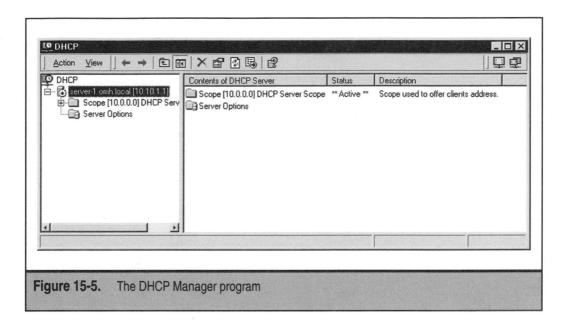

Figure 15-5. The DHCP Manager program

CONFIGURING A SERVER CLIENT

Before you can *really* finish setting up a new server, you need to test its ability to allow a client computer to connect to it. To do this, you need to perform the following steps:

▼ Create a test user account.

■ Create a shared resource on the server for the client computer to access.

■ Configure a Windows 9x client to connect to the server.

▲ Actually log into the server with the client computer and verify everything is working properly.

The following discussions show you how these tasks are carried out.

Creating a User Account

The first order of business to confirm server functionality is to create a test user account, with which you can log into the server from a network computer. You can use the Administrator account for this if you wish to skip this step, but using a sample user account is better.

Start by opening the Start menu, then Programs, then Administrative Tools, and, finally, select the entry called Active Directory Users and Computers. This opens the Windows Management Console application with the Active Directory Users and Computers settings, as shown in Figure 15-6.

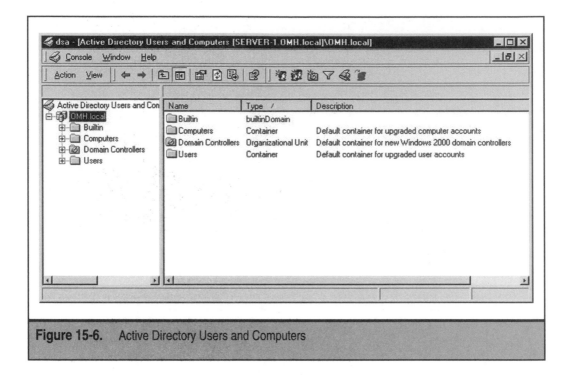

Figure 15-6. Active Directory Users and Computers

As with most Windows programs, the left pane enables you to navigate a tree (in this case, the tree of user and computer objects) and the right pane shows the details for the selected branch of the tree. To add a user, right-click the server in the left-hand pane, choose New, and then choose User from the pop-up menu. You see the Create New Object (User) dialog box shown in Figure 15-7.

Enter in the first and last name for the user you wish to create and then enter in the User Logon Name in the field provided. The remaining fields are generated automatically based on the information you just entered, although you can change them if required. In the example given, the user FredF will log into Active Directory using the user account **fredf@omh.local**. After entering in the information, click Next to continue.

Now, you enter in a starting password for the account you just created. For this example, simply use the password **password**. (Remember to remove this test user account after you finish with your testing. You don't ever want to leave a user account active on the system with a password that can be guessed easily.) Click Next to continue and then click Finish to complete creating the user account.

Creating a Shared Folder

The next step is to create a resource—in this case a folder—that the test user should be able to access from a computer on the network. Windows 2000 Server shares folders

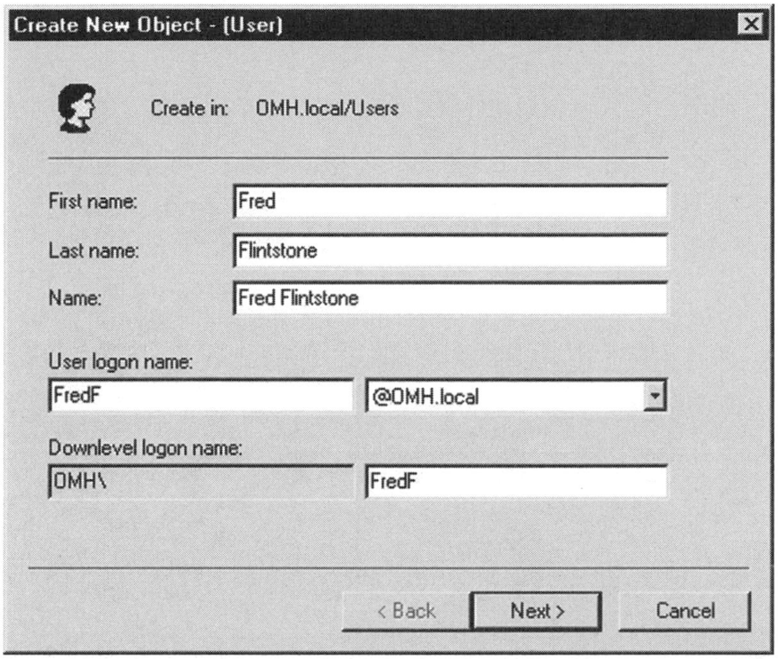

Create New Object - (User)   ☒

Create in: OMH.local/Users

First name: Fred

Last name: Flintstone

Name: Fred Flintstone

User logon name:

FredF   @OMH.local ▾

Downlevel logon name:

OMH\   FredF

< Back   Next >   Cancel

Figure 15-7.   Create New Object (User) dialog box

through a mechanism called a *share*. A *share* is a browsable resource remote users can access, provided they have sufficient privileges to do so.

To set a folder so it can be accessed over the network, create a normal folder on one of the server's disk drives. Right-click the folder and choose Sharing from the pop-up menu. This displays the Sharing tab of the folder's properties dialog box, as shown in Figure 15-8.

To make the folder shared, first click the Share This Folder option button. Next, review the share name (which is automatically assigned based on the folder name) and modify it, if you like. Then, click OK to finish sharing the folder.

NOTE: By default, new shares created on the server allow everyone full control of their contents. To change this, you need to click the Permissions button and then modify the permissions. This is discussed in more detail in Chapter 16.

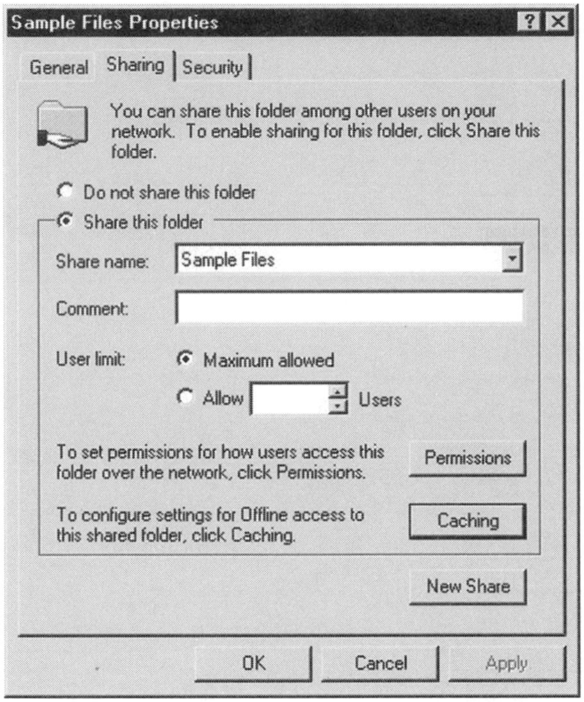

Figure 15-8. The Sharing tab of a folder's properties

Setting Up a Windows 9x Client to Access the Server

To set up a Windows 95 or Windows 98 client to access the new server, follow these steps:

1. In the Control Panel, open the Network object.

2. Click Add, choose Client in the Select Network Component Type dialog box, and then click Add.

3. Choose Microsoft from the list of Manufacturers, and then choose Client for Microsoft Networks in the right-hand pane (see Figure 15-9). Click OK to continue.

4. After a short while, the Network Properties dialog box will reappear in the foreground, with both the Client for Microsoft Networks and the TCP/IP protocol installed, as shown in Figure 15-10.

5. Select Client for Microsoft Networks and click the Properties button.

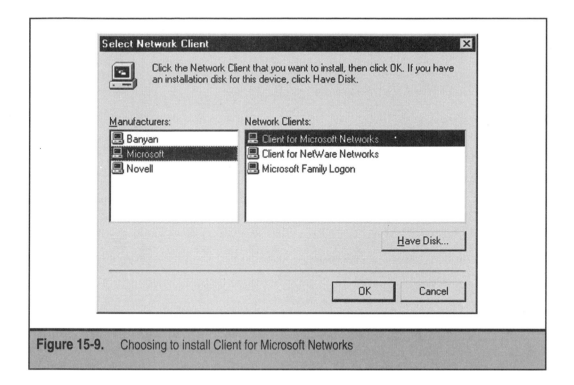

Figure 15-9. Choosing to install Client for Microsoft Networks

6. In the Client for Microsoft Networks Properties dialog box, select the checkbox Log Onto Windows NT Domain, and then type the name of the domain in the field provided. For the example used in this chapter, the domain name is simply OMH.

7. Click OK to close the Network Properties dialog box.

Once you close the Network Properties dialog box, you may be prompted for your Windows 9x CD-ROM so the necessary components can be installed. After the installation of the network components is complete, you are prompted to restart the computer, which you must do before the network settings are made active.

Testing the Client Connection

After completing the preceding steps, you can now log onto the domain being administered by Windows 2000 Server and browse the files you placed into the shared folder.

When the computer restarts after the steps in the preceding section are complete, you are prompted to log into the domain before you see the Windows 9x desktop. Enter the test user account name (FredF), the domain name (OMH), and the password you assigned (password) to log into the domain. If you have entered the information correctly,

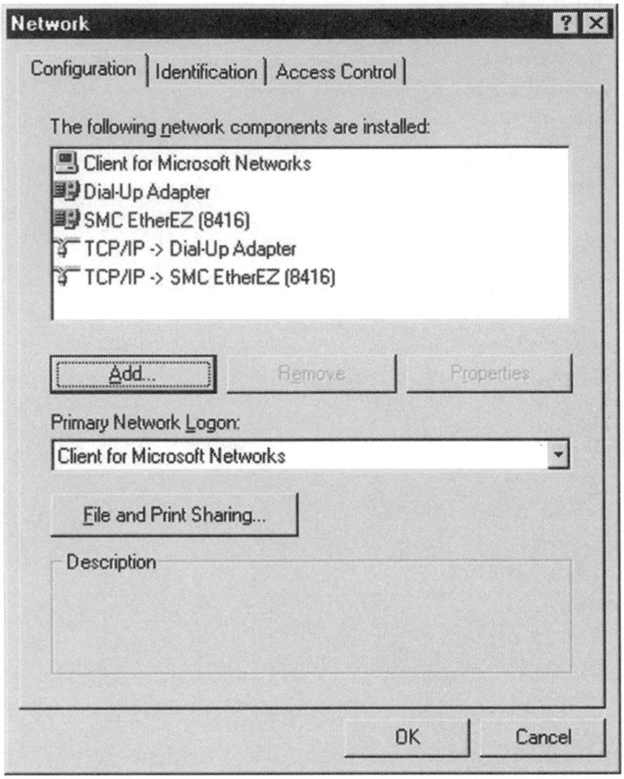

Figure 15-10. Network Properties dialog box with installed components

you will log into the domain. If any problems occur, such as an unrecognized user name, password, or domain name, you are warned and will have a chance to correct them.

Once Windows 9x starts, you should be able to open Network Neighborhood and see the server you installed appear in the list. Opening the server then shows you any shares on the server to which you have access. Among those folders, you will see **netlogin** and **sysvol**, as well as the folder you created and shared. You should be able to open the sample share and see the files you placed in the folder. You should be able to manipulate those files, delete them, rename them, open them, and so forth just as if you were working with files on a local hard disk.

TIP: Sometimes a server may not appear automatically in Network Neighborhood, particularly if it's recently been installed. If this is true for you, open the Start menu, choose Find, and then choose Computer. Type the name of the server you set up in the Find dialog box and click Find Now. After a moment, the server should appear in the Find dialog box and you can double-click to open it.

CHAPTER SUMMARY

In this chapter, you saw how Windows 2000 Server is installed and set up, using basic installation choices that will be appropriate for many servers in small businesses. You also learned how to set up and test a client computer to verify the network and the server are working properly.

The purpose of this chapter is to familiarize you with the basic installation procedures for Windows 2000 Server. However, this chapter neither covers all the myriad choices available to you during the installation of Windows 2000 Server nor discusses more complex installation topics appropriate for larger networks. Instead, this chapter is intended to help beginners to networking understand the basic steps to install Windows 2000 Server and to teach them enough to get a basic server up and running with minimal problems.

If you will be installing Windows 2000 Server into a production environment—no matter how small—it's vital for you to learn much more about Windows 2000 Server and about its installation and configuration than this book can discuss. Fortunately, many fine training classes and books are available to teach you all you must do to set up and administer a Windows 2000 Server-based network.

Installing a NOS is only a small part of the battle. Even more important is that you know how to administer the server and perform various administrative tasks for the NOS. These include managing user accounts, groups, printers, and other required maintenance tasks. Chapter 16 discusses the basics of Windows 2000 Server administration. Chapter 17 completes the discussion of Windows 2000 Server by teaching you about various features that are available for Windows 2000 Server, such as Cluster Services, Internet Information Server, and so forth.

CHAPTER 16

Administering Windows 2000 Server: The Basics

Installing and setting up Windows 2000 Server is only the tip of the iceberg. Far more important and more time consuming is the process of administering the server. This includes regular and common duties such as adding new users, deleting old users, assigning permissions to users, performing backups, and so forth. These topics are the subject of this chapter. Learning how to do all these things and to do them well will ensure the network and the server remain productive and secure.

THINKING ABOUT NETWORK SECURITY

Before diving into the administrative activities discussed in this chapter, you should spend some time thinking about network security and how it relates to your specific company. Network security is an important subject and administering a server must be predicated on maintaining appropriate security for your network.

The key here is to remember that every network has an appropriate level of security. The security requirements for a Department of Defense contractor who designs military equipment will be different from the security requirements for a company that operates a few restaurants. The important thing, therefore, is first to determine the appropriate security needs of your network. Many beginning network administrators forget this important fact and set up their networks to follow the strongest security measures available. The problem with this approach is these measures almost always reduce the productivity of people using the network. You need to strike a balance between productivity and security, and the answer will be different for every company.

For example, Windows 2000 Server enables you to set various security policies that apply to users. These include forcing password changes at intervals you specify, requiring passwords be of a certain minimum length, causing new passwords always to be unique and not re-uses of old passwords, and so on. You can set up these policies to require passwords that are at least 20 characters long and must be changed weekly. Provided users don't resort to writing down their passwords so they can remember them from week to week, these settings would be secure. A 20 character-long password is virtually impossible to crack using standard methods and weekly password changes reduce the chance someone else will discover a user's password and be free to use it for an extended period of time. The problem with policies this strict, however, is users will frequently forget their passwords, be locked out of the system for periods of time, and require a lot of help from the network administrator (you!) to clear up these problems each time they occur. For the DoD contractor in our example, these tradeoffs may be worthwhile. For the restaurant operator, however, they would be inappropriate and would end up hurting the company more than they help it. So, the first point to remember is network security should always be appropriate to the company and its specific network, and to define appropriate security levels early on is important, and to get the necessary support from management for the tradeoffs you think appropriate.

A related point is this: Sometimes security that is too strong results in reduced security over the long run, at least for certain things. For example, in the preceding example with the frequently changing, 20-character-long passwords, you can be assured a large percentage of users will have to write down their passwords so they can remember them and gain access to the system. The problem here, of course, is a written password is far less secure than one that is remembered because someone else can find the written password and bypass security easily once they have done so.

The final point—and the reason you should pay attention to this subject before learning about administration—is you should determine the appropriate network security early, so you can allow for it as you administer the network on a daily basis. Network security doesn't have to take up much of your time, provided you set up your administrative procedures so they presuppose the level of security you require. For example, if you know what your password policies will be on the network, it only takes a few seconds to ensure each new user has those policies set for their account. If you know you maintain a paper-based log of changes to security groups in the network, then it only takes a second to follow this procedure as you change group membership occasionally. Failing to determine these security practices and policies early on will result in having to undertake much larger projects as part of a security review or audit. This is an area where you're much better off to do things right the first time!

WORKING WITH USER ACCOUNTS

For anyone—including the administrator—to gain access to a Windows 2000 Server, he or she must have an account established on the server or in the domain (a *domain* is essentially a collection of security information shared among Windows 2000 servers). The account defines the *user name* (the name by which the user is known to the system) and the user's password, along with a host of other information specific to each user. Creating, maintaining, and deleting user accounts is easy with Windows 2000 Server.

NOTE: Every account created for a Windows 2000 Server domain is assigned a special number, called a *Security ID* (SID). The user is *really* known to the server by this number. SIDs are said to be "unique across space and time." What this means is no two users will ever have the same SID, even if they have the same user name or even the same password. This is because the SID is made up of a unique number assigned to the domain and then a sequential number assigned to each created account (with billions of unique user-specific numbers available). If you have a user called "frank," then delete that account, and then create another account called "frank," both accounts will have different SIDs. This means no user account will accidentally receive permissions originally assigned to another user of the same name.

To maintain user accounts, you use the Active Directory (AD) Users and Computers management console found in Start/Programs/Administrative Tools. Once the console is open, open the tree for the domain you are administering and then click the Users folder. Your screen should look similar to Figure 16-1 at this point.

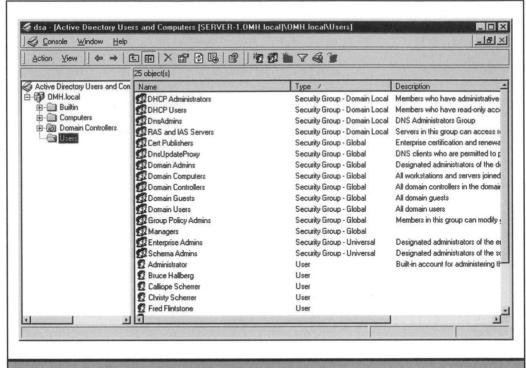

Figure 16-1. The Active Directory Users and Computers console

Activities in the console are accomplished by first selecting either a container in the left-hand pane or an object in the right-hand pane, and then either right-clicking the container or object, or pulling down the Action menu and choosing from the available options. Because the available options change based on the selected container or object, first selecting an object with which to work is important.

Adding a User

To add a user with the AD Users and Computers console, start by selecting the Users container in the left-hand pane, within the domain you are administering. Then, right-click the Users container, choose New from the pop-up menu, and then User from the sub-menu. You see the Create New Object (User) dialog box shown in Figure 16-2.

Fill in the First Name, Last Name, and User Logon Name fields. Then click the Next button to move to the next dialog box, which is shown in Figure 16-3.

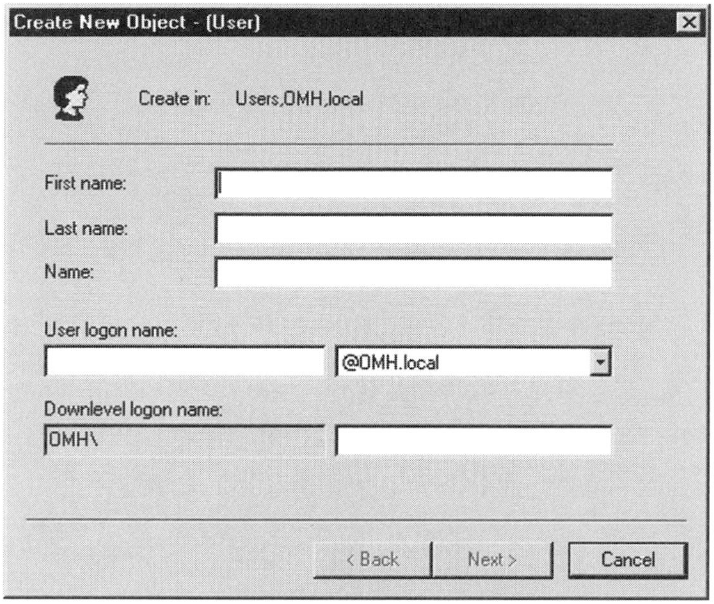

Create New Object - (User)   ⊠

Create in: Users,OMH,local

First name: |

Last name: |

Name: |

User logon name:
| |@OMH.local   ▼|

Downlevel logon name:
|OMH\ | |

                              | < Back | Next > | | Cancel |

Figure 16-2.   Use the Create New Object (User) dialog box to add a new user

NOTE: You should establish standards by which you assign logon names on your network. Small networks (fewer than 50 users) often just use people's first names, followed by the first initial of their last names when conflicts arise. A more commonly seen standard is to use the user's last name followed by the first initial of their first name. This latter standard allows far more combinations before conflicts arise and any conflicts that do arise can then be resolved by adding the person's middle initial, or a number, or some other change so all user names at any given time on the system are unique.

In the second dialog box, which has no name, you enter the initial password the account will use. You also select several options that will apply to the account, as follows:

▼   **User Must Change Password at Next Login**   Selecting this checkbox forces users to choose their own password when they first log into the system.

■   **User Cannot Change Password**   This option is sometimes used for resource accounts where you require the password not change. Generally, this option should be cleared, however.

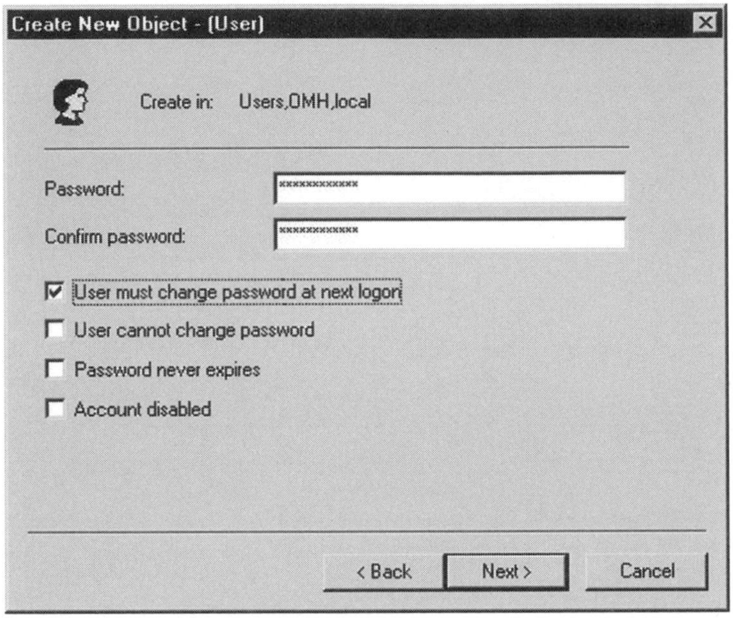

Figure 16-3.   The second dialog box for adding a new user

- ■ **Password Never Expires**   Choose this option to cause the system to allow the password in question to remain viable for as long as the user chooses to use it. Activating this option for most users is generally considered a poor security practice, so consider carefully if you enable this option.

- ▲ **Account Disabled**   Selecting this option causes the new account to be disabled. It can be enabled when needed (see the section later in this chapter on disabling and enabling user accounts).

After entering the password and selecting the options you want, click Next to continue. You will then see a confirmation screen. Click Next a final time to create the account or click Back to return to make any needed changes.

Modifying a User Account

The dialog boxes you see when creating a user account are much simpler than the one you see when modifying a user account. The dialog box in which you modify the information about a user contains many other fields that can be used to document the account and to set some other security options.

To modify an existing user account, right-click the user object you wish to modify and choose Properties from the pop-up menu. You see the tabbed dialog box shown in Figure 16-4.

In the first two tabs, General and Address, you can enter some additional information about the user, such as his or her title, mailing address, telephone number, e-mail account, and so forth. Because Active Directory also integrates with new versions of Exchange Server, this information may be important to enter for your network.

The third tab, Account, is where you can set some important user account options. Figure 16-5 shows the Account tab.

The first line of the dialog box defines the user's Windows 2000 logon name, as well as the Windows 2000 domain in which the user has primary membership. The second line defines the user's Windows NT logon name, which the user can optionally use if he or she needs to log into the domain from a Windows NT computer or using an application that doesn't yet support Active Directory logins. (While you can set these two logon names to be different, this rarely is a good idea.)

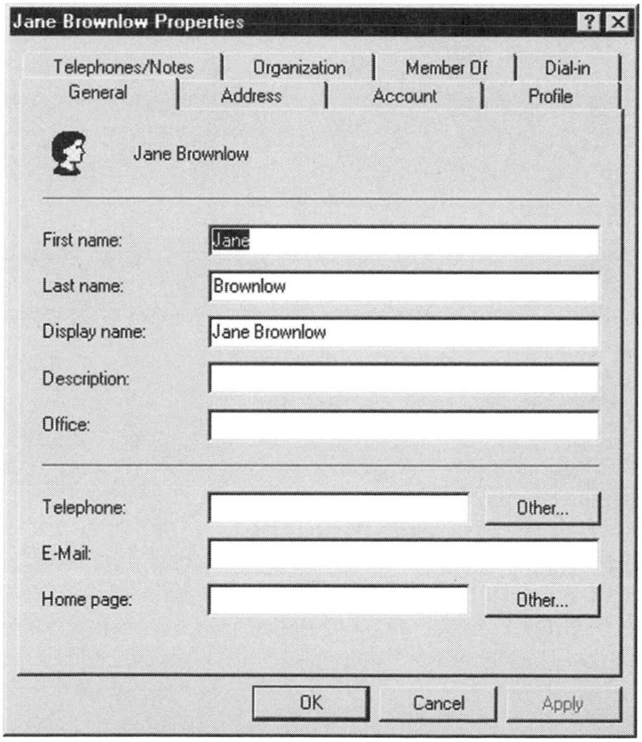

Figure 16-4.   A user's Properties dialog box

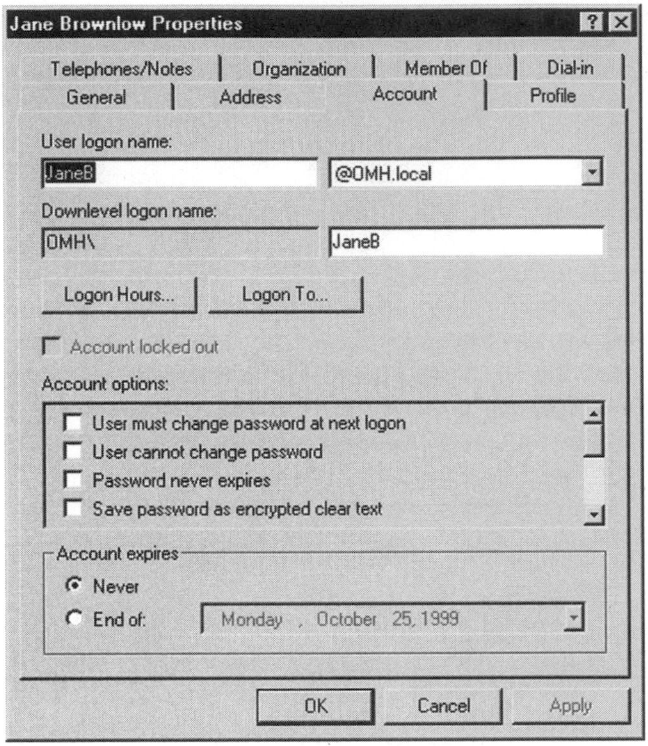

Figure 16-5.   The Account tab of a user's Properties dialog box

Clicking the Logon Hours button displays the dialog box shown in Figure 16-6. You use this dialog box by selecting different blocks of time within a standard week and then clicking the option button to permit or deny access to the network for that time period. In Figure 16-6, logon times have only been permitted for normal work hours, with some cushion before and after those times to allow for slightly different work hours. By default, users are permitted to log on to the network at any time, any day of the week. For most networks, particularly smaller networks, permitting logon at any time is generally acceptable.

Another button on the Account tab of the user properties dialog box (refer to Figure 16-5) is the Logon To button, which opens the dialog box shown in Figure 16-7. By default, users can log on to any workstation in the domain and the domain authenticates them. In some cases, stricter security may be called for, where you control which computers a user account can log on to. For example, you may set up a network backup account you use to back up the network and you may leave this account logged on all the time in your locked computer room. Because the backup account has access to all files on the network (or it couldn't do its job), a good idea is to limit that account only to log on to the

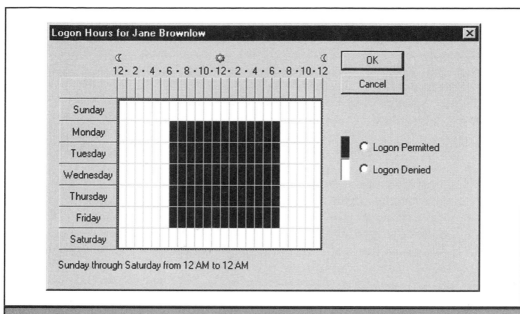

Figure 16-6. Setting logon time restrictions for a user

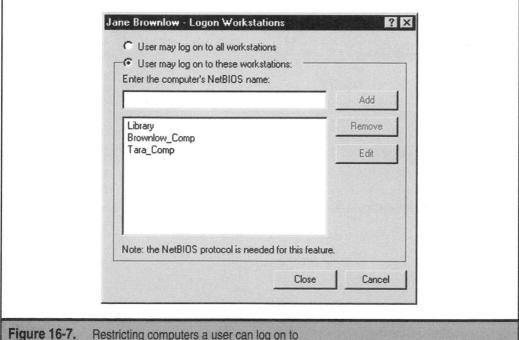

Figure 16-7. Restricting computers a user can log on to

computer designated for this purpose in the computer room. You use the Logon To button to set up this type of restriction.

> **NOTE:** The Logon To feature only works if NetBIOS or NetBEUI protocols are being used on the network. This feature will not work with TCP/IP-only networks.

You should be aware that allowing a user (let's call this user George) to log on to another user's computer does not mean George can log on with the other user's permissions or access anything that only the other user can access. This simply means George can use the listed physical computer to log on to his own account from that computer.

The Account Options section of the Account tab enables you to select various binary (On/Off) account options. Some of the options, such as requiring a user to change his password at the next logon, you set as you added the account. Some options listed are unique to the user's properties dialog box. The two most important of these additional options are Account Is Disabled and Account Is Trusted for Delegation. *Account Is Disabled,* if selected, disables the user account while leaving it set up within Active Directory. This is useful if you need to deny access to the network, but may need to re-enable it again in the future. (Also, Account Is Disabled is handled as a high-priority change within the domain and its effects are made immediately.) Because deleting an account also deletes any permissions the user may have, you should always disable an account if you may need to grant access to the network again to that user. (For example, if someone is on vacation, you could disable her account while she's gone and then clear the Account Is Disabled checkbox on her return.) The second option, *Account Is Trusted for Delegation,* must be selected if you want to designate the user account to administer some part of the domain. Windows 2000 Server enables you to grant administrative rights to portions of the Active Directory tree without having to give administrative rights to the entire domain.

The last option on the Account tab of the user properties dialog box is the expiration date setting. By default, it is set to Never. If you wish to define an expiration date, you may do so in the End Of field. When the date indicated is reached, the account is automatically disabled (but not deleted, so you can re-enable it if you wish).

Another tab you will use often in the user's properties dialog box is the *Member Of tab,* in which you define the security groups for a user. Figure 16-8 shows this tab. Security groups are discussed later in this chapter.

Deleting a User Account

Deleting a user account is easy using the Active Directory Users and Groups Management Console. Use the left-hand pane to select the Users folder and then select the user in the right-hand pane. Either right-click the user and choose Delete, or pull down the Action menu and choose Delete.

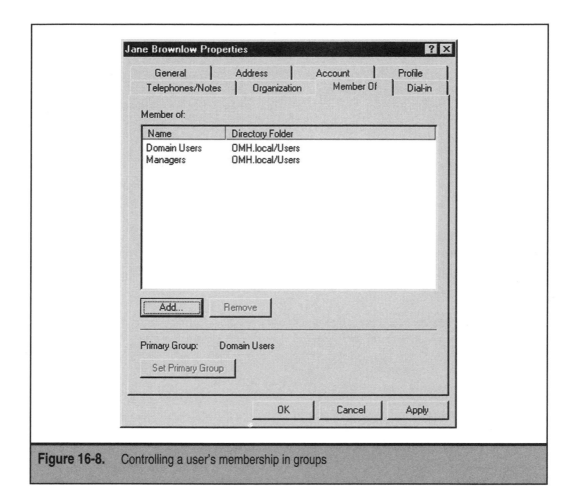

Figure 16-8.   Controlling a user's membership in groups

TIP: If you need to delete a large number of accounts, you can select them all before choosing the Delete or Disable Account commands to save time. Just be sure you haven't selected accounts you didn't want to delete or disable!

Disabling an account is just as easy. As before, first select the user account. Then, right-click it and choose Disable Account, or pull down the Action menu and choose Disable Account.

WORKING WITH GROUPS

On any network, you usually have to administer permissions to many different folders and files. If only you were able to grant access by user account, you'd quickly go crazy trying to keep track of it all. For example, say a group of people, like an accounting department, has different permissions to access 20 different folders on the server. When a new accountant is hired, do you have to remember or look up what all those 20 folders are, so you can give her the same permissions as the rest of her department? Or, say a user with many different permissions changes departments. Do you have to find each permission the user has so you can make sure he only has the appropriate permissions for his new department?

To answer difficulties like these, all network operating systems support the concept of *security groups* (or just *groups*). The way groups work is you create the group and then you assign all the appropriate users into the group, so you can administer their permissions more easily. When you grant permission to a folder on the server, you do so by giving the group the network permission. All the members of the group automatically *inherit* those permissions. This makes maintaining network permissions over time much easier. In fact, you shouldn't try to manage network permissions without using groups this way. You may quickly become overwhelmed trying to keep track of everything and you're almost certain to make mistakes over time.

Not only can users be members of groups, but groups can be members of other groups. This way, you can build a hierarchy of groups that makes administration even easier. For instance, say you have a group defined for each department in your company. Half those departments are part of a larger division called R&D (Research and Development) and half are part of SG&A (Sales, General, and Administration). On your network, some folders are specific to each department, some are specific to all of R&D or SG&A, and some can be accessed by every user on the network. In a situation like this, you would first create the departmental groups and then you would create the R&D and SG&A groups. Each departmental group would then become a member in either R&D or SG&A. Finally, you would use the built-in Domain Users group, or another one you created that represents everyone, and you would assign R&D and SG&A into that top-level group for every user.

Once you've done this, you can then grant permissions in the most logical way. If a resource is just for a specific department, you assign that departmental group to the resource. If a resource is for R&D or SG&A, you assign that grouping to the resource and all the individual departmental groups within that division will inherit permission to access the resource. If a resource is for everyone, you would assign the master, top-level group to the resource. Using hierarchical group levels like this makes administering permissions even easier and it's required for larger networks with hundreds of users.

Creating Groups

You create groups using the same console as you use for users: the Active Directory Users and Computers. Groups appear in two of the domain's containers: Built-In and Users.

The Built-In groups are fixed and cannot be deleted, and they can't be made members of other groups. The Built-In groups have certain important permissions already assigned to them and other groups you create can be given membership in the Built-In groups. Similarly, if you want to disable a particular Built-In group, you would do so simply by removing all its member groups. Figure 16-9 shows the list of Built-In groups for Windows 2000 Server.

CAUTION: Be careful changing the membership of the Built-In groups. For most networks, while it's important to understand what they are and how they work, you generally want to leave them alone.

Generally, you only work with groups defined in the Users container. Figure 16-10 shows the default groups in the Users container, which you can distinguish from user accounts by both the two-person icon and the Type designation.

To add a new group, first select the Users container in the left-hand pane. Then, pull down the Action menu and choose New and then choose Group. You see the Create New Object (Group) dialog box shown in Figure 16-11.

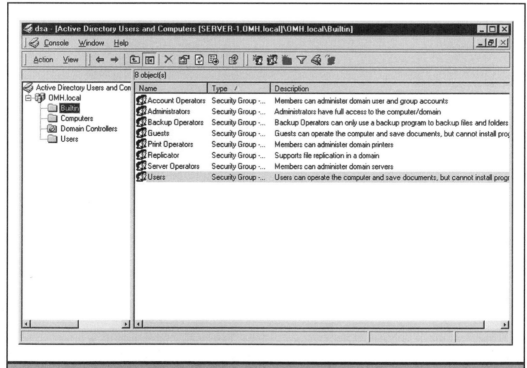

Figure 16-9.   Viewing the list of built-in groups

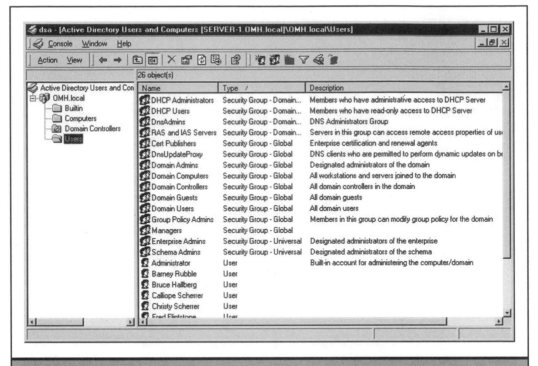

Figure 16-10. Default groups in the Users container

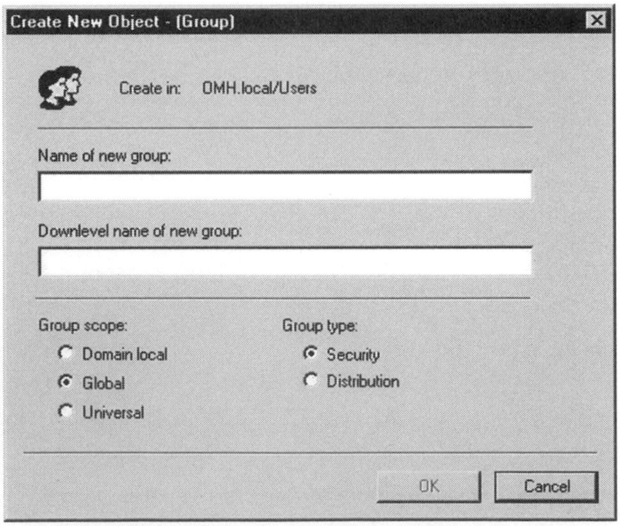

Figure 16-11. The Create New Object (Group) dialog box

First, enter the name of the group in the field provided. You'll see the name you enter echoed in the Downlevel Group field. The Downlevel field enables you to specify a different group name for Windows NT computers, which is generally not a good idea because it can quickly get confusing.

After naming the group, you need to select from the available option buttons in the lower half of the dialog box. Group Scope refers to how widely the group is populated throughout a domain. A *Universal group* exists throughout an organization, even when the organization's network is made up of many individual domains. Universal groups can also contain members from any domain in an organization's network. A *Global group,* on the other hand, can only contain members from the domain in which they exist. However, Global groups can be assigned permissions to any domain within the network, even across multiple domains. Finally, *Domain Local groups* only exist within a single domain and can only contain members from that domain.

TIP: Don't worry if you create a group with the wrong scope. You can easily change the group's scope, providing its membership doesn't violate the new scope's rules for membership. To change a domain scope, select the group and open its properties dialog box (right-click and choose Properties from the pop-up menu). Providing the group membership allows the change, you can select a different group scope option button.

After you set the group's scope, you can also select whether it will be a Security group or a Distribution group. *Distribution groups* are only used to maintain distribution lists and have no security impact in Windows 2000 Server. They are only used for e-mail applications like Microsoft Exchange Server.

Maintaining Group Membership

After you complete the Create New Object (Group) dialog box entries and click OK, the group is created, but it starts out with no membership. To set the membership for a group, follow these steps:

1. Select the group and open its properties dialog box (right-click and choose Properties from the pop-up menu).

2. Click the Members tab. You see the group properties dialog box shown in Figure 16-12.

3. Click the Add button. You see the Select Users, Contacts, Computers, or Groups dialog box shown in Figure 16-13.

4. Scroll through the list to select each member you want to add to the group and click the Add button to add them to the list of members. Only objects that can be made members of the group are shown.

If you want the group to be a member of another group, move to the Member Of tab and use its Add button, similar to how you added members to the group.

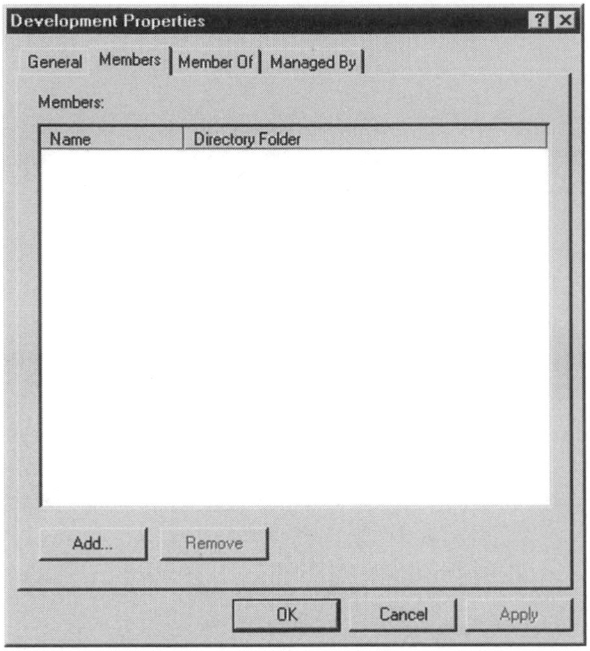

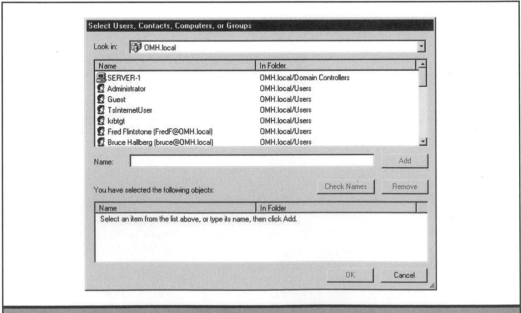

Figure 16-12.   The Members tab of the group properties dialog box

Figure 16-13.   The Select Users, Contacts, Computers, or Groups dialog box

WORKING WITH SHARES

Drives and folders under Windows 2000 Server are made available to users over the network as shared resources, simply called *shares* in Windows 2000 parlance. You select a drive or folder, enable it to be shared, and then set the permissions for the share.

Understanding Share Security

Both drives and folders can be set as distinct shared resources (or *shares*), whether they are located on a FAT-formatted drive or on a NTFS-formatted drive. In the case of an NTFS-formatted drive (only), however, you can also set permissions on folders and files within the share that are separate from the permissions on the share itself. Understanding how Windows 2000 Server handles security for shares, folders, and files on NTFS drives is important.

Let's say you created a share called RESEARCH and you gave the R&D security group read-only access to the share. Within the share, you set the permissions on a folder called PROJECTS to allow full read and write access (called *Change permission*) for the R&D security group. The question is: will the R&D group have Read-Only permission to that folder or Change permission? The answer is they will have Read-Only permission because when security permissions differ between folders within a share and the share itself, the most-restrictive permissions apply. A better way to set up share permissions is to allow everyone Change permission to the share and then control the actual permissions by setting them on the folders within the share itself. This way, you can assign any combination of permissions you want and the permissions you set on those folders will be what the users receive, even though the share is set to Change permission.

Also, remember users receive permissions based on the groups in which they have membership and these permissions are cumulative. So, if I'm a member of the Everyone group who has Read-Only permission for a particular file, but I'm also a member of the Admins group who has Full Control permission for that file, I'll have Full Control permission in practice. This is an important rule: permissions set on folders and files are always cumulative and take into account permissions set for the user individually as well as any security groups in which he is a member.

The next thing to remember is permissions within a share (sometimes called *NTFS permissions*) can be set on both folders and files, and these permissions are also cumulative. So, for instance, you can set Read-Only permission on a folder for a user, but Change for some specific files. The user then has the ability to read, modify, and even delete those files without having that permission for other files in the same folder.

The last thing to remember is that there's a permission called No Access. *No Access* overrides all other permissions, no matter what. If you set No Access permission for a user on a file or folder, then that's it; the user will have no access to that file or folder. An extremely important corollary to this is No Access permission is also cumulative. So, if the Everyone security group has Change permission for a file, but you set a particular user to No Access for that file, that user will receive No Access permission. If I set No Access permission for the Everyone group, however, then all members of that group will also receive No Access because it overrides any other permissions they have. Be careful about using No Access with security groups! There are many other fine points to setting and maintaining permissions that go beyond the scope of this book, but you can resolve most permission problems if you remember the rules discussed here:

1. When share permissions conflict with file or folder permissions, the *most-restrictive* always wins.

2. Aside from Rule #1, permissions are cumulative, taking into account permissions assigned to users and groups, files and folders.

3. When a permission conflict occurs, the No Access permission always wins.

Creating Shares

To create a new share, use either My Computer or Windows Explorer on the server. Right-click the folder or drive you want to share and choose Sharing from the pop-up menu. You will see the Sharing tab of its properties dialog box, as shown in Figure 16-14.

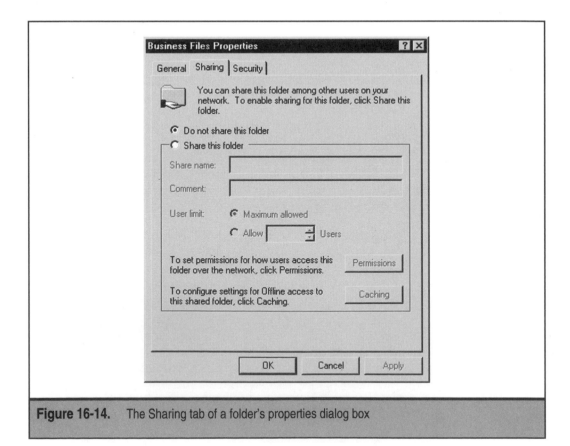

Figure 16-14.   The Sharing tab of a folder's properties dialog box

Click the Share This Folder option button and then assign a Share Name and, if you like, a Comment for the share (users will be able to see the comment you enter). After naming the share, you can select a limit to how many users can simultaneously access the share, if you wish. Normally, leave User Limit set to Maximum Allowed.

The last step you should take is to check the permissions for the share. Click the Permissions button, which reveals the Permissions dialog box shown in Figure 16-15. As you can see, the default settings for a share are for the group Everyone to have the fullest possible access to the share. Normally, this is what you want. (See the discussion in the preceding section about share permissions for more information about this.) Still, if you need to restrict access to the share in some fashion, the Permissions dialog box enables you to accomplish this. Clicking Add brings up the Select Users, Contacts, Computers, or Groups dialog box, from which you can choose those entities and assign them permissions to the share. Once an entity is added, you can use the checkboxes in the Permissions window of the Permissions dialog box to set the exact permissions you want.

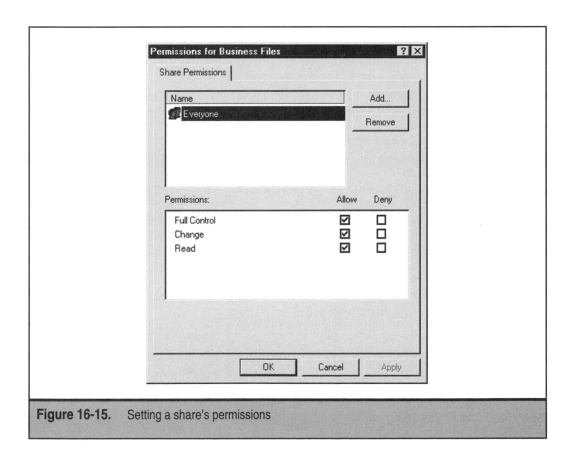

Figure 16-15.   Setting a share's permissions

NOTE: When you click an entity and some of their permission boxes are grayed, this means the permissions were inherited from a higher-level granting of permissions.

Once a share is created, users can browse it through either Network Neighborhood (Windows 9x and NT) or My Network Places (Windows 2000). Double-clicking the share will open it, depending on the permissions.

Making a share hidden but still available for users who know the share name is possible. To do this, create the share normally, but append the $symbol to the end of its name. For example: FILES$ is an example of a share that is not seen when browsing available network shares.

Mapping Drives

Shares are usable by opening them in Network Neighborhood or My Network Places, and they function just like the folders in My Computer. However, you may frequently want to simulate a connected hard disk on your computer with a share from the network. For example, many applications that store files on the network require the network folders are accessible as a normal drive letter. The process of simulating a disk drive with a network share is called *mapping*, where you create a map (link) between the drive letter you want to use and the actual network share to remain attached to that drive letter.

You can create a drive mapping in many ways. The easiest way is, from the client computer, open Network Neighborhood and locate the share you want to map. Right-click it and choose Map Network Drive. In the dialog box that appears, the name of the domain and share will appear already typed in for you; simply select an appropriate drive letter for the mapping and click OK. From then on, the share will appear as that drive letter to your computer and can be seen as such in My Computer.

To connect to a hidden share, right-click Network Neighborhood (or My Network Places for Windows 2000) and choose Map Network Drive. Choose a drive letter for the mapping and then enter in the complete share name (with the appended $ symbol) and click OK. Provided you have permission to access that share, the mapping will take place normally.

You can also map drives using a command line utility called NET. The *NET command* takes many different forms and can fulfill many different needs, depending on what parameters you give it. For mapping a drive, you use the NET USE command. Typing NET USE by itself and pressing ENTER will list all currently mapped drives. To add a new drive mapping, you would type:

NET USE *drive_letter: UNC_for_share*

Most network resources in a Windows network use a naming system called the *Universal Naming Convention* (UNC). To supply a UNC, you start with two backslashes, then the name of the server, another backslash, and the name of the share (additional backslashes and names can refer to folders and files within the share). So, if you want to map drive G: to a share called GROUP located on the server SERVER, the command would be:

NET USE G: \\SERVER\GROUP

TIP: You can use the NET command from any Windows client for any Windows network.

WORKING WITH PRINTERS

Before setting and working with printers on a network, understanding the components involved in network printing and how they interact is important, as follows:

▼ A *print job* is a set of binary data sent from a network workstation to a network printer. A print job is the same data as a computer would send to a locally connected printer—it's just redirected to the network for printing.

■ The network workstation that sends the print job to the print queue is responsible for formatting the print data properly for the printer. This is done through software installed on the workstation—called *print drivers*—that is specific to each type of printer being worked with. Printer drivers are also specific to each operating system that uses them. In other words, an HP LaserJet 5si driver for a Windows 95 computer is different from an HP LaserJet 5si driver for a Windows NT Workstation computer. More troublesome, different versions of the same operating system usually use different drivers, so a driver for a Windows 95 computer may not work with a Windows 98 computer and vice versa.

■ Print jobs are often sent to the network through a captured printer port. What happens is one of the printer ports on a networked workstation, such as LPT1:, is redirected to the network by the network client software. The process of redirecting a printer port to a network printer is called *capturing*. Usually, captured ports are persistent and continue through multiple logins until they are turned off.

Many applications are currently intelligent enough so they don't require a captured printer port. Instead, they are able to work closely with the operating system (such as Windows 9*x* or Windows 2000) and simply send their output to a printer defined by the local operating system. Behind the scenes, the operating system sends the print job to the printer queue on the network. Captured printer ports are usually only required by DOS or Windows 3.*x* applications because applications designed for those older operating systems don't have the capacity to print directly to a network printer.

■ Print jobs sent to the network go to a place called a *printer queue*. There, the print job sits until the network is able to service the print job and send it to the printer. Printer queues can hold many jobs from many different users and, typically, they are managed in a first-in, first-out fashion.

▲ Print jobs are removed from print queues and sent to actual printers by *print servers*. Once the job is completely sent to the printer, the print server removes the job from the queue. Print serving can be accomplished in many different ways. If the printer being used is connected to a server or workstation on the network, then that server or workstation handles the print server duty. If the printer is directly connected to the network (if it has its own network port), then the printer usually has a built-in print server as part of its network hardware. This built-in print server has the intelligence to log in to the network and to service a particular printer queue.

Print jobs start at the printing application, which sends its printer output to the local operating system. The local operating system uses the printer driver requested by the application to format the actual print job for the printer in question. Then, the local operating system works with the installed network client software to send the formatted print job to the print queue, where the job sits until the printer is available. Then, the print server takes the print job from the queue and sends it to the actual printer. Many steps are involved, but once everything is set up it works smoothly, as you see in the next section. Figure 16-16 shows an overview of how network printing works.

Setting Up a Network Printer

For this example, I'll assume you're setting up a printer connected directly to a Windows 2000 Server and you want to make it available to network users. In this case, the printer and its Windows 2000 driver are already installed properly, as they would normally be during the installation of Windows 2000 Server. If they are not properly installed, then open the Printers folder and use the Add Printers icon to set up the printer on the server itself.

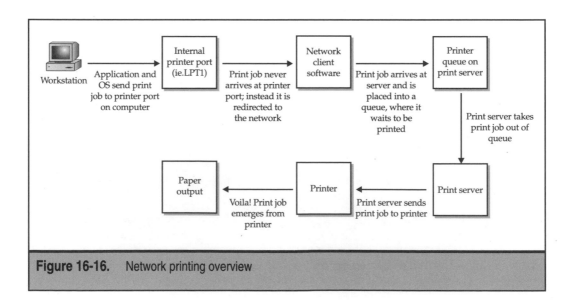

Figure 16-16.   Network printing overview

TIP: While you can easily set up a printer connected to a server (or workstation) so other network users can access it, for networks larger than about 20 users you're better off either buying printers with network interfaces and built-in print servers, or using dedicated print server boxes that interface between a printer and the network. For most laser printers, adding a dedicated network interface and server increases the cost of the printer by about $300. This is money well spent because the process of sending a print job to a printer carries a lot of processing impact to the print server and, if it's also your main file server, its overall performance will be significantly decreased (particularly when large print jobs are being serviced). Also, printers with built-in print servers are far easier to relocate on the network. They can go anywhere a network connection exists and where power is available. Once connected to the network at a new location, the printer logs into the network and starts doing its work immediately.

To share a printer connected to a Windows 2000 Server, first open the server's Printers folder. (Open the Start menu, choose Settings, and then choose Printers.) You will see all the installed printers in the Printers folder. Right-click the one you want to share and choose Sharing from the pop-up menu. The properties dialog box for the printer will appear, with the Sharing tab activated, as shown in Figure 16-17.

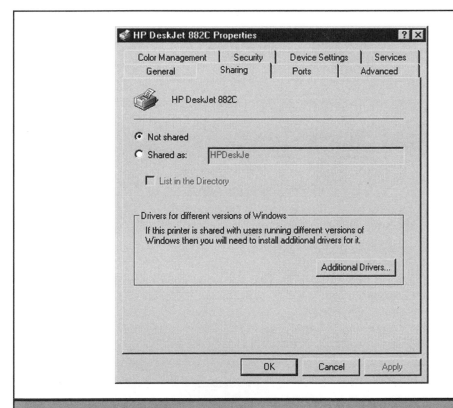

Figure 16-17. A printer's Sharing tab

Click the Shared As option button and then assign the printer a share name, by which it will be known to the client computers. At this point, you can click the OK button because the default permissions for a shared printer are for the Everyone group to be able to print to it. Usually, though, you need to check at least two other available settings, as follows:

▼ For high-throughput requirements, you may want to use a feature called *printer pooling*, which enables you to set up a number of identical printers, all connected to a single printer queue, which appear as one printer to the network. Users print to the listed printer and the first available real printer takes care of servicing their job. Using printer pooling, you could have a whole bank of printers appear as one printer to the users and dramatically increase the amount of print requests you can handle. Remember, pooled printers must be identical, however, because they will all use the same print driver.

To turn on printer pooling, move to a shared printer's Ports tab. Click the Enable Printer Pooling checkbox and then select the additional ports that also have the same type of printer installed. Figure 16-18 shows the Ports tab set up this way.

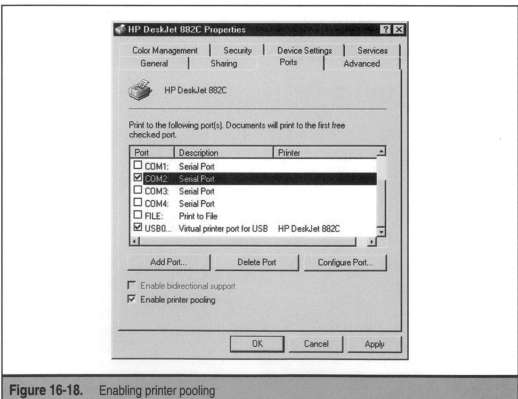

Figure 16-18. Enabling printer pooling

- ■ To set the permissions for a shared printer, use the Security tab of the printer's properties dialog box, shown in Figure 16-19. The groups you see assigned in Figure 16-19 are the default assignments for a shared printer, with the Administrators permissions shown. As you can see, three main permissions are assigned to each entity: Print, Manage Printers, and Manage Documents. The Everyone group has permission to Print, but not to manage documents in the queue. However, a special group called Creator Owner has permission to manage documents. This means the user who sent the print job automatically has permission to modify or delete his own print job, but not others waiting in the queue.

- ▲ Windows 2000 Server can store the appropriate printer drivers for a number of different Windows-based clients that may connect to it and use its printers. For example, the printer drivers for a particular printer will be different depending on whether the client computer is running Windows 95, Windows 98, Windows NT 4, Windows 2000, or some other version of Windows. When a client computer opens a shared printer on the network, the printer driver is automatically installed for the client computer. You control this back on the Sharing tab by clicking the Additional Drivers button, which reveals the Additional Drivers dialog box shown in Figure 16-20. To add new drivers, click the appropriate client types that may use the shared printer on the network and then click OK. You will then be prompted for the appropriate disks or CD-ROMs to install those drivers and Windows 2000 Server will then take care of distributing those printer drivers to the client computers when they first use the printer.

As you can see, setting up networked printers with Windows 2000 Server is a relatively straightforward process that gives you considerable flexibility in how you set up and manage your shared printers. Remember, too, other printing models are also possible, such as network-connected printers. Consult the documentation that comes with such printers for details on setting them up on your network.

WORKING WITH BACKUPS

One single task is more important than any other for a network administrator. This task doesn't have to do with making a network secure from hackers, maintaining users, designing new network segments, or solving server or workstation problems. What is it? Making regular and reliable backups of data on the system. Taking care to make regular and reliable backups is often a thankless job, *until something happens and the backups are needed*, at which point it becomes the most thank*ful* job in the company! And make no mistake about this, while computers are far more reliable than ever, there are still myriad ways in which they can fail and lose or corrupt important data. Remember, there are only two types of network administrators: *those who have had system crashes and those who will*. It's

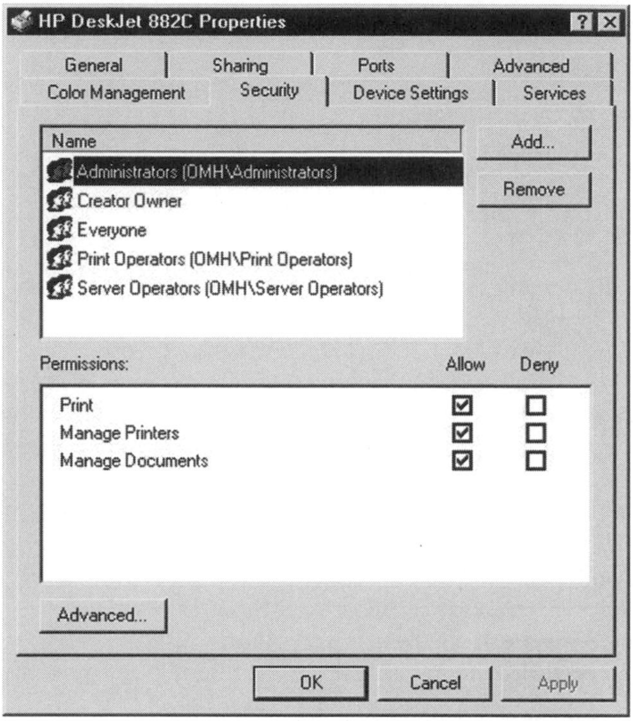

Figure 16-19.   Setting a shared printer's permissions

not just hardware failures, either. Applications or users often make mistakes that lose important data and having good copies of that data on multiple backup tapes can save the day.

Before delving into the details of how Windows 2000 Server's backup software works, you should review some key terms and concepts important in backups.

Every file and folder object on a server has a number of attribute bits attached to it. Some designate the files as being read-only, as system files, or even as hidden files. One is called *archive* (often referred to as the *archive bit*) that marks whether a file has been backed up. Windows 2000 Server keeps track of files that have been modified. Any time a file is modified on the disk, the archive bit is set to "on." (Bits like this are usually referred to as being *set,* which means they are on and are set to the value 1, or as being *clear,* which means they are off and are set to the value 0.) When a backup is made of the system, the backed-up files have the archive bit cleared again. This is how the system knows which files need to be backed up and which ones have been backed up.

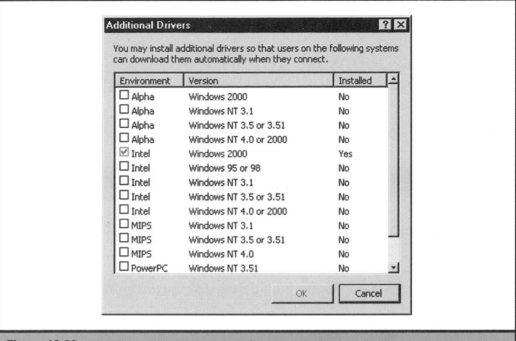

Figure 16-20.   Loading additional print drivers for a shared printer

Treating the archive bit in different ways results in different types of backups, as follows:

NOTE: The following are terms used with Windows 2000 Server backup. Some systems have slightly different names for these types of backups, even though the concepts are always the same. For example, what Microsoft calls a *Normal backup*, many call a *Full backup*.

▼ **Normal backups** back up everything selected for the backup regardless of whether the archive bits are set. All archive bits are set to off as each file is backed up.

■ **Copy backups** back up everything selected for the backup, regardless of whether the archive bits are set. Copy backups do not change the state of the archive bits, however; they remain untouched. Copy backups are used to make a backup without disturbing a sequence of Normal, Incremental, and Differential backups.

■ **Incremental backups** back up only those files that have their archive bits set within the selection set. The archive bits are cleared by the backup.

- ■ **Differential backups** also back up only those files that have their archive bits set, but the archive bits are left unchanged by the backup.
- ▲ **Daily backups** are a special type of backup in Windows 2000 Server that is like a Differential backup, except only files modified on a given day are backed up.

Now that you understand the different types of backups available, you can consider different tape rotation schemes that make use of these different types of backups.

The simplest backup scheme is just to run Normal backups every night and rotate tapes. In this model, there are many good ways to rotate tapes. One of the best ways I've found that doesn't consume too many tapes is to have four tapes labeled Monday through Thursday and to use them on those days. Then, have four tapes labeled Friday 1, Friday 2, up to Friday 4, and rotate those each week. Then, make a month-end tape on the last day of the month and keep it forever. The nice thing about this scheme is it makes a good tradeoff between using tapes and being able to go back in time to restore files. This scheme will use 20 tapes in a year, at which point the rotating tapes should probably be replaced.

TIP: No matter what tape rotation scheme you set up, a good idea is to set up a tape called "Employee Archive." Whenever an employee leaves the company, append his or her files to that tape before you remove those files from the system and keep a list of what employees are on the tape. This gives you a ready reference and quickly available restoration source if a particular person's files are needed at some future time (which happens often).

Another tape rotation scheme involves using the same tapes as listed in the preceding scheme, making full (Normal) backups of the system every Friday night, but then making Incremental backups on Monday through Thursday nights. Because only changed files are backed up during the week, backups during the week happen quickly. The big drawback to this scheme is, should the system crash on Friday morning, you must restore a lot of tapes to get the system to its most-recent backup state. First, you must restore the previous Friday's Normal backup and then, in sequence, restore each of the incremental tapes up to the day when the system crashed. The risk here is this: what do you do if one of those tapes goes bad? Things can get messed up if one of the tapes doesn't work. While this is always true, it's especially true in this scheme.

TIP: The Backup program included in Windows 2000 Server doesn't do this, but most third-party backup solutions include automatic tape rotation schemes where they'll keep track of what tapes you need, how long you've been using them, and what tapes you need to restore any given set of files. Using the built-in rotation scheme of any third-party backup software is generally easy and they're usually good schemes.

One way around the limitations of the preceding scheme is to use Differential backups during the week, instead of Incremental backups. So, you make a Normal backup Friday night and then a Differential on each day of the week. If you had to restore the system after a crash on Friday morning, all you would need to restore is two tapes: the previous

Friday and the one from Thursday night. This is because Differential backups back up all changed files since the last Normal backup. Monday's Differential backs up the files changed on Monday, Tuesday's Differential backs up the files changed on Monday and Tuesday, and so on.

NOTE: A good idea is to keep a recent set of tapes off site, in case a fire or some other catastrophe destroys your computer room. I recommend sending the next to most-recent full backup of your system off site and keeping the most recent tape available for use. This is because situations frequently occur when you must quickly restore files from a recent backup, so you always want to have the most recent backups available for this purpose. But you also need to keep a rotating tape off site that doesn't loose too much data, in case the worst happens.

Frequency of Backups

Is there such a thing as too many backups?

If you followed the Department of Justice versus Microsoft antitrust trial, you were probably astounded at all the old e-mails the government was able to subpoena from the company because Microsoft had good backup schemes for everything on its network and, apparently, the company never got rid of anything. As demonstrated in the trial, keeping everything isn't necessarily the best idea in the world! I'm sure Microsoft would answer the question posed at the beginning of this section with a resounding "Yes, you can have too many backups!"

Discuss with your Legal department setting up a document retention policy and applying it to your e-mail database and backups. Most Legal departments are terrified of getting involved in a lawsuit and having "All e-mails relating to such-and-such a matter from June 1993 to September 1999" subpoenaed. If you think about the effort involved in satisfying such a request, you should be terrified, too. For an e-mail system, this would mean restoring every backup for the time period in question and then searching the e-mail database for all e-mails that fit the criterion, restoring the next tape, and repeating the whole process. If you have hundreds of long-term archival tapes of your e-mail, you're going to be in big trouble trying to fill such a request.

This is where document retention policies can save you. For example, you may work with the Legal department to set up a policy where you only keep four backup tapes of your e-mail system, two tapes that rotate every day, and two that rotate every week. So, on Monday you use Daily A, on Tuesday you use Daily B, on Wednesday you overwrite Daily A with Wednesday's data, and so forth. You do the same thing on Fridays with the two weekly tapes. A minimal scheme like this gives you a good chance to restore the e-mail system should something happen, but it doesn't keep hundreds of copies at the same time. Of course, every company will have to come up with its own balance between the security of having more backups vs. the risks that may be involved.

Using Windows 2000 Server's Backup Software

Windows 2000 Server includes a reliable, easily used backup software program. While it doesn't have all the bells and whistles of some of the third-party backup software programs available (like ArcServe or Backup Exec) it does a good job and will meet most needs. You access the Backup program using this path in the Start menu: Start menu | Programs | Accessories | System Tools | Backup. When you start it, you will first see its welcome screen, as shown in Figure 16-21.

Backup does three important things—it backs up files, restores those files, and can help you prepare for a total system rebuild in case of catastrophic failure. The wizards accessed from the Welcome tab work well and enable you to access all the features of the Backup program easily.

To set up a backup, click the Backup Wizard button on the Welcome tab and then click Next once the opening screen of the Backup Wizard appears. You then see the screen shown in Figure 16-22.

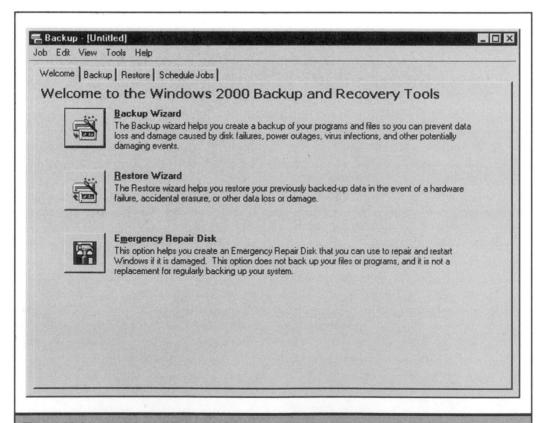

Figure 16-21. Windows 2000 Server backup program

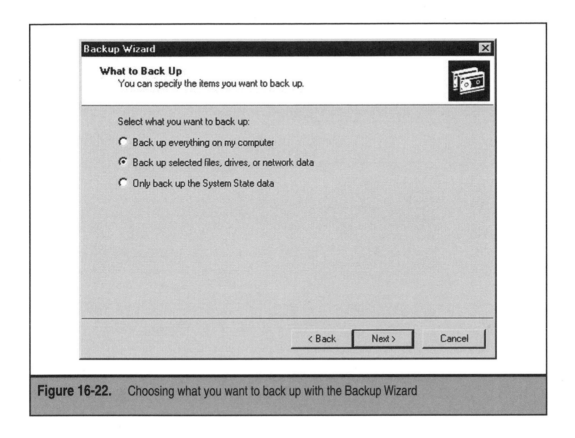

Figure 16-22.   Choosing what you want to back up with the Backup Wizard

Choose the appropriate option, such as "Back up selected files, drives, or network data" and click Next to continue. You then have a chance to select what you want to back up with the Items to Back Up screen shown in Figure 16-23.

Use the tree views in the left-hand pane to select the drives, files, or other computer contents you want to back up. You can also select a special category called *System State*, which includes all the information necessary to rebuild a Windows 2000 Server from scratch, such as key system files, registry data, and so forth. (A good idea is generally to include System State in most backups.) After selecting what you want to back up, click Next to continue. You see the Where to Store the Backup dialog box shown in Figure 16-24.

One nice feature of the Backup program is you can store a backup on any kind of media attached to the computer, including another disk drive, or removable media-like tapes, writable CDs, or JAZ or Zip drives. In the Where to Store the Backup dialog box, choose the destination type and, if you are performing a file-based backup, assign a name to the backup set. After clicking Next another time, you will see a confirmation screen showing all the pertinent details about the backup you are preparing. An important button on the con-

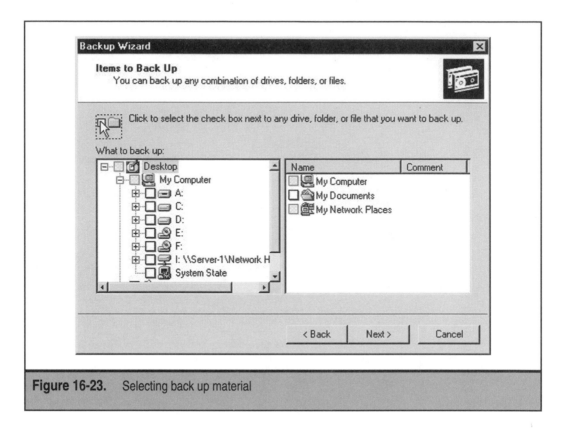

Figure 16-23. Selecting back up material

firmation screen is labeled Advanced. Clicking the Advanced button takes you through another sequence of dialog boxes in which you can set the following properties:

▼ Backup type, where you can choose between Normal, Copy, Incremental, Differential, and Daily backup types

■ Whether the backup data will be verified by reading it after it is written and comparing its contents to the source contents to ensure the backup is correct

■ Whether to append or overwrite any existing backup data on the media target you chose

■ A label for the backup set and media, if you wish to change the default names

▲ Scheduling information for the backup, which can be used to schedule a backup to take place later, and can also be used to set up automatically recurring backup jobs, which will be managed by the Windows 2000 Server Scheduler service

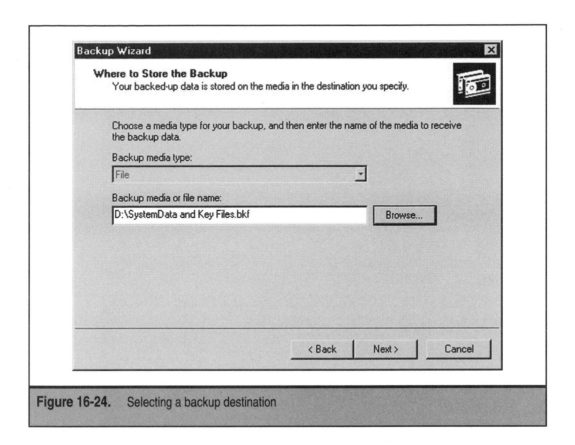

Figure 16-24. Selecting a backup destination

After completing the Advanced settings, if desired, you can click Next on the final Backup Wizard screen either to start the backup or to set it to run at the time you've scheduled.

Restoring files is easier than backing them up. You can either use the Restore tab or the Restore Wizard. Both methods first prompt you to select either the media or the file you used for the backup from which you want to restore and then enable you to browse the list of backed up files and select the ones for restoration. You will have an opportunity to choose whether to overwrite files or to restore the backup to another location on the disk.

CHAPTER SUMMARY

No single chapter can do justice to all the tools and knowledge needed to administer a Windows 2000 Server professionally. In this chapter, though, you saw how the most common and important tasks are handled. If you are or will be administering a Windows 2000 Server, you should pursue even more detailed knowledge about the topics discussed in this chapter and the many other subjects you will need to master.

In particular, start out by researching and learning about these important tools:

▼ Performance Monitor for troubleshooting, performance tuning, and ongoing monitoring of important server statistics. Performance Monitor can be configured to take certain actions when triggers that you set occur, such as beeping you or sending alert messages to other computers on the network. It is also an extremely useful tool for resolving any performance problems you encounter.

■ Event Viewer is key to your ability to find and diagnose Windows 2000 Server problems. You should use Event Viewer on a regular basis (I recommend using it daily) to view new events and decide whether they need your immediate attention. You can use Event Viewer to save the Windows 2000 logs periodically, creating a long-term record of error and informational messages stored in its logs.

■ Network Monitor is an advanced tool for capturing network packets and displaying information about them. It also reports various network statistics that can be useful in troubleshooting network performance problems.

▲ Scheduled Tasks can be used to schedule recurring tasks you want to run frequently on your server, such as virus scans (with third-party virus software), disk defragmentation, and disk testing.

These are some of the core tools you should learn for basic Windows 2000 Server administration. You can also read about some other tools used to administer advanced Windows 2000 Server features in the next chapter.

CHAPTER 17

Understanding Other Windows 2000 Server Services

O ne of the real strengths of Windows 2000 is that it can do many things and fill many roles. Not only is Windows 2000 Server a powerful and effective file and print server, but it's also extremely capable of performing these other tasks right out of the box:

▼ TCP/IP management with DHCP and DNS services

■ Web, FTP, and Telnet services with Internet Information Server

■ Dial-up remote access with Remote Access Service

■ Virtual Private Network access with Routing and Remote Access Service

▲ Mainframe-like Windows terminal support with Terminal Services

The preceding two chapters showed you how Windows 2000 Server is set up in a basic file and print server role, and how Windows 2000 Server is administered on a daily basis. This chapter overviews other available Windows 2000 services, emphasizing services that come with Windows 2000 Advanced Server. To get the most out of Windows 2000 Server, you need to know what additional services are available, how they work, and what they do. However, detailed instructions for implementing these services should be found in a dedicated Windows 2000 Server book, such as *Windows 2000 Administration,* by George Spalding (ISBN: 0-07-212582-2, Osborne/McGraw-Hill).

DHCP SERVER

If you've been involved with computers for long, you probably remember what it was like to manage TCP/IP addresses manually (you may still do this now!). You had to visit every computer on the network to set their TCP/IP address manually. You also had to keep track of which computers used which addresses because you had a limited number of addresses with which to work. Plus, as you probably know, when two computers on a network try to use the same TCP/IP address, trouble quickly follows, and so you had to spend time sorting out these problems.

Dynamic Host Control Protocol (DHCP) saves the day in situations like this. A DHCP server is a computer on the network that keeps track of what TCP/IP addresses are available and parcels them out to computers and other devices that boot up and request a TCP/IP address from the server. With a DHCP server, you needn't worry about address conflicts and you needn't worry about having to renumber the addresses used on computers if your TCP/IP address range ever has to change (as it does when you change ISPs for your network).

NOTE: Because TCP/IP is the default protocol for Windows 2000 Server-based networks and because Windows 2000 Server is designed to operate correctly over a TCP/IP-only network, DHCP services are important and *are installed* with Windows 2000 Server by default. The DHCP services *are not enabled* by default, however, as it's important never to set up conflicting DHCP servers on a network.

DHCP servers work by having a scope defined, which is simply the range (or ranges) of TCP/IP addresses they are allowed to parcel out, along with other associated TCP/IP settings they give to client computers, such as the addresses for DNS or WINS servers also on the network. When they assign a TCP/IP address to a client computer, the address is said to be *leased* and it remains assigned to that client computer for a set period of time. Leases are usually configured to last for two to seven days. During this period, the assigned TCP/IP address is not given out to a different computer.

When a client computer boots up and joins the network, if it is configured to seek a DHCP server, the client computer does so while initializing its TCP/IP protocol stack. Any available DHCP servers respond to the client's request for an address with an available address from its address database. The client computer then takes this address and uses it for the duration of its lease.

The administrator can cancel and reassign scope information when needed. (Usually this is done after-hours when the client computers are turned off.) The administrator can then make changes to the DHCP scope information, which then gets communicated to the clients when they reconnect to the network. In this way, changes such as DNS server addresses or even TCP/IP address ranges can be easily made without having to visit all the computers.

TIP: To access DHCP on a Windows 2000 Server, choose Start menu | Programs | Administrative Tools | DHCP.

While DHCP is a great tool for managing TCP/IP addresses, it should only be used for client computers not hosting any TCP/IP services themselves. For example, you would not want to set up a Web server to use DHCP to get a dynamic TCP/IP address because then clients wishing to connect to the Web server will be unable to find it when its address changes. Instead, you should assign fixed addresses to computers that offer TCP/IP-enabled services either to the local network or through the Internet. This can be done in one of two ways: First, you can simply assign those computers fixed TCP/IP addresses locally and then set up *exclusion ranges* to the scope the DHCP server manages, which prevents it from using or offering those addresses to client computers. Second, you can set up a *reservation* on the DHCP server, which forces it to always assign the reserved address to a specific computer.

DNS

The *Domain Name System* (DNS) is a technology that allows easily used names to be mapped to TCP/IP addresses and ports. For instance, when you use a Web browser and enter the address http://www.yahoo.com, you are using a DNS server to resolve the domain name www.yahoo.com into a particular TCP/IP address, at which point your Web browser transparently uses the TCP/IP address to communicate with the server in question. The DNS system makes the Internet much easier to use than it otherwise would be. (Imagine how excited advertisers would be to say "Visit our Web site at http://65.193.55.38!")

NOTE: General DNS information is discussed in Chapter 5.

Windows 2000 Server includes a full DNS server and, in fact, a DNS server is required for Active Directory to function. If you install the first Active Directory server into a Windows 2000 domain, DNS services are automatically installed; otherwise, you select them manually if you want to add them.

You manage the DNS services with the DNS Management Console plug-in, which you access by choosing Start menu | Programs | Administrative Tools | DNS. Figure 17-1 shows the DNS plug-in.

When you set up DNS for an organization, you first establish a root namespace, usually using the domain name you have registered for the Internet, such as omh.com. You can then create your own subdomains by pre-pending organizational or geographic units, such as italy.omh.com or accounting.omh.com. A Windows 2000 Server running

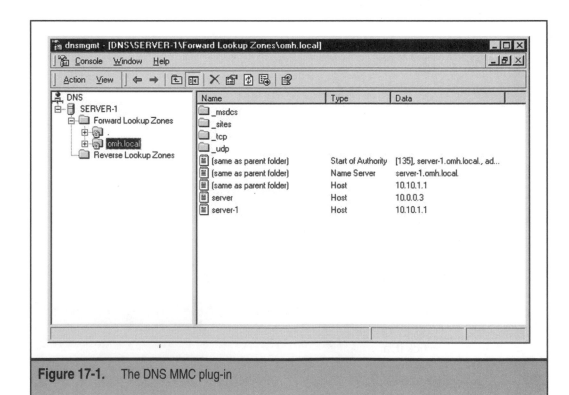

Figure 17-1.   The DNS MMC plug-in

DNS services can manage your own domains and subdomains, and you can also set up multiple DNS servers that each manage a portion of the domain namespace. Each DNS server is responsible for storing all the DNS names used for its managed namespace and for communicating any changes to other DNS servers. When you use multiple DNS servers to each manage portions of your DNS namespace, each DNS server manages a *zone*. Updates between different zones are called *zone transfers*. Windows 2000 DNS services support both full and incremental zone transfers (incremental zone transfers only exchange updated information, which cuts down on network traffic considerably on networks with large DNS namespaces).

Because DNS is integral to Active Directory, it's important for you to establish redundancy for your DNS servers. Microsoft recommends each domain controller also act as a DNS server and you have at least one primary and secondary DNS server for each managed zone. (On small networks, it is possible—and probably desirable because of cost issues—to use only a single DNS server.)

NOTE: Prior to Windows 2000 Server, Windows-based TCP/IP networks actually use two different naming systems. The first, used with TCP/IP, is DNS. The second, used with NetBIOS and NetBEUI, is *Windows Internet Name Service* (WINS). With Windows 2000 Server, DNS services also can be configured to provide WINS services to the network.

RAS AND RRAS

Remote Access Service, usually just called RAS, provides a way for you to set up dial-in support to your network, where remote client computers form a remote-node connection to the network using some form of dial-up connection. Dial-up connections can be made with modems and telephone lines or ISDN connections. (Of course, both sides of a RAS connection must support the connection type!) RAS services easily enable you to set up a Windows 2000 Server to act as a RAS server to the network, to which remote users connect and gain access to the network's resources.

Routing and Remote Access Service (RRAS) is also a remote-access technology, but it includes routing capabilities that enables connections to the network over a public network—like the Internet—using *Virtual Private Network* (VPN) technology. A VPN works by setting up a secure "tunnel" between a client and the RRAS server through which encrypted packets pass. The client computer dials up its normal Internet ISP and then forms a VPN connection to the RRAS server over the Internet, in a secure fashion.

RAS and RRAS are administered through the same tool on Windows 2000 Server. Choose Start menu | Programs | Administrative Tools | Routing and Remote Access to access the MMC plug-in. Once started, select the server on which you want to enable remote access, right-click it, and choose Configure and Enable Routing and Remote Access. A helpful wizard guides you through the process and enables you to choose whether to enable only remote access, only routing/remote access, or both. Figure 17-2 shows the Routing and Remote Access plug-in once RRAS has been enabled.

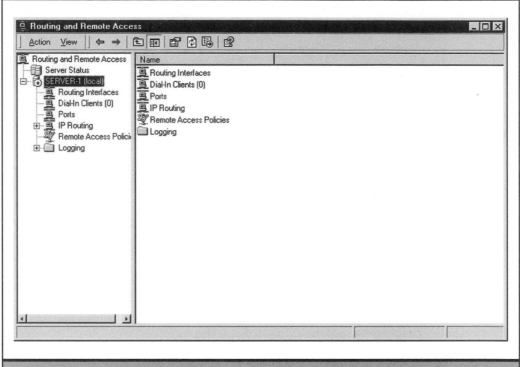

Figure 17-2.   Use the Routing and Remote Access MMC plug-in to administer remote access

Remote access services under Windows 2000 Server are secure and offer considerable flexibility in setting them up to work in the way you want. First, you must enable a user to access the network remotely, which can be done by editing the user's properties dialog box (see Chapter 16). Then, you can configure RRAS to use a number of control features that enable you to keep remote access secure, including:

▼ Setting times and days when remote access is operational.

■ Setting times and days when specific users or groups can use remote access.

■ Limiting access to only the RRAS server or to specific services on the network.

■ Using call-back features, where a remote client dials into the network and logs in. The network then disconnects the connection and dials the user back at a predefined phone number.

▲ Setting access policies based on remote client computer name or TCP/IP address.

Through the use of RAS and RRAS, you can easily set up Windows 2000 Server to provide important remote access services to remote users, both over dial-up connections and through the Internet, in a secure and productive fashion.

INTERNET INFORMATION SERVER

Windows 2000 Server includes a set of Internet services that run as part of *Internet Information Server* (IIS). IIS includes Web, FTP, SMTP, and NNTP services, each of which can be started or stopped independently. IIS is administered through the Internet Services Manager program found in the Administrative Tools program group. Figure 17-3 shows the Internet Services Manager.

IIS Web services provide comprehensive Web hosting software. You can define multiple Web sites with IIS, each one administered separately. For each site, you specify the

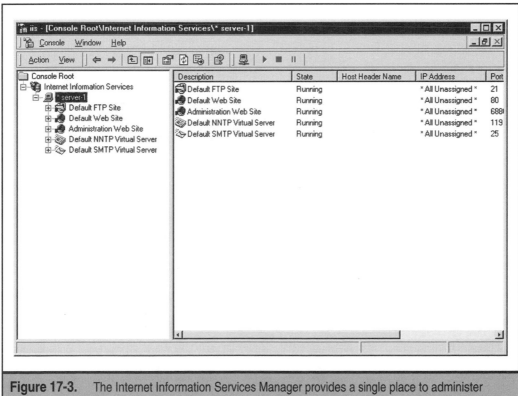

Figure 17-3.   The Internet Information Services Manager provides a single place to administer Internet services

directory in which the site's files can be found, as well as security settings for the site and performance parameters to optimize the performance of the Web site.

IIS FTP services enable you to set up an FTP site on a Windows 2000 Server computer. You define the FTP directory, as well as whether directory listings will be shown in UNIX- or MS-DOS-style formats. You can also set security settings to allow or disallow different client computers or client networks access to the FTP server, and whether you will permit anonymous FTP logins.

The NNTP server in IIS enables you to set up your own Usenet-style site using the NNTP protocol. Clients can connect to your NNTP server using tools like Outlook Express or other Usenet newsreaders.

Finally, the *Simple Mail Transfer Protocol* (SMTP) server allows SMTP connections to be formed between the system running IIS and remote SMTP mail systems. SMTP is the standard protocol for exchanging e-mail over the Internet.

CLUSTER SERVICES

Windows Cluster Services enables you to combine together two or more servers into a *cluster*. These clusters can be configured to fill one of several different cluster roles:

▼   Network Load Balancing clusters enable you to share TCP/IP-based services—such as a Web server—among up to 32 Windows 2000 servers

▲   *Server clusters* provide fail-over support in case one of the servers in the cluster fails. The two servers share a common disk array and share access to the array for the various services and applications each runs. You can perform limited load balancing by running some services on one server and others on the other server. If one server fails, the other one seamlessly takes over its duties. Server clusters also enable you to move services onto one server or another, which is useful when doing in-place upgrades.

Cluster Services is an invaluable tool when building high-availability, high-performance networks. However, the setup, care, and feeding of clusters is a complicated subject. If you need to deploy clusters, you should carefully read the Microsoft documentation related to their setup and maintenance, and consider purchasing a book dedicated to clustering with Windows 2000.

WINDOWS TERMINAL SERVICES

The final service discussed in this chapter, but possibly one of the most powerful, is *Windows Terminal Services* (WTS). WTS enables you to set up a Windows 2000 Server almost as if it's a mainframe—where terminals can connect and all the work is performed on the central computer—in this case, a Windows 2000 Server computer. A client computer connects to the Terminal Server using a TCP/IP connection, either over a dial-up or a LAN/WAN connection, and logs in. From then on, the client computer is only responsible for displaying screens and accepting keyboard and mouse input; all work is actually being done on the Terminal Server through the creation of a virtual Windows machine on the server. A *Terminal Server* can create many virtual Windows machines, each one carrying out its own tasks and running its own programs.

When would you use a Terminal Server connection to a network instead of a remote node connection, such as the remote node connections offered via RAS and RRAS? The answer is dependent on a number of factors, of which the following are possible considerations:

▼ The remote computer doesn't have adequate resources to run some application or perform some task. By running its programs on the Terminal Server, the remote computer can take advantage of the Terminal Server's resources. For example, say some application runs optimally only when it has 2GB of RAM with which to work. In a case like this, a simple Windows 98 client with 64MB of RAM can connect to the Terminal Server (that has 2-4GB of RAM) and run the application in question. Similarly, some applications may require many processors or direct access to large disk arrays, or to some other centrally located resource to which the Terminal Server has access.

■ Over low-bandwidth connections, such as 33.6Kbps modem connections, some applications work far more effectively using a remote-control approach rather than a remote-node approach. Most remote access connections are low-bandwidth and yet some applications need high-bandwidth requirements to work properly. Because a remote computer connected to a Terminal Server only has to transfer display and input information, the application running on the Terminal Server can run much faster than it could over a remote-node connection.

▲ Some applications and tasks, such as administration of a Windows 2000 Server, cannot be fully performed by another computer even if it has a connection running at LAN speeds. Terminal Services allows a remote computer to—with the appropriate permissions—run such applications. For instance, say your company has a remote network located somewhere in Asia, but the network is not large enough to justify a local administrative person. Using Terminal Services, you could connect to that network over the company WAN and perform all necessary administrative tasks, such as configuring hard disks, shares, additional network protocols, and so forth.

Aside from being driven by certain applications that may need Terminal Services, you may want to consider Terminal Services anyway, as an adjunct to your remote access services. If you have many remote users to support, you may find some users have needs best served by remote node connections and some have needs best served by remote-control connections. Running both services on your network adds considerable flexibility in your ability to support remote users and anything they may throw at you.

NOTE: If you implement Terminal Services, make sure you carefully review Microsoft's license agreement and pricing models, which differ when you use Terminal Services.

CHAPTER SUMMARY

The Windows 2000 Server family is perhaps the richest NOS environment available today. While other NOS products can perform all the tasks described in this chapter, none include all these capabilities with their NOS offerings; add-on purchases are required. Because of the richness with which Windows 2000 Server is packaged, you can more easily put together a server to meet nearly any need you may have. And because the various Windows 2000 Server services work so well together, you can easily implement nearly all these advanced services on just a single server! This "out-of-the-box" flexibility is one of the reasons the Windows NT Server NOS has been gaining market share so rapidly over the past several years and why it's a safe bet Windows 2000 Server will continue this trend.

CHAPTER 18

Installing Linux in a Server Configuration

A key attribute in Linux's recent success has been the remarkable improvement in installation tools. What once was a mildly frightening process many years back has now become almost trivial. The improvement in different ways the software can be installed has been even better; CD-ROM's (although still the most common) are not the only choice. Network installations are part of the default list of options as well, which can be a wonderful thing when installing a large number of hosts.

Most default configurations Linux gets installed in are already capable of becoming servers. This is, unfortunately, due to a slightly naïve design decision: a server means it serves everything—from disk services to printers to mail to news to. . . . It's all turned on from the start. As you know, the reality of most servers is they are dedicated to performing one or two tasks and any other installed services simply take up memory and drag on performance.

In this chapter, the installation process of Red Hat Linux 6.1 as it pertains to servers is discussed. This requires us to do two things: differentiate between what a server and client workstation are, and streamline a server's operation based on what it will be dedicated on doing.

NOTE: With a variety of Linux distributions available, why was Red Hat the choice here? The answer is simple: Red Hat is both popular and technically sound. Red Hat is friendly to a lot of different crowds and, from the standpoint of having to install it for the first time, it is also friendly to the user (that the entire distribution is available free from the Internet is also a plus!). As you become more experienced with Linux, you may find other distributions interesting and you should look into them. It is, after all, one of the war cries of Linux users everywhere—freedom of choice is crucial. You should never feel locked into a proprietary system.

BEFORE THE INSTALLATION

Before getting into the actual installation phase, evaluating two things is important:

▼   What hardware is the system going to run on?

▲   How should the server be best configured to provide the services you need from it?

Let's start with examining hardware issues.

Hardware

Like any operating system, determining what hardware configurations work before getting started with an installation process is prudent. Each commercial vendor publishes a Hardware Compatibility List (HCL) and makes the lists available on its Web sites. Be sure you obtain the latest versions of these lists so you are confident in the hardware selected. In general, most popular Intel-based configurations work without difficulty. Red Hat's

Web page is at http://www.redhat.com/hardware and Caldera's HCL is at http://www.calderasystems.com/products/openlinux/hardware.html.

A general suggestion that applies to all operating systems is to avoid bleeding-edge hardware and software configurations. While these appear impressive, they haven't had the maturing process some of the slightly older hardware has already gone through. For servers, this usually isn't an issue because no need exists for a server to have the latest and greatest toys, such as fancy video cards. After all, the main goal is to provide a highly available server for our users, not to play Doom. (Although I've heard some people have found Linux to remain stable as a fileserver, even with Doom running.)

Server Design

When a system becomes a server, its stability, availability, and performance become a significant issue. These three are usually tackled through the purchase of more hardware, which is unfortunate. Paying thousands of dollars extra to get a system capable of achieving all three, when the desired level of performance could have been extracted from existing hardware with a little tuning, is a shame, which everyone should make an effort to avoid. With Linux, this is not hard. Even better, the gains are outstanding!

The most significant design decision you must make when managing a server configuration is not technical, but administrative. You must design a server *not* to be friendly to casual users. This means no cute multimedia tools, no sound card support, and no fancy Web browsers (when at all possible). In fact, someone should make a rule that casual use of a server is strictly prohibited. This means not only site users, but site administrators as well.

Another important aspect of designing a server is making sure it has a good environment. As a systems administrator, you must insure the physical safety of your servers by keeping them in a separate room under lock and key (or the equivalent). The only access to the servers for nonadministrative personnel should be through the network. The server room itself should be well ventilated and kept cool. Not doing so is a cookbook formula for an accident waiting to happen. Systems that overheat and nosy users who "think" they know how to fix problems can be as great a danger to sever stability as bad software (arguably, even more so).

Once the system is safely located behind locked doors, installing battery backup is also crucial. This serves two key purposes: the first is (obviously) to keep the system running during a power failure so it may gracefully shut down, thereby avoiding having to lose any files. The second is to insure voltage spikes, drops, and other noises don't interfere with the health of your system.

Some specifics you can do to improve your server situation are:

▼ Take advantage of the fact that the GUI is uncoupled from the core operating system and avoid starting X-Windows unless someone needs to sit on the console and run an application. After all, X-Windows, like any other application, requires memory and CPU time to work, both of which are better off going to the server processes instead.

■ Determine what functions you want the server to perform and disable all other functions. Not only are unused functions a waste of memory and CPU, but they are just another issue you need to deal with on the security front.

▲ Linux, unlike some other operating systems, enables you to pick and choose features you want in the kernel. The default kernel you get is already reasonably well tuned, so you needn't worry about it. If you do need to change a feature or upgrade a kernel, though, be picky about what you add and what you don't. Make sure you need a feature before adding it.

NOTE: You may hear an old recommendation that you recompile your kernel to make the most effective use of your system resources. This is no longer true—the only reason you should want to recompile your kernel is to upgrade or add support for a new device. This falls into the philosophy of "don't screw around with what's stable and performs reasonably."

Uptime

All this chatter about taking care of servers and making sure silly things don't cause them to crash stems from a long-time UNIX philosophy: *Uptime is good. More uptime is better.*

The **uptime** command tells the user how long the system has been running since its last boot, how many users are currently logged in, and how much load the system is experiencing. The latter two are useful measures necessary for daily system health and long-term planning, for example, server load has been staying high lately, maybe it's time to buy a faster/bigger/better server.

But the all-important number is how long the server has been running since its last reboot. Long uptimes are a sign of proper care, maintenance, and, from a practical standpoint, system stability. You often find UNIX administrators boasting about their server's uptimes the way you hear car buffs boast about horsepower. This is also why you hear UNIX administrators cursing at Windows installations that require a reboot for every little change. In contrast, you'll be pressed to find any changes to a UNIX system that require a reboot to take effect.

You might deny caring about it now. In six months, you may scream at anyone who reboots a system unnecessarily. Don't bother trying to explain this to a nonadmin because he or she will just look at you oddly. You'll know in your heart your uptime is better than theirs.

Dual-Booting Issues

If you are new to Linux, you may not be ready to commit a complete system for the sake of "test-driving." Understanding that we live in a hetereogeneous world, all distributions of Linux can be installed on only certain partitions of your hard disk, while leaving others alone. Typically, this means allowing Microsoft Windows to co-exist with Linux.

Because the focus here is on server installations, the details of building a dual-booting system won't be covered. Anyone with a little experience in creating partitions on a disk, however, should be able to figure this out. If you are having difficulty, you may want to reference the installation guide that came with your distribution or another one of the many beginner's guides to Linux available on the market.

Some quick hints: If Windows 95 or Windows 98 currently consumes an entire hard disk as drive C:, you can use the **fips** tool to repartition the disk. Simply defragment and then run **fips.exe**. If you are using Windows NT and have already allocated all the disk with data on each partition, you may have to do a little moving around of data by hand to free a partition. Don't bother trying to shrink an NTFS partition, though, because it is a journaling file system and it cannot be defragmented and resized.

NOTE: From the perspective of flexibility, NTFS doesn't sound like a good thing but, in reality, it is. If you have to run NT, use NTFS.

In either case, you may find using a commercial tool like Partition Magic especially helpful.

Methods of Installation

With the improved connectivity and speed of both local area networks and Internet connections, an increasingly popular option is to perform installations over the network, rather than needing a local CD-ROM.

In general, you'll find network installations become important once you decide to deploy Linux over many machines and you require a fast installation procedure where many systems can install in parallel.

Typically, server installations aren't well suited to automation because each server usually has a unique task, thus, each server has a slightly different configuration. For example, a server dedicated to handling logging information sent to it over the network is going to have especially large partitions set up for the appropriate logging directories, as compared to a file server that performs no logging of its own.

Because of this, the focus here is exclusively on the technique for installing a system from a CD-ROM. Of course, once you have gone through the process from a CD-ROM once, you will find performing the network-based installations straightforward to do.

If It Just Won't Work Right . . .

You've gone through the installation procedure . . . twice. This book said it should work. The installation manual said it should work. The Linux guru you spoke with last week said it should work.

But it's just not working.

In the immortal words of Douglas Adams, "Don't panic." No operating system installs smoothly 100 percent of the time. (Yes, even for the MacOS!) Hardware doesn't always work as advertised, combinations of hardware conflict with each other, or that CD-ROM your friend burned for you has CRC errors on it. (Remember: it is legal for your buddy to burn you a copy of Linux!) Or, (hopefully not), the software has a bug.

With Linux, you have several paths you can traverse to get help. If you have purchased your copy from Caldera or Red Hat, you can always call their tech support lines and get a knowledgeable person on the phone, who is dedicated to working through the problem with you. If you didn't purchase a box set, you can try contacting companies, such as LinuxCare (www.linuxcare.com), which is a commercial company dedicated to providing help. Last, but certainly not least, is the option of going online for help. An incredible number of Web sites are available to help you get started. They contain not only useful tips and tricks, but also documentation and discussion forums where you can post your questions. Obviously, you want to start with the site dedicated to your distribution, www.redhat.com for Red Hat Linux and www.caldera.com for Caldera Linux. (Other distributions have their own sites. Check your distribution for its appropriate Web site information.)

Some recommended sites for installation help:

▼ **comp.os.linux.admin**   This is a newsgroup, not a Web site. You can read it through the Web at http://www.deja.com.

■ **http://www.ojichan.com/linux-admin/**   This site contains a book titled *Linux Administration Made Easy.* The book is geared toward cookbook administration tasks and contains some useful tips for installing Red Hat Linux.

▲ **http://www.linuxdoc.org/**   This site is a collective of wonderful information about all sorts of Linux-related topics, including installation guides. Just a warning, though: Not all documents are current. Be sure to check the last time the document was updated before following the directions. A mix of cookbook-style help guides exist, as well as guides that give more complete explanations for what is happening.

INSTALLING RED HAT LINUX

In this section, the steps necessary to install Red Hat Linux 6.1 on a stand-alone system are documented. A liberal approach to the process is taken, installing all the tools possibly relevant to server operations. Later chapters explain each subsystem's purpose and help you determine whether you need to keep it.

You have two ways to start the boot process: you can use a boot floppy disk or the CD-ROM. This installation guide assumes you will boot off the CD-ROM to start the Red Hat installation procedure. If you have an older machine incapable of booting from the CD-ROM, you need to use a boot disk and start the procedure from there.

NOTE: Using the boot disk alters the order of some of the steps during the installation, such as which language to use and whether to use a hard disk or a CD-ROM for installation. Once you pass the initial differences, you will find the graphical steps are the same.

If your system supports bootable CD-ROM's, this is obviously the faster approach. If your distribution did not come with a boot disk and you cannot boot from the CD-ROM, you need to create the boot disk. I assume you have a working installation of Windows to create the boot disk.

NOTE: Users of other UNIX operating systems can use the **dd** command to create the boot image onto a floppy disk. Follow the instructions that came with your distribution on using the **dd** command with your floppy device.

TIP: "But I don't want to use the graphical installer!" Don't worry, Red Hat realized plenty of people still exist who prefer text-based installation tools and some who need to use them for systems that do not support graphics. If you fall into one of these categories, type **text** at the boot: prompt when starting Linux from either the CD-ROM or floppy disk.

Creating a Boot Disk

Once Windows has started and the CD-ROM is in the appropriate drive, open up a MS-DOS Prompt window (Start | Program Menu | MS-DOS prompt), which gives you a command shell prompt. Change over to the drive letter where the CD-ROM is and go into the **dosutils** directory. There you find the **rawrite.exe** program. Simply run the executable and you will be prompted for the source file and destination floppy disk.

The source file is on the same drive and is called \images\boot.img.

Starting the Installation

To start the installation process, boot off the CD-ROM. This presents you with a splash screen introducing you to Red Hat 6.1. At the bottom of the screen is a prompt that reads:

```
boot:
```

If you do not press any keys, the prompt automatically times out and begins the installation process. You can press ENTER to start the process immediately.

If you have had some experience with Red Hat installations in the past and you do not want the system to probe your hardware automatically, you can type in **expert** at the boot: prompt. For most installations, though, you want to stick with the default.

NOTE: As the initial part of the operating system loads and autodetects hardware, do not be surprised if it does not detect your SCSI subsystem. SCSI support is activated later in the process.

Choosing a Language

The first menu you are prompted with asks in which language you want to continue the installation process (see Figure 18-1).

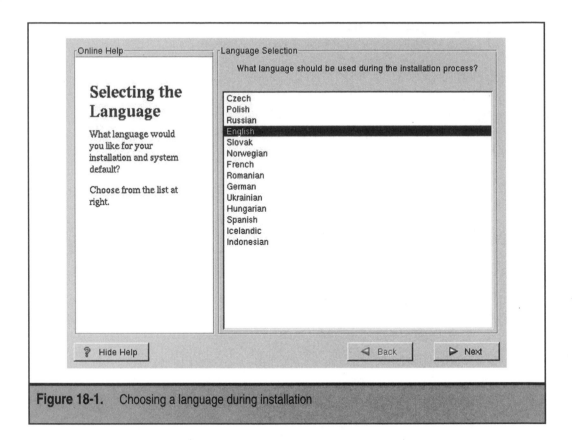

Figure 18-1. Choosing a language during installation

The interface works much like any other Windows-style interface. Simply point and click on your selection. When you are ready, click the Next button in the lower-right portion of the screen.

On the left side of the screen is context-sensitive help. If you don't want to see it, you can click the Hide Help button at the lower-left part of the screen.

The Back button in the lower-right of the screen is grayed out at this point because there have been no prior options to select.

Selecting a Keyboard Type

This next menu enables you to select what kind of keyboard you have. The options are broken into three dialog boxes: the first lists the types of keyboards supported, the second lists available layouts the keyboard can have, and the third enables us to pick available additional variants. The bottommost dialog box is meant for you to type in, thereby enabling you to test whether your keyboard works. You don't have to type anything in there if you don't want to do so.

For most of us, the keyboard type will be one of the Generic options, the layout will be U.S. English, and the variant will be set to None (see Figure 18-2).

TIP: If you ever want to change your keyboard layout or type, you can run the program /usr/sbin/kbdconfig.

When you finish, click Next to continue or select Back to go back to the language selection menu.

Selecting a Mouse

You now can select the type of mouse you want to use with the X-Windows environment (X-Windows is Linux's graphical user interface). More than likely, the auto-probe will have been able to highlight what you already have.

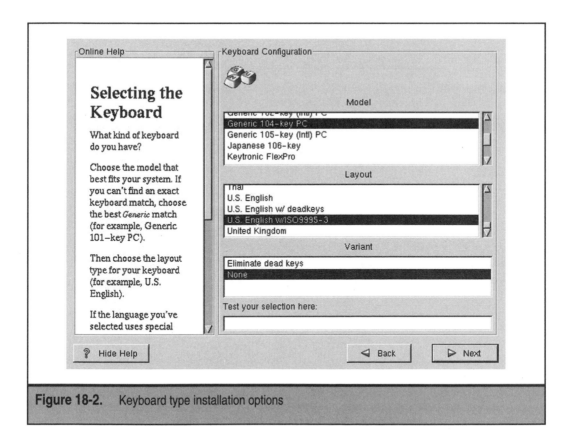

Figure 18-2. Keyboard type installation options

If you need to help Linux, simply pick the type of mouse you have in the top menu box (see Figure 18-3). If you see the name brand of the mouse with a plus sign (+) to the left of it, clicking the plus sign will open a new level of choices for that particular brand. If you have a serial mouse, you also need to select the serial port it is using. That is done in the lower box in the screen.

If you have a two-button mouse, you want to click Emulate 3 Buttons at the bottom of the screen. This is because some features of the X-Windows environment only work with a three-button mouse. Doing so enables you to click both buttons of a two-button mouse to emulate the middle button.

TIP: If you change the type of mouse you have later, you can run /usr/sbin/mouseconfig to reconfigure your mouse.

Welcome to Red Hat Linux

With the input devices and language selected, you are now ready to begin the actual installation phase of Red Hat Linux. This starts with a splash screen whose corresponding help bar tells you how to register Red Hat Linux if you purchased the boxed version.

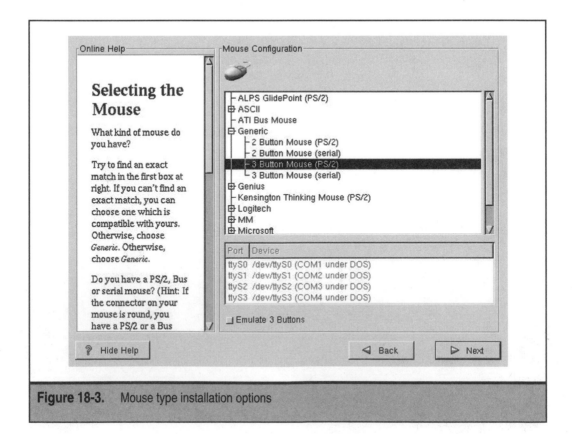

Figure 18-3.   Mouse type installation options

Once you have read the information about registering, you can simply click Next to continue.

Upgrading or Installing?

Now you see a screen that enables us to pick how you want to install Red Hat Linux. If you are on an upgrade path, this selection is easy. Simply click Upgrade and then click Next. This leads you through some screens that inform you what is being upgraded as it performs the upgrades.

For this chapter, you can assume you're doing a clean installation. This will wipe out all the existing contents of the disk before freshly installing Red Hat 6.1.

Note that there is an option to install Linux in a server configuration (see Figure 18-4). This method has all the packages preselected for you, as well as a disk partitioning scheme. For this chapter, you want to choose Custom, so you can fine tune what you install and how you configure it.

Creating Partitions for Linux

Because you selected to go via the custom-installation route, you need to create partitions for Linux to install on. If you are used to the Windows installation process, you will find this is a little different than the way partitioning Windows into separate drives works.

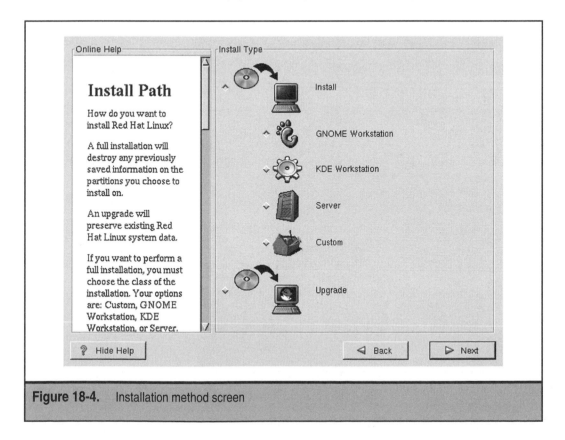

Figure 18-4. Installation method screen

In short, each partition is *mounted* at boot time. The mount process makes the contents of that partition available as if it were just another directory on the system. So, for example, the root directory (/) is on the first (*root*) partition. A subdirectory called /usr exists on the root directory, but it has nothing in it. A separate partition can then be mounted so going into the /usr directory enables you to see the contents of the newly mounted partition (see Figure 18-5).

Because all the partitions, when mounted, appear as a unified directory tree rather than separate drives, the installation software does not differentiate between one partition and another. All it cares about is which directory each file goes into. As a result, the installation process automatically distributes its files across all the mounted partitions, so long as the mounted partitions represent different parts of the directory tree where files are usually placed. Under Linux, the most significant grouping of files happens in the /usr directory, where all of the actual programs reside. (In Windows terms, it's similar to Program Files.)

Because you are configuring a server, you must be aware of the additional large grouping of files that will exist over the life of the server. They are

▼ **/usr**   Where all the program files will reside (similar to C:\Program Files).

■ **/home**   Where everyone's home directory will be (assuming this server will house them). This is useful for keeping users from consuming an entire disk and leaving other critical components without space, for example, log files.

■ **/var**   The final destination for log files. Because log files can be affected by outside users (for example, individuals visiting a Web site), partitioning these

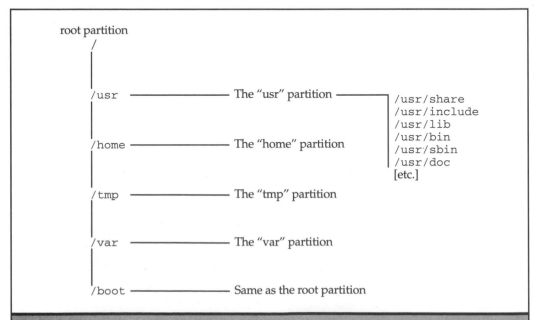

Figure 18-5.   A visualization of how separate partitions exist in a single directory tree

off is important, so no one can perform a Denial of Service (DoS) attack by generating so many log entries the entire disk fills up.

- **/tmp** Temporary files are placed here. Because this directory is designed so it is world writable by any user (similar to the C:\TEMP directory under Windows), you need to make sure arbitrary users don't abuse this and fill the entire disk by keeping it on a separate partition.

- ▲ **Swap** This isn't a user-accessible file system, but it is where the virtual memory file is stored. Although Linux (and other UNIX's as well) can use a normal disk file to hold virtual memory the way Windows does, you'll find by having it on its own partition improves performance.

This is why it is a good idea to create multiple partitions on a disk, rather than a single large partition, which you may be used to doing under Microsoft Windows. As you become more familiar with the hows and whys of partitioning disks under Linux, you may choose to go back to a single large partition. At that point, of course, you will have enough knowledge of both systems to understand why one may work better for you than the other.

Now that you have some background on partitioning under Linux, let's get back to the installation process itself. You should be at a screen that looks like Figure 18-6.

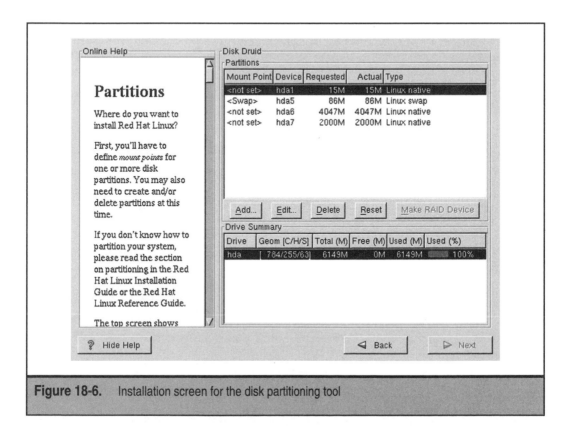

Figure 18-6. Installation screen for the disk partitioning tool

The Disk Druid partitioning tool was developed by Red Hat as an easy way to create partitions and associate them to the directories to which they will be mounted. When starting Disk Druid, you see all the existing partitions on your disk. Each partition entry shows the following information:

▼ **Mount point**   The location where the partition is mounted. Initially, this should not have any entries in it.

■ **Device**   Linux associates each partition with a separate *device*. For the purpose of installation, you only need to know that under IDE disks, each device begins with /dev/hdXY where X is:

- ■ **a** for Primary chain, primary disk
- ■ **b** for Primary chain, secondary disk
- ■ **c** for Secondary chain, primary disk
- ■ **d** for Secondary chain, secondary disk

and Y is the partition number of the disk. For example, /dev/hda1 is the first partition on the primary chain, primary disk. SCSI follows the same basic idea except, instead of starting with /dev/hd, each partition starts with /dev/sd and follows the format /dev/sdXY, where X is a letter representing a unique physical drive (**a** is for SCSI id 1, **b** is for SCSI id 2, etc.). The Y represents the partition number. Thus, /dev/sdb4 is the fourth partition on the SCSI disk with id 2. The system is a little more complex than Windows, but each partition's location is explicit—no more guessing "to what physical device does E: correspond?"

■ **Requested**   The minimum size requested when the partition was defined.

■ **Actual**   The actual amount of space allocated for that partition.

▲ **Type**   The partition's type. Linux's default type is Linux Native, but Disk Druid also understands many others, including FAT, VFAT, and NTFS.

The second half of the screen shows the drive summaries. Each line represents a single drive and its characteristics. Among the information presented is:

▼ The drive name (without the preceeding /dev/)

■ The disk geometry in Cylinders/Heads/Sectors format

■ Total size of the disk

■ Amount of disk that has been allocated (partitioned)

▲ Amount of available disk that can still be partitioned

In the middle of the screen are the menu choices for what you can do with Disk Druid. These buttons are

▼ **Add**   Create a new partition.

■ **Edit**   Change the parameters on the highlighted partition.

- **Delete** Delete the highlighted partition.
- **Reset** Reset all of the changes back to the original settings.
- **Make RAID Device** Begin the process of setting up a RAID configuration. On any operating system, setting up a RAID configuration is non-trivial and has implications that are not always obvious. This is out of the scope for this chapter.
- **Next** Commit changes to disk.
- ▲ **Back** Abort all changes made using Disk Druid and exit the program.

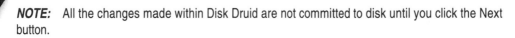

NOTE: All the changes made within Disk Druid are not committed to disk until you click the Next button.

ADDING A PARTITION To create a new partition, click the Add button. This brings up a dialog box that should resemble Figure 18-7.

Each of the elements in the dialog box are as follows:

- ▼ **Mount Point** The directory where you want this partition to be automatically mounted at boot time.
- **Size (Megs)** The size of the partition in megabytes.
- **Grow to fill disk?** By using the space bar to check this box, you are telling Disk Druid you want to grow this partition later. If you have an especially large disk and you don't know how much to allocate to what, you may find it handy to size each partition as you need it now and select the "Grow to fill disk?" option. Thus, as the system gets used and you see which partitions need more space than others, you can easily grow the necessary partitions without repartitioning your disk.

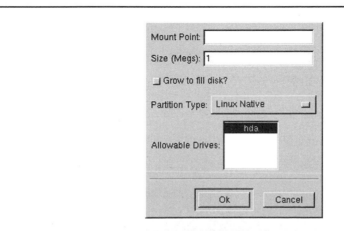

Figure 18-7.   The Add Partition dialog box

- **Partition Type**   The type of partition that will reside on that disk. By default, you want to select Linux Native, except for the swap partition that should be Linux Swap.

▲ **Allowable Drives**   Specifies onto which drives the partition should be created.

Once you finish entering all the information, click OK to continue.

At a minimum, you need to have two partitions: one for holding all the files and the other for swap space. *Swap space* is usually sized to be double the available RAM if less than 128M of RAM exists or the exact same amount of RAM if there is 128M+.

Realistically, you want to separate partitions out for /usr, /var, /home, and /tmp in addition to a root partition. You can adjust this equation based on the purpose of the server.

OTHER PARTITION MANIPULATION TASKS   Once you have gone through the steps of adding a partition and you are comfortable with the variables involved (mount points, sizes, types, devices, and so forth), the actual process of editing and deleteing partitions is quite simple. *Editing an entry* means simply changing the same entries you established when you added the partition. *Deleting an entry* requires only that you confirm you want to perform the deletion.

Formatting Partitions

This screen presents you with a list of all the newly created partitions (see Figure 18-8). Because you are wiping the disk of previous installations, you want to select all the partitions to be formatted. (More accurately, Red Hat will be creating a file system on it.)

TIP: If you are using an older drive and you aren't sure about its reliability, click the "Check for bad blocks while formatting" option, listed directly below all the partitions. This causes the formatting process to take significantly longer, but at least you will know for sure whether the disk is reliable.

Installing LILO

LILO is the boot manager for Linux. A *boot manager,* if you aren't already familiar with what it does, handles the process of actually starting the load process of an operating system. If you're familiar with Windows NT, you have already dealt with the NT Loader (NTLDR), which presents the menu at boot time, enabling you to select whether you want "Windows NT" or "Windows NT (vga only)." LILO effectively does the same thing, just without flashy menus.

In the Red Hat tool for setting up LILO, three sections of the screen appear (see Figure 18-9). The top of the screen enables you to select whether you want a boot disk to be made. For obvious reasons, having a boot disk is a good idea.

The middle block of the screen enables you to select whether you want to have LILO set up on the master boot record (MBR) or the first partition on which Linux resides. The MBR is the first thing the system reads when booting a system. The MBR is essentially the point where the built-in hardware tests finish and pass control off to the software. If you choose to have LILO installed here, LILO loads with a **boot:** prompt when you turn on your system or reboot it, and enables you to select which operating system to load. In a server configuration, only one choice should exist!

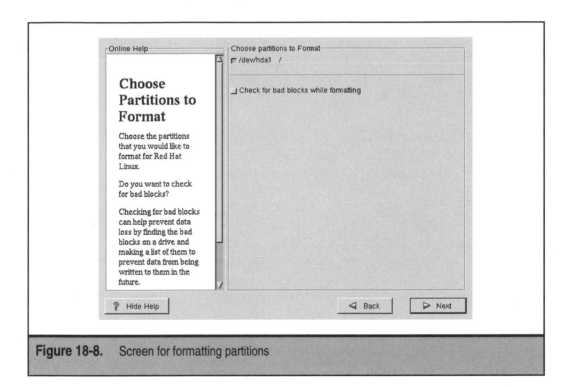

Figure 18-8.   Screen for formatting partitions

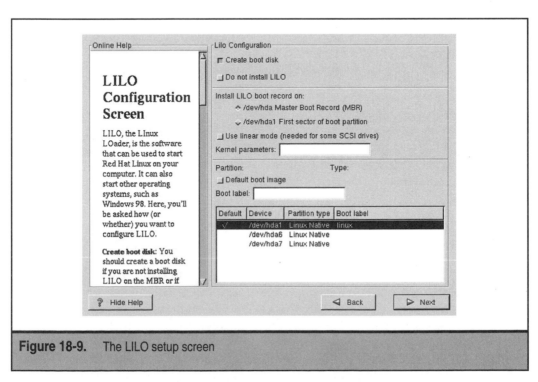

Figure 18-9.   The LILO setup screen

If you are already using another boot loader and prefer it, then you will want to place LILO on the first sector of the root partition. This will allow your preferred boot loader to run first and then pass control off to LILO if you decide to start Linux.

Also in the middle block is an option to use linear mode. This only applies to some SCSI drives or drives that are accessed in LBA mode.

The last option in the middle block is a box that enables you to enter kernel parameters to be used at boot time. For most people, nothing needs to be placed here. If the documentation for a particular feature or device requires you to pass a parameter here, add it. Otherwise, leave it blank.

Finally, the bottom part of the screen enables you to select which operating systems LILO enables you to select at boot time. On a system configured to support both Windows and Linux, you will see your choices here. Because our system is only meant for Linux, one choice is seen.

NOTE: The exception is for SMP-based systems, which have two choices. The first choice, "linux," is set up to support multiple processors. If this doesn't work out for you, "linux-up" is also available, which uses only one processor, but at least gets you up and going.

Setting up Networking

Red Hat is now ready to configure your network interface cards (see Figure 18-10).

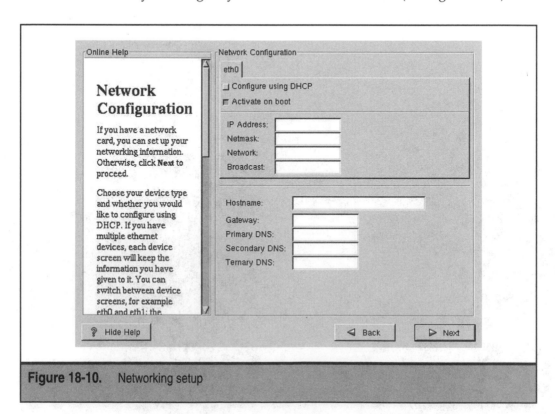

Figure 18-10.   Networking setup

Each interface card you have is listed as a tabbed menu on the top of your screen. Ethernet devices are enumerated eth0, eth1, eth2, and so forth. For each interface, you can either configure it using DHCP or setting the IP address by hand. If you choose to configure by hand, be sure to have the IP address, netmask, network, and broadcast addresses ready. Finally, click the "Activate on boot" option if you want the interface to be enabled at boot time.

On the bottom half of the screen, you see the configuration choices for giving the machine a host name, gateway, and related DNS information. Once you have all this filled out, click Next to continue.

Time Zone Configuration

The time zone configuration screen (see Figure 18-11) enables you to select in which time zone the machine is located. If your system's hardware clock keeps time in UTC, be sure to click the UTC button, so Linux can determine the difference between the two and correctly display the local time.

Creating Accounts

The Red Hat Installation tool creates one account for you called *root*. This user account is similar in nature to the Administrator account under Windows NT—the user who is allowed access to this account has full control of the system.

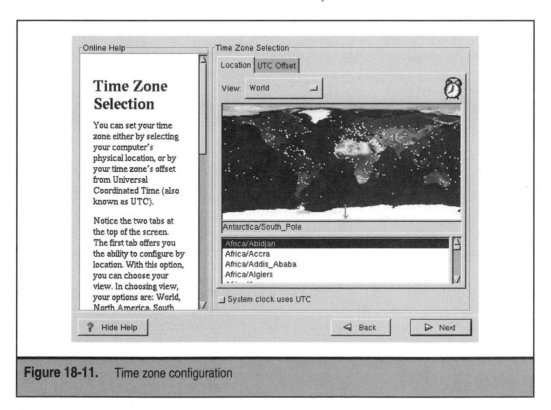

Figure 18-11. Time zone configuration

Thus, it is crucial for you to protect this account with a good password. Be sure not to pick dictionary words or names as passwords because they are easy to guess and crack.

Part of protecting root means not allowing users to log in as the root user over the network. This keeps crackers from being able to guess your root password by using automated login scripts. To allow legitimate users to become the root user, you need to log in as yourself, and then use the *su (switch user)* command. Thus, setting the root password isn't enough if you intend to perform remote administration; you also need to set up a real user.

In general, setting up a normal user to do daily work is considered a good idea. This gives you the protection of being unable to break configuration files accidentally or other important components while you're just surfing the net or performing nonadministrative tasks. The exception to this rule is certain server configurations where there should never be any users except the root user, for example, firewalls.

In Figure 18-12, you see the screen that enables you to set the root password, as well as create new users.

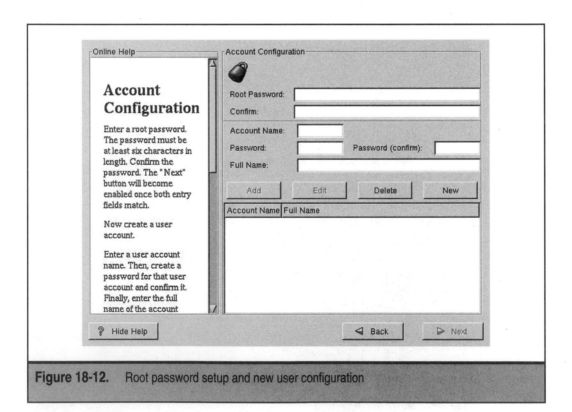

Figure 18-12.   Root password setup and new user configuration

Begin by picking a root password and entering it into the root password box at the top of the screen. Enter it again in the root password confirmation box right below it. Having to enter the password twice protects you from locking yourself out of the system in case you make a typo.

The remainder of the screen is meant for creating new users. To do so, simply enter the user name in the Account Name box, the user's real name in the Full Name box, and the user's password in the Password and Password (confirm) boxes. Click add to insert this new user into the list below these boxes.

NOTE: You do not need to add the root user.

If you make any mistakes while adding new users, you can also delete and edit them. Click Next to continue.

Authentication Configuration

Linux keeps its list of users in the /etc/passwd file. Each system has its own copy of this file and a user listed in one /etc/passwd cannot log in to another system unless the user has an entry in the other /etc/passwd file. To enable users to log in to any system in a network of computers, Linux uses the Network Information System (NIS) to handle the remote password file issues.

In addition to listing users, the /etc/passwd file contains all the passwords for each user in an encrypted format. For a long time, this was acceptable because the process of attacking such files to crack passwords was so computationally expensive, it was almost futile to try. Within the last few years, affordable PC's have gained the necessary computational power to present a threat to this type of security and, thus, a push to use shadow passwords has come. *Shadow passwords* are a mechanism by which the actual encrypted password entry is not kept in the /etc/passwd file but, rather, in a /etc/shadow file. The /etc/passwd file remains readable by any user in the system, but /etc/shadow is readable by the root user only. This is obviously a good step up in security. Unless you have a specific reason not to do this, be sure to check the "Enable shadow passwords" checkbox (see Figure 18-13).

Another good security trick is to use passwords encrypted with MD5. This algorithm supports longer passwords (256 characters instead of just 8) and because it takes longer to compute the hash, it takes longer for crackers to attack your system if they try to do so.

If your site has an existing NIS infrastructure, enter the relevant NIS domain and server name in this window. If you don't know it or you simply want to deal with this later, you can safely ignore it.

Once you have selected all checkboxes and filled out the relevent entries, click Next to continue on to the next screen.

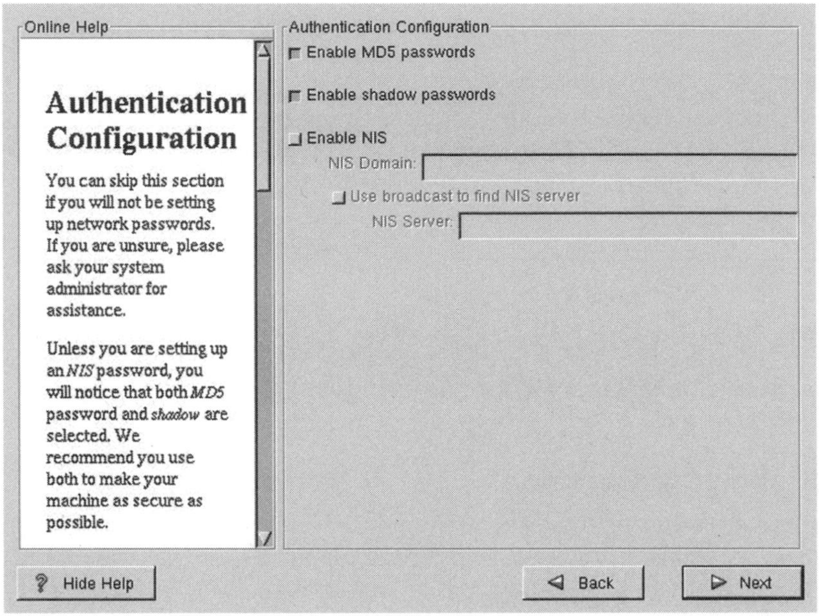

Figure 18-13. Authentication Configuration screen

Selecting Package Groups

This is where you can select what packages get installed onto the system. Red Hat categorizes these packages into several high-level descriptions. This enables you to make a quick selection of what type of packages you want installed and safely ignore the details. You can also select to install all the packages that come with Red Hat but, be warned, that can be upwards of 1.5 Gbytes of software!

Looking at the choices (Figure 18-14), you see the menu of top-level groups Red Hat gives us. You can simply pick the groups that look interesting, you can pick everything to have all the packages installed, or you can click a button at the bottom of the screen labeled "Select individual packages." Once you have made your decisions, simply click Next.

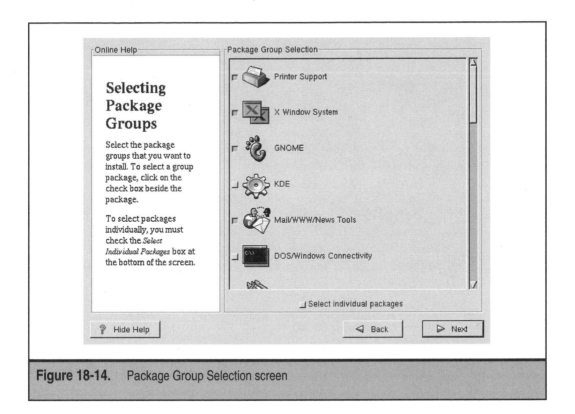

Figure 18-14.   Package Group Selection screen

If you pick, "Select individual packages," you see a screen looking somewhat like Figure 18-15. On the left side of the screen, you see the logical groupings of packages. On the right side of the screen, you see what the packages that exist in that group are. When you click a package, the bottom of the screen shows the name of the package and a brief description. Directly above the description is a button to click if you want that package installed.

If you opted to select individual packages, Red Hat goes through and verifies that all the prerequisites necessary for the packages you picked are met. If any are not met, you are shown these packages in a screen that looks like Figure 18-16.

If any packages need to be installed to allow all your selected packages to work, simply make sure the button at the bottom of Figure 18-16 labeled "Install packages to satisfy dependencies" is selected. Click Next when you finish picking packages.

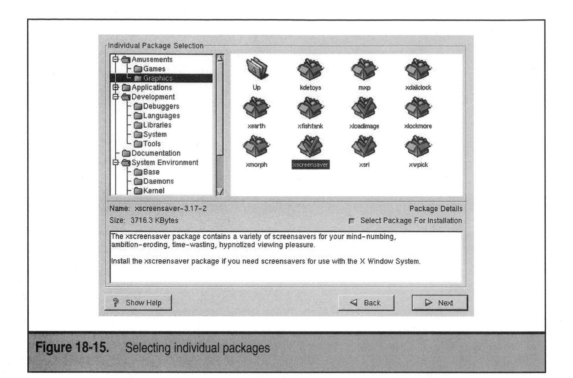

Figure 18-15. Selecting individual packages

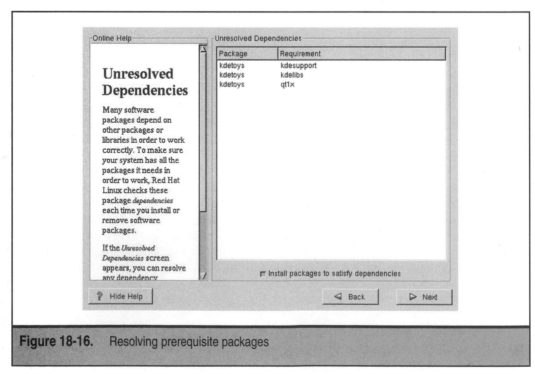

Figure 18-16. Resolving prerequisite packages

Configuring X-Windows

CAUTION: This is the last step in configuring Red Hat Linux before all the changes you selected through this process get committed. After this screen, partitions are written out and packages installed. This is your last chance to abort.

X-Windows is the basis for Linux's graphical user interface. It is what communicates with the actual video hardware. Programs such as KDE and GNOME, which you are more likely to have heard about, use X-Windows as a standard mechanism for communicating with the hardware.

What makes X-Windows interesting is it is decoupled from the base operating system. In fact, the version of X Linux uses—Xfree86—is also available for many other UNIX based systems, such as those from Sun. This means running a server without ever starting the graphical environment is possible and, as mentioned earlier in this chapter, it is often a good idea to do so. By having the GUI turned off, you save memory and system resources that can, instead, be used for the actual server processes.

This doesn't change the fact that many nice administrative tools are only available under X-Windows, so getting it set up is still a good idea.

Red Hat begins by trying to auto-sense the type of network card and monitor you have. If you have a brand name monitor and card, you'll likely have the easiest time. If Linux cannot determine the type of video card and monitor, you are then prompted for the necessary information.

NOTE: You should have the frequency information about your monitor before entering the information. Trying to send your monitor too high a frequency can cause physical damage. This author managed to toast his first color monitor this way, back when monitors were far less robust and X-Windows configuration tools didn't exist.

Once Red Hat has the necessary information, you see a screen similar to Figure 18-17.

Four choices exist under the description of the hardware configuration: Test the configuration, customize X-Windows, use a graphical login, and don't configure X-Windows.

The first choice is a button which, when pressed, immediately tests your X-Windows configuration. This enables you to verify the settings work. The second choice is a toggle switch that when selected, enables you to select the resolution at which X-Windows will start and how many colors it will use. By default, Xconfigurator tries to use the highest resolution with the maximum number of colors available. For some people, this resolution setting is too high and makes fonts hard to read.

The third choice, of using a graphical login, is just that—you can have X-Windows automatically start up on boot, so the first log in everyone sees is graphical instead of text based. This choice is often nice for novice users who have a Linux system at their desk.

The fourth choice is, if you don't need X-Windows or you want to configure it later, you can select the button not to configure X-Windows. When you finish selecting, click Next to continue.

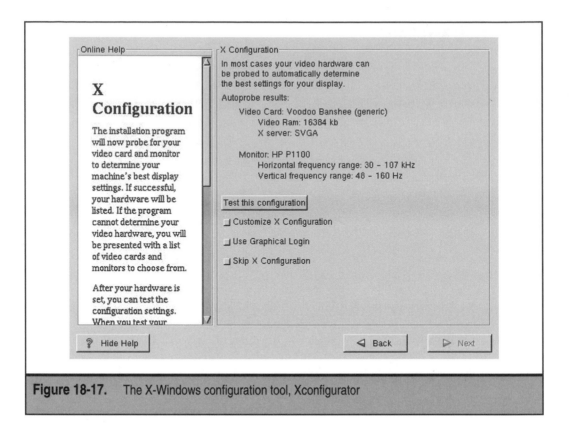

Figure 18-17.   The X-Windows configuration tool, Xconfigurator

And It's Off!

Red Hat now goes through the process of installing all the packages you selected as part of the installation process. Depending on the speed of your hard disk, CD-ROM, and machine, this could take from just a few minutes to 10-20 minutes. A status indicator (see Figure 18-18) lets you know how far the process has gotten and how much longer the system expects to take.

Boot Disk Creation

If you opted to create a boot disk earlier in the installation process, you are prompted here to insert a blank disk (see Figure 18-19). This disk enables you to boot the system in a failure, so you can reconfigure/resetup those components giving you a problem.

At this point, if you decide you don't want to create a boot disk now, you can click the button marked "Skip boot disk creation" to skip the process.

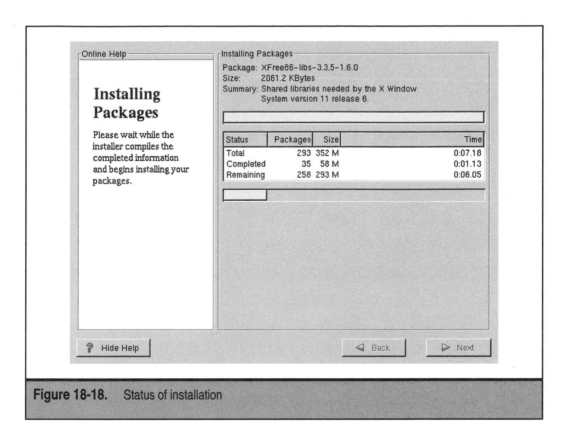

Figure 18-18. Status of installation

And You're Done!

That's it! The installation process is over. You are prompted to press a key to reboot the system. As the system reboots, be sure to remove any CD-ROMs or floppy disks you have in your system that are capable of booting before your hard disk.

CHAPTER SUMMARY

In this chapter you learned about the process of building up a server, choosing the right hardware, establishing the right environment, and, finally, installing Red Hat 6.1. All the comments before we got to the actual process of installing Red Hat Linux apply to any server you build, regardless of operating system.

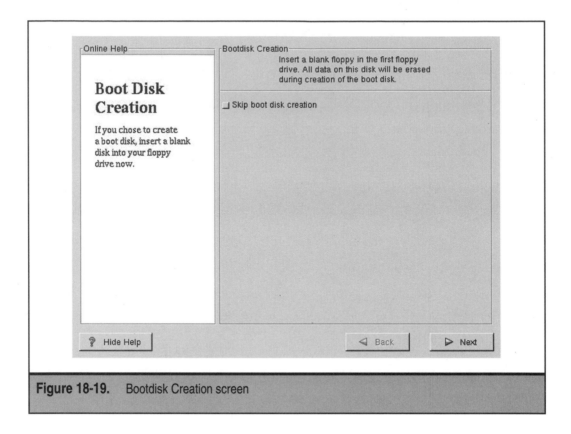

Figure 18-19. Bootdisk Creation screen

The steps to installing Red Hat itself are also quite straightforward. Anyone who witnessed the procedure from prior versions should have noted how much easier the process has become and how many fewer configuration choices need to be made to begin. What makes Linux wonderful is, even though those options are no longer part of the installation process, you can still change them and tweak them to your heart's delight once you complete the install and start the system for real.

Don't forget to search those places mentioned earlier in the chapter if you need help and, once you become a whiz at doing it, don't forget to help others.

CHAPTER 19

Introduction to Linux Systems Administration

When Linux first came out in 1991, you either had to be a systems administrator with lots of time or a good hacker to use the system effectively. While this was great for folks who were willing to spend the time, it wasn't great for the vast majority who saw potential for using Linux, but shied away from the learning curve.

Thankfully, the folks at Red Hat (among others) have realized this and have gone to great lengths to make Linux not only easy to install, but relatively painless to perform basic administrative duties.

In this chapter, you learn about some of the basic administrative chores necessary to keep your machine going and useful. This is, of course, by no means a complete guide to systems administration, but it is a start in the right direction. If, after reading this chapter, you're interested in learning more about Linux systems administration, look at *Linux Systems Administration: A Beginner's Guide*, published by Osborne/McGraw-Hill.

NOTE: This chapter makes a few assumptions. Namely, I assume you have Red Hat Linux already installed and the graphical user interface (X-Windows) configured. I also assume you are logging in to the system and running all programs as the user root. If you find your login prompt is in straight text mode, you should log in as root and run the program **startx** to get X-Windows started. If X-Windows is erroring out, use the Xconfigurator program to set it up correctly.

CAUTION: The root user is almighty under Linux. If you are familiar with Windows NT, you can think of root as being somewhat equivalent to the Administrator account. With root access, you have full control of the system, including the ability to break it. If you are new to Linux, I highly recommend you take some time and practice on a nonproduction system before trying things out on your user base! (Would you let a Windows 95 user go crazy with your PDC?)

This chapter is broken into two distinct sections. The first section deals with Linuxconf, the GUI front end to a great number of system administration functions. We step through using several components of it that are commonly used when initially configuring a host.

The second part of the chapter deals with the command line interface. While this isn't about systems administration per se, it is the foundation work for basic system administration tasks. In general, you'll find the section on Linuxconf to be much more geared toward "point here, click there, enter data here, and click Accept," whereas the command line section gets more verbose and explains the purpose of the command. This is because I assume you are familiar with the high-level features of Linux (such as what DNS is and its theory of operation), but are not familiar with the details of the UNIX command line.

ABOUT LINUXCONF

The *Linuxconf tool*, the basis for most of the administrative tasks you need to do, handles user administration, network administration, disk administration, and so on. What makes Linuxconf especially nice is it provides a consistent view of the world. The only downside to Linuxconf is, like other GUIs, it has limitations. You may find that for more advanced tasks, you need to use the command line interface.

Linuxconf can be started by running Linuxconf from a terminal window like so:

```
[root@ford /root]# linuxconf &
```

The ampersand following it allows Linuxconf to detach itself from the terminal window, enabling you to get your prompt back. (This is similar to when you start a program from the DOS command prompt in Windows and, once the new window opens, you get your C:\> prompt back.)

The first time you run Linuxconf, you see a window that looks like Figure 19-1. Take a moment to read through this window because it explains how the user interface works with Linuxconf. If you are already comfortable with graphical user interfaces, this shouldn't be too different for you.

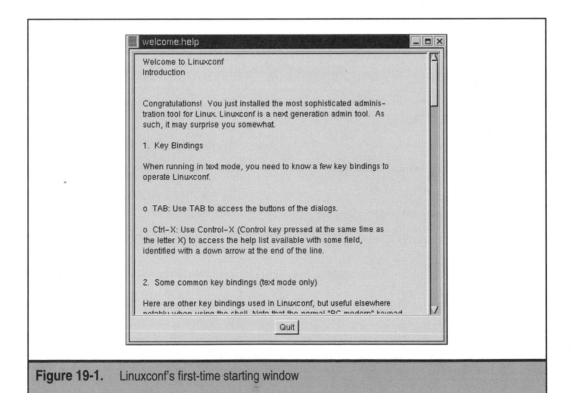

Figure 19-1.　Linuxconf's first-time starting window

When you're done reading it, simply click Quit at the bottom of the window to exit the introduction screen and start Linuxconf. The opening window to Linuxconf looks like Figure 19-2.

The left of the window is the hierarchical display of all the features Linuxconf offers. Use this tree of features to move around Linuxconf and see the various features it is capable of doing. Whenever you click an item, it will appear on the right side of the window. For example, when you click the Add User menu, you see the options for that menu appear on the right (see Figure 19-3).

When you finish with the Add User option (or whatever option is being displayed), be sure to click its Quit button. This will cause the menu option to exit, but it won't cause Linuxconf to exit. To exit Linuxconf altogether, click the Quit button in the lower-left corner of the window.

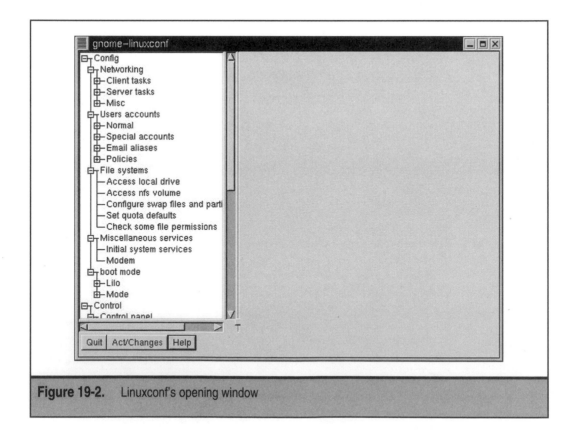

Figure 19-2.   Linuxconf's opening window

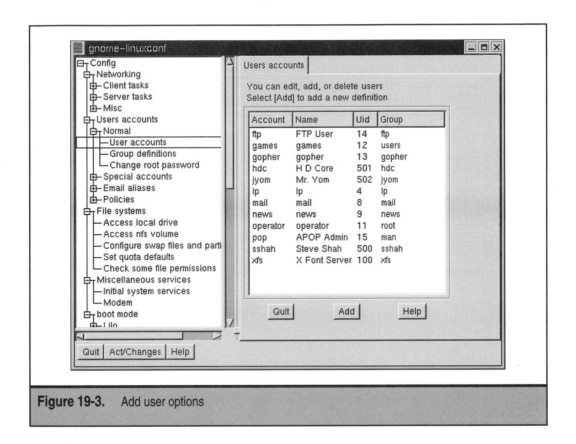

Figure 19-3.   Add user options

MANAGING USERS

One aspect of Linux that makes it useful is that multiple users of the system can work on it at the same time. From each user's point of view, the system appears dedicated to serving only his or her needs. Each user has his or her own home directory where configuration specific to that user is kept. You can think of this as multiple user profiles capable of being active in parallel without affecting each other. Pretty neat, isn't it?

To take advantage of the multiuser nature of Linux, it is necessary to add, edit, and re-move users from the system. All this can be done through Linuxconf.

Adding Users

To add a user to the system using Linuxconf, do the following:

1. Click the Config | Users Accounts | Normal | User Accounts menu option
    on the left side of the Linuxconf window. This brings up something that looks
    like Figure 19-3.

2. Click the Add button, which is on the bottom of the list of users. This brings up four tabbed windows (see Figure 19-4).

3. You must, at a minimum, fill in the login name (less than eight characters) and the full name of the user. If you aren't sure about where the user's home directory should be, the type of shell, and so forth simply leave that information blank and Linuxconf will determine the correct values for you based on the user's login name.

4. By clicking the tabs at the top of the window for Mail Settings, Disk Quota, and Privileges you can control user-specific features. Under Mail Settings, you can enter an e-mail alias and possibly a forwarding address. Under Disk Quota,

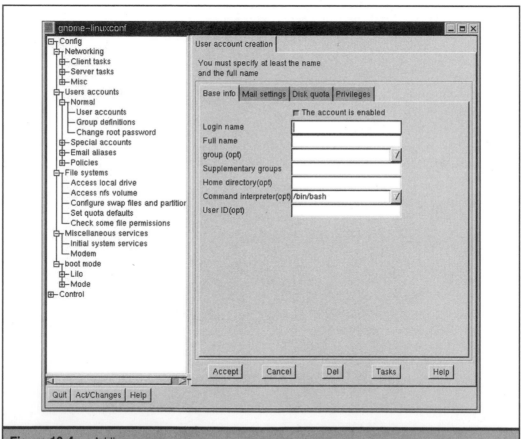

Figure 19-4. Adding a user

you can set up the maximum disk space that can be used in that user's home directory. (*Soft limits* are those the user can exceed for some temporary time; *hard limits* cannot be exceeded.) Under the Privileges tab is a second-level series of menus that enable you to control finely what services this new user can access.

5. Once you are done, click the Accept button at the bottom of the window.

6. You now have a window prompting you for the new user's password. Enter the new user's password here. Once you click OK, you are prompted again to enter the user's password. This is not a bug—the system wants to be sure no typos are in the new password, thereby preventing the new user access. Click Accept when you finish.

In general, you can simply specify the user's login name and real name only to get him or her on to the system and working.

TIP: Picking a good password means not picking a dictionary word, no matter how bizarre or strange it may seem. This includes words from foreign languages. Many crackers trying to break into systems use automated programs that take large multilingual dictionaries and go through each word, one at a time, trying all of them to see if any words match any passwords. A good technique for picking passwords is to use a phrase and then to take the first letter of each word in the phrase. For example: "Snacking on Oatmeal Squares is good for you" translates into SoOSgfy. The phrase is easy to remember, even if the password is horribly cryptic. This is an example of a good password, but remember to create your own.

Removing Users

A good idea is to keep track of who may log in to a system and who cannot. Thus, when someone should have his or her access revoked (for example, if a user leaves the company, changes departments, and so forth) the access *is* revoked. This is important to system security.

To remove a user, do the following:

1. Click the Config | Users Accounts | Normal | User Accounts menu option on the left side of the Linuxconf window. This brings up something that looks like Figure 19-3.

2. Click the user you want to remove. This takes you to a screen that looks like the Add User screen, except this time the user information is already filled out.

3. Click the Del button at the bottom of the window.

4. The system will ask you what to do with that user's data. You can either archive the data, delete the data, or leave it in its place. If you need to get to this

user's work files, the best solution is to leave the user's data in its place. If you think the user might come back, archive the data. Otherwise, delete it and reclaim the disk space. Click the appropriate choice and then click Accept. This brings you back to the user list in Step 1, minus the user you just removed.

Editing Users

If you want to change a user's settings, for example, his or her Full Name entry, you can do so using Linuxconf. To edit a user, do the following:

1. Click the Config | Users Accounts | Normal | User Accounts menu option on the left side of the Linuxconf window. This brings up something that looks like Figure 19-3.

2. Click the user you want to edit. This takes you to a screen that looks like the Add User screen, except this time the user information is already filled out.

3. Change the information you want to change. Click Accept when you are done.

Changing Root's Password

As previously mentioned, the root user is a special user who has a lot of power on the system. Obviously, an account with this much power needs to be protected with a good password. If you think someone may have gotten the root password or someone who had the root password should no longer have it (for example, an old employee), you should immediately change it.

To change root's password, do the following:

1. Click Config | Users Accounts | Normal | Change Root Password. This brings up a window like the one shown in Figure 19-5.

2. Enter root's current password in the box. You must enter the current password. This is in case you leave your screen logged in as root, and someone walks by and changes the password on you! Click Accept when you finish.

3. Enter root's new password. Follow the suggestion given for the "Adding Users" section to make sure you select a good root password. Click Accept when you're done.

4. You are prompted again to enter root's new password. This is to make sure that if any typos occurred the first time you entered, you won't be locked out. Click Accept when you finish.

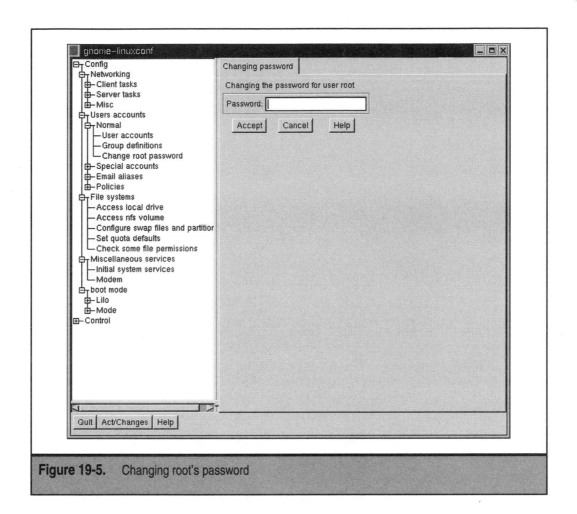

Figure 19-5.   Changing root's password

NETWORK CONFIGURATION

Linux is at home in a networked environment. In fact, its design from the onset supports it. But networks are dynamic and things change—and Linux is easy to change with it. In the next section, you see how to use Linuxconf to change the network configuration in Linux.

Changing Your Host Name

Changing the name of your system is quite easy with Linuxconf. Here are the steps to follow:

1. Click Config | Networking | Client tasks | Basic host information. This brings you to a window that looks like Figure 19-6.

2. Enter the new host name into the box and click Accept.

That's all it takes.

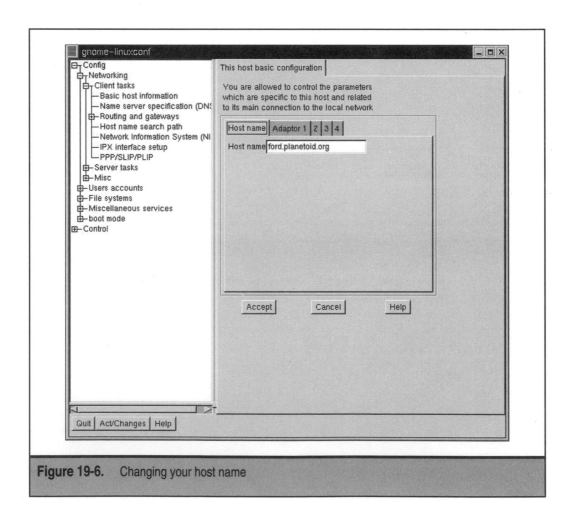

Figure 19-6. Changing your host name

CAUTION: Changing your host name on the network may be easy, but it does have repercussions to other members of the network and your relationship to them. Specifically, DNS records should be updated to reflect the new host name, as well as host files for any systems that refer to the system directly. Any tools or applications that rely on your host name also need to be told about the change. And, most importantly, other users on the network should know about the change if they have a need to contact your system (for example, if your system is the company intranet Web server and you change your name, no one will be able to find your server!).

Changing Your IP Address

To change the IP address of your system, do the following steps:

1. Click Config | Networking | Client tasks | Basic host information, just like for changing the host name. This brings you to a window that looks like Figure 19-6.

2. Click the tab Adaptor 1. This brings up the configuration information for the first network adaptor on your system, which looks like Figure 19-7. If you want to change the IP address to another adaptor, simply click the corresponding numbered tab.

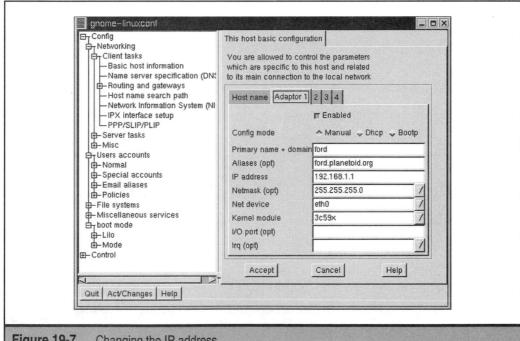

Figure 19-7.   Changing the IP address

3. Change the relevant information for that adaptor. This includes being able to change the kernel module driver for the adaptor. Immediately above the information are three buttons that enable you to select whether the information comes from manually configuring the device, DHCP, or BOOTP.

4. Once you have made all your selections, click Accept to accept the changes.

The /etc/hosts File

The /etc/hosts file contains a list of host names to IP mappings. Most systems use this so they find other machines on the network if DNS is inaccessible. Typical entries include the host itself, servers for common services (for example, the DNS server), and gateway entries.

The steps to adding entries into the /etc/hosts file are as follows:

1. Click Config | Networking | Misc | Information About Other Hosts. This brings you to a window that looks like Figure 19-8.

2. Click the Add button.

3. Fill in the form and click Accept.

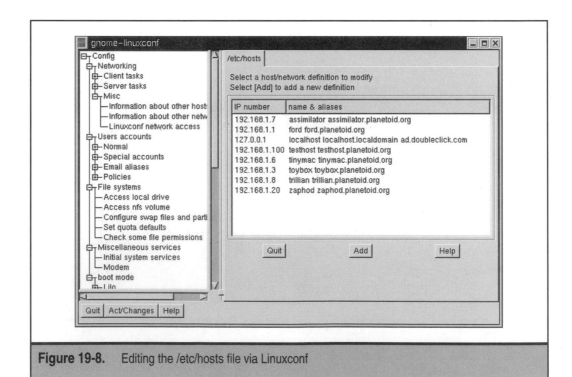

Figure 19-8. Editing the /etc/hosts file via Linuxconf

The steps to editing an entry in the /etc/hosts file is as follows:

1. Click Config | Networking | Misc | Information About Other Hosts.
2. Click the entry you want to change.
3. Change the relevant information and click Accept to commit the changes.

The steps to removing an entry in the /etc/hosts file are as follows:

1. Click Config | Networking | Misc | Information About Other Hosts.
2. Click the entry you want to remove.
3. Click the Del button that appears below the entry information.

Changing DNS Client Configuration

If your system needs to work with a larger network (such as the Internet), a good idea is to have it configured to point to a DNS server, so it can resolve host names to IP addresses and vice versa. You can set up this information in Linuxconf by doing the following:

1. Click Config | Networking | Client tasks | Name Server Specification (DNS). This brings you to a window that looks like Figure 19-9.

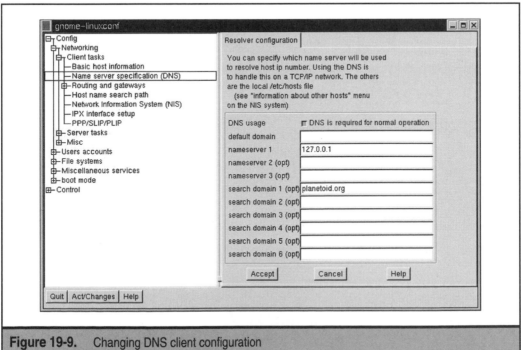

Figure 19-9. Changing DNS client configuration

2. Enter your domain name information and IP numbers for DNS servers in the appropriate boxes.

3. Click Accept to commit these changes.

Changing Your Default Route

In large networks, it is impossible for a single machine to know how to get to every other machine on the network, especially one as large as the Internet. Thus, when your machine doesn't know where to send a packet, it should have a default that either does know or can find out. Typically, this is a router of some kind that speaks the necessary protocols to learn where other components of the network are located.

To set the default route, do the following:

1. Click Config | Networking | Client Tasks | Routing and Gateways | Defaults. This brings you to a window that looks like Figure 19-10.

2. Enter the IP address of your default route here. If you don't want to use a default route, you can also deselect the Enable Routing button on this page.

3. Click Accept to commit the changes.

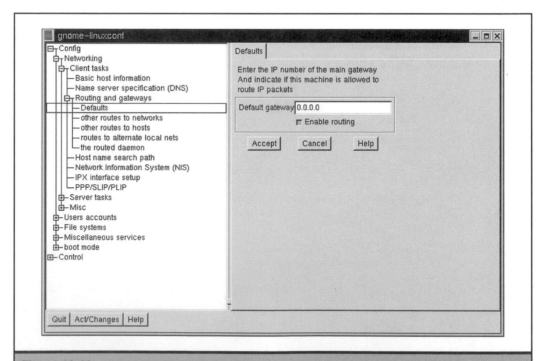

Figure 19-10. Changing your default route

Changing How Host Names Are Looked Up

Linux enables you to change the method by which host name resolution is done. The purpose in enabling you to do this is so you have the option of not having to run more advanced services, such as DNS and NIS, if you don't need to do so.

To select the order in which host names are looked up, do the following:

1. Click Config | Networking | Client Tasks | Host Name Search Path. This brings you to a window that looks like Figure 19-11.

2. Select the order in which you prefer host names to be resolved. If you aren't sure, a safe bet is "hosts, dns."

3. Click Accept to commit your changes.

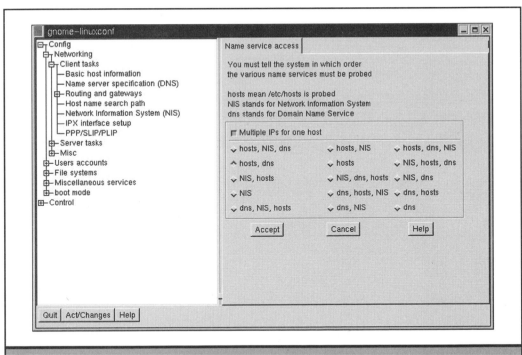

Figure 19-11.   Changing the order in which host names are looked up

MANAGING CLIENT NFS FILE SYSTEMS WITH LINUXCONF

If an existing UNIX infrastructure is at your site, you may want to use Linux as a NFS client to access remote disks. Adding, changing, and removing NFS mounts is easy to manage with Linuxconf.

To add an NFS mount, do the following:

1. Click Config | File Systems | Access NFS Volume. This brings you a window that looks like Figure 19-12.

2. Click the Add button.

3. Enter the server name, the volume you are mounting, and the local directory to which you are going to mount the volume. You can, in addition, go through the tab menus for this mount and modify the parameters for how the partition is to be mounted. Do this only if you are familiar with NFS. Don't forget, the servers must be configured to enable your client to mount his or her volumes.

4. Once you have the information entered, click Accept to commit your changes.

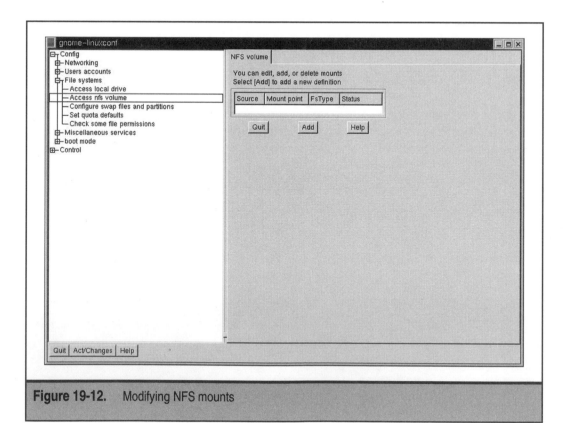

Figure 19-12. Modifying NFS mounts

To edit a mount point:

1. Click Config | File Systems | Access NFS Volume. This brings you a window that looks like Figure 19-12.

2. Click the mount point you want to edit.

3. You can change any of the parameters for the mount. When you are done with the changes, you can click Accept to commit the changes.

To remove a mount point:

1. Click the Config | File Systems | Access NFS Volume. This brings you to a window that looks like Figure 19-12.

2. Click the mount point you want to remove.

3. Click the Del button below the configuration information.

NOTE: Creating, changing, or removing a mount point does not affect whether the partition is mounted or unmounted. To do that, you must select the partition and click the Mount or the Unmount button. Any partitions listed in this table automatically get mounted the next time the system is rebooted.

LINUX COMMAND LINE BASICS

Historically, the aspect of UNIX that makes it so powerful and flexible has been the options available through the command line. Casual observers of UNIX gurus are often astounded at how a few carefully entered commands can result in powerful actions. Unfortunately, this power comes at the expense of ease of use! For this reason, graphical user interfaces (GUIs) have proliferated and have become the de facto standard for so many tools.

As you become more experienced, however, you will find presenting all the available options to a user is difficult for GUIs. Doing so would make the interface just as complicated as the command line equivalent. Thus, the GUIs have remained overly simplified and experienced users have had to drop back down to the command line.

TIP: Before you get into a "which interface is better" argument with someone, remember, both types of interfaces serve a purpose: each has weaknesses as well as benefits. In the end, the person who chooses to master both comes out ahead.

Before jumping into the nitty-gritty of the command line interface under Linux, you must remember this section is a far cry from an exhaustive list of Linux command-line tools. Instead of trying to cover many tools without any depth, this chapter covers in detail a smaller handful of tools that are believed most crucial to daily work.

NOTE: All the commands discussed in this section are to be performed in a terminal window. If you are using the GNOME environment, you can start this by clicking the picture of a monitor on the control bar at the bottom of the screen. If you are using KDE, you can use the menu in the lower-left corner of your screen. Go to Utilities and then click Terminal Window. This brings you a prompt that looks something like **[root@hostname /root]#**, where host name is the name of your machine.

Environment Variables

The concept of environment variables is the same under Windows NT as it is under UNIX; the only difference is how they are set, viewed, and removed.

Printing Environment Variables

To list all your environment variables, use the **printenv** command. For example:

```
[root@ford /root]# printenv
```

To show a specific environment variable, specify the variable as a parameter to **printenv**. For example, to see the environment variable OSTYPE, type:

```
[root@ford /root]# printenv OSTYPE
```

Setting Environment Variables

To set an environment variable, use the following format:

```
[root@ford /root]# variable=value
```

where *variable* is the variable name and *value* is the value you want to assign the variable. For example, to set the environment variable FOO with the value BAR, type:

```
[root@ford /root]# FOO=BAR
```

Once the value is set, use the **export** command to finalize it. The format of the **export** command is:

```
[root@ford /root]# export variable
```

where *variable* is the name of the variable. In the example of setting FOO, type:

```
[root@ford /root]# export FOO
```

TIP: You can combine the steps of setting the environment variable with the **export** command, like so:

```
[root@ford /root]# export FOO=BAR
```

If the value of the environment variable you want to set has spaces in it, you need to surround the variable with quote marks. Using the previous example, if you want to set FOO to "Welcome to the BAR of FOO," you would type:

```
[root@ford /root]# export FOO="Welcome to the BAR of FOO."
```

Unsetting Environment Variables

To remove an environment variable, use the **unset** command, like so:

```
[root@ford /root]# unset variable
```

where *variable* is the name of the variable you want to remove. For example, to remove the environment variable FOO, type:

```
[root@ford]# unset FOO
```

Nuances on the Command Line Itself

One of the difficulties in moving to the command line interface, especially coming from using command-line tools, such as command.com, is dealing with a shell that has a great number of short cuts. These short cuts may surprise you if you're not careful. In this section, the most common of these nuances are reviewed, and why they behave as they do is explained.

File Name Expansion

Under UNIX-based shells—such as bash—wild cards seen on the command line are expanded *before* being passed as a parameter to the application. This is in sharp contrast to the default mode of operation for DOS-based tools, which often have to perform their own wild card expansion. This also means you must be careful as to where you use the wild card characters.

The wild card characters themselves are identical to those in command.com: the asterisk (*) matches against all filenames and the question mark (?) matches against single characters. If you need to use these characters as part of another parameter for whatever reason, you can *escape* them by placing a backslash (\) in front of them. This causes the shell to interpret them as just another character instead of wild cards.

Environment Variables as Parameters

Although command.com also does this, it isn't commonly done and, thus, is often forgotten about: you can use environment variables as parameters on the command line. This means issuing the parameter $FOO results in the value of the FOO environment variable to be passed instead of the string $FOO.

Multiple Commands

Under the bash shell, executing multiple commands on the same line by separating them by semicolons (;) is possible. For example, to execute the sequence of commands:

```
[root@ford /root]# ls -l
[root@ford /root]# cat /etc/passwd
```

on a single line, you could, instead, type:

```
[root@ford /root]# ls -l ;cat /etc/passwd
```

Backticks

How's this for wild: you can take the output of one program and make it the parameter of another program. Sound bizarre? Well, it's time to get used to it! This is one of the most creatively used features available in all UNIX shells. And, as a result, it's also very powerful.

What *backticks* enable you to do is embed commands as parameters to other commands. (The backticks feature uses the accent symbol [`], which is sometimes called a "backtick," and thus the name.) A common instance of this in this book is taking a number sitting in a file and passing that number as a parameter to the **kill** command. A typical instance of this occurs with the DNS server, named starts, it writes its process identification number into the file /var/run/named.pid. Thus, the generic way of killing the named process is to look at the number in /var/run/named.pid using the **cat** command and then issuing the **kill** command with that value. For example:

```
root@ford /root]# cat /var/run/named.pid
253
[root@ford /root]# kill 253
```

One problem with killing the named process this way is it cannot be automated. We are counting on a human reading the value in /var/run/named.pid, so she can kill the number.

The second problem isn't so much a problem as it is a nuisance: it takes two steps to stop the DNS server.

Using backticks, however, you can combine the steps into one *and* do it in a way that can be automated. The backticks version would look like this:

```
[root@ford /root]# kill `cat /var/run/named.pid`
```

When bash sees this command, it first runs cat /var/run/named.pid and stores the result. It then runs **kill** and passes the stored result to it. From our point of view, this happens in one graceful step.

Documentation Tools

Linux comes with two tremendously useful tools for making documentation accessible: man and info. Currently, a great deal of overlap exists between the two documentation systems, as many applications are moving their documentation to the info format. The *info format* is considered superior to man because it allows the documentation to be hyperlinked together in a World Wide Web-like way, without actually having to be written in HTML format. The *man format,* on the other hand, has been around for decades. Thousands of utilities have only one source of documentation: their man pages. Furthermore, many applications continue to release their documentation in man format because many other UNIX-like operating systems—such as Sun Solaris—default to their documentation being in man format. As a result, both these documentation systems will be around for a long while and you should try to become comfortable with both of them.

Man

Man (short for *manual*) *pages* are documents found online covering the use of tools and their corresponding configuration files. The format of the **man** command is:

```
[root@ford /root]# man program_name
```

where *program_name* is the name of the program for which you want to read the manual page. For example:

```
[root@ford /root]# man ls
```

While reading about UNIX and UNIX-related sources for information (for example, newsgroups) you may find references to commands followed by parenthesized numbers—for instance, ls(1). The numeral represents the *section* of the manual pages. Each section covers various subject areas. Some tools, such as **printf**, are both commands in the C programming language and a command-line command, thus, two entries would exist for **printf** under two different sections.

To refer to a specific section, simply specify the section number as the first parameter and then specify the command as the second parameter. For example, to get the C programmer's information on **printf**, you would enter:

```
[root@ford /root]# man 3 printf
```

whereas, to get the command line information, you would enter:

```
[root@ford /root]# man 1 printf
```

by default, the lowest section number gets its manual page printed first.

The section numbers' meanings are as follows:

1	User tools
2	System calls
3	C library calls
4	Device driver-related information

5	Configuration files
6	Games
7	Packages
8	System tools

The unfortunate side effect of this method of organization is that it can be difficult to use. A graphical interface to this library of documentation has been developed as part of the GNOME project, called *gnome-help-browser*. You should find a large icon for it on your tool bar at the bottom of your screen or in the menu selection on the lower-left corner of your screen. If you don't see the icon, you can always start it from a terminal window yourself by typing the following:

```
[root@ford /root]# gnome-help-browser
```

TIP: A handy option to the **man** command is **-k**. With this option, man searches the summary information of all the man pages and lists which pages have a match, along with those pages' section numbers. For example:

```
[root@ford /root]# man -k printf
```

Texinfo

In addition to man pages, texinfo pages are another common form of documentation. Established as the GNU standard, *texinfo* is a documentation system that has a closer resemblance to the Web in the sense that documents can be hyperlinked together, whereas man pages are single, static documents. Thus, texinfo tends to be easier to read, follow, and find information.

To read the texinfo documents on a specific tool or application, simply invoke **info** with the parameter specifying the tool's name. For example, to read about **emacs**, simply type:

```
[root@ford /root]# info emacs
```

In general, you want to check if a man page exists first. This is because a great deal more information is still available in this format than in texinfo format. Some man pages explicitly state the texinfo pages are more authoritative and should be read instead.

File Listings, Ownerships, and Permissions

Managing files under Linux is different from managing files under Windows NT and especially different from managing files under Windows 95/98. In this section, the tools necessary to perform basic file management are discussed. The order taken is unusual because it starts with learning about some commands and then you learn some background information. Doing this actually makes some of the concepts easier to understand because you'll already be familiar with some of the simpler tools discussed.

ls—Listing Files

The **ls** command is used to list all the files in a directory. Over 26 options exist; however, the most common of these are

Option	Description
-l	Long listing—in addition to the filename, show the file size, date/time, permissions, ownership, and group information.
-a	All files—show all files in the directory, including those that are *hidden*. Hidden files begin with a period.
-1	Single column listing.
-R	Recursively list all files and subdirectories.

These options can be used in any combination with one another. See the texinfo page for the complete list of options.

Example: To list all files in a directory with a long listing, type:

```
[root@ford /root]# ls -la
```

Example: To list non-hidden files in a directory that starts with *A*, type:

```
[root@ford /root]# ls A*
```

About Files and Directories

Under Linux (and UNIX, in general), you will find almost everything is abstracted to a file. This was originally done to simplify the programmer's job. Thus, instead of having to communicate directly with device drivers, special files (which appear as ordinary files to the application) are used as a bridge instead. To accommodate all these uses of files, different types of files exist.

NORMAL FILES   Normal files are just that—normal. They contain data or executables, and the operating system makes no assumptions about their contents.

DIRECTORIES   *Directory files* are a special instance of normal files, in that their contents list the location of other files. Among the files the directory file points to may be other directories. From a daily standpoint, this won't matter to you much unless you try to open and read the file yourself, rather than use existing applications to navigate directories. (One might compare this with electing to read the DOS File Allocation Table directly, rather than using command.com to navigate directories or the findfirst/findnext system calls.)

HARD LINKS   Each file in the Linux file system gets its own i-node. An *i-node* keeps track of a file's attributes and location on the disk. If you need to refer to a single file using two separate filenames, you can create a hard link. The *hard link* has the same i-node as the original file and, therefore, looks and behaves just like the original. With every hard link that is created, a *reference count* is incremented. When a hard link is removed, the reference count is decremented. Until the reference count reaches zero, the file remains on disk.

Note, a hard link cannot exist between two files on separate partitions. This is because the hard link refers to the original file by i-node. What file is referred to by one i-node on one file system also refers to another file on another file system.

SYMBOLIC LINKS   Unlike hard links that point to a file by its i-node, a *symbolic link* (often abbreviated *symlinks*) points to another file by its name. This allows symbolic links to point to files located on other partitions or even on other network drives.

BLOCK DEVICES   Because all device drivers are accessed through the file system, files of type block device are used to interface with devices such as disks. The three identifying traits of a *block device* are it has a major number, a minor number, and when viewed using the **ls -l** command, it shows the first character of the permissions to be a *b*. For example:

```
[root@ford /root]# ls -l /dev/hda
brw-rw----  1 root     disk     3,   0 May  5  1998 /dev/hda
```

In this case, you see the *b* at the beginning of the file's permissions, the 3 is the major number, and the 0 is the minor number.

The significance of the major number is it identifies which device driver that file represents. When accessing this file, the minor number is passed to the device driver as a parameter to tell it which device it is accessing, for example, if there are two serial ports, they will share the same device driver and, thus, the same major number, but each serial port will have a unique minor number.

CHARACTER DEVICES   Similar to block devices, *character devices* are special files that enable you to access devices through the file system. The obvious difference between block and character devices are block devices communicate with the actual devices in large blocks, whereas character devices work one character at a time. (A hard disk is a block device; a modem is a character device.) The distinguishing characteristic of a character device is its permissions start with a *c* and it has a major and a minor number. For example:

```
[root@ford /root]# ls -l /dev/ttyS0
crw-------  1 root     tty      4,  64 May  5  1998 /dev/ttyS0
```

NAMED PIPES   *Named pipes* are a special type of file that allow for interprocess communication. Using the **mknod** command (discussed later), you can create this special kind of file, which one process can open for reading and another process can open for writing, thus allowing the two to communicate with one another. This works especially well when packages refuse to take input from a command line pipe, but you have another program that needs to feed it data and you don't have the disk space for a temporary file.

You can tell a file is a named pipe because the first character of its file permissions is a *p*. For example:

```
[root@ford /root]# ls -l mypipe
prw-r--r--  1 root     root         0 Jun 16 10:47 mypipe
```

chown—Change Ownership

The **chown** command enables you to change the ownership of a file to someone else. This is only doable by the root user. (Normal users may not "give away" or "steal" ownership of a file from another user.) The format of the command is:

```
[root@ford /root]# chown [-R] username filename
```

where username is the user's login to which you want to change the ownership and filename is the name of the file that will have its ownership changed. Filename may also be a directory.

The **-R** option applies when the specified *filename* is a directory name. It tells the command to descend recursively through the directory tree and to apply the new ownership not only to the directory itself, but also to all the files and directories within it.

chgrp—Change Group

chgrp is another command line utility that enables you to change the group settings of a file. It works in much the same way as **chown** does. The format of the command is:

```
[root@ford /root]# chgrp [-R] groupname filename
```

where *groupname* is the name of the group to which you want to change *filename*. *Filename* may also be a directoryl.

The **-R** option applies when the specified *filename* is a directory name. Like **chown**, it tells the command to descend recursively through the directory tree and to apply the new ownership not only to the directory itself, but also to all the files and directories within it.

chmod—Change Mode

Permissions are broken into four parts. The first part is the first character of the permissions. If the file is "normal," then it has no value and is represented with a - character. If the file has a special attribute, it is represented with a letter. The two special files that are most interesting are directories, which are represented with a *d*, and symbolic links, which are represented with an *l*.

The second, third, and fourth parts are represented in three-character chunks. The first part is the permissions for the owner of the file. The second part is the permissions for the group. Finally, the last part is the permissions for the world. In the context of UNIX, the world is simply all the users in the system, regardless of their group settings.

The letters used to represent permissions are:

Letter	Meaning
r	Read
w	Write
x	Execute

Each permission has a corresponding value. The read attribute is equal to 4, the write attribute is equal to 2, and the execute attribute is equal to 1. When you combine attributes, you add their values. See the following examples.

The reason these attributes need values is so you can use the **chmod** command to set them. Although the **chmod** command does have more readable ways to set permissions, it is important for you to understand the numbering scheme because it is used while programming. Plus, not everyone uses the naming scheme and people often assume if you understand file permissions, you also understand the numeric meanings.

The most common groups of three and their meanings are:

Permission	Values	Meaning
---	0	No permissions
r--	4	Read only
rw-	6	Read and write
rwx	7	Read, write, and execute
r-x	5	Read and execute
--x	1	Execute only

While other combinations do exist (for example, **-wx**) they are nonsensical and the likelihood you'll ever run across them is almost nil.

Each of these three-letter chunks is then grouped together, three at a time. The first chunk represents the permissions for the owner of the file, the second chunk represents the permissions for the group of the file, and the third chunk represents the permissions for all the users on the system. Some common permissions are:

Permission	Numeric Equivalent	Meaning
-rw-------	600	The owner has read and write permissions. This is what you want set on most of your files.
-rw-r--r--	644	The owner has read and write permissions. The group and world has read-only permissions. Be sure you want to let other people read this file.
-rw-rw-rw-	666	Everybody has read and write permissions on a file. This is bad. You don't want other people to be able to change your files.

Permission	Numeric Equivalent	Meaning
-rwx------	700	The owner has read, write, and execute permissions. This is what you want for programs you want to run (the file that results from compiling a C or C++ program).
-rwxr-xr-x	755	The owner has read, write, and execute permissions. The rest of the world has read and execute permissions.
-rwxrwxrwx	777	Everyone has read, write, and execute privileges. Like the 666 setting, this is bad. Letting others edit your files is the cookbook formula for disaster.
-rwx--x--x	711	The owner has read, write, and execute permissions. The rest of the world has execute-only permissions. This is useful for programs you want to let others run, but not copy.
drwx------	700	This is a directory created with the **mkdir** command. Only the owner can read and write into this directory. Note, all directories must have the executable bit set.
drwxr-xr-x	755	This directory can be changed only by the owner, but everyone else can view its contents.
drwx--x--x	711	A handy trick to use when you need to keep a directory world readable, but you don't want people to be able to **ls**. Only if the person knows the filename they wish to retrieve will they be allowed to read it.

File Management and Manipulation

In this section, you learn about the basic command line tools for managing files and directories. Most of this should be familiar if you have previously used a command line interface. Same old functions, new commands to do them with. . . .

cp—Copy Files

The **cp** command is used to copy files. Like the **ls** command, the **cp** command has a large number of options. See the man page for additional details. By default, this command works silently, only displaying status information if an error condition exists. The most common of these options are:

Option	Description
-f	Force copy—do not ask for verification.
-i	Interactive copy—verify with the user that each file should be verified before it is copied.

Example: To copy index.html to index-orig.html, type:

```
[root@ford /root]# cp index.html index-orig.html
```

Example: To copy all files interactively ending in .html to the /tmp directory, type:

```
[root@ford /root]# cp -i *.html /tmp
```

mv—Move Files

mv is used to move files from one location to another. Files can also be moved across partitions. Because that requires a real copy to occur as well, the move command can at times take longer.

The most common options to this command are:

Option	Description
-f	Force move
-i	Interactive move

Example: To move a file from /usr/src/myprog/bin/* to /usr/bin, type:

```
[root@ford /root]# mv /usr/src/myprog/bin/* /usr/bin
```

Example: Because no explicit rename tool exists, you can use **mv**. To rename /tmp/blah to /tmp/bleck, type:

```
[root@ford /root]# mv /tmp/bleck /tmp/blah
```

ln—Link Files

This tool enables you to establish one of two types of links, hard links and soft links. (See the section on file types earlier in this chapter for additional information.) The general format of this tool is:

```
[root@ford /root]# ln original_file new_file
```

ln has many options, most of which you'll never need to use. The most common option is **–s**, which creates a symbolic link instead of a hard link.

Example: To create a symbolic link so /usr/bin/myadduser points to /usr/local/bin/myadduser, type:

```
[root@ford /root]# ln -s /usr/local/bin/myadduser /usr/bin/myadduser
```

find—Find a File

This tool enables you to find files based on a number of criteria. Like the tools already discussed, a large number of options exist that you can read about on the **find** man page. The general format of the command is:

```
[root@ford /root]# find start_dir [options]
```

where *start_dir* is the directory from which the search should start. Here is a list of the most common options used:

Option	Description
-mount	Do not search file systems other than the file system from which you started.
-atime *n*	File was accessed at least $n*24$ hours ago.
-ctime *n*	File was changed at least $n*24$ hours ago.
-inum *n*	File has inode *n*.
-amin *n*	File was accessed *n* minutes ago.
-cmin *n*	File was changed *n* minutes ago.
-empty	File is empty.
-mmin *n*	File was modified *n* minutes ago.
-mtime *n*	File was modified $n*24$ hours ago.
-nouser	File's UID does not correspond to a real use in /etc/passwd.
-nogroup	File's GID does not correspond to a real group in /etc/group.
-perm *mode*	File's permissions are exactly set to *mode*.

Option	Description
-size *n[bck]*	File is at least *n* blocks/characters/kilobytes big. One block equals 512 bytes.
-print	Print the filenames found.
-exec *cmd*\;	On every file found, execute *cmd*. Be sure to follow every *cmd* with a \; or bash becomes confused.
-name *name*	File's name should be *name*. You can use regular expressions here.

Example: To find all files in /tmp that have not been accessed in at least seven days, type:

```
[root@ford /root]# find /tmp -atime 7 -print
```

Example: To find all files in /usr/src whose names are core and remove them, type:

```
[root@ford /root]# find /usr/src -name core -exec rm {} \;
```

Example: To find all files in /home that end in .jpg and are over in 100KB in size, type:

```
[root@ford /root]# find /home -name "*.jpg" -size 100k
```

dd—Convert and Copy a File

The **dd** command reads the contents of a file and sends it to another file. What makes the **dd** command different from **cp** is it can perform on-the-fly conversions on the file and it can accept data from a device (such as tape and floppy drives). When the **dd** command accesses a device, it does not assume anything about the file system and, instead, pulls the data in a raw format. Thus, it can be used to generate images of disks, even if the disk is of foreign format.

The most common parameters for **dd** are:

Option	Description
if=infile	Specifies the input file as *infile*.
of=outfile	Specifies the output file as *outfile*.
count=blocks	Specifies *blocks* as the number of blocks that **dd** should operate on before quitting.
ibs=size	Sets the block size of the input device to be *size*.
obs=size	Sets the block size of the output device to be *size*.
seek=blocks	Skip *blocks* number of blocks on the output.
skip=blocks	Skip *blocks* number of blocks on the input.
swab	Convert big endian input to little endian or vice versa.

Example: To generate an image of a floppy disk (especially useful for foreign file formats), type:

```
[root@ford /root]# dd if=/dev/fd0 of=/tmp/floppy_image
```

gzip—The File Compression Tool

In the original distributions of UNIX, a tool to compress a file was appropriately called *compress*. Unfortunately, the algorithm was patented by someone hoping to make a great deal of money. Instead of paying out, most sites sought and found a different compression tool with a patent-free algorithm, **gzip**. Even better, **gzip** consistently achieves better compression ratios than compress does.

TIP: You can usually differentiate files compressed with **gzip** versus compress by their extensions. Files compressed with **gzip** typically end in **.gz,** whereas files compressed with compress end in **.z**.

The most used optional parameters to **gzip** are:

Option	Description
-c	Write compressed file to the stdout (thereby allowing the output to be piped to another program)
-d	Decompress
-r	Recursively find all files that should be compressed
-9	Best compression
-1	Fastest compression

See the man page for a complete list. Note, **gzip** compresses the file *in place,* meaning after the compression takes place, the original file is removed and the only thing left is the compressed file.

NOTE: **gzip** does not share file formats with either PkZip or WinZip; however, WinZip can decompress **gzip** files.

Example: To compress a file and then decompress it:

```
[root@ford /root]# gzip myfile
[root@ford /root]# gzip -d myfile.gz
```

Example: To compress all files ending in .html using the best compression possible:

```
[root@ford /root]# gzip -9 *.html
```

mknod—Make Special Files

As discussed earlier, Linux accesses all its devices through files. To create a file the system understands as an interface to a device, the file must be of type block or character and have a major and minor number. To create this kind of file with the necessary values, you use the **mknod** command. In addition to creating interfaces to devices, **mknod** can be used to create named pipes.

The use of this command is:

```
[root@ford /root]# mknod name type [major] [minor]
```

where *name* is the name of the file, *type* is either the character *b* for block device, *c* for character device, or *p* for named pipe. If you choose to create a block or character device, you need to specify the *major* and *minor* number. The only time you need to create a block or character device is when installing some kind of device driver that requires it. The documentation that comes with that driver should tell you what values to use for the major and minor numbers.

Example: To create a named pipe called /tmp/mypipe, type:

```
[root@ford /root]# mknod /tmp/mypipe p
```

mkdir—Create a Home Directory

The **mkdir** in Linux is identical to the one in other UNIX's, as well as in MS-DOS. The only option available is **–p**, which creates a parent directories if none exist. For example, if you need to create /tmp/bigdir/subdir/mydir and the only directory that exists is /tmp, using **–p** causes bigdig and subdir to be automatically created along with mydir.

Example: To create a directory called mydir, type:

```
[root@ford /root]# mkdir mydir
```

NOTE: The **mkdir** command cannot be abbreviated as **md** as it can under DOS.

rmdir—Remove Directory

The **rmdir** command offers no surprises for those who are familiar with the DOS version of the command. It simply removes an existing directory. The only command line parameter available for this is **–p**, which also removes parent directories. For example, if the directory /tmp/bigdir/subdit/mydir exists and you want to get rid of all the directories from bigdir to mydir, you only need to issue the command:

```
[root@ford /tmp]# rmdir -p bigdir/subdir/mydir
```

Example: To remove a directory called mydir, type:

```
[root@ford /root]# rmdir mydir
```

NOTE: The **rmdir** command cannot be abbreviated to **rd** as it can under DOS.

pwd—Show Present Working Directory

Inevitably, you will sit down in front of an already logged in workstation and not know where in the directory tree you are. To get this information, you need the **pwd** command. It has no parameters and its only task is to print the current working directory. The DOS equivalent is typing **cd** alone; however, under the bash shell it results in taking you back to your home directory.

Example: To get the current working directory:

```
[root@ford src]# pwd
/usr/local/src
```

tar—Tape Archive

If you are familiar with the pkzip program, you are used to compression tools not only reducing file size, but also combining multiple files into a single large file. Under Linux, this process is separated into two tools. The compression tool, of course, being **gzip**.

The *tar program* combines multiple files into a single large file. The reason for separating this from the compression tool is it enables you to select which compression tool to use or whether you even want compression. Additionally, **tar** is able to read and write to devices in much the same way **dd** is able to, making it a good tool for doing backups to tape devices.

NOTE: Although the name of the program includes the word "tape," it is unnecessary to read or write to a tape drive when creating archives. In fact, you rarely you use **tar** with a tape drive in daily work (backups aside).

The structure of the **tar** command is:

```
[root@ford /root]# tar [commands and options] filenames
```

The commands and options available to **tar** are as follows:

Options	Descriptions
-c	Create a new archive.
-t	View the contents of an archive.
-x	Extract the contents of an archive.
-f	Specify the name of the file (or device) in which the archive is located.
-v	Be verbose during operations.
-z	Assume the file is already (or will be) compressed with **gzip**.

Many more options exist that are less commonly used. Refer to the man page for the complete list.

Example: To create an archive called apache.tar containing all the files from /usr/src/ apache, type:

```
[root@ford src]# tar -cf apache.tar /usr/src/apache
```

Example: To create an archive called apache.tar containing all the files from /usr /src/apache and show what is happening as it happens, type:

```
[root@ford src]# tar -cvf apache.tar /usr/src/apache
```

Example: To create a **gzip**ped compressed archive called apache.tar.gz containing all the files from /usr/src/apache and show what is happening as it happens, type:

```
[root@ford src]# tar -cvzf apache.tar.gz /usr/src/apache
```

Example: To extract the contents of a **gzip**ped tar archive called apache.tar.gz and show what is happening as it happens, type:

```
[root@ford /root]# tar -xvzf apache.tar.gz
```

cat—Concatenate Files

The *cat program* provides an extremely simple purpose: to display files. While more creative things can be done with the **cat** program, almost all its use will be in the form of simply displaying the contents of text files, much the way the type command under DOS does. Because multiple filenames can be specified on the command line, it is possible to concatenate files into a single large continuous file. This is different from **tar** in that the resulting file has no control information to show the boundaries of different files.

Example: To display the /etc/passwd file, type:

```
[root@ford /root]# cat /etc/passwd
```

Example: To display the /etc/passwd file and the /etc/group file, type:

```
[root@ford /root]# cat /etc/passwd /etc/group
```

Example: To concatenate the /etc/passwd file with the /etc/group file into the file /tmp/complete file, type:

```
[root@ford /root]# cat /etc/passwd /etc/group > /tmp/complete
```

Example: To concatenate the /etc/passwd file to an existing file called /tmp/orb, type:

```
[root@ford /root]# cat /etc/passwd >> /tmp/orb
```

more—Display a File One Screen at a Time

The *more command* works in much the same way the DOS version of the program does: it takes an input file and displays it one screen at a time. The input file can either come from its stdin or from a command-line parameter.

Additional command line parameters exist for this command; however, their use is extremely rare. See the man page for additional information.

Example: To view the /etc/passwd file one screenful at a time, type:

```
[root@ford /root]# more /etc/passwd
```

Example: To view the directory listing generated by the **ls** command one screen at a time, type:

```
[root@ford /root]# ls | more
```

du—Disk Utilization

You will often come across the need to determine where and by whom disk space is being consumed, especially when you're running low on it! The **du** command enables you to determine the disk utilization on a directory-by-directory basis.

Some of the options for **du** are:

Options	Description
-c	Produce a grand total at the end of the run.
-h	Print sizes in human readable format.
-k	Print sizes in kilobytes rather than block sizes. (Note: under Linux, one block is equal to 1KB, however, this is not true for all UNIX's.)
-s	Summarize. Print only one output for each argument.

Example: To display the amount of space each directory in /home is taking up in a human readable format, type:

```
[root@ford /root]# du -sh /home/*
```

which—Show Which Directory a File Is Located

The **which** command searches your entire path to find the name of the file specified on the command line. If the **which** command finds the name of the file, it displays the actual path of the requested file. The purpose of this command is so fully qualified paths can be easily found.

Example: To find out which directory the **ls** command is in, type:

```
[root@ford /root]# which ls
```

whereis—Locate the Binary, Source, and Manual Page for a Command

As the description states, this program searches your path and displays not only the name of the program and its absolute directory, it finds the source file (if available) and the man page for the command (again, if available).

Example: To find the location of the binary, source, and manual page for the command **grep**, type:

```
[root@ford /root]# whereis grep
```

df—Disk Free

This program displays the amount of free space on a partition-by-partition basis. The drives/partitions must be mounted to get this information. NFS information can also be gathered this way.

Some of the parameters you can use for this tool are:

Options	Description
-h	Generate human readable free size numbers, rather than blocks free.
-l	List only the mounted file systems that are local. Do not display any information about network-mounted file systems.

Additional command-line options are available; however, they are rarely used. You can read about them in the **df** manual page.

Example: To show the free space for all locally mounted drivers, type:

```
[root@ford /root]# df -l
```

Example: To show the free space in a human readable format for the file system on which our current working directory is located, type:

```
[root@ford /root]# df -h
```

Example: To show the free space in a human readable format for the file system on which /tmp is located, type:

```
[root@ford /root]# df -h /tmp
```

sync—Synchronize Disks

As most other modern operating systems do, Linux maintains a disk cache in an effort to improve efficiency. This means however, at any given moment, not everything you want written to disk, has been written to disk.

To schedule the disk cache to be written out to the disk, use the **sync** command. If **sync** detects that writing the cache out to disk has already been scheduled, it causes the kernel to immediately flush the cache.

No command-line parameters exist.

Example: To insure the disk cache has been flushed, type:

```
[root@ford /root]# sync ;   sync
```

Process Manipulation

Under Linux (and UNIX, in general), each running program is composed of at least one process. From the operating system's standpoint, each process is independent of one another and, unless they specifically asked to share resources with other processes, they are confined to the memory and CPU allocation assigned to them. Processes that overstep their memory allocation (which could potentially corrupt another running program and make the system unstable) are immediately killed. This method of handling processes has been one of the key reasons UNIX has been able to sustain its claims to system stability for so long: user applications cannot corrupt other user programs or the operating system.

In this section, the tools used to list and manipulate processes are discussed. This is important in a system administrator's daily work because it's always important to keep an eye on what's happening.

ps—List Processes

The *ps command* enables you to list all the processes in a system, their state, size, name, owner, CPU time, wall clock time, and much more. Many command-line parameters exist, but only the most common are covered here. They are:

Options	Descriptions
-a	Show all processes with a controlling terminal, not just the current user's.
-r	Show only running processes (read the following comments about the different states a process can be in).
-x	Show processes that do not have a controlling terminal.
-u	Show the process owners.
-f	Visually show which processes are the parents to which other processes.
-l	Produce long format.
-w	Show process's command line parameters (up to half a line).
-ww	Show all of a process's command-line parameters, despite length.

The most common set of parameters used with the **ps** command are **-auxww**, which shows all the processes (regardless of whether they have a controlling terminal), each process's owners, and all the processes' command-line parameters. Let's examine the output of an invocation of **ps -auxww**.

```
USER     PID %CPU %MEM   VSZ  RSS TTY   STAT START   TIME COMMAND
root       1  0.0  0.3  1096  476 ?     S    Jun10   0:04 init
root       2  0.0  0.0     0    0 ?     SW   Jun10   0:00 [kflushd]
root       3  0.0  0.0     0    0 ?     SW   Jun10   0:00 [kpiod]
root       4  0.0  0.0     0    0 ?     SW   Jun10   0:00 [kswapd]
```

```
root       5  0.0  0.0     0     0 ?      SW<  Jun10  0:00 [mdrecoveryd]
bin      253  0.0  0.2  1088   288 ?      S    Jun10  0:00 portmap
root     300  0.0  0.4  1272   548 ?      S    Jun10  0:00 syslogd -m 0
root     311  0.0  0.5  1376   668 ?      S    Jun10  0:00 klogd
daemon   325  0.0  0.2  1112   284 ?      S    Jun10  0:00 /usr/sbin/atd
root     339  0.0  0.4  1284   532 ?      S    Jun10  0:00 crond
root     357  0.0  0.3  1232   508 ?      S    Jun10  0:00 inetd
root     371  0.0  1.1  2528  1424 ?      S    Jun10  0:00 named
root     385  0.0  0.4  1284   516 ?      S    Jun10  0:00 lpd
root     399  0.0  0.8  2384  1116 ?      S    Jun10  0:00 httpd
xfs      429  0.0  0.7  1988   908 ?      S    Jun10  0:00 xfs
root     467  0.0  0.2  1060   384 tty2   S    Jun10  0:00 /sbin/mingetty tty2
root     468  0.0  0.2  1060   384 tty3   S    Jun10  0:00 /sbin/mingetty tty3
root     469  0.0  0.2  1060   384 tty4   S    Jun10  0:00 /sbin/mingetty tty4
root     470  0.0  0.2  1060   384 tty5   S    Jun10  0:00 /sbin/mingetty tty5
root     471  0.0  0.2  1060   384 tty6   S    Jun10  0:00 /sbin/mingetty tty6
root     473  0.0  0.0  1052   116 ?      S    Jun10  0:01 update (bdflush)
root     853  0.0  0.7  1708   940 pts/1  S    Jun10  0:00 bash
root    1199  0.0  0.7  1940  1012 pts/2  S    Jun10  0:00 su
root    1203  0.0  0.7  1700   920 pts/2  S    Jun10  0:00 bash
root    1726  0.0  1.3  2824  1760 ?      S    Jun10  0:00 xterm
root    1728  0.0  0.7  1716   940 pts/8  S    Jun10  0:00 bash
root    1953  0.0  1.3  2832  1780 ?      S    Jun11  0:05 xterm
root    1955  0.0  0.7  1724   972 pts/1  S    Jun11  0:00 bash
nobody  6436  0.0  0.7  2572   988 ?      S    Jun13  0:00 httpd
nobody  6437  0.0  0.7  2560   972 ?      S    Jun13  0:00 httpd
nobody  6438  0.0  0.7  2560   976 ?      S    Jun13  0:00 httpd
nobody  6439  0.0  0.7  2560   976 ?      S    Jun13  0:00 httpd
nobody  6440  0.0  0.7  2560   976 ?      S    Jun13  0:00 httpd
nobody  6441  0.0  0.7  2560   976 ?      S    Jun13  0:00 httpd
root   16673  0.0  0.6  1936   840 pts/1  S    Jun14  0:00 su - sshah
sshah  16675  0.0  0.8  1960  1112 pts/1  S    Jun14  0:00 tcsh
root   18243  0.0  0.9  2144  1216 tty1   S    Jun14  0:00 login --sshah
sshah  18244  0.0  0.8  1940  1080 tty1   S    Jun14  0:00 -tcsh
```

The first line of the output is the header showing which column means what. Most of these are self-explanatory:

Heading	Description
USER	Who owns what process.
PID	Process identification number.
%CPU	Percentage of the CPU taken up by a process. Remember, a system with multiple processors will have this column add up to be larger than 100 percent!
%MEM	Percentage of memory taken up by a process.
VSZ	How much virtual memory a process is taking.

Heading	Description
RSS	How much actual (resident) memory a process is taking.
TTY	The controlling terminal for a process. A '?' means the process is no longer connected to a controlling terminal.
STAT	Tells the process's state. **S** means the process is sleeping. Remember, all processes ready to run (are being multitasked, but the CPU is focused on another process at the moment) will be asleep. **R** means the process is actually on the CPU, **D** is an uninterruptible sleep (usually I/O related). **T** means a process is being traced by a debugger or has been stopped. **Z** means the process has gone zombie. *Going zombie* means one of two things: either the parent process has not acknowledged the death of its child using the **wait** system call or the parent was improperly killed and, until the parent is completely killed the init process cannot reap the child itself. A zombied process usually indicates poorly written software.
	Each process state can have a modifier suffixed to it. These modifiers are: **W** means the process has no resident pages in memory (it has been completely swapped out), **<** means it is a high-priority process, **N** means it is a low-priority task, and, finally, **L** means pages in memory are locked into memory (usually signifying the need for real-time functionality).
START	Date the process was started.
TIME	Amount of time the process has spent on the CPU.
COMMAND	Name of the process and its command-line parameters.

top—Show an Interactive List of Processes

The *top command* is an interactive version of **ps**. Instead of giving a static view of what is going on, it refreshes the screen with a list of processes every 2-3 seconds (user adjustable). From this list, you can reprioritize or kill processes.

The key problem with the **top** program is it is a CPU hog. On a congested system, this program tends to make the problem worse as users start running **top** to see what is going on, only to find several other people are also running **top** and, collectively, they have made the system even slower than before!

By default, **top** is shipped so everyone can use it. You may find it prudent, depending on your environment, to allow only root to run it. To do this, change the permissions on **top** with the command:

```
[root@ford /root]# chmod 0700 /usr/bin/top
```

kill—Send a Signal to a Process

For some reason, this program was horribly named—the **kill** program doesn't really kill processes! What it does do is send *signals* to running processes. The operating system by default supplies each process a standard set of *signal handlers* to deal with incoming signals. From a system administrator's standpoint, the most important handler is for signal numbers 9 and 15: kill process and terminate process. (Okay, maybe using **kill** as a name wasn't so bad after all. . . .)

When **kill** is invoked, it requires at least one parameter: the process identification number (PID) as derived from the **ps** command. When only passed the PID number, kill, by default, sends signal 15, terminate process. This is a lot like politely asking a process to stop what it's doing and shut down. Some programs intercept this signal and perform a number of actions so they can cleanly shut down. Others just stop running in their tracks. Either way, it isn't a guaranteed method for making a process stop.

The optional parameter is a number prefixed by a dash character (-) where the number represents a signal number. The two signals of most interest as sysadmins are 9 and 1: kill and hang up. The kill signal is the impolite way of making a process stop. Instead of asking a process to stop, the operating system takes it upon itself to kill the process. The only time this fails is when the process is in the middle of a system call (such as a request to open a file), in which case the process dies once it returns from the system call.

The hang-up signal is a bit of a throwback to when most users of UNIX connected to the system via VT100 style terminals. When a user's connection would drop in the middle of his session, all his running processes would receive a hang-up signal (often called a SIGHUP or HUP, for short). This gave the processes an opportunity to perform a clean shutdown or, in the case of some programs designed to keep running in the background, they could safely ignore it.

Currently, the HUP signal is used to tell certain server applications to go and re-read their configuration files. Most applications otherwise ignore the signal.

SECURITY ISSUES OF KILL   The power to terminate a process is obviously a powerful one. The developers of the **kill** command realized this and made sure security precautions existed so users could only kill processes they had permission to kill. In the case of nonroot users, the only processes they can send signals to are their own processes. Attempts to send signals to processes they do not own result in error messages being sent back to them. The root user is the exception to this: root may send signals to all processes in the system. This means the root user needs to exercise great care when using the **kill** command to insure she doesn't accidentally kill the wrong process!

Example: To terminate process number 2059, type:

```
[root@ford /root]# kill 2059
```

Example: To kill process number 593 in an almost guaranteed way, type:

```
[root@ford /root]# kill -9 593
```

Example: To send the init program (which is always process ID 1) the HUP signal, type:

```
[root@ford /root]# kill -1 1
```

Miscellaneous Tools

If an entire book were dedicated to the commands available in your Linux system, these tools could definitely be categorized. But, because this covers just the important stuff for daily administrative chores, these tools don't have their own labels. However, just because they don't get their own category, doesn't mean they aren't important!

uname—Show System Name

The **uname** program enables you to learn some details about a system. This is often helpful when you've managed to log in remotely to a dozen different computers and you have lost track of where you are! This is also helpful for script writers because it enables them to change the path of a script based on the system information.

The command line parameters for **uname** are as follows:

Options	Description
-m	Print machine hardware type (for example, i686 for Pentium Pro and better architectures)
-n	Print ghte machine's host name
-r	Print the operating system's release name
-s	Print the operating system's name
-v	Print the operating system's version
-a	Print all of the above

While it may appear odd that **uname** prints such things as the operating system name when everyone knows this is Linux, it is actually quite useful because you can find **uname** across almost all UNIX-like operating systems. Thus, if you sit down at an SGI workstation, **uname –s** will return IRIX, a Sun workstation would return SunOS, and so forth. Folks who work in heterogeneous environments often find it useful to write their scripts so they behave differently depending on the operating system type; **uname** provides a wonderfully consistent way to determine that information.

Example: To get the operating system's name and release, type:

```
[root@ford /root]# uname -s -r
```

who—Who Is Logged In

When administering systems that enable people to log in to other people's machines or specially set up servers, you want to know who is logged in. This report is generated by using the **who** command. Simply type:

```
[root@ford]# who
```

to get a report that looks like:

```
sshah     tty1      Jun 14 18:22
root      pts/9     Jun 14 18:29 (:0)
root      pts/11    Jun 14 21:12 (:0)
root      pts/12    Jun 14 23:38 (:0)
```

su—Switch User

Once you have logged in to the system as one user, it is unnecessary to have to log back out and log in again to assume another identity (for example, you logged in as yourself and you want to become the root user). Simply use the **su** command to switch to another user. This command has only two command line parameters, both of which are optional.

By default, running **su** without any parameters results in your trying to become the root user. You are prompted for the root password and, if you enter it correctly, dropped down to a root shell. If you are the root user and you want to take the identity of another user, you needn't enter their password.

Example: If you are logged in as yourself and you want to switch to the root user, type:

```
[sshah@ford ~]$ su
```

Example: If you are logged in as root and you want to switch over to user sshah, type:

```
[root@ford /root]# su sshah
```

The optional parameter you can use is a dash character. This character tells **su** not only to switch identities, but to run the login scripts for that user as well.

Example: If you are logged in as root and want to switch over to user sshah, with all his login and shell configurations, type:

```
[root@ford /root]# su -sshah
```

CHAPTER SUMMARY

This chapter covered two basic methods of systems administration and laid the ground work for learning more about it. You learned how the Linuxconf program worked and how to set many of the higher level features of Linux using it. In the second half of the chapter, you learned even more about the Linux command line and how to control the system using it.

In both halves of this chapter, we've obviously had to leave out information. After all, most system administration books are hundreds of pages and this chapter isn't even 50 pages long. But, given what you learned here, you should be able to perform basic administrative duties.

The easiest way to gain more information is to spend time playing with both the command-line tools and the Linuxconf utility. Linuxconf is capable of so much more than was discussed. For simple servers, performing system maintenance using Linuxconf alone is entirely possible! The command line, on the other hand, is Linux's secret weapon to flexibility.

On a final note, if you want to learn more about systems administration for Linux, be sure to check out *Linux Systems Administration: A Beginner's Guide,* from Osborne/McGraw-Hill, which should be available by January 2000.

GLOSSARY

10Base-2 Specification for 10Mbps (baseband) carried over coaxial cable. Also called *thin Ethernet* or *ThinNet*.

10Base-5 Specification for 10Mbps (baseband) carried over thick coaxial cable. Also called *thick Ethernet* or *ThickNet*.

10Base-Fx Specification for 10Mbps (baseband) carried over fiber-optic cable.

10Base-Tx Specification for 10Mbps (baseband) carried over twisted-pair cable.

100Base-T Specification for 100Mbps (baseband) carried over twisted-pair cable.

802.x Specification for Ethernet networks. Both 802.2 and 802.3 are in use.

access control list (ACL) A list of security permissions for a network's files, directories, and other resources.

access rights The rights that control what a user can and cannot do for a particular network resource.

account The definition for a user on a network. Access to a network cannot be had without a valid account.

Address Resolution Protocol (ARP) A protocol that resolves a destination's Media Access Control (MAC) address from its Internet Protocol (IP) address.

administrator The chief administrator of a network, who generally has permission to perform any task on a network and access any resource, and who can assign rights to network users. Sometimes called *supervisor* and *super user*.

American National Standards Institute (ANSI) A private nonprofit organization that coordinates standards in the United States.

analog A multistate electrical signal that usually has an infinite number of values. For example, a volume knob on a radio is usually an analog adjustment.

Apple Attachment Unit Interface (AAUI) A connector for connecting a Macintosh to an Ethernet network.

Apple Filing Protocol (AFP) A file access protocol for working with files through a network.

AppleTalk A set of networking protocols for Macintosh computers.

application layer The seventh and highest layer in the OSI networking model, which handles communication between applications across a network.

archive bit A bit flag indicating which files need to be archived (backed up). When a full backup is done, the archive bit is cleared. Any subsequent changes to the file cause the archive bit to be set to on, indicating the need for an archive.

ARCnet A token-passing network protocol rarely used currently.

Asynchronous Transfer Mode (ATM) A high-speed switched and multiplexed network specification.

Attachment Unit Interface (AUI) A box that connects a network cable to a transceiver.

attributes (file) Characteristics given to files. For example, in DOS files can be Read-Only, System, Hidden, and Archive. Network systems generally add to this list with attributes like Shareable and Delete Inhibit.

backbone A common cable shared by segments of a network. Usually, the backbone portion of a network operates at a higher speed than the individual segments because it must carry most of the connected segments' traffic.

bandwidth The amount of data that can be carried over a network, usually expressed in mega (million) bits per second, or Mbps. Sometimes bandwidth is also specified in hertz, such as 10 megahertz (MHz).

baseband A network cable that can carry only one signal at a time. See *broadband*.

Basic Rate Interface (BRI) A package of ISDN services that includes two bearer channels at 64Kbps each, plus a single data channel that carries 16Kbps. BRI is sometimes also called *2B+D*.

baud rate The speed at which an analog signal is carried. Baud rate is analogous to bits per second (bps); thus, 2,400 baud is roughly equivalent to 2,400 bits per second.

B-channel A channel in an ISDN connection that carries (normally) 64Kbps of data.

bindery A database that contains account and security information for Novell networks versions 3 and earlier.

bit   Short for *binary digit*, a single digit having a value of either 0 or 1.

BNC connector   Bayonet-Neill-Concelman connector. A bayonet-style connector used in 10Base2 (thin) Ethernet networks.

bottleneck   In a complex system, the rate-limiting part of the system.

bridge   A networking device that connects two networks to each other using layers 1 and 2 of the OSI network model.

broadband   A network cable that can carry multiple signals at once. See *baseband*.

broadcast   A network transmission sent to all nodes of a network or subnetwork.

browser   An application that interprets and displays data formatted using Hypertext Markup Language (HTML) on the World Wide Web.

buffer   Memory set aside to cache data between two devices, providing faster access to frequently used data. Buffers are often used by operating systems to hold frequently used data stored on disks.

bus   (1) A network topology in which a cable runs from node to node, terminating on each end.
(2) A connection backbone used in a computer, to which most peripherals connect.

byte   A collection of 8 bits, bytes can represent up to 256 distinct values.

cache   Memory set aside expressly for holding frequently accessed data from a disk.

capture   A mechanism whereby a network printer acts like a local printer for a specific computer. Output sent to the computer's printer port is captured and redirected to a network printer.

central office (CO)   A local switching facility run by the Regional Bell Operating Company (RBOC) that provides an access point to their network.

Challenge Handshake Authentication Protocol (CHAP)   An Internet communication standard for validating encrypted passwords.

client A computer on a network that uses data provided by a server.

client/server A network concept in which data processing work is divided between a client's processor and a server's processor, letting each perform the jobs to which they are best suited.

CNE A Certified NetWare Engineer.

coaxial cable Cable with a center conductor surrounded by a shield. Common coaxial cable types are RG-58 and RG-8.

Common Gateway Interface (CGI) A programming standard that connects databases and web browsers.

concentrator A network device that connects multiple user devices to a network. Sometimes called a *hub*.

console A NetWare server's administrative interface.

CSMA/CD Carrier Sense Multiple Access with Collision Detection. A method used with Ethernet networks to manage packets on a segment.

CSU/DSU Channel Service Unit/Data Service Unit. A hardware device that interfaces between a network's signals and the signals carried over a public network connection, like a T-1 line.

customer premises equipment (CPE) Telephone company lingo for interconnection equipment located on a company's premises.

cyclic redundancy check (CRC) A method to detect errors in transmitted or stored data. A *checksum* is a simpler, less reliable method that serves the same purpose.

data communications Equipment (DCE) One end of an RS-232C or other serial connection. See *data terminal equipment*.

datagram A collection of network data, along with its associated addressing and header information. Also called a *packet*.

data-link layer The second layer of the OSI network model, the data-link layer handles error-free connections between two devices over a common physical connection.

data terminal equipment (DTE) One end of an RS-232C or other serial connection. A DTE device only communicates with a DCE device, and vice-versa. See *data communications equipment*.

DBMS   Database management system. Usually a relational database.

D-channel   Data channel. One of the channels used in all ISDN interfaces, it carries 16Kbps of data and is for call setup and other signal control duties. It carries no user data.

deadlock   A situation in which two computers or two processes attempt to access a resource simultaneously and both wait indefinitely for the other one to finish using the resource.

delayed write   A method used in writing new or changed data to a network server's disks to improve overall performance. Data to be written is temporarily held in memory until the system is not busy (or for a set maximum amount of time), at which time the data is committed to the disk.

Dial-Up Networking (DUN)   A Microsoft term for a dial-up network connection over a modem.

differential backup   A backup that copies all files with their archive bit set and does not clear the archive bit when done.

digital   A signaling method in which all signals are binary (1's and 0's only) in nature.

digital audio tape (DAT)   A digital tape often used in network backup devices.

digital signature   An authentication code embedded in a network message.

direct cable connection   A serial (RS-232C) connection between two computers.

directory   In the tree-shaped structure of a disk's file system, a logical container for files.

disk mirroring   Also known as *RAID 1*, a method whereby data is redundantly written to two separate disks.

domain   (1) On the Internet, a domain is a network identified by a name, such as yahoo.com.
(2) On Microsoft Windows NT networks, a domain is the smallest administrative unit in a network.

Domain Name System (DNS)   An Internet system whereby domain names are resolved to IP addresses.

drive map   A method that uses a network directory to simulate a local drive for a client computer.

DS0   A basic telephone line.

DS1   A digital telephone line used for both voice and data applications. A DS1 carries up to 1.544Mbps of data, split across 28 separate channels, or that carries up to 28 voice channels. Often called a *T-1 line*.

DS3   A digital telephone line that carries up to 44.736Mbps of data. Often called a *T-3 line*.

Ethernet   A network standard that uses CSMA/CD methods to carry network data over many different types of media at many different speeds.

EtherTalk   An Apple protocol for connecting Macintosh computers to an Ethernet network.

Fast Ethernet   An Ethernet network that runs at 100Mbps.

FAT   File allocation table. Used by several operating systems to allocate space for files on physical disks.

Fiber Distributed Data Interface (FDDI)   Fiber-optic LAN that operates at 100Mbps.

file server   A network server primarily responsible for storing, sharing, and retrieving files for network clients.

File Transfer Protocol/Program (FTP)   An Internet protocol for copying files between two computers. Also, a program that uses the FTP protocol to do its job.

firewall   A network device that protects a network from outside intruders.

Fractional T-1   A T-1 telecommunications connection in which only some of the channels are leased for use.

frame   A data-link layer unit of transmission in the OSI network model. Frames can be of variable length.

full backup   A process where all files on a network drive are copied to tape or other archival media. Each file's archive bit is cleared as part of a full backup.

full-duplex   A connection in which both ends can transmit and receive simultaneously.

gateway	A device that connects two networks together at all layers of the OSI network model. An example is an e-mail gateway that transmits e-mail from one network to another.
GB	Gigabyte. GB represents one billion bytes.
generational backup	A tape-swapping methodology that gives good restoration granularity without consuming too many tapes. Also called the *Grandfather-Father-Son method.*
half-duplex (simplex)	A connection in which only one end can transmit at a time.
handshaking	The process of negotiating a connection and data transmission between two devices.
header	Control information carried along with a file or a unit of network data, such as a packet.
hub	A network device that connects multiple nodes to a network segment.
Hypertext Markup Language (HTML)	A formatting language used to format Web pages.
Hypertext Transfer Protocol (HTTP)	A network protocol used to retrieve Web pages from a Web server.
IEEE	Institute of Electrical and Electronics Engineering. A body that defines standards for electrical devices.
incremental backup	Backs up files that have their archive attribute set and then clears the archive attribute.
Internet	A world-wide public network of services for businesses and consumers.
intranet	A company-specific network modeled after the Internet.
IPv6	Internet Protocol version 6. Increases the number of IP addresses available dramatically and includes other enhancements to the IP protocol.
IPX	Internetwork Package Exchange. A network protocol used with NetWare networks.
IRQ	Interrupt request. A hardware switch in a computer that allows a device to signal the processor.
ISA bus	Industry Standard Architecture bus. A computer bus originally developed for the IBM PC-AT.

ISDN Integrated Services Digital Network. A telecommunications standard for providing digital telephony services to consumers and businesses.

ISO International Standards Organization. A body that defines many computer standards, including networking standards.

ISP Internet service provider. A company that provides Internet services directly to businesses and/or consumers.

Java A programming language, derived from C, which allows automation of Internet Web pages.

KB Kilobyte. 1,024 bytes.

key A digital password used to sign electronic documents to guarantee their authenticity.

LAN Local area network. A building-specific network.

LAN Manager An older Microsoft network operating system.

leased line A dedicated, always-on, telephone connection.

LocalTalk An Apple networking system for connecting Macintoshes and Apple laser printers together on a low-speed (230Kbps) network over twisted-pair wire.

login The act of providing account and authentication information to a computer or network to gain access to its resources.

login script A set of commands that runs automatically when a user logs into a computer or network.

MAC Media Access Control. A sublayer of layer 2 of the OSI networking model that is defined by Ethernet standard 802.3.

MB Megabyte. 1,048,576 bytes.

MCA bus Micro Channel Architecture bus. A computer bus standard introduced by IBM, which was not widely accepted.

MCSE Microsoft Certified System Engineer. A person who has completed a set of tests given by Microsoft to certify them as a networking engineer.

MHz Megahertz, or one million Hertz (signals per second). Roughly equivalent to Mbps (million bits per second).

MIME Multipurpose Internet Mail Extensions. A standard for the attachment of binary data (attachments) to Internet e-mail messages. Also available as S/MIME, which is a secure form of MIME.

modem	Modulator/demodulator. A device that allows digital signals to travel over an analog telephone line. A modem is required on each end of the connection.
MSAU	Multistation Access Unit (or MAU). A hub used to connect Token Ring nodes together.
multiplexing	A technique that allows multiple signals to be aggregated onto a single channel.
multiprocessor	A computer, operating system or application that uses more than one processor to accomplish its work.
multitasking	The act of running multiple programs simultaneously on a single computer.
NetBEUI	NetBIOS Extended User Interface. An enhancement to the NetBIOS protocol.
NetBIOS	Network Basic Input/Output System. An older and slower networking protocol, originally developed by IBM.
NetWare	A network operating system developed by Novell Corporation.
NetWare Core Protocol (NCP)	An underlying protocol that manages server and workstation communications on a NetWare network.
NetWare Loadable Module (NLM)	A special program that runs only on NetWare servers.
network interface card (NIC)	A peripheral card attached to a computer that lets it interface to a network.
network layer	Layer 3 of the OSI networking model.
nibble	Four bits.
node	A computer or device that is a distinct network entity, such as a computer or printer.
NOS	Network operating system. An operating system that runs on network servers.
Novell Directory Services (NDS)	A directory service for NetWare networks.
OSI	Open Systems Interconnection. A reference model that conceptually describes how networks work.

packet A collection of data sent as a single entity from one node on a network to another node.

packet filtering The act of examining packets coming into and going out of a network to prevent unauthorized traffic.

partition A logical division of a hard disk.

patch cable A cable that connects between a patch panel and a network hub, or from a wall jack to a computer.

PCI Peripheral Component Interconnect. A very fast bus introduced by Intel corporation to allow high-speed communications between peripherals and the computer in which they are installed.

peer-to-peer network A network that spreads shareable resources among all the client computers on the network. A peer-to-peer network has no central network servers.

physical layer Layer 1 of the OSI networking model.

Point-to-Point Protocol (PPP) An IP-specific protocol that allows remote nodes to connect to a network over telephony connections.

Post Office Protocol (POP) A communications protocol for the exchange of e-mail over the Internet.

presentation layer Layer 6 of the OSI networking model.

Primary Rate Interface (PRI) An aggregation of ISDN B-channels plus one D-channel that provides 1.544Mbps of network bandwidth through the telephone network.

print job A unit of printing from a client computer to a network printer.

print queue A place on a network server that accepts and accumulates user print jobs and then sends them to the network printer in sequence.

print server A computer or dedicated device on a network that accepts jobs from print queues and interfaces them to the individual printers.

protocol A syntax for communication over a network.

RAID Redundant Array of Inexpensive Disks. A variety of methods that allow high-speed failsafe arrays of disks to be used in concert.

Registry	A database used on Microsoft Windows operating systems that stores computer and user settings.
remote access (node and control)	The process of accessing a network from a remote computer, usually over a telephone line or sometimes through the Internet. Remote node makes the remote computer a node on the network. Remote control lets the remote computer "take control" of a computer that is already a local node on a network.
Remote Access Service (RAS)	A Windows NT service that provides remote node access to remote computers.
repeater	A device that extends the distance a network segment can be run.
requestor	Special networking software that runs on a client computer that interfaces between the computer's operating system and the network operating system. Requestors are specific to each different type of NOS.
ring topology	An electrical arrangement of nodes on a network in a ring configuration.
RJ-45	A snap-in connector used with some kinds of network media, similar to modular telephone connectors used in homes, but larger.
router	A device that routes network traffic from one network to another.
Routing Information Protocol (RIP)	A protocol that allows routers to communicate with each other to discover the best route between networks.
SCSI	Small Computer Systems Interface. A high-speed interface used primarily to interface hard disks to network servers.
segment	An individual part of a network that connects two or more computers together.
server	A computer on a network that provides some kind of network service to client computers.
session layer	Layer 5 of the OSI networking model.
share	A Windows NT shared directory, available for use over a network, provided the user has permission.

SMTP Simple Mail Transfer Protocol. An Internet standard for the exchange of e-mail between systems on the Internet.

SNMP Simple Network Management Protocol. A protocol that allows for the management of network devices by special management software.

SPX Sequenced Packet Exchange. A NetWare protocol used in concert with IPX.

star topology A network arrangement whereby a central hub connects to the nodes it services by individual cables.

switch An Ethernet device that switches traffic between two or more network segments.

TB Terabyte. One trillion bytes.

TCP/IP Transmission Control Protocol/Internet Protocol. A standard network protocol used on the Internet and on many private networks.

token An electrical signal circulated around Token Ring networks. Only the computer that "has the token" can transmit on the Token Ring network.

Token Ring A network designed by IBM that uses a ring topology and circulates a token to manage traffic on the network.

transceiver A device that connects a computer to a network cable. Often transceivers are built-into NIC cards.

transport layer Layer 4 of the OSI networking model.

twisted-pair Cable that uses small-gauge wires twisted together within a common sheath to carry network or telephone signals. Twisted-pair cable comes in unshielded (UTP) and shielded (STP) varieties.

UPS Uninteruptable power supply. A battery-driven power supply that allows a server to continue operating when a building's power supply is cut off.

URL Uniform Resource Locator. An address that allows a resource on the Internet to be located and accessed.

Virtual Private Network (VPN) A secure, virtual network connection formed over a public network, like the Internet.

wiring closet   A closet or room in which all the cables needed for a building's network are brought together.

workstation   A generic computer client on a network. Sometimes this also refers to a high-powered computer used for engineering purposes.

INDEX

T

X

 Z